SCHAUM'S OUTLINE OF

THEORY AND PROBL...

OF

MANAGERIAL ECONOMICS

DOMINICK SALVATORE, Ph.D.

Professor of Economics and Business
Fordham University

SCHAUM'S OUTLINE SERIES
McGRAW-HILL PUBLISHING COMPANY

New York   St. Louis   San Francisco   Auckland   Bogotá   Caracas
Hamburg   Lisbon   London   Madrid   Mexico   Milan   Montreal
New Delhi   Oklahoma City   Paris   San Juan   São Paulo
Singapore   Sydney   Tokyo   Toronto

DOMINICK SALVATORE received his Ph.D. in 1971 and is currently Professor of Economics and Business at Fordham University. He is the author of numerous books, including: *Managerial Economics* (McGraw-Hill, 1989), *Microeconomic Theory* (1986), and *International Economics*, 2nd ed. (1987). He has also written Schaum's Outlines in *Microeconomics*, 2nd ed. (1983), *Statistics and Econometrics* (1982), and *International Economics*, 2nd ed. (1984), and coauthored *Principles of Economics* (1980) and *Development Economics* (1977). His research has been published in leading scholarly journals and presented at national and international conferences.

Schaum's Outline of Theory and Problems of

MANAGERIAL ECONOMICS

2 3 4 5 6 7 8 9 10 11 12 13 14 15 16 17 18 19 20 SHP SHP 8 9 2 1 0 9

ISBN 0-07-054513-8

Sponsoring Editor, Elizabeth Zayatz
Production Supervisor, Janelle Travers
Editing Supervisors, Marthe Grice, Meg Tobin

Library of Cogress Cataloging-in-Publication Data

Salvatore, Dominick.
    Schaum's outline of theory and problems of managerial economics/
by Dominick Salvatore.
        p.   cm.—(Schaum's outline series)
    Includes index.
    ISBN 0-07-054513-8
    1. Managerial economics.   I. Title.
HD30.22.S248 1989
338.5′024658—dc19   88-27630
                                                       CIP

Preface

Managerial Economics refers to the application of economic theory (mostly micro-economic theory) and the tools of analysis of decision science (such as statistics and quantitative methods) to examine how an organization can achieve its aims or objectives most efficiently. As such, it has traditionally been one of the most important courses in all business and in many economics curricula in practically all colleges and universities.

Managerial Economics is an overview course that brings together many aspects of economic theory and the tools of analysis from the various fields of business adminis-tration. It is also one of the most difficult courses and often becomes a stumbling block for many students. The purpose of this book is to help students overcome this difficulty by approaching managerial economics from a learn-by-doing methodology. This book is intended as a supplement to all current standard textbooks in managerial economics, including my own (McGraw-Hill, 1989).

Each chapter begins with a clear statement of theory, principles, or background information, and is fully illustrated with examples. This is followed by a set of multiple-choice review questions with answers. Subsequently, numerous theoretical and numer-ical problems are presented with their detailed, step-by-step solutions. These solved problems serve to illustrate and amplify the theory, to bring into sharp focus those fine points without which the student continually feels on unsafe ground, and to provide the applications and the reinforcement so vital to effective learning.

Topics are arranged in the order in which they are usually covered in managerial economics courses and texts in both undergraduate and M.B.A. programs. There is no prerequisite for its study other than some knowledge of principles of economics. Knowl-edge of statistical and quantitative methods is useful but is not required, since these topics are covered in chapters 2, 3, and 4 of the book. The presentation is conducted exclusively in terms of simple graphs and algebra, but Appendix A (which is optional) at the end of the book presents the full range of the mathematical techniques used in managerial-decision courses that utilize calculus.

The methodology of this book and much of its content have been tested in the under-graduate and the M.B.A. courses that I have been teaching at Fordham University over the past 15 years. The students were enthusiastic and made many valuable suggestions for improvements. To all of them I am deeply grateful.

In writing this book, I greatly benefited from detailed comments from my colleagues Victor M. Borum, Katherin Marton, and George C. Logush of the Fordham Business School, and Joseph Cammarosano, James Heilbrun, and Timothy Weithers of the Department of Economics at Fordham. My former colleague, Frank Fabozzi, now a visiting professor at the Sloane School of Management at M.I.T. also made many valuable suggestions, as did Louis Lopilato (Marcy College), Patrick O'Sullivan (State University of New York), Siamack Shojai (Lafayette College), and Michael Szenberg (Pace University). Alan Anderson assisted me throughout this project. No professor could ask for a better graduate assistant. I also received much help from my other assis-tants Gregory Burton and Emily Tusaneza. Finally, I would like to express my gratitude to the entire Schaum's staff at McGraw-Hill for their skillful assistance and especially to Elizabeth Zayatz, John Aliano, and Marthe Grice.

DOMINICK SALVATORE

Contents

CONTENTS

CONTENTS

Chapter 1

The Scope and Nature
of Managerial Economics

1.1 DEFINITION OF MANAGERIAL ECONOMICS

Managerial economics refers to the use of economic theory (microeconomics and macroeconomics) and the tools of analysis of decision science (mathematical economics and econometrics) to examine how an organization can achieve its aims and objectives most efficiently.

EXAMPLE 1.   A firm may seek to maximize profits subject to limitations on the availability of essential inputs (skilled labor, capital, and raw materials) and legal constraints (minimum wage laws, health and safety standards, and pollution emission standards). Not-for-profit organizations (such as hospitals, universities, museums) and government agencies also seek to reach some goal or objective subject to some constraints (see Problems 1.1 and 1.2). While the goals and constraints may differ from case to case, managerial economics studies the decision-making process, that is, the means by which an organization can achieve its objective most efficiently.

1.2 RELATIONSHIP OF MANAGERIAL ECONOMICS TO OTHER FIELDS OF STUDY

The relationship between managerial economics and other fields of study can be examined with the aid of Fig. 1-1. *Economic theory* refers to microeconomics and macroeconomics. *Microeconomics* is the study of the economic behavior of *individual* decision-making units such as individual consumers, resource owners, and business firms in a free-enterprise system. *Macroeconomics* is the study of total, or *aggregate*, output, income, employment, consumption, investment, and prices of the economy *viewed as a whole*. Managerial economics utilizes the tools of mathematical economics and econometrics. *Mathematical economics* is used to formalize the economic models postulated by economic theory. *Econometrics* applies statistical tools

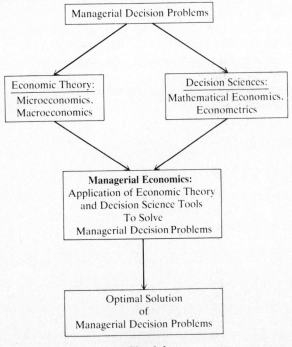

Fig. 1-1

1

(primarily regression analysis) to real-world data to estimate the models postulated by economic theory and for forecasting. (For the relationship between managerial economics and the functional areas of business administration studies, see Problem 1.5.)

EXAMPLE 2.   Economic theory postulates that the quantity demanded of a commodity (Q) is a function of, or depends on, the price of the commodity (P), the income of consumers (Y), and the prices of related (i.e., complementary and substitute) commodities (P_c and P_s, respectively). Assuming constant tastes, we may postulate the following formal (mathematical) model:

$$Q = f(P, Y, P_c, P_s) \qquad (1\text{-}1)$$

Collecting data on Q, P, Y, P_c, and P_s for a particular commodity, we can then estimate the empirical (econometric) relationship. This will permit the firm to determine how much Q would change as a result of a change in P, Y, P_c, and P_s and to forecast the future demand for the commodity. These steps are essential in order for management to achieve the goal, or objective, of the firm (profit maximization) most efficiently.

1.3 THE THEORY OF THE FIRM

Firms exist because the economies they generate in production and distribution confer great benefits to entrepreneurs, workers, and other resource owners. The *theory of the firm* postulates that the primary goal, or objective, of the firm is to maximize wealth or the *value of the firm*. This is given by the present value of the expected future profits of the firm. Formally,

$$\begin{aligned} \text{PV} &= \frac{\pi_1}{(1+r)^1} + \frac{\pi_2}{(1+r)^2} + \cdots + \frac{\pi_n}{(1+r)^n} \\ &= \sum_{t=1}^{n} \frac{\pi_t}{(1+r)^t} \end{aligned} \qquad (1\text{-}2)$$

where PV is the present value of all expected future profits of the firm; π_1, π_2, $\cdots$, π_n represent the expected profits in each of the n years considered; and r is the discount rate. With Σ denoting the summation of the expression that follows it and t having values from 1 to the n years considered, we can see that the second formulation of PV given above is an abbreviated but equivalent form of the first. Since the firm faces many resource, legal, and other constraints, we speak of *constrained optimization*. Alternative theories of the firm postulate other objectives for the firm (Problems 1.13 to 1.15), but profit or value maximization predicts the behavior of the firm more accurately than any alternative criteria.

EXAMPLE 3.   At a discount rate of 10 percent, the value of a firm that generates $100 of profits for each of two years and is sold for $800 at the end of the second year is

$$\begin{aligned} \text{PV} &= \frac{\$100}{(1+0.10)^1} + \frac{\$100}{(1+0.10)^2} + \frac{\$800}{(1+0.10)^2} \\ &= \frac{\$100}{1.10} + \frac{\$100}{1.21} + \frac{\$800}{1.21} \\ &= \$90.91 + \$82.64 + \$661.16 \\ &= \$834.71 \end{aligned}$$

According to the theory of the firm, it is this value (PV) that the firm seeks to maximize.

1.4 THE NATURE AND FUNCTION OF PROFITS

Business profit is the revenue of a firm minus its explicit costs. *Explicit costs* are the actual out-of-pocket expenditures of the firm to hire labor, borrow capital, rent land and buildings, and purchase raw materials. *Economic profit*, however, equals the revenue of the firm minus its explicit and implicit costs. *Implicit costs* are the money values of the inputs owned and used by the firm in its own production processes. These include the salary that the entrepreneur could earn in managing another firm and the return that the firm could earn by investing its capital and renting its land and other inputs to other firms. Economic profit can result from frictional disturbances, monopoly power, the introduction of innovations, above-average managerial efficiency, risk-bearing, or a combination of these (see Problems 1.18 and 1.19). Economic profit provides the signals for the efficient allocation of society's resources. The general public and the business community use the terms *profit* and *cost* when speaking of business profit and explicit costs, but in the rest of this book, by *profit*, we will mean economic profit, and by *cost*, the sum of explicit and implicit costs.

EXAMPLE 4. Suppose that during a year a firm has revenues of $100,000 and explicit costs of $80,000 for hiring labor, borrowing capital, and purchasing raw materials. Suppose also that the entrepreneur could have earned $30,000 by managing another firm and an additional $5,000 by lending out the capital invested in the firm to another firm facing similar risks. The business profit of this firm is then $20,000, and it is derived from the firm's revenue of $100,000 minus its explicit costs of $80,000. The economic profit of the firm, on the other hand, is −$15,000 (an economic loss), and it is derived from the firm's revenue of $100,000 minus both its explicit costs of $80,000 and its implicit costs of $35,000 ($30,000 of salary plus $5,000 of interest forgone). Thus, a business profit of $20,000 per year corresponds to an economic loss of $15,000. Therefore, the entrepreneur should sell the firm and become manager of someone else's firm at a salary of $30,000. Thus, it is the concept of economic profit that provides the signal for the efficient allocation of society's resources.

Glossary

Business profit   The revenue of a firm minus its explicit, or accounting, costs.

Constrained optimization   The process of maximizing or minimizing an objective function subject to some constraints.

Econometrics   The empirical estimation and testing of economic relationships and models.

Economic profit   The revenue of a firm minus its economic costs.

Economic theory   The study of microeconomics and macroeconomics.

Explicit costs   The actual out-of-pocket expenditures of a firm to purchase or hire the inputs it requires in production.

Implicit costs   The value of the inputs owned and used by a firm in its own production processes.

Macroeconomics   The study of the total, or aggregate, level of output, income, employment, consumption, investment, and prices for the economy *viewed as a whole*.

Managerial economics   The study of the application of economic theory and the tools of decision science to examine how an organization can achieve its aims or objectives most efficiently.

Mathematical economics   The study of the formal (equational) relationship among economic variables in economic models and their theoretical implications.

Microeconomics   The study of the economic behavior of *individual* decision-making units such as individual consumers, resource owners, and business firms in a free-enterprise system.

Theory of the firm   It postulates that the primary goal or objective of the firm is to maximize wealth or the value of the firm.

Value of the firm   The present value of all expected future profits of the firm.

Review Questions

1. The principles of managerial economics apply to

    (a) business firms.

    (b) not-for-profit organizations.

    (c) government agencies.

    (d) all of the above.

    Ans.   (d) See Section 1.1.

2. Which of the following fields is not used by managerial economics?

    (a) Economic theory

    (b) Economic history

    (c) Mathematical economics

    (d) Econometrics

    Ans.   (b) See Sections 1.1 and 1.2.

3. Which of the following statements is false?

    (a) Economic theory refers to microeconomics and macroeconomics.

    (b) Decision sciences utilize the tools of analysis of mathematical economics and econometrics.

    (c) Mathematical economics uses statistical tools to estimate economic relationships.

    (d) None of the above.

    Ans.   (c) See Section 1.2.

4. The statement that quantity demanded of a commodity during a particular period of time is a function of, or depends on, the price of the commodity, consumers' income, and the price of related commodities, is an example of

    (a) an economic theory.

    (b) a mathematical relationship.

    (c) an economic relationship.

    (d) decision science.

    Ans.   (a) See Section 1.2.

5. Which are the functional areas of business administration studies?

    (a) Accounting, decision science, finance, personnel, production

    (b) Accounting, finance, marketing, personnel, production

    (c) Finance, marketing, mathematics, personnel, production

    (d) Accounting, econometrics, finance, marketing, personnel

    Ans.   (b) See Problem 1.5.

6. Which of the following statements is correct?

    (a) Firms combine and organize resources for the purpose of producing goods and services for sale.

    (b) Firms exist because of the economies they generate in production and distribution.

    (c) The existence of firms benefits entrepreneurs, workers, and other resource owners.

    (d) All of the above.

    Ans.   (d) See Section 1.3.

7.   The theory of the firm postulates that the firm maximizes

   (*a*)   short-term profits.

   (*b*)   the value of the firm.

   (*c*)   sales.

   (*d*)   growth.

   Ans.   (*b*) See Section 1.3.

8.   We accept the theory that the objective of the firm is to maximize its value because

   (*a*)   that theory is the simplest one available.

   (*b*)   that theory accurately predicts the firm's behavior.

   (*c*)   that theory was the first developed.

   (*d*)   none of the above.

   Ans.   (*b*) See Section 1.3.

9.   The salary that an entrepreneur could earn by managing another firm rather than the entrepreneur's own is

   (*a*)   an implicit cost.

   (*b*)   an explicit cost.

   (*c*)   a business cost.

   (*d*)   a business profit.

   Ans.   (*a*) See Section 1.4.

10.   Economic profit is equal to

   (*a*)   business profit minus implicit costs.

   (*b*)   business profit minus explicit costs.

   (*c*)   explicit costs plus implicit costs.

   (*d*)   a normal return on investment.

   Ans.   (*a*) See Section 1.4.

11.   An economic profit can arise from

   (*a*)   risk-bearing or disequilibrium.

   (*b*)   monopoly power.

   (*c*)   the introduction of innovations or above-average managerial efficiency.

   (*d*)   all of the above.

   Ans.   (*d*) See Section 1.4.

12.   Which of the following statements about economic profit is false?

   (*a*)   It provides the signal for the efficient allocation of society's resources.

   (*b*)   It can exist in the short run but not in the long run.

   (*c*)   It refers to above-normal return on investment.

   (*d*)   None of the above.

   Ans.   (*b*) See Section 1.4.

Solved Problems

THE SCOPE OF MANAGERIAL ECONOMICS

1.1   With regard to a hospital, a state university, and a museum, define (*a*) a possible primary aim, or goal, of each, (*b*) some of the constraints under which they operate, and (*c*) the relationship of (*a*) and (*b*) to the study of managerial economics.

(*a*)   The goal, or objective, of a hospital may be to seek to treat as many patients as possible at an "adequate" level of medical care. The objective of a state university may be to provide an adequate education to as many students as possible. The objective of a museum may be to maximize the number of visitors and/or the size of its art collection.

(*b*)   The constraints faced by a hospital may be the number of physicians, medical technicians, and nurses; quantity of diagnostic equipment; number of beds; and budget. The constraints of a state university may be the number of professors and secretaries, extent of library and computer facilities, amount of classroom space, and budget. The constraints of a museum may be the amount of space for its art display, its budget, and the requirements imposed by some large contributor.

(*c*)   Just as in the case of a business firm, not-for-profit organizations (such as hospitals, state universities, museums) also have some goal(s), or objective(s), that they seek to achieve subject to the constraints they face. While the goals and constraints of business firms and not-for-profit organizations may differ, managerial economics is very important and relevant to both types of organizations because it shows how each enterprise can reach its objective most efficiently.

1.2   With regard to a government agency, indicate (*a*) its possible objective, (*b*) its constraints, and (*c*) the usefulness of managerial economics in the operation of the agency.

(*a*)   The aim, or goal, of a government agency may be to provide a particular service (such as fire protection, which cannot be provided as efficiently by private firms) to as many people as possible at the lowest possible cost.

(*b*)   All government agencies face budgetary constraints on their operation. After all, most funds to provide government services are raised by general taxation, and there are limits on how much taxes can be raised to provide additional or better services.

(*c*)   Managerial economics studies the process of efficient decision making and is therefore very important in the operation of government agencies as they seek to achieve their objectives subject to the constraints under which they operate.

1.3   Explain briefly the importance and usefulness of (*a*) microeconomics and (*b*) macroeconomics in the study of managerial economics. (*c*) Which is more important? Why?

(*a*)   An important aspect of microeconomics is the theory of the firm, and this is the single most important element in managerial economics.

(*b*)   Macroeconomics is important and useful to managerial economics because macroeconomics studies the general conditions of the economy (such as the level of aggregate demand, the rate of inflation, and interest rates), within which the firm operates.

(*c*)   While macroeconomics is important to the study of managerial economics, microeconomics has a more central role. In fact, some people refer to managerial economics as *applied* microeconomics.

1.4   Explain briefly the methodology of science in general and economics in particular.

According to Milton Friedman (a Nobel prize winner in economics), a theory or model should be accepted if it predicts accurately, even if it is based on unrealistic assumptions. That is, a theory or model can be tested only by its predictive ability and not in terms of the realism or lack of realism of the assumptions on which it is based. For example, while a firm may have multiple aims or objectives, we accept the theory of the firm based on the assumption of profit maximization because the theory then accurately predicts the behavior of the firm.

1.5   Managerial economics is often said to help the business student integrate the knowledge gained in other courses. Explain how this integration is accomplished.

Managerial economics utilizes the theoretical tools of microeconomics and macroeconomics and the mathematical and econometric techniques of decision sciences as well as knowledge of accounting, finance, marketing, personnel, and production (the functional areas of business administration studies) to examine how any organization can achieve its objectives most efficiently. To that extent, managerial economics integrates all of these fields and illustrates to the student the relationship among the various fields and how they interact in the decision-making process.

THE THEORY OF THE FIRM

1.6   (a) Explain the function of a business firm, (b) describe its major forms of organization, and (c) indicate its place in the "circular flow of economic activity."

(a)   A firm is an organization that combines and organizes resources for the purpose of producing goods and services for sale. There are millions of firms in the United States, and they produce more than 80 percent of all goods and services consumed.

(b)   Firms are organized in three major forms: (1) proprietorships (i.e., firms owned by one individual), (2) partnerships (firms owned by two or more individuals), and (3) corporations (firms owned by stockholders).

(c)   Firms hire resources from resource owners in order to produce goods and services for sale to the public. Firms then use the revenues generated from the sale of goods and services to the public to pay for the resources purchased from the resource owners.

1.7   Explain (a) the reason business firms exist and (b) the reason they do not continue to grow indefinitely.

(a)   Firms exist because it would be very inefficient and costly for entrepreneurs to enter into and enforce contracts with workers and owners of capital, land, and other resources to perform each separate step of the production and distribution process. By entering into long-term broader contracts with labor and other resources, contractual costs are sharply reduced. The resulting increase in efficiency leads to higher profits for the entrepreneur and higher incomes for other resource owners. By internalizing many transactions (i.e., by performing many functions within the firm) the firm also saves on sales taxes and is not subject to other government regulations that apply only to transactions among firms.

(b)   The reason firms do not grow larger and larger indefinitely is that there are limitations on management ability to effectively control and direct the operation of the firm as it becomes ever larger. It is true that up to a point, a firm can overcome these internal disadvantages of large size, or diseconomies of scale, by establishing a number of semiautonomous divisions (i.e., by decentralizing). Eventually, however, the increased communications traffic that is generated and the ever-increasing distancing of top management from the operation of each division imposes sufficient diseconomies of scale to limit the growth of the firm. Furthermore, the firm will reach a point at which the cost of supplying additional services within the firm exceeds the cost of purchasing those services from other firms. An example of this is some highly technical (legal, medical, or engineering) service that the firm may need only occasionally.

1.8   The owner of a firm expects to receive a profit of $100 in each of the next three years and to be able to sell the firm at the end of the third year for $700. The owner believes that the appropriate discount rate for the firm is 10 percent per year. Calculate the value of the firm.

We use equation (1-2) to calculate the value of the firm (PV).

$$PV = \frac{\pi_1}{(1+r)^1} + \frac{\pi_2}{(1+r)^2} + \cdots + \frac{\pi_n}{(1+r)^n}$$

$$= \frac{\$100}{(1.1)^1} + \frac{\$100}{(1.1)^2} + \frac{\$100}{(1.1)^3} + \frac{\$700}{(1.1)^3}$$

$$= \frac{\$100}{1.1} + \frac{\$100}{1.21} + \frac{\$100}{1.331} + \frac{\$700}{1.331}$$

$$= \$90.91 + \$82.64 + \$75.13 + \$525.92$$

$$= \$774.60$$

1.9 Recalculate the value of the firm, using a discount rate of 20 percent. What is the effect on the value of the firm of using a higher discount rate?

From equation (*1-2*),

$$PV = \frac{\$100}{(1.2)^1} + \frac{\$100}{(1.2)^2} + \frac{\$100}{(1.2)^3} + \frac{\$700}{(1.2)^3}$$

$$= \frac{\$100}{1.2} + \frac{\$100}{1.44} + \frac{\$100}{1.728} + \frac{\$700}{1.728}$$

$$= \$83.33 + \$69.44 + \$57.87 + \$405.09$$

$$= \$615.73$$

Using a higher discount rate reduces the value of the firm.

1.10 Calculate the present value of an investment that yields a net cash flow of $100 in each future year indefinitely if the discount rate is (*a*) 10 percent, (*b*) 5 percent, and (*c*) 20 percent.

(*a*) $PV = R/r$, where R is equal to the net cash flow received in each future year indefinitely and r is the discount rate. At $r = 10\%$, $PV = \$100/0.1 = \$1,000$.

Note in the answer to Problem 1.8 that the present value of $100 declines year by year. The present value of a sum received more than 30 years from now is very close to zero. A PV based on $100 received indefinitely in each future year at a discount rate of 10 percent approaches or converges toward $1,000. (For the actual derivation of the formula for the present value of a so-called annuity, see your managerial economics texts.)

(*b*) At $r = 5\%$, $PV = R/r = \$100/0.05 = \$2,000$.

(*c*) At $r = 20\%$, $PV = R/r = \$100/0.2 = \$500$.

Thus, the value of an annuity is inversely related to the discount rate.

1.11 (*a*) Restate the summary or abbreviated form of the formula for the value of a firm presented in Section 1.3 in terms of total revenue and total cost. (*b*) Explain how the formula for the value of the firm in part (*a*) provides an integrated framework for the analysis of managerial decision making in all the functional areas of business administration studies.

(*a*) Since profits are equal to total revenue (TR) minus total costs (TC), the equation for the value of a firm can be rewritten as

$$\text{Value of firm} = PV = \sum_{t=1}^{n} \frac{TR_t - TC_t}{(1 + r)^t}$$

(*b*) The formula for the value of a firm in terms of total revenue and total cost shown in part (*a*) provides the unifying theme for the analysis of managerial decision making. Specifically, TR depends on sales, or the demand for a firm's output, and the firm's pricing decisions. These are the major responsibility of the marketing department. TC depends on the technology of production and resource prices. These are the major responsibility of the production and personnel departments. The discount rate (r) depends on the perceived risks of the firm and on the cost of borrowing funds, which are the major responsibility of the finance department. The accounting department, of course, is concerned with keeping records on revenues and costs and is, therefore, involved with all the other departments.

1.12 In managerial economics, we often speak of "constrained optimization." (*a*) Explain the meaning of this expression. (*b*) Specify the constraints usually faced by firms.

(*a*) Constrained optimization refers to the maximization or minimization of an objective function by an organization subject to the constraints that the organization faces. For example, a firm may want to maximize profits or minimize costs subject to the limitations it faces regarding the availability of essential inputs, the size of the budget, and the legal controls or regulations to which it is subject.

(b)   Firms usually face limitations on the number of skilled workers they can hire and the amounts of specific inputs they can purchase, especially in the short run. They may also face limitations on factory and warehouse space and in the quantity of capital funds available for a given project or purpose. Besides resource constraints, firms also face many legal constraints. These take the form of minimum wage laws, health and safety standards, and pollution emission standards as well as laws and regulations that prevent firms from adopting unfair business practices. So pervasive are the constraints faced by firms and other organizations that we usually refer to the process by which they strive to achieve their objective as constrained optimization.

1.13   Some economists have advanced a theory of the firm that postulates that firms seek to maximize sales rather than profits or the value of the firm. (a) Explain what the motivation of managers might be in seeking to maximize sales rather than profits. (b) Explain the reason that we retain the theory of the firm in terms of value rather than sales maximization.

(a)   According to the sales maximization model introduced by William Baumol and others, managers of modern corporations, after generating an "adequate" rate of profit to satisfy stockholders, seek to maximize sales rather than profits because managers' salaries are more closely correlated with sales than with profits. Indeed, some early empirical studies found a strong correlation between executives' salaries and sales but not between salaries and profits. More recent empirical studies, however, found the opposite.

(b)   One reason for favoring the theory of the firm that postulates value maximizing is that the results of some recent empirical studies seem to indicate a stronger correlation between executives' salaries and profits than between salaries and sales. Another reason is that the value-maximization model predicts the behavior of the firm more accurately than the sales-maximization model. Thus, we retain the theory of the firm presented in Section 1.3.

1.14   Another model advanced as an alternative to the value-maximization model of the firm postulates that with the advent of the modern corporation and the resulting separation of management from ownership, managers are more interested in maximizing their own utility than corporate profits. (a) Indicate how you would measure managers' utility. (b) Explain the reason that this theory cannot supplant our theory of the firm in terms of value maximization.

(a)   Managers' utility can be measured in terms of their compensation (salaries, fringe benefits, stock options, etc.), the size of their staff, the extent of their control over the corporation and its investment decisions, the lavishness of their offices, their access to chauffeured limousines, etc.

(b)   The theory of the firm in terms of management utility maximization cannot supplant the theory in terms of profit or value maximization because those managers who seek to maximize their own utility rather than the corporation's profits are likely to be replaced either by action of the stockholders of the corporation or as a result of the corporation's being taken over (merged) with another firm that sees the unexploited profits of the first.

1.15   Still another model advanced as an alternative to the value-maximization model of the firm postulates that because of the great complexity of running the large modern corporation, including the problems of uncertainty and lack of data, managers are not able to maximize profits but can only strive for some satisfactory goal in terms of sales, profits, growth, market share, and so on. Herbert Simon (a Nobel prize winner in economics) called this *satisficing behavior*. That is, the large corporation is a satisficing rather than a maximizing organization.

Evaluate this theory in relation to the profit- or value-maximizing theory of the firm presented in Section 1.3.

The satisficing theory of the firm is not necessarily inconsistent with profit or value maximization. Presumably, with more and better data and search procedures, the modern corporation could conceivably approach profit or value maximization. Indeed, the stiff competition prevailing today in most product and resource markets, as well as in the market for managerial and entrepreneurial talent, today, forces managers to pay close attention to profits—lest the firm go out of business or the managers be replaced. As a result, we retain our theory of the firm in terms of profit or value maximization. The assumptions of this theory are somewhat unrealistic, but the theory predicts the behavior of the firm more accurately than any alternative theories.

THE NATURE AND FUNCTION OF PROFITS

1.16 The costs of attending a state college for one year are $2,000 for tuition, $1,500 for the room, $1,000 for meals, and $500 for books and supplies. As an alternative the student could earn $13,000 by getting a job instead of going to college and, in addition, earn 8 percent interest by saving the money not spent on attending college. Calculate (a) the explicit costs, (b) the implicit costs, and (c) the total economic costs that the student faces by attending the college for one year.

(a) The explicit costs are $2,000 for tuition, $1,500 for the room, $1,000 for meals, and $500 for books and supplies, for a total of $5,000 per year.

(b) The implicit costs are the sum of $13,000 that the student could have earned by getting a job instead of going to college and $400 interest at 8 percent forgone on the $5,000 of expenses for the year [i.e., $5000 × 0.08 = $400], for a total of $13,400.

(c) The total economic costs to this student of attending the college for one year equal the sum of the explicit costs of $5,000 and the implicit costs of $13,200, or $18,200. Note that the implicit costs are almost three times larger than the explicit costs.

1.17 A person managing a dry-cleaning store for $30,000 per year decides to open a dry-cleaning store. The revenues of the store during the first year of operation are $100,000 and the expenses are $35,000 for salaries, $10,000 for supplies, $8,000 for rent, $2,000 for utilities, and $5,000 for interest on a bank loan. Calculate (a) the explicit costs, (b) the implicit costs, (c) the business profit, (d) the economic profit, and (e) the normal return on investment in this business. (f) Indicate whether the person should open the dry-cleaning store.

(a) The explicit costs are $60,000 (obtained by adding together the $35,000 for salaries, $10,000 for supplies, $8,000 for rent, $2,000 for utilities, and $5,000 for interest on the bank loan).

(b) The implicit costs are equal to $30,000 (i.e., the entrepreneur's forgone salary).

(c) The business profit equals total revenues minus the explicit costs, or $100,000 − $60,000 = $40,000.

(d) The economic profit equals total revenues minus the explicit costs of $60,000 and implicit costs of $30,000, or $100,000 − $90,000 = $10,000.

(e) The normal return on investment equals the implicit costs of the entrepreneur (i.e., the salary forgone) of $30,000.

(f) The person would earn an economic profit of $10,000 per year and, therefore, should open the dry-cleaning store.

1.18 Explain how economic profit arises according to (a) the frictional theory of profit and (b) the monopoly theory of profit.

(a) According to the frictional theory of profit, economic profit arises from frictions, or displacements from long-run equilibrium. That is, in long-run, perfectly competitive equilibrium, firms tend to earn only a normal return (adjusted for risk) or zero (economic) profit on their investment. At any point in time, however, firms are not likely to be in long-run equilibrium and may earn a profit or incur a loss. For example, at the time of the energy crisis in the early 1970s, firms producing insulating material faced a sharp increase in demand. This led to large profits, and more firms entered the industry. With the sharp decline in petroleum prices in the mid-1980s, many of these firms began to incur losses and left the industry.

(b) According to the monopoly theory of profit, economic profit arises from the monopoly power that some firms have, which allows them to restrict output and charge higher prices than they would in a perfectly competitive market. Because of the restricted entry into the industry, monopoly profit can persist in the long run.

1.19   Explain how profits arise according to (*a*) the risk-bearing theory of profit, (*b*) the innovation theory of profit, and (*c*) the managerial efficiency theory of profit.

   (*a*)   According to the risk-bearing theory of profit, above-normal returns (i.e., economic profits) are required by firms in order to enter and remain in fields with above-average risks, such as petroleum exploration. Similarly, the expected return on stocks has to be higher than on bonds because of the greater risk associated with the former.

   (*b*)   The innovation theory of profit postulates that (economic) profit is the reward for the introduction of a successful innovation. As other firms imitate the innovation, the profits of the innovator are reduced and, eventually, are eliminated.

   (*c*)   The managerial efficiency theory of profit rests on the observation that if the average firm tends to earn only normal returns on its investment in the long run, firms that are more efficient than the average would earn above-average returns and (economic) profits.

1.20   (*a*) Explain the crucial function that economic profit performs in a free-enterprise system such as our own. (*b*) Why, then, does government regulate telephone, electric power, and other public utility companies?

   (*a*)   Economic profit provides the signal for the efficient allocation of society's resources in a free-enterprise system such as our own. Economic profit signals that society wants more of the output of the industry and/ or is the reward for above-average efficiency. The opposite is true for economic loss. In the process of reallocation of resources that arises in response to the profit signals, more of the goods and services that society wants the most are produced.

   (*b*)   The government often allows only one electric power company in each area in order to foster large-scale economies in production, with lower costs per unit. But then it regulates the company in order to allow just enough (i.e., normal) return on investment to attract and retain investments in the industry. Regulation is required to prevent the company from using the monopoly power conferred on it by the government to charge higher prices to consumers and earn above-normal returns (i.e., economic profits) on investment.

1.21   According to some economists, the only responsibility of business is to make as much profit as possible within the legal and moral rules set by society. Imposing additional societal goals on business would not be in the long-term interest of society. Explain why you agree or disagree with this.

   In the course of maximizing profits or the value of the firm, business supplies the goods and services that society wants the most, provides employment, and pays taxes. According to some economists, trying to impose additional explicit societal goals on business would interfere with the allocative efficiency of the free-enterprise system. It is true that society often wants to modify the operation of the economic system so as to achieve some explicit social goals (such as reducing the overall level of unemployment, hiring the handicapped, controlling inflation, etc.). But this, according to those economists, can best be achieved through government regulations and incentives rather than by interfering with the profit motive and the allocative efficiency to which the profit motive gives rise.

Chapter 2

Techniques of Analysis: Optimization

2.1 OPTIMIZATION AND OTHER TECHNIQUES OF ANALYSIS IN MANAGERIAL ECONOMICS

We have seen in Chapter 1 that managerial economics examines how an organization can achieve its objectives most efficiently. For example, the optimal behavior of a firm is to maximize profits or the present value of the firm. Thus, *optimization analysis*, the subject of this chapter, is one of the most important techniques of analysis in managerial economics. Other important techniques of analysis in managerial economics are *risk analysis* and *estimation*, which are examined in the next two chapters.

EXAMPLE 1. The total profit of a firm is equal to total revenue minus total cost. Thus, the firm maximizes its profit when the positive difference between total revenue and total cost is greatest. The total profit of the firm will increase as long as the extra or marginal revenue that the firm receives from producing and selling each extra unit of output exceeds the extra or marginal cost that the firm incurs to produce the extra unit of output. The process of profit maximization, as a most important example of optimization by the firm, is examined in this chapter, using total and marginal revenue and cost curves. Since most managerial decisions are made in the face of risk or uncertainty, it is also very important to examine risk and to show how it can be incorporated into the managerial decision process. Finally, it is very important in the managerial decision process to estimate the quantitative relationship among economic variables. Optimization analysis, risk analysis, and estimation are techniques used throughout the rest of the book in the study of managerial economics.

2.2 TOTAL, AVERAGE, AND MARGINAL ECONOMIC RELATIONSHIPS

To study the process of optimization by the firm, we begin by examining the relationship between total revenue, average revenue, and marginal revenue on the one hand, and total cost, average cost, and marginal cost on the other. In the next section, we bring together the revenue and cost concepts and curves presented in this section to examine the process of optimization by the firm.

Average revenue (AR) equals total revenue (TR) divided by quantity (Q), and marginal revenue (MR) is the change in total revenue (i.e., ΔTR) per unit change in output (ΔQ). Similarly, average cost (AC) equals total cost (TC) divided by quantity (Q), and marginal cost (MC) is the change in total cost (i.e., ΔTC) per unit change in output (ΔQ).

EXAMPLE 2. Suppose that the total revenue function of a firm is given by TR $= 8Q - Q^2$. By substituting various values of Q into the TR function, we generate the TR schedule shown in the first and the third columns of Table 2.1. From the TR schedule, we can then derive the AR and MR schedules (fourth and fifth columns, respectively, of Table 2.1): AR $=$ TR$/Q$. MR $= \Delta$TR$/\Delta Q$. By plotting the TR, AR, and MR schedules in Table 2.1, we get the TR, AR, and MR curves in Fig. 2-1. Note that AR is equal to the slope of a ray from the origin to the TR curve. In Fig. 2-1, AR declines continuously but remains positive as long as TR is positive. Since MR is the change in TR per unit change in

Table 2.1

Q	$8Q - Q^2$	TR	AR	MR
0	$8(0) - (0)^2$	\$ 0	—	—
1	$8(1) - (1)^2$	7	\$7	\$ 7
2	$8(2) - (2)^2$	12	6	5
3	$8(3) - (3)^2$	15	5	3
4	$8(4) - (4)^2$	16	4	1
5	$8(5) - (5)^2$	15	3	-1

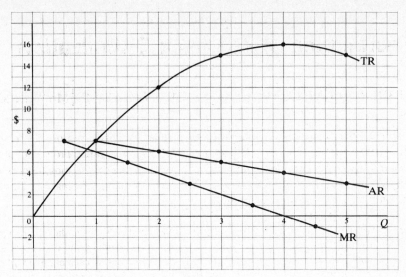

Fig. 2-1

output, the MR values of Table 2.1 are plotted halfway between successive levels of output in Fig. 2-1. At any particular point on the TR curve, MR is equal to the slope of the TR curve at that point. MR declines continuously and is less than AR at every level of output. At $Q = 4$, TR is at its maximum and MR is zero. At larger outputs, TR declines and MR is negative.

EXAMPLE 3.   Suppose that the total cost schedule of a firm is the one given in the first two columns of Table 2.2. We can then derive the corresponding average and marginal cost schedules in the third and fourth columns, respectively: $AC = TC/Q$. $MC = \Delta TC/\Delta Q$. By plotting the schedules of Table 2.2, we get the TC, AC, and MC curves in Fig. 2-2. AC is equal to the slope of a ray from the origin to the TC curve. This declines to point B and then rises. The slope of the TC curve, or MC, falls to point A (the point of inflection) and then rises, and is equal to AC at point B. Note that when the AC curve falls, the MC curve is below it. When the AC curve rises, the MC curve is above it, and when AC is lowest, $MC = AC$.

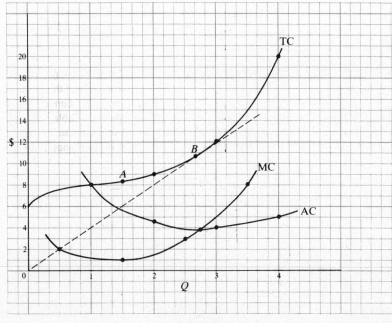

Fig. 2-2

Table 2.2

Q	TC	AC	MC
0	$ 6	—	—
1	8	$8	$2
2	9	4.50	1
3	12	4	3
4	20	5	8

2.3 OPTIMIZATION ANALYSIS: PROFIT MAXIMIZATION

Optimization analysis can best be explained by examining the process by which the firm determines the output level at which it maximizes total profit. A firm maximizes total profit at the level of output at which the positive difference between total revenue and total cost is greatest. At this level of output, the firm's total revenue curve and total cost curve are parallel and marginal revenue equals marginal cost. This is one of the most important concepts in managerial economics. That is, according to *marginal analysis*, as long as the marginal benefit of an activity (such as expanding output or sales) exceeds the marginal cost, it pays for the organization (firm) gains by increasing the activity (output or sales). The total benefit (profit) is maximized when the marginal benefit (revenue) equals the marginal cost.

EXAMPLE 4.   The determination of the output level at which the firm maximizes total profit is shown in Fig. 2-3. In the top panel of Fig. 2-3, the TR and MR curves are those of Fig. 2-1, while the TC and MC curves are those of Fig.

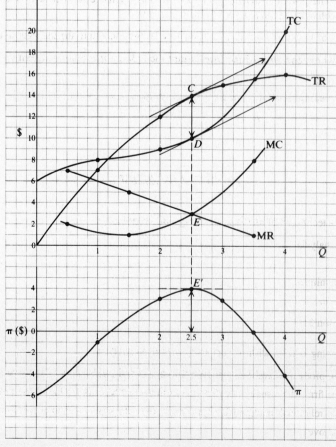

Fig. 2-3

2-2. The total profit (π) curve in the bottom panel of Fig. 2-3 is derived by subtracting the TC curve vertically from the TR curve. The maximum π (of \$4) occurs at $Q = 2.5$, where the π curve has zero slope. At $Q = 2.5$, the TR curve is above and parallel to the TC curve, so that the vertical distance between them (π) is greatest. This is also the output level at which the slope of the TR curve, or MR, equals the slope of the TC curve, or MC. AT $Q < 2.5$, MR > MC and the firm would be adding more to TR than to TC, so that π would increase by expanding output and sales. (The symbols < and > mean "smaller than" and "larger than," respectively.) However, at $Q > 2.5$, MR < MC and the firm would be adding less to TR than to TC, so that π would increase by *reducing* output. As a result, π is maximized at $Q = 2.5$, where MR = MC. This is a most important example of optimization by marginal analysis.

Glossary

Average cost (AC)   Total cost divided by output (i.e., TC/Q).

Average revenue (AR)   Total revenue divided by output or sales (i.e., TR/Q).

Estimation techniques   Methods of calculating quantitative relationships among economic variables.

Marginal analysis   An analytical technique which postulates that an activity should be carried out until the marginal benefit of the activity equals the marginal cost.

Marginal cost (MC)   The change in total cost per unit change in output (i.e., $\Delta TC/\Delta Q$).

Marginal revenue (MR)   The change in total revenue per unit change in output or sales (i.e., $\Delta TR/\Delta Q$).

Optimization analysis   The process whereby an organization can achieve its objective most efficiently; for a firm this involves maximizing profits or the value of the firm.

Risk analysis   The study of how risk and uncertainty can be incorporated into the managerial decision process.

Total cost (TC)   The total expenditures of the firm to hire the inputs, or resources, required to produce and sell its output.

Total revenue (TR)   The earnings of the firm in selling its output; price times quantity sold.

Review Questions

1.   The most important technique of analysis in managerial economics is

   (*a*)   optimization analysis.

   (*b*)   risk analysis.

   (*c*)   estimation techniques.

   (*d*)   all of the above.

   Ans.   (*d*) See Section 2.1.

2.   Which of the following is false with respect to optimization analysis?

   (*a*)   It refers to the process whereby an organization achieves its objectives most efficiently.

   (*b*)   For a business firm, this usually involves maximizing profits or the value of the firm.

   (*c*)   It relies on the relationship among total, average, and marginal concepts or measures.

   (*d*)   None of the above.

   Ans.   (*d*) See Section 2.1.

3.   The firm maximizes profits when

   (*a*)   the positive difference between total revenue and total cost is at the maximum.

   (*b*)   total revenue is at its maximum.

   (*c*)   total cost is at its minimum.

   (*d*)   all of the above.

   Ans.   (*a*) See Section 2.1 and Example 1.

4.   Which of the following statements is *false* with respect to risk?

   (*a*)   Most managerial decisions are made in the face of risk.

   (*b*)   Risk and uncertainty arise when there is more than one possible outcome of a decision.

   (*c*)   Risk analysis cannot be incorporated into the optimization calculations of the firm.

   (*d*)   None of the above.

   Ans.   (*c*) See Section 2.1 and Example 1.

5.   If the price of the commodity declines as the firm sells more units of the commodity, the total revenue (TR) curve of the firm

   (*a*)   is negatively sloped.

   (*b*)   is a positively sloped straight line.

   (*c*)   first rises, reaches a maximum, and then declines.

   (*d*)   is convex.

   Ans.   (*c*) See Example 2 and Fig. 2-1.

6.   Which of the following statements about average revenue (AR) is false?

   (*a*)   If the TR curve is concave, the AR curve declines continuously.

   (*b*)   When the TR curve begins to decline, AR becomes negative.

   (*c*)   If the TR curve is a positively sloped straight line, the AR curve is horizontal.

   (*d*)   AR is given by the slope of a ray from the origin to the TR curve.

   Ans.   (*b*) See Section 2.2, Example 2, and Fig. 2-1.

7.   Which of the following statements about marginal revenue is false?

   (*a*)   It is positive when total revenue rises.

   (*b*)   It is zero when total revenue is zero.

   (*c*)   It is negative when total revenue declines.

   (*d*)   None of the above.

   Ans.   (*b*) See Section 2.2.

8.   Which of the following statements about the relationship between marginal revenue and average revenue is false?

   (*a*)   When the AR curve is falling, MR is negative.

   (*b*)   When the AR curve is falling, the MR curve is below the AR curve.

   (*c*)   When AR is positive, MR can be positive or negative.

   (*d*)   None of the above.

   Ans.   (*a*) See Section 2.2 and Fig. 2-1.

9.   Which of the following statements about the total cost (TC) curve is true?

      (a) The TC curve is always positively sloped.

      (b) The TC curve can be positive at zero output.

      (c) The TC curve can first be concave and then convex to the origin.

      (d) All of the above.

      Ans.   (d) See Fig. 2-2.

10.   Which of the following statements about the average and marginal cost curves is true?

      (a) The AC curve falls when the MC curve falls.

      (b) The AC curve rises when the MC curve rises.

      (c) At the lowest point on the AC curve, MC = AC.

      (d) All of the above.

      Ans.   (c) See Section 2.2 and Fig. 2-2.

11.   A firm maximizes total profits when

      (a) MR = MC and the MC curve intersects the MR curve from below.

      (b) the positive difference between TR and TC is at the maximum.

      (c) the TR and TC curves have equal slopes, and the TR curve is above the TC curve.

      (d) all of the above.

      Ans.   (d) See Section 2.3.

12.   At the point of profit maximization

      (a) MR is at its maximum.

      (b) profit per unit is at its maximum.

      (c) MC is at its minimum.

      (d) none of the above.

      Ans.   (d) See Section 2.3 and Fig. 2-3.

Solved Problems

OPTIMIZATION AND OTHER TECHNIQUES OF ANALYSIS IN MANAGERIAL ECONOMICS

2.1   (a) Explain what is meant by optimization by the firm. (b) How is optimization analysis conducted?

       (a) Optimization by the firm refers to the process by which the firm seeks to achieve its objectives most efficiently. The optimal behavior of the firm is usually taken to be profit maximization, or the maximization of the present value of the firm. Sometimes, optimization may involve minimizing the total costs of the firm. This would be the case if the firm had a contract to supply a specific quantity of a commodity at a given price. By minimizing total costs for the given total revenue (since price per unit and sales are given), the firm would also be maximizing total profits. Thus, optimization may involve the maximization of profits or the minimization of costs by the firm.

       (b) To a large extent, optimization analysis rests on the relationship among total, average, and marginal concepts and measures. The average is equal to the total divided by the quantity, while the marginal value is equal to the change in the total per unit change in quantity. The firm maximizes profits when the positive difference between total revenue and total cost is greatest. The total profits of the firm will increase as long as the extra or marginal revenue that the firm receives from producing and selling one extra unit of output exceeds the extra or marginal cost that the firm incurs to produce the extra unit of output. The total profit of the firm increases as long as marginal revenue exceeds marginal cost and until they are equal.

2.2   (*a*) What is meant by risk? (*b*) Why is it important to incorporate risk in managerial decision making?

(*a*)   Risk refers to the situation in which there is more than one possible outcome to a decision. For example, a firm may be anticipating sales of $100 million next year. However, depending on the general economic conditions that will prevail in the economy next year, the behavior of competitors, and other conditions, the sales of the firm could be as high as $150 million or as low as $75 million. If the firm can attach some probabilities to the occurrence of the events that affect its sales (e.g., if the firm knows or can forecast the probability of a recession next year), we say that the firm faces a risk.

(*b*)   Most managerial decisions are made in the face of risk. Thus, it is extremely important that the firm consider the effect of risk in optimizing its behavior. For example, a firm may have a choice of drilling in one of two oil fields, one with very high profitability but with a low probability of finding petroleum and the other with a large probability of finding less petroleum. The entire future of the firm may depend on the choice it makes. Thus, it is crucial for the firm to be able to incorporate (i.e., take into consideration) the information about the amount of oil and the probability of striking it in determining the optimal course of action. Risk analysis is one of the most important techniques of analysis in managerial economics. Because of the importance of risk analysis and because it is used throughout the book, we devote all of Chapter 3 to the topic before beginning to study the formal subject matter of managerial economics (i.e., the analysis of demand, supply, costs, prices, market structures, government regulations, and so on).

2.3   (*a*) What is meant by estimation techniques? (*b*) Why are these important to managerial economics?

(*a*)   Estimation techniques are the methods of determining the quantitative relationship between a dependent variable, or variable that we seek to explain, and one or more independent or explanatory variables. For example, economic theory postulates that the quantity demanded of a commodity is a function of, or depends on, the price of the commodity, the income of consumers, and the price of related commodities (complements and substitutes). One of the most important estimation techniques used in managerial economics is regression analysis. This can be used, for example, to estimate how much the quantity demanded of a commodity declines, given a specific increase in the price of the commodity and in the price of the complementary commodity, and how much the quantity demanded of a commodity increases upon a specific increase in consumers' income and in the price of a substitute commodity. Estimation techniques (mostly regression analysis) are examined in Chapter 4.

(*b*)   In order for a firm to maximize its total profits, or its value, the firm must have some estimates of the quantitative relationships among the variables that affect its revenues and costs. It is not sufficient to know, for example, that the quantity demanded of a commodity is inversely related to the price of the commodity and the price of complementary commodities, and directly related to consumers' income and the price of substitute commodities. In order to maximize profits, a firm needs also to know how much the quantity demanded of the commodity changes for a given change in the commodity price, in consumers' income, and in the price of related commodities.

TOTAL, AVERAGE, AND MARGINAL ECONOMIC RELATIONSHIPS

2.4   Indicate (*a*) the different forms in which economic relationships can be expressed and (*b*) the advantage of each.

(*a*)   Economic relationships can be expressed in equational, tabular, and graphical forms. Example 2 gave a hypothetical TR function (equation). By substituting various values of *Q* into the TR function, we generated the TR schedule in Table 2.1 and, from it, the AR and MR schedules. By then plotting the TR, AR, and MR schedules of Table 2.1, we obtained the corresponding TR, AR, and MR curves shown in Fig. 2-1.

(*b*)   The advantage of expressing economic relationships in tabular form is that a table can readily summarize a large amount of data. The advantage of a figure is that it provides a quick visual overview of changes in the data over time or across units of observation. Expressing an economic relationship in functional or equational form allows us to utilize the powerful techniques of mathematics (e.g., differential calculus) in determining the optimal solution to problems.

2.5　Given the total revenue function $TR = 12 - 2Q^2$ (a) derive the total revenue, average revenue, and marginal revenue schedules. (b) On the same set of axes, plot the total revenue, the average revenue, and the marginal revenue schedules of part (a). (c) Using the figure you drew for part (b), explain the relationship among the total, average, and marginal revenue curves.

(a)　The total, average, and marginal revenue schedules are derived in Table 2.3.

Table 2.3

Q	$12 - 2Q^2$	TR	AR	MR
0	$12(0) - 2(0)^2$	\$ 0	—	—
1	$12(1) - 2(1)^2$	10	\$10	\$ 10
2	$12(2) - 2(2)^2$	16	8	6
3	$12(3) - 2(3)^2$	18	6	2
4	$12(4) - 2(4)^2$	16	4	−2

(b)　The TR, AR, and MR schedules of Table 2.3 are plotted in Fig. 2-4. The AR curve is the demand curve (D) for the product that the firm faces. Note that the MR values are plotted halfway between successive levels of output because MR represents the change in TR per unit change in output.

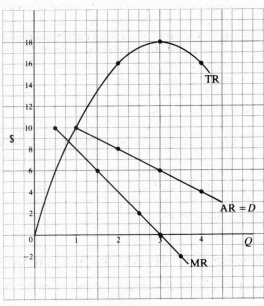

Fig. 2-4

(c)　The slope of a ray from the origin to the TR curve, (i.e., the average revenue), falls continuously and is positive as long as TR is positive. Since the TR curve is concave, its slope, or MR, also falls continuously. MR is positive as long as TR increases, MR = 0 when TR is at its maximum, and MR is negative when TR declines. Since the AR, or D, curve falls continuously, the MR curve is always below it.

2.6   Given the following total product (TP) schedule, (*a*) derive the average product (AP) and marginal product (MP) schedules. (*b*) On the same set of axes plot the total, average, and marginal product schedules of part (*a*). (*c*) Using the figure you drew for part (*b*), explain the relationship among the total, average, and marginal product curves.

Q	0	1	2	3	4	5	6	7
TP	0	3	8	12	15	17	17	16

(*a*)   The average and marginal product schedules are derived in Table 2.4.

Table 2.4

Q	TP	$AP = TP/Q$	$MP = \Delta TP/\Delta Q$
0	0	—	—
1	3	3	3
2	8	4	5
3	12	4	4
4	15	$3\frac{3}{4}$	3
5	17	$3\frac{2}{5}$	2
6	17	$2\frac{5}{6}$	0
7	16	$2\frac{2}{7}$	-1

(*b*)   The TP, AP, and MP schedules of Table 2.4 are plotted in Fig. 2-5. Note that the MP values are plotted halfway between successive levels of output.

(*c*)   The slope of a ray from the origin to the TP curve, or (i.e., the average product), rises to point *B* in Fig. 2-5 and then falls, but it remains positive as long as TP is positive. Thus, the AP curve rises to point *B'* and then declines. At the same time, the slope of the TP curve (i.e., the marginal product) rises to point *A*

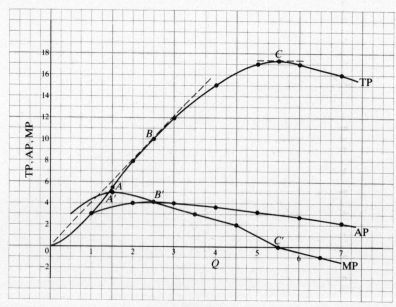

Fig. 2-5

(the point of inflection of the TP curve) and falls thereafter. Thus, the MP curve rises to point A' and then declines. When TP is at its maximum, the slope of the TP curve is zero (point C), and so is MP (point C'). Past point C, the TP curve declines and MP is negative. Note also that when the AP curve rises, the MP curve is above it, and when the AP curve declines, the MP curve is below it. The MP curve intersects the AP curve at the highest point of AP (point B'), so that AP = MP at that level of output (2.5 units in Fig. 2-5).

2.7 (a) Derive the average and marginal profit schedules for the total profit curve in the bottom panel of Fig. 2-3 in Example 4. (b) Plot the total profit curve of Fig. 2-3, and below it, on a separate set of axes, plot the corresponding average and marginal profit schedules of part (a). (c) Using the figure you drew for part (b), explain the relationship among the total, average, and marginal profit curves.

(a) The average profit ($\overline{\pi}$) and the marginal profit ($\dot{\pi}$) schedules are derived in Table 2.5.

Table 2.5

Q	π	$\overline{\pi} = \pi/Q$	$\dot{\pi} = \Delta\pi/\Delta Q$
0	$-6	—	—
1	-1	$-1	$ 5
2	3	1.50	4
3	3	1	0
4	-4	-1	-7

(b) The π, $\overline{\pi}$, and $\dot{\pi}$ schedules of Table 2.5 are plotted in Fig. 2-6.

(c) The slope of a ray from the origin to the π curve, (i.e., average profit, $\overline{\pi}$), is negative but rises up to $Q =$ 2.33, after which it declines, becomes zero at $Q = 3.5$, and is negative thereafter (because π is once again

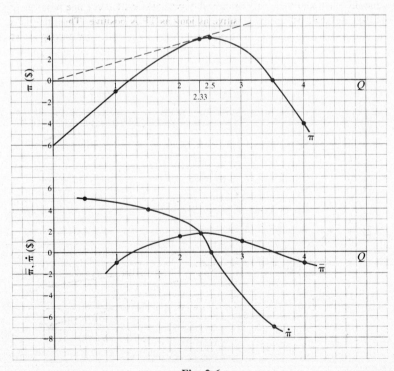

Fig. 2-6

negative). At the same time, the slope of π, (i.e., marginal profit, $\dot{\pi}$), declines continuously, but it is positive up to $Q = 2.5$ and negative thereafter. As the $\overline{\pi}$ curve rises, reaches its highest point, and declines, the $\dot{\pi}$ curve lies above it, intersects it, and lies below it. Note that $\overline{\pi}$ is highest at a smaller level of output ($Q = 2.33$) than the one ($Q = 2.5$) at which π is maximum.

2.8 Given the following total cost schedule, (a) derive the average and marginal cost schedules. (b) On the same set of axes, plot the total, average, and marginal cost schedules of part (a). (c) Using the figure you drew for part (b), explain the relationship among the total, average, and marginal cost curves.

Q	0	1	2	3
TC	$2	10	12	18

(a) The average and marginal cost schedules are derived in Table 2.6.

Table 2.6

Q	TC	AC = TC/Q	MC = ΔTC/ΔQ
0	$ 2	—	—
1	10	$10	$8
2	12	6	2
3	18	6	6

(b) The TC, AC, and MC schedules of Table 2.6 are plotted in Fig. 2-7.

(c) The slope of a ray from the origin to the TC curve, or (i.e., average case), falls to the point $Q = 2.5$ in Fig. 2-7 and rises thereafter. Thus, the AC curve declines to the point $Q = 2.5$ and then rises. At the same time, the slope of the TC curve, (i.e., marginal cost), falls to the point of inflection on the TC curve at $Q = 1$ and rises thereafter. Thus, the MC curve declines to the point $Q = 1$ and then rises. At $Q = 2.5$, a ray from the origin has the smallest slope (so that we are at the lowest point on the AC curve) and equals the slope of the TC curve, or MC, at that point. Thus, at $Q = 2.5$, AC = MC. As the AC curve declines, reaches its minimum point, and then rises, the MC curve lies below it, intersects it, and lies above it.

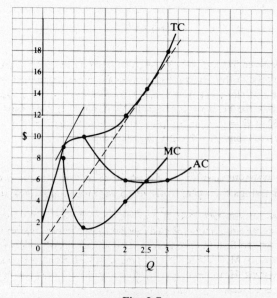

Fig. 2-7

OPTIMIZATION ANALYSIS: PROFIT MAXIMIZATION

2.9   Using the total revenue curve in Fig. 2-4 and the total cost curve in Fig. 2-7, derive the total profit function and show how the firm determines the profit-maximizing level of output.

      In Fig. 2-8, the TR curve is that of Fig. 2-4 and the TC curve is that of Fig. 2-7. The total profit (π) curve is derived from the vertical distance between the TR and the TC curves. The firm maximizes π at $Q = 2$, where

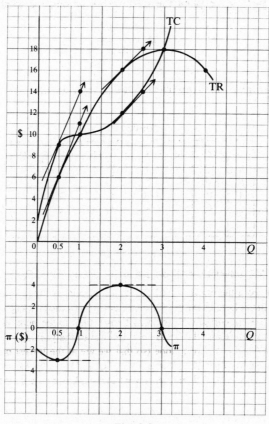

Fig. 2-8

the positive difference between TR and TC ($4) is greatest. At $Q = 2$, the TR and TC curves are parallel, so that their vertical distance (with the TR curve above the TC curve) is greatest and the π curve lies above the horizontal axis and has a zero slope. At $Q = 0.5$, the π curve also has a zero slope and the TR and TC curves are parallel. But at $Q = 0.5$, the TC curve is above the TR curve, so that the firm's loss ($3) is at its maximum. To summarize, $\pi = -\$2$ at $Q = 0$, $\pi = -\$3$ at $Q = 0.5$ (the largest loss), $\pi = 0$ at $Q = 1$ and $Q = 3$ (the break-even points of the firm), and $\pi = \$4$ (the largest profit) at $Q = 2$.

2.10   Draw the marginal revenue curve of Fig. 2-4 and the marginal cost curve of Fig. 2-7 on the same set of axes, and use the drawings to explain why the best level of output of the firm is two units.

      In Fig. 2-9, the profit-maximizing level of output is $Q = 2$. This is the level of output at which the MC curve intersects the MR curve from below. We can explain why the firm maximizes total profits (π) at $Q = 2$ by showing that it pays for the firm to expand an output smaller than 2 units and reduce a larger output. For example, at $Q = 1.5$, MR > MC. Therefore, the firm is adding more to its TR than to its TC, and so π is increased by expanding output. However, at $Q = 2.5$, MR < MC. Therefore, the firm is adding less to its TR than to its TC, and so π is increased by *reducing* output. At $Q = 2$, MR = MC. Therefore, the firm is adding as much to TR as to TC and π is at its maximum.

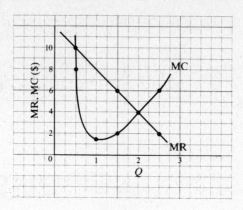

Fig. 2-9

Note, however, that MR = MC at $Q = 0.5$ also. But at $Q = 0.5$, the firm has produced all the (fractional) units of the commodity for which MC < MR, and so the firm maximizes its total loss. To distinguish between the loss-maximizing and the profit-maximizing level of output (since at both levels of output MR = MC), we seek the level of output at which MR = MC *and* the MC curve intersects the MR curve from below. This is the same as finding the level of output at which the π curve has a zero slope and faces down (i.e., its slope diminishes from positive values to zero to negative values).

2.11 How should a firm determine the best level of (*a*) advertising, (*b*) input use, and (*c*) investment?

(*a*) The best level of advertising for a firm is the one at which the marginal benefit of advertising (in the form of increased sales and revenue) is equal to the marginal cost of advertising.

(*b*) A firm should use each unit of input until the marginal revenue gained from sales of the resulting product (good or service) equals the marginal cost of hiring or using that unit of input.

(*c*) A firm should continue to invest until the marginal return on the investment is equal to the marginal cost of the investment (the extra interest that must be paid for the last dollar invested).

2.12 (*a*) How does the value of a business manager's time affect the person's decision to fly or drive on a business trip? (*b*) How much time should a consumer spend on shopping (searching) for lower prices? (*c*) For which type of goods would you expect consumers to spend more time on comparative shopping, or shopping for lower prices?

(*a*) The total cost of a business trip includes not only the transportation cost but also the imputed cost of the business manager's time. Often, the latter is greater than the former. The manager should fly or drive depending on which method of transportation will lead to a lower total cost for the trip (which includes the imputed value of the manager's time).

(*b*) A consumer should shop (search) for lower prices until the marginal benefit of the search (in the form of the savings resulting from the lower prices) is equal to the marginal cost of the search (i.e., the forgone earnings for the time of the search). The more valuable a consumer's time is, the smaller is the amount of optimal search time.

(*c*) Given the marginal cost of comparative shopping, or shopping for lower prices, for the consumer, we would expect the consumer to spend more time searching for lower prices for more expensive items than for cheaper ones. The reason is that usually the more expensive the item, the greater is the potential benefit (saving) of the search.

Chapter 3

Risk Analysis

3.1 MEANING AND MEASUREMENT OF RISK

In many managerial decisions, the manager does not know the exact outcome of each possible course of action. In such cases, we say that the firm faces risk or uncertainty. *Risk* refers to the situation in which there is more than one possible outcome to a decision and the probability of each specific outcome is known or can be estimated. If such probabilities are not known and cannot be estimated, we have *uncertainty*. In evaluating and comparing investment projects that are subject to risk, we use the concepts of expected value, standard deviation, and coefficient of variation.

The *expected profit* of a project subject to risk is obtained by multiplying each possible outcome or profit from the project by its probability of occurrence, and then adding these products (see Example 1). That is,

$$\text{Expected profit} = E(\pi) = \overline{\pi} = \sum_{i=1}^{n} \pi_i P_i \qquad (3\text{-}1)$$

where π_i is the profit level associated with outcome i, P_i is the probability or chance that outcome i will occur, $i = 1$ to n refers to the number of possible outcomes or states of nature, and Σ refers to the "sum of." For investment projects facing equal risk, the firm will choose the project with the largest expected profit.

The *absolute* risk of an investment project can be measured by the *standard deviation* of the possible profits from the project. The standard deviation, σ (read "sigma"), is given by

$$\text{Standard deviation} = \sigma = \sqrt{\sum_{i=1}^{n} (\pi_i - \overline{\pi})^2 \cdot P_i} \qquad (3\text{-}2)$$

The greater is the possible dispersion of the profits from a project, the greater is the project's standard deviation and risk.

To compare the relative dispersion of the possible profits, or risk, of two or more projects, we will use the *coefficient of variation* (v). This is given by the ratio of the standard deviation to the expected profit of each project. That is, an investor will usually prefer a more risky project only if its expected profit is sufficiently higher than that of a less risky project (see Example 2).

EXAMPLE 1. Suppose that the possible profits of two investment projects (A and B) under three possible states of the economy (boom, normal, and recession) are those of column (3) in Table 3.1. To obtain the expected profit from each project in column (4) of the table, multiply the probability of occurrence of each state of the economy by the profit from the project under that particular state, and then add these products. Note that the sum of the probabilities for the possible profits from each project in column (2) is 1 or 100 percent, since one of the three states of the economy must occur with certainty. In column (4) we see that the expected profit from each project is $400. However, in column (3) we see that the range of profits for project A (from $500 to $300) is smaller than for project B (from $600 to $200). Figure 3-1 shows the probability distribution of profits from the two projects.

EXAMPLE 2. Table 3.2 shows how to calculate the standard deviation (σ) of the probability distribution of profits in projects A and B. In Table 3.2, we see that for project A, $\sigma = \$70.71$, while for project B, $\sigma = \$141.42$. These values provide a numerical measure of the absolute dispersion of profits in each project from the project mean and confirm the smaller dispersion of profits and risk for project A than for project B, which is shown graphically in Fig. 3-1. Note in Table 3.2 that σ is the square root of the variance (σ^2).

To measure relative dispersion or risk, we use the coefficient of variation (v):

For project A, $\quad v = \sigma/\overline{\pi} = \$70.71/\$400 = 0.18$

For project B, $\quad v = \sigma/\overline{\pi} = \$141.42/\$400 = 0.36$

Table 3.1

State of Economy (1)	Probability of Occurrence (2)	Profit (3)	Expected Value (2) × (3) (4)
Project A			
Boom	0.25	$500	$125
Normal	0.50	400	200
Recession	0.25	300	75
Expected profit from project A = $400			
Project B			
Boom	0.25	$600	$150
Normal	0.50	400	200
Recession	0.25	200	50
Expected profit from project B = $400			

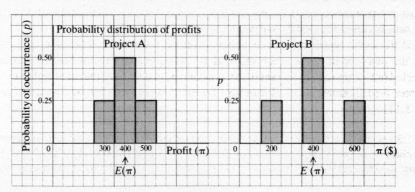

Fig. 3-1

Table 3.2

Deviation $(\pi_i - \overline{\pi})$	Deviation Squared $(\pi_i - \overline{\pi})^2$	Probability (P_i)	Deviation Squared Times Probability $(\pi_i - \overline{\pi})^2 \cdot P_i$
Project A			
$500 - $400 = $ 100	$10,000	0.25	$2,500
400 - 400 = 0	0	0.50	0
300 - 400 = -100	10,000	0.25	2,500
Variance = σ^2 = $5,000 Standard deviation = $\sigma = \sqrt{\sigma^2} = \sqrt{\$5,000}$ = $70.71			
Project B			
$600 - $400 = $ 200	$40,000	0.25	$10,000
400 - 400 = 0	0	0.50	0
200 - 400 = -200	40,000	0.25	10,000
Variance = σ^2 = $20,000 Standard deviation = $\sigma = \sqrt{\sigma^2} = \sqrt{\$20,000}$ = $141.42			

Since the expected profit is the same for the two projects, but project A has a smaller relative dispersion (v), or risk, than project B, a risk-averse investor would choose project A. (Note that in this case, since the expected profit from each project is the same, this conclusion can be inferred from the value of σ for each project, without the need to calculate the v's.)

3.2 INCORPORATING RISK INTO MANAGERIAL DECISIONS

Most managers are *risk-averse* and face *diminishing marginal utility for money*. That is, doubling money or profits less than doubles their total utility or satisfaction, so that the marginal or extra utility diminishes. Under such conditions, a manager will not undertake an investment project even though it has a positive *expected profit*, if its *expected utility* is negative (see Example 3). While some managers are *risk neutral* or *risk seekers*, most are risk-averse. A risk-averse individual will not accept a fair bet (i.e., one with a 50-50 chance of winning or losing a specific sum of money) because the utility gained by winning the bet is smaller than the utility lost by losing the bet.

Risk can also be incorporated into decisionmaking by the *risk-adjusted discount rate approach* or by the *certainty-equivalent approach*. According to the first, a risk-averse manager adds a *risk premium* to the *risk-free* discount rate (as shown by a *risk-return trade-off function*, or indifference curve) in calculating the present value of the expected profits for a risky investment. Alternatively, the risk-averse manager can substitute equivalent *certain* sums in place of larger but risky sums (net cash flows) and use the *risk-free* discount rate to calculate the present value of the project (see Example 4). The ratio of an equivalent certain sum to a larger risky sum is called the *certainty-equivalent coefficient* (α).

Managerial decisions involving risk are often made in stages, with subsequent decisions and events depending on the outcome of earlier decisions and events. The sequence of possible managerial decisions and their expected outcomes under each set of circumstances or states of nature can be represented graphically by *decision trees* (see Example 5). Risk can also be incorporated into managerial decisions by simulation (see Problem 3.11).

EXAMPLE 3.   Suppose that a manager wants to determine whether or not to undertake an investment project that has a 40 percent probability of providing a profit of $40,000 and a 60 percent probability of producing a loss of $20,000. Suppose also that the manager's utility function is that shown in Fig. 3-2, with money measured along the horizontal

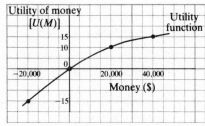

Fig. 3-2

axis and the utility of money (measured in arbitrary or fictitious units called *utils*) measured along the vertical axis. Since the utility function for money is concave, or faces down, its slope, or marginal utility, is diminishing, and so the manager is risk-averse. In column (4) of Table 3.3, we see that the expected profit from the project is positive ($4,000), but the manager will not undertake the project because the corresponding expected utility of the project (column 5) is negative (-3 utils).

EXAMPLE 4.   Suppose that the risk-return trade-off function of a manager is that shown in Fig. 3-3. It indicates that the manager is indifferent between a 10 percent rate of return on a risk-free investment with $\sigma = 0$ (point A) and a 14 percent rate of return on an investment with risk given by $\sigma = 0.5$ (point B), so that the risk premium is 4 percent. Suppose also that the firm is contemplating an investment project that is expected to generate a net cash flow of $20,000 per year for three years and to cost initially $48,000. From Table 3.4, we see that the firm would undertake the project

Table 3.3

State of Nature	Probability (1)	Monetary Outcome (2)	Associated Utility (3)	Expected Profit (4) = (1) × (2)	Expected Utility (utils) (5) = (1) × (3)
Success	0.40	$ 40,000	15	$ 16,000	6
Failure	0.60	−20,000	−15	−12,000	−9
				$ 4,000	−3

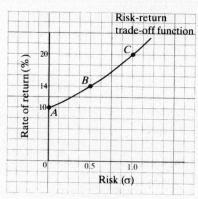

Fig. 3-3

Table 3.4   Present Value (PV) of a Project

At a Rate of Return of 10 Percent	At a Rate of Return of 14 Percent
$$PV = \frac{\$20,000}{1.10} + \frac{\$20,000}{(1.10)^2} + \frac{\$20,000}{(1.10)^3}$$ $$- \$48,000$$ $$= \frac{\$20,000}{1.10} + \frac{\$20,000}{1.21} + \frac{\$20,000}{1.331}$$ $$- \$48,000$$ $$= \$18,181.82 + \$16,528.93 + \$15,026.30$$ $$- \$48,000$$ $$= \$1,737.05$$	$$PV = \frac{\$20,000}{1.14} + \frac{\$20,000}{(1.14)^2} + \frac{\$20,000}{(1.14)^3}$$ $$- \$48,000$$ $$= \frac{\$20,000}{1.14} + \frac{\$20,000}{1.2996} + \frac{\$20,000}{1.481544}$$ $$- \$48,000$$ $$= \$17,543.86 + \$15,389.35 + \$13,499.43$$ $$- \$48,000$$ $$= -\$1,567.36$$

at the risk-free rate of interest, or discount, of 10 percent because the present value of the project is positive ($1,737.05), but not at the rate of 14 percent because the present value of the project is negative (−$1,567.36).

Alternatively, if the manager regarded the certain sum of $18,600 as equivalent to the risky net cash flow of $20,000 (implying a certainty-equivalent coefficient, $\alpha = \$18,600/\$20,000 = 0.93$) and used the certain sum of $18,600 and the risk-free discount rate of 10 percent, the net present value of the project would be −$1,744.55 (the calculations are left to the reader). This result is similar to that obtained by using the risky net cash flow of $20,000 and the risk-adjusted discount rate of 14 percent, and so the firm would not undertake the project. While the choice of the risk-adjusted discount rate and the certainty-equivalent coefficient is subjective, the latter is somewhat superior because it explicitly considers the manager's attitude toward risk.

EXAMPLE 5. Figure 3-4 shows a decision tree that a firm can use to determine whether to build a $2 million plant or a $1 million plant [section (1) of the figure]. Three states of the economy (boom, normal, or recession) can occur [section (2)]. Thus, we have six possible outcomes, each with its probability of occurrence [section (3)] and present value of net cash flows [section (4)]. Multiplying the probability of each outcome by the present value of its net cash flow, we get

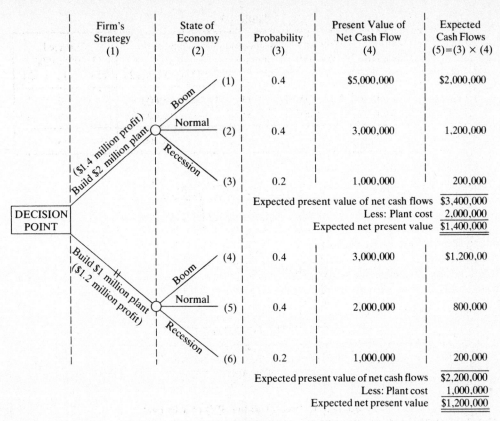

Firm's Strategy (1)	State of Economy (2)		Probability (3)	Present Value of Net Cash Flow (4)	Expected Cash Flows (5)=(3) × (4)
	Boom	(1)	0.4	$5,000,000	$2,000,000
	Normal	(2)	0.4	3,000,000	1,200,000
	Recession	(3)	0.2	1,000,000	200,000

Expected present value of net cash flows $3,400,000
Less: Plant cost 2,000,000
Expected net present value $1,400,000

	Boom	(4)	0.4	3,000,000	$1,200,00
	Normal	(5)	0.4	2,000,000	800,000
	Recession	(6)	0.2	1,000,000	200,000

Expected present value of net cash flows $2,200,000
Less: Plant cost 1,000,000
Expected net present value $1,200,000

Fig. 3-4

the corresponding expected net cash flow [section (5)]. Adding the expected cash flows from each strategy, we get $3.4 million for the $2 million plant and $2.2 million for the $1 million plant. Thus, the firm should build the larger plant because its profit of $1.4 million is larger than the $1.2 million profit for the smaller plant (which is, therefore, crossed off in section (1) of the figure as suboptimal).

3.3 DECISION MAKING UNDER UNCERTAINTY

Uncertainty exists when the decision maker does not know and cannot estimate the probability of occurrence of each specific outcome. Two decision rules applicable under uncertainty are the maximin criterion and the minimax regret criterion.

The *maximin criterion* postulates that the decision maker should determine the worst possible outcome of each strategy and then pick the strategy that provides the best of the worst possible outcomes (see Example 6). This very conservative criterion is appropriate when the firm has a very strong aversion to risk, as for example, when the survival of a small firm depends on avoiding losses.

The *minimax regret criterion* postulates that the decision maker should select the strategy that minimizes the maximum regret or opportunity cost of the wrong decision, whatever the state of nature that actually occurs. Regret is measured by the difference between the payoff of a given strategy and the payoff of the best strategy *under the same state of nature* (see Example 7). Which of the above two decision rules a firm might apply depends on its objectives and circumstances. (The maximin criterion and the minimax regret criterion very occasionally lead to the same conclusion, i.e., both may lead either to a decision to invest or a decision not to invest.)

EXAMPLE 6. Suppose that a manager wants to determine whether to undertake an investment project that provides a profit of $40,000 if successful and a loss of $20,000 if a failure (as in Example 3), but now does not know and cannot

Table 3.5

Strategy	State of Nature		Maximin
	Success	Failure	
Invest	$40,000	−$20,000	−$20,000
Do not invest	0	0	0*

*Maximin choice.

estimate the probability of success or failure. To apply the maximin criterion, the manager first determines the worst possible outcome of each strategy (row) in Table 3.5. This is −$20,000 for the strategy of investing and 0 for the strategy of not investing (shown in the "Failure" column of the table). Hence, the manager picks the strategy of not investing, which is indicated by an asterisk next to its zero return, because it provides the best (*max*imum) of the worst (*min*imum) possible outcomes (i.e., maximin).

EXAMPLE 7.   Table 3.6 presents the payoff and regret matrices for the investment project that we examined in Example 6. The regret matrix is constructed by determining the maximum payoff for each state of nature [columns (1) and (2)]

Table 3.6

Strategy	State of Nature		Regret Matrix		Maximum Regret (5)
	Success (1)	Failure (2)	Success (3)	Failure (4)	
Invest	$40,000	−$20,000	$ 0	$20,000	$20,000*
Do not invest	0	0	40,000	0	40,000

*Minimax regret choice.

and then subtracting the payoff of the strategy chosen from the maximum payoff. For example, if the manager chooses to make the investment and the state of nature that actually occurs is one of success, the manager has no regret because that was the correct strategy. Thus, the regret value of zero is entered at the top of the first column in the regret matrix. However, if the firm had chosen not to invest, the regret value would be $40,000, which is entered at the bottom of the first column of the regret matrix. The payoffs in the second column of the regret matrix under the state of nature of failure are similarly determined. The manager then chooses the strategy of investing because it provides a minimum regret value of $20,000 (indicated by the asterisk in the last column of the table), as compared with the maximum regret of $40,000 that results from the strategy of not investing.

Glossary

Certainty   The situation in which a decision has only one possible outcome and this outcome is known precisely; that is, the decision is risk-free.

Certainty-equivalent approach   The method of using the risk-free discount rate and equivalent smaller sums in place of larger but risky sums or profits to adjust the valuation model for risk.

Certainty-equivalent coefficient (α)   The ratio of the certain sum equivalent to the expected risky sum, or profit, from an investment, that is used to adjust the valuation model for risk.

Coefficient of variation (v)   The ratio of the standard deviation to the expected value.

Decision tree A graphical technique for showing and analyzing the sequence of possible managerial decisions and their expected outcomes under each set of circumstances or states of nature.

Diminishing marginal utility for money The decline in the extra utility received for each dollar increase in income.

Expected profit The sum of the products of each possible profit from an investment times the probability of its occurrence.

Expected utility The sum of the products of the utility of each possible outcome times its probability of occurrence.

Maximin criterion The decision rule under uncertainty that postulates that the decision maker should determine the worst possible outcome of each strategy and then pick the strategy that provides the best of the worst possible outcomes.

Minimax regret criterion The decision rule under uncertainty that postulates that the decision maker should select the strategy that minimizes the maximum regret, or opportunity cost, of the wrong decision, whatever the state of nature that occurs.

Risk The situation in which a decision has more than one possible outcome and the probability of each possible outcome is known or can be estimated.

Risk-adjusted discount rate approach The method of using a higher rate of discount to calculate the present value of the net cash flows or profits of an investment project in order to compensate for risk.

Risk-averse Term applied to someone who has a diminishing marginal utility for money.

Risk-neutral Term applied to someone whose marginal utility for money is constant.

Risk premium The excess in the expected or required rate of return on a risky investment over the rate of return on a riskless asset; the premium compensates for risk.

Risk-return trade-off function A curve showing the various risk-return combinations among which a manager or investor is indifferent.

Standard deviation (σ) A measure of the amount of difference between possible outcomes and the expected value of the outcome.

Uncertainty The case in which there is more than one possible outcome to a decision and the probability of occurrence of each specific outcome is not known and cannot be estimated.

Review Questions

1.   Risk refers to the situation in which there is

   (*a*)   one possible outcome to a decision.

   (*b*)   more than one possible outcome to a decision.

   (*c*)   more than one possible outcome to a decision and the probability of each specific outcome is known or can be estimated.

   (*d*)   more than one possible outcome to a decision and the probability of each specific outcome is not known and cannot be estimated.

   Ans.   (*c*) See Section 3.1.

2.   If the profit associated with project A under conditions of boom in Table 3.1 had been $600 instead of $500, the expected profit from project A would have been

   (*a*) $425.

   (*b*) $450.

   (*c*) $500.

   (*d*) $600.

   Ans.   (*a*) See Example 1.

3.   Which of the following measures can be used to compare the risk of two or more investment projects?

(*a*)   Expected profit.

(*b*)   Standard deviation of possible profits.

(*c*)   Coefficient of variation.

(*d*)   Variance.

Ans.   (*c*) See Section 3.1.

4.   The coefficient of variation for a given project is given by the

(*a*)   ratio of the standard deviation to the expected profit of the project.

(*b*)   ratio of the expected profit to the standard deviation of the project.

(*c*)   expected profit of the project.

(*d*)   standard deviation of the actual profits of the project.

Ans.   (*a*) See Section 3.1.

5.   If the utility function of a manager is concave, or faces down, the

(*a*)   manager is a risk seeker.

(*b*)   manager is risk-averse.

(*c*)   manager is risk-neutral.

(*d*)   manager's marginal utility of money increases.

Ans.   (*b*) See Example 3.

6.   Who, if any, of the following individuals will not accept a fair bet?

(*a*)   A risk averter.

(*b*)   A risk-neutral person.

(*c*)   A risk seeker.

(*d*)   None of the above.

Ans.   (*a*) See Section 3.2 and Example 3.

7.   A risk-averse manager

(*a*)   will always undertake a project with a positive expected profit.

(*b*)   would never undertake a project with a positive expected profit.

(*c*)   may or may not undertake a project with a positive expected profit.

(*d*)   disregards risk; otherwise the manager would never undertake a risky project.

Ans.   (*c*) See Section 3.2.

8.   Which of the following statements is false?

(*a*)   The risk-return trade-off function shows the various combinations of risk and return among which the manager is indifferent.

(*b*)   The certainty-equivalent coefficient is the ratio of a risky sum to its equivalent certain sum.

(*c*)   The risk-adjusted discount rate is equal to the risk-free discount rate plus a risk premium.

(*d*)   The certainty-equivalent approach uses a smaller certain sum as equivalent to a larger risky sum and the risk-free discount rate to find the present value of profits.

Ans.   (*b*) See Section 3.2.

9. Which of the following statements is false with regard to decision trees?

    (a)   Since the firm has control over the strategies open to it, no probabilities are attached to strategies.

    (b)   States of nature are uncontrollable events for the firm, and so probabilities of occurrence are attached to them.

    (c)   In the construction of decision trees, boxes are used to show decision points and circles to show states of nature.

    (d)   None of the above.

    Ans.   (*d*) See Section 3.2 and Example 5.

10. The decision rule that postulates that the decision maker should determine the worst possible outcome for each strategy and then pick the strategy that provides the best of the worst possible outcomes is

    (a)   a decision rule applicable under uncertainty.

    (b)   applicable when the firm has a very strong risk aversion.

    (c)   called the maximin criterion.

    (d)   all of the above.

    Ans.   (*d*) See Section 3.3.

11. Which of the following statements is false with regard to the minimax regret criterion?

    (a)   It postulates that the decision maker should select the strategy that minimizes the maximum regret whatever the state of nature that actually occurs.

    (b)   Regret is measured by the difference between the payoff of a given strategy and the payoff of the best strategy under the same state of nature.

    (c)   It is a more sophisticated decision rule than the maximin criterion.

    (d)   None of the above.

    Ans.   (*c*) See Section 3.3.

12. The maximin criterion and the minimax regret criterion

    (a)   can never lead to the same decision.

    (b)   will always lead to the same decision.

    (c)   may or may not lead to the same decision.

    (d)   would never be used by the same firm.

    Ans.   (*c*) See Section 3.3 and Examples 6 and 7.

Solved Problems

MEASURING RISK IN MANAGERIAL DECISION MAKING

3.1   (*a*) Give an example of decision making under certainty, risk, and uncertainty. (*b*) What is the meaning of strategy? State of nature? Payoff matrix? (*c*) What is meant by probability? By probability distribution?

    (*a*)   An example of decision making under certainty is the purchase of Treasury bills. This leads only to one outcome (the amount of the yield) and the outcome is known with certainty by the investor. The reason is that there is virtually no chance that the federal government will fail to redeem these securities at maturity or that it will default on interest payments. An example of decision making in the fact of risk is the purchase of a stock or the introduction of a new product. These can lead to one of a set of possible outcomes, and the probability of each possible outcome can be estimated from past experience or from market studies.

An example of decision making under uncertainty may be an undertaking to drill for oil in a completely unproven field when the investor does not know and cannot estimate either the possible oil outputs or their probabilities of occurrence.

(b) A *strategy* refers to one of several alternative courses of action that a decision maker can take to achieve a goal. For example, a decision maker can choose between the strategy of building a large plant or of building a small plant in order to maximize profits or the value of the firm.

A *state of nature* refers to conditions in the future that will have a significant effect on the degree of success or failure of any strategy, but over which the decision maker has little or no control. For example, the economy may be booming, normal, or in a recession.

A *payoff matrix* is a table that shows the possible outcomes, or results, of each strategy under each state of nature. For example, a payoff matrix may show, for each of the three states of the economy (booming, normal, and recessionary), the level of profit that would result if the firm were to build a large or a small plant.

(c) The *probability* of an event is the chance, or odds, that the event will occur. For example, if we say that the probability of booming conditions in the economy is 0.25, or 25 percent, we mean that there is one chance in four that this condition will occur.

The *probability distribution* of an event, say the probability distribution of profits from an investment project, is a list of all the possible outcomes of an event (profits from the investment) and the probability of occurrence of each. The sum of the probabilities is equal to 1, or 100 percent, since one of the possible events must occur with certainty.

3.2 A computer software company has to decide which of two advertising strategies to adopt: spot TV commercials or newspaper ads. The marketing department has estimated sales and their probabilities under each alternative plan as given in the following table:

Strategy A (TV commercials)		Strategy B (newspaper ads)	
Sales	Probability	Sales	Probability
$ 8,000	0.25	$ 8,000	0.3
12,000	0.50	10,000	0.4
16,000	0.25	12,000	0.3

The firm's profit margin is 50 percent of sales. (a) Calculate the expected profit under each strategy. (b) Chart the probability distribution of the profits under each strategy.

(a) To find the expected profit under each promotion strategy we proceed as indicated in Table 3.7. The table shows that the expected profit from strategy A (TV commercials) is $6,000 as compared with the expected profit from strategy B (newspaper ads) of $5,000. Note that the expected profit from a strategy is a weighted average of all possible profit levels that can result from the strategy, with the probabilities of those profit levels used as weights. Note also that the expected profit from a strategy need not equal any of the profit levels of the strategy (although in this case it does).

(b) The probability distributions of profits from strategy A and strategy B are shown in Fig. 3-5.

3.3 Using the data in Problem 3.2, (a) calculate the standard deviation of the distribution of profits for each promotion strategy. (b) Which of the two promotion strategies is more risky? (c) Which promotion strategy should the firm choose?

(a) The standard deviations of the distribution of profits under each strategy are calculated in Table 3.8.

(b) Strategy B is less risky than strategy A, but it also has a lower expected profit. Therefore, the information given is insufficient to decide which strategy is best. The choice depends on whether the lower expected

Table 3.7

Sales (1)	Profit (2)	Probability (3)	Expected Profit (4) = (2) × (3)
Strategy A (TV commercials)			
$ 8,000	$4,000	0.25	$1,000
12,000	6,000	0.50	3,000
16,000	8,000	0.25	2,000
Expected profit from strategy A = $6,000			
Strategy B (newspaper ads)			
$ 8,000	$4,000	0.3	$1,200
10,000	5,000	0.4	2,000
12,000	6,000	0.3	1,800
Expected profit from strategy B = $5,000			

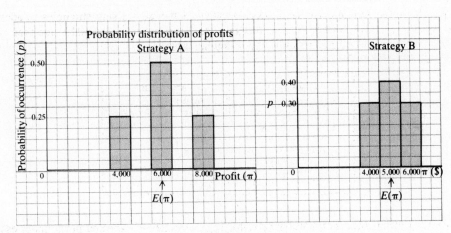

Fig. 3-5

profit from strategy B is more or less balanced by its lower risk. This determination depends on the attitude of the manager toward risk.

(c)   To determine which promotion strategy the firm should choose, we must find the coefficient of variation (v) of the distribution of profits from each strategy. This measures the risk per dollar of profit for each investment. That is,

$$v_A = \frac{\sigma_A}{\pi_A} = \frac{\$1,414.21}{\$6,000} = 0.24$$

$$v_B = \frac{\sigma_B}{\pi_B} = \frac{\$774.60}{\$5,000} = 0.15$$

Since the coefficient of variation is higher for strategy A than for strategy B, strategy B is less risky than strategy A. This confirms the greater dispersion of profits for strategy A than for strategy B shown graphically in Fig. 3-5.

Table 3.8

Deviation $(\pi_i - \overline{\pi})$	Deviation Squared $(\pi_i - \overline{\pi})^2$	Probability (P_i)	Deviation Squared Times Probability $(\pi_i - \overline{\pi})^2 \cdot P_i$
Strategy A			
$4,000 - $6,000 = $-2,000	$4,000,000	0.25	$1,000,000
6,000 - 6,000 = 0	0	0.50	0
8,000 - 6,000 = 2,000	4,000,000	0.25	1,000,000
Variance $= \sigma^2 = $2,000,000$			
Standard deviation $= \sigma = \sqrt{\sigma^2} = \sqrt{$2,000,000} = $1,414.21$			
Strategy B			
$4,000 - $5,000 = $-1,000	$1,000,000	0.3	$300,000
5,000 - 5,000 = 0	0	0.4	0
6,000 - 5,000 = 1,000	1,000,000	0.3	300,000
Variance $= \sigma^2 = $600,000$			
Standard deviation $= \sigma = \sqrt{\sigma^2} = \sqrt{$600,000} = 774.60			

3.4   In Problem 3.2 we have specified only three possible profit levels and obtained the steplike *discrete* probability distribution of profits shown in Fig. 3-5. If we specify more and more profit levels and their respective probabilities, each bar becomes thinner and thinner and approaches a vertical line at the limit. With the above in mind, (*a*) sketch on the same set of axes the approximate *continuous* (smooth) probability distribution of profits from each promotion strategy examined in Problem 3.2. (*b*) Determine the probability that the profit level from each promotion strategy will fall within a specific range.

(*a*)   The approximate continuous probability distribution of profits from each promotion strategy of Problem 3.2 is shown in Fig. 3-6. Note that the probability distribution of each strategy is centered on its expected profit.

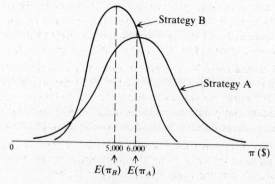

Fig. 3-6

Also note that the probability distribution for strategy B is "tighter" or less dispersed around its expected profit than the probability distribution for project A and reflects the smaller risk of the former compared with the latter.

(*b*)   When dealing with a continuous probability distribution, the probability that the profit level from each promotion strategy will fall within a specific range is given by the area under the curve between the profit levels defining the range of relevant profits. Note that in a continuous probability distribution, there are theoretically an infinite number of profit levels, and so the probability of occurrence of each specific profit level is zero.

3.5   Given that the probability distribution of many strategies or experiments follows a normal distribution, the probability that a particular outcome (profit) falls within a particular range of outcomes can be found by the area under the standard normal curve within the specific range. The *standard normal curve* is a bell-like distribution that is symmetrical about its zero mean and has a standard deviation of 1; the area under the curve represents a total probability of 1. To find the probability that a particular outcome (profit) falls within a specific range of the mean, subtract the expected value, or mean, of the distribution under consideration from the outcome, or profit, defining the range. Then, divide the result by the standard deviation of the distribution. Finally, look up the resulting (so-called z) value of the standard normal curve in Table C.1 in Appendix C.

With the above in mind, determine from the information for strategy A (with mean, $\bar{\pi} = \$6,000$ and standard deviation, $\sigma = \$1,414.21$) the probability that profit (*a*) falls between $6,000 and $7,000, (*b*) falls between $5,000 and $6,000, (*c*) is more than $7,000 or less than $5,000, and (*d*) falls between $7,500 and $8,500.

(*a*)   To determine the probability that profit will fall between $6,000 (the expected profit, or $\bar{\pi}$) and $7,000, we first find the value of z for $7,000, as follows:

$$z = \frac{\pi_i - \bar{\pi}}{\sigma} = \frac{\$7,000 - \$6,000}{\$1,414.21} = 0.71$$

and then look up the value of $z = 0.71$ in Table C.1 in Appendix C. Going down the column headed z to 0.7 and then moving across the table until we are directly below the column headed 0.01 (so as to have $z = 0.71$), we get a value of 0.2611. This means that the area under the standard normal curve between the zero mean [i.e., $z = (\$6,000 - \$6,000)/\$1,414.21 = 0$] and $z = 0.71$ standard deviation to the right of the mean is 0.2611, or 26.11 percent. Thus, the probability that the profit from strategy A falls between $6,000 and $7,000 is also 0.2611, or 26.11 percent.

(*b*)   To find the probability that profit will fall between $5,000 and $6,000 we find the value of z for $5,000, as follows:

$$z = \frac{\pi_i - \bar{\pi}}{\sigma} = \frac{\$5,000 - \$6,000}{\$1,414.21} = -0.71$$

Since the standard normal curve is symmetrical about its zero mean, the area under the curve between the zero mean and 0.71 standard deviation to the *left* of the mean is the same as the area under the curve between the zero mean and 0.71 standard deviation to the *right* of the mean. Thus, the probability that profit will fall between $5,000 and $6,000 is also 0.2611, or 26.11 percent.

(*c*)   Since the standard normal curve is symmetrical about its zero mean, half, or 0.5, of the area under the curve is to the right of the mean and half is to the left. Thus, the probability that profit will be greater than $7,000 is equal to 0.5 minus the probability that profit will be between the means of $6,000 and $7,000. That is, the probability that profit will be larger than $7,000 is $0.5000 - 0.2611 = 0.2389$, or 23.89 percent. By symmetry, the probability that profit will be less than $5,000 is also 0.2389, or 23.89 percent.

(*d*)   To find the probability that profit falls between $7,500 and $8,500, we first find the value of z for $7,500 and $8,500, look up these values in Table C.1 in Appendix C, and then subtract the value in the table corresponding to $7,500 from the value corresponding to $8,500.

$$\text{For } \$7,500, \quad z = \frac{\$7,500 - \$6,000}{\$1,414.21} = 1.06$$

$$\text{For } \$8,500, \quad z = \frac{\$8,500 - \$6,000}{\$1,414.21} = 1.77$$

Looking up the value of $z = 1.06$ and 1.77 in Table C.1, we get 0.3554 and 0.4616, respectively. Thus, the probability that profit falls between $7,500 and $8,500 is equal to $0.4616 - 0.3554 = 0.1062$, or 10.62 percent.

3.6   Using Table C.1 for the standard normal distribution, show that the area under the standard normal curve within (*a*) $\pm 1\sigma$ is 68.26 percent, (*b*) $\pm 2\sigma$ is 95.44 percent, (*c*) $\pm 3\sigma$ is 99.74 percent. (*d*) Draw a figure showing the above results.

(*a*)   To determine that the area under the curve of the standard normal distribution within $\pm 1\sigma$ is 68.26 percent, we look up the value of $z = 1.0$ in Table C.1. This is 0.3413. This means that the area to the right of the zero mean of the standard normal distribution to $z = 1$ is 0.3413, or 34.13 percent. Because of symmetry, the area between the mean and $z = -1$ is also 0.3413, or 34.13 percent. Therefore, the area within $z = \pm 1\sigma$ under the curve of the standard normal distribution is double 0.3413, which is 0.6826, or 68.26 percent.

(*b*)   From Table C.1, we get the value of 0.4772 for $z = 2$. Thus, the area under the standard normal curve within $z = \pm 2\sigma$ is $2(0.4772)$, which equals 0.9544, or 95.44 percent.

(*c*)   From Table C.1, we get the value of 0.4987 for $z = 3$. Thus, the area under the standard normal curve within $z = \pm 3\sigma$ is 0.9974, or 99.74 percent.

(*d*)   See Fig. 3-7

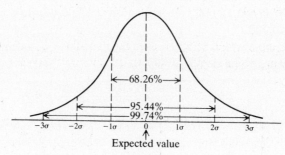

Fig. 3-7

INCORPORATING RISK INTO MANAGERIAL DECISIONS

3.7   For the investment project in Example 3 in Section 3.2 (*a*) draw a figure and (*b*) construct a table showing that a risk-neutral or risk-seeking manager would undertake the project.

(*a*)   Figure 3-8 shows three total utility functions: for the risk-averse manager, a function that is concave, or faces down (so that its slope, or marginal utility of money, is diminishing, as in Fig. 3-2); for the risk-neutral manager, a total utility function that is a straight line (so that its slope, or marginal utility of money, is constant); and for the risk-seeking manager, a total utility function that is convex, or faces up (so that its slope, or marginal utility of money, increases).

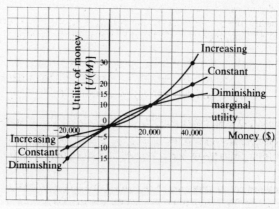

Fig. 3-8

Table 3.9

State of Nature	Probability (1)	Monetary Outcome (2)	Associated Utility (utils)		Expected Utility (utils)	
			Risk Neutral (3)	Risk Seeker (4)	Risk Neutral (5) = (1) × (3)	Risk Seeker (6) = (1) × (4)
Success	0.4	$ 40,000	20	30	8	12
Failure	0.6	−20,000	−10	−5	−6	−3
					2	9

(b) Since the expected utility of the project is positive for the risk-neutral [see column (5) of Table 3.9] and the risk-seeking manager [see column (6) of Table 3.9], both types of manager will undertake the project. Note that the associated utility of the project under success and failure for the risk-neutral and risk-seeking managers [columns (3) and (4), respectively, of Table 3.9] was read off from Fig. 3-8 in part (a).

3.8   A manager must determine which of two projects to undertake. Using market studies, the manager constructed the following payoff matrix of the present value of all future profits under all the different states of the economy:

State of Economy	Probability	Profit	
		Project A	Project B
Boom	0.3	$80	$60
Normal	0.4	40	30
Recession	0.3	0	20

The manager's utility function is

$$U = 200M - M^2$$

where M refers to dollars of profit. (a) Is this manager a risk averter, risk neutral, or a risk seeker? Why? (b) If the manager's objective is profit maximization regardless of risk, which project should be undertaken? (c) If the manager's objective is utility maximization regardless of risk, which project should be undertaken?

(a)   We can determine the manager's attitude toward risk by substituting two dollar amounts (one double the other) for M in the utility function formula and determining what happens to the level of utility. For example, by substituting $M = \$10$ and then $M = \$20$ in the formula for the manager's utility function, we get

$$U = 200M - M^2$$
$$= 200(10) - (10)^2 = 2,000 - 100 = 1,900 \text{ utils}$$
$$= 200(20) - (20)^2 = 4,000 - 400 = 3,600 \text{ utils}$$

Although M is doubled, U is less than doubled; therefore, the manager is risk averse.

(b)   If the manager's objective is to maximize profits regardless of risk, project A should be undertaken because the expected profit from project A is larger than the expected profit from project B. This is shown in Table 3.10.

(c)   To determine which project to undertake if the manager wants to maximize utility, we must calculate the expected utility resulting from each project. This is shown in Table 3.11. The utility associated with each profit level shown in Table 3.11 is obtained by substituting the profit level for M in the manager's utility

Table 3.10

	Project A		
State of Nature (1)	Probability (2)	Profit (3)	Expected Profit (4) = (2) × (3)
Boom	0.3	$80	$24
Normal	0.4	40	16
Recession	0.3	0	0
	Expected profit from project A = $40		
	Project B		
Boom	0.3	$60	$18
Normal	0.4	30	12
Recession	0.3	20	6
	Expected profit from project B = $36		

Table 3.11

State of Economy (1)	Probability (2)	Profit (3)	Associated Utility (4)	Expected Utility (5) = (2) × (4)
		Project A		
Boom	0.3	$80	9,600 utils	2,880 utils
Normal	0.4	40	6,400	2,560
Recession	0.3	0	0	0
		Expected utility from project A = 5,440		
		Project B		
Boom	0.3	$60	8,400 utils	2,520 utils
Normal	0.4	30	5,100	2,040
Recession	0.3	20	3,600	1,080
		Expected utility from project B = 5,640		

function. Since the expected utility from project B (5,640 utils) exceeds the expected utility from project A (5,440 utils), the manager should choose project B.

3.9 The manager of a movie theater must decide on which of two vending machines to install in the theater, machine 1 or machine 2. Both machines initially cost $100,000. The manager anticipates that machine 1 will generate a net cash flow of $34,000 in each of five years while machine 2 will generate a net cash flow of $40,000 in each of four years. Which of the two machines should the manager install if (a) the risk-adjusted discount rate is 10 percent? (b) the risk-adjusted discount rate is 20 percent? (c) the certainty-equivalent coefficient, $\alpha = 0.75$ for machine 1 and 0.8 for machine 2, and the risk-free discount rate is 8 percent?

(a) The net present value of machines 1 (NPV_1) and 2 (NPV_2) at the risk-adjusted discount rate of 10 percent can be found as in Table 3.4 in Example 4, or more quickly as follows:

$$NPV_1 = \sum_{t=1}^{5} \frac{\$34,000}{(1.10)^t} - \$100,000 \qquad NPV_2 = \sum_{t=1}^{4} \frac{\$40,000}{(1.10)^t} - \$100,000$$

$$= \$34,000 \left(\sum_{t=1}^{5} \frac{1}{(1.10)^t} \right) - \$100,000 \qquad = \$40,000 \left(\sum_{t=1}^{4} \frac{1}{(1.10)^t} \right) - \$100,000$$

$$= \$34,000(3.7908) - \$100,000 \qquad = \$40,000(3.1699) - \$100,000$$

$$= \$28,887 \qquad = \$26,796$$

The interest factor of 3.7908 for $\sum_{t=1}^{5} 1/(1.10)^t$ in the above calculations is obtained from Table B.4 in Appendix B by moving across the table until the column headed 10 percent is reached, and then moving down five rows for $t = 5$. The interest factor of 3.1699 for $\sum_{t=1}^{4} 1/(1.10)^t$ is similarly obtained. Since NPV_1 exceeds NPV_2, the manager should install machine 1. (See Chapter 13, on capital budgeting, for a discussion of present value concepts.)

(b)   At the risk-adjusted discount rate of 20 percent, we have

$$NPV_1 = \sum_{t=1}^{5} \frac{\$34,000}{(1.20)^t} - \$100,000 \qquad NPV_2 = \sum_{t=1}^{4} \frac{\$40,000}{(1.20)^t} - \$100,000$$

$$= \$34,000 \left(\sum_{t=1}^{5} \frac{1}{(1.20)^t} \right) - \$100,000 \qquad = \$40,000 \left(\sum_{t=1}^{4} \frac{1}{(1.20)^t} \right) - \$100,000$$

$$= \$34,000(2.9906) - \$100,000 \qquad = \$40,000(2.5887) - \$100,000$$

$$= \$1,680.40 \qquad = \$3,548$$

Since NPV_2 now exceeds NPV_1, the manager should install machine 2.

(c)   With a certainty-equivalent coefficient of $\alpha = 0.75$, the risky sum of $34,000 for machine 1 is equivalent to a certain sum of $(0.75)(\$34,000) = \$25,500$. With $\alpha = 0.8$, the risky sum of $40,000 for machine 2 is equivalent to a certain sum of $(0.8)(\$40,000) = \$32,000$. Using the risk-free discount rate, we have:

$$NPV_1 = \sum_{t=1}^{5} \frac{\$25,500}{(1.08)^t} - \$100,000 \qquad NPV_2 = \sum_{t=1}^{4} \frac{\$32,000}{(1.08)^t} - \$100,000$$

$$= \$25,500 \left(\sum_{t=1}^{5} \frac{1}{(1.08)^t} \right) - \$100,000 \qquad = \$32,000 \left(\sum_{t=1}^{4} \frac{1}{(1.08)^t} \right) - \$100,000$$

$$= \$25,500(3.9927) - \$100,000 \qquad = \$32,000(3.3121) - \$100,000$$

$$= \$1,813.85 \qquad = \$5,987.20$$

The manager should install machine 2. Note that this result is similar to that reached in part (b).

3.10   A manager faces the choice of a high- or a low-price strategy for the firm's product. If the firm adopts a high-price strategy, there is a 70 percent probability that competitors will also adopt a high-price strategy, but if the firm adopts a low-price strategy, there is only a 40 percent probability that competitors will do the same. Regardless of the price strategy adopted by the firm, the state of nature in the future can be one of high demand for the product, medium demand, or low demand, with respective probabilities of 20, 50, and 30 percent. The present value of the firm's profits under each price strategy, plus the competitors' price response, is indicated in Table 3.12.

Construct a decision tree to show which of the two price strategies the manager should follow, on the assumption that the manager has already considered risk in estimating the present value of the firm's profits under each price strategy.

The decision tree that the firm can use to determine whether to adopt a high- or a low-price strategy is shown in Fig. 3-9. Note that in a decision tree, boxes show decision points and circles show states of nature. Since the firm has control over its price strategy, no probabilities are attached to the branches in section 1. However, since the firm has no control over competitors' price reactions (section 2) or the state of nature, or demand (section 3), probabilities are attached to each of these branches. The joint or *conditional probability* of each of the 12 possible outcomes (section 4) is obtained by multiplying the probability of each competitor's price reaction by the probability of occurrence of the particular state of demand. For example, the conditional proba-

Table 3.12

Firm's Price Strategy	Competitors' Price Response	State of Nature (Level of Demand)	Present Value of Firm's Profit
High price	High price	High	$50,000
		Medium	$40,000
		Low	$30,000
	Low price	High	$40,000
		Medium	$30,000
		Low	$20,000
Low price	High price	High	$50,000
		Medium	$35,000
		Low	$25,000
	Low price	High	$40,000
		Medium	$35,000
		Low	$30,000

bility of occurrence of outcome 1 is given by the probability of the competitor's high-price reaction (0.7) times the probability of high demand (0.2), or 14 percent. The best price strategy for the firm is a high-price one, since its expected profit of $36,000 exceeds the expected profit of $34,700 for the low-price strategy (which is, therefore, crossed off as suboptimal). In the real world, decision trees can become much more complex than the one shown in Fig. 3-9 and usually involve many decisions (boxes) by the firm.

3.11 (*a*) What is meant by simulation? How can it be used to analyze real-world decision-making situations involving risk? (*b*) What is the shortcoming of simulation analysis? What is its advantage?

(*a*) *Simulation* involves the construction of a mathematical model of the managerial decision-making situation and the use of the model to estimate the effect of a strategy (such as expanding the firm's output of a commodity) on the outcome of the strategy (i.e., on the profit of the firm). This is often referred to as *sensitivity analysis* and is the simplest type of simulation. In full-fledged simulation models, the model builder must estimate or specify the probability distribution of each variable in the model. Randomly selected values of each variable of the model are then fed into the computer program to determine the present value of the firm's profit. This process is repeated a large number of times so as to generate the probability distribution of the firm's profit. (The repetitions of one process are *iterations*.) The distribution is then used to calculate the expected value and standard deviation (as a measure of risk) of the firm's profit resulting from each strategy, so as to determine the optimal strategy of the firm.

(*b*) One shortcoming of simulation is that it is usually a very expensive technique. Its advantage is that it explicitly and simultaneously considers all the interactions among the variables of the model in decision-making situations that are too complex to be analyzed by decision trees. Simulation is becoming more and more widely used today in evaluating large, risky projects involving millions of dollars.

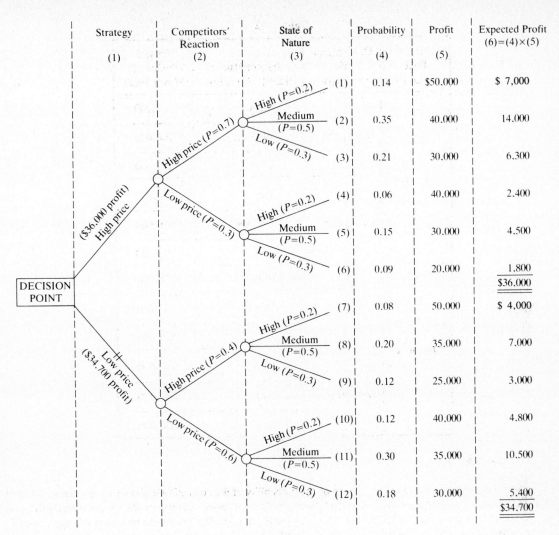

Strategy (1)	Competitors' Reaction (2)	State of Nature (3)		Probability (4)	Profit (5)	Expected Profit $(6)=(4)\times(5)$
		High ($P=0.2$)	(1)	0.14	$50,000	$ 7,000
	High price ($P=0.7$)	Medium ($P=0.5$)	(2)	0.35	40,000	14,000
		Low ($P=0.3$)	(3)	0.21	30,000	6,300
($36,000 profit) High price		High ($P=0.2$)	(4)	0.06	40,000	2,400
	Low price ($P=0.3$)	Medium ($P=0.5$)	(5)	0.15	30,000	4,500
		Low ($P=0.3$)	(6)	0.09	20,000	1,800 $36,000
		High ($P=0.2$)	(7)	0.08	50,000	$ 4,000
	High price ($P=0.4$)	Medium ($P=0.5$)	(8)	0.20	35,000	7,000
		Low ($P=0.3$)	(9)	0.12	25,000	3,000
Low price ($34,700 profit)		High ($P=0.2$)	(10)	0.12	40,000	4,800
	Low price ($P=0.6$)	Medium ($P=0.5$)	(11)	0.30	35,000	10,500
		Low ($P=0.3$)	(12)	0.18	30,000	5,400 $34,700

Fig. 3-9

3.12 Given the following payoff matrix for investment projects A, B, and C, determine the best investment project for the firm according to (*a*) the maximin criterion and (*b*) the minimax regret criterion.

Project	State of Economy		
	Recession	Normal	Boom
A	$70	$90	$ 95
B	60	80	105
C	75	80	85

(*a*) According to the maximin criterion, the firm should choose the project that provides the best of the worst possible outcomes. This is project C, which has a payoff of $75 (indicated by an asterisk in Table 3.13).

(*b*) According to the minimax regret criterion, the firm should choose the project that minimizes the maximum regret resulting from the wrong decision, after the fact. Hence, the firm should choose project A, for which

Table 3.13

Project	State of Economy			Maximin
	Recession	Normal	Boom	
A	$70	$90	$ 95	$70
B	60	80	105	60
C	75	80	85	75*

*Maximin choice.

the minimum maximum regret is $10 (marked by an asterisk in Table 3.14). Note that while the best project for the firm is project C according to the maximin criterion, it is project A according to the minimax regret criterion.

Table 3.14

Project	State of Economy			Regret Matrix			Maximum Regret
	Recession	Normal	Boom	Recession	Normal	Boom	
A	$70	$90	$ 95	$ 5	$ 0	$10	$10*
B	60	80	105	15	10	0	15
C	75	80	85	0	10	20	20

*Minimax regret choice.

Chapter 4

Regression Analysis

4.1 SIMPLE REGRESSION ANALYSIS

Regression analysis is a statistical technique for estimating the quantitative relationship between the economic variable that we seek to explain (the dependent variable, denoted by Y) and one or more independent or explanatory variables (denoted by X's). When there is only one independent variable, we have *simple regression*. If we plot data for X and Y on a graph, we can use regression analysis to estimate the line that minimizes the sum of the squared vertical deviations of the XY observations from the line. This is called the *least-squares method*. The slope of the regression line is obtained by:

$$\hat{b} = \frac{\sum_{t=1}^{n} (X_t - \overline{X})(Y_t - \overline{Y})}{\sum_{t=1}^{n} (X_t - \overline{X})^2} \qquad (4\text{-}1)$$

where $\overline{X}$ and $\overline{Y}$ are the means, or averages, of X and Y, respectively, Σ is the summation sign, and t marks the number of years, or observations, from 1 to n. The symbol $\hat{b}$ measures $\Delta Y/\Delta X$. The vertical intercept of the line ($\hat{a}$) is then obtained by:

$$\hat{a} = \overline{Y} - \hat{b}\overline{X} \qquad (4\text{-}2)$$

so that the estimated equation of the regression line is:

$$\hat{Y}_t = \hat{a} + \hat{b}X_t \qquad (4\text{-}3)$$

To test for the statistical significance of $\hat{b}$, we must first find the *standard deviation, or error, of* $\hat{b}$ ($s_{\hat{b}}$). This is given by

$$s_{\hat{b}} = \sqrt{\frac{\sum (Y_t - \hat{Y}_t)^2}{(n-k)\sum (X_t - \overline{X})^2}} = \sqrt{\frac{\sum e_t^2}{(n-k)\sum (X_t - \overline{X})^2}} \qquad (4\text{-}4)$$

where e_t is the error, or deviation, of the actual value of Y from its estimated value ($\hat{Y}$) in year t, and k is the number of estimated coefficients (which in a simple regression is 2). Then we divide $\hat{b}$ by $s_{\hat{b}}$ and get the *t statistic*

$$t = \frac{\hat{b}}{s_{\hat{b}}} \qquad (4\text{-}5)$$

If the value of the t statistic exceeds the critical value of the t distribution (Table C.2 in Appendix C) at the 0.05 level of significance with $n - k$ (here $n - 2$) degrees of freedom, we accept the hypothesis that $\hat{b}$ is statistically significant.

Finally, the *coefficient of determination* (R^2) measures the proportion of the total variation in Y (measured from its mean) that is explained by the variation in X. R^2 is given by

$$R^2 = \frac{\text{Explained variation in } Y}{\text{Total variation in } Y} = \frac{\sum (\hat{Y}_t - \overline{Y})^2}{\sum (Y_t - \overline{Y})^2} \qquad (4\text{-}6)$$

EXAMPLE 1. Suppose that a firm wants to determine the relationship between its advertising expenditures (X) and its sales revenues (Y), both in millions of dollars, using the data in the first three columns of Table 4.1. To do so, the

Table 4.1

t (Year)	X_t (Advertising)	Y_t (Sales)	$X_t - \overline{X}$	$Y_t - \overline{Y}$	$(X_t - \overline{X})(Y_t - \overline{Y})$	$(X_t - \overline{X})^2$
1	4	44	-3	-11	33	9
2	5	42	-2	-13	26	4
3	6	52	-1	-3	3	1
4	6	48	-1	-7	7	1
5	7	50	0	-5	0	0
6	8	60	1	5	5	1
7	7	58	0	3	0	0
8	9	62	2	7	14	4
9	8	64	1	9	9	1
10	10	70	3	15	45	9
$n = 10$	$\sum X_t = 70$ $\overline{X} = 7$	$\sum Y_t = 550$ $\overline{Y} = 55$	$\sum (X_t - \overline{X}) = 0$	$\sum (Y_t - \overline{Y}) = 0$	$\sum (X_t - \overline{X})(Y_t - \overline{Y}) = 142$	$\sum (X_t - \overline{X})^2 = 30$

firm calculates the rest of Table 4.1 and uses the results to estimate $\hat{b}$ and $\hat{a}$, as follows:

$$\hat{b} = \frac{\sum\limits_{t=1}^{n} (X_t - \overline{X})(Y_t - \overline{Y})}{\sum\limits_{t=1}^{n} (X_t - \overline{X})^2} = \frac{142}{30} = 4.733$$

$$\hat{a} = \overline{Y} - \hat{b}\overline{X} = 55 - 4.733(7) = 21.87$$

Thus, the equation of the regression line is

$$\hat{Y}_t = 21.87 + 4.73X_t \tag{4-7}$$

This regression line indicates that with zero advertising expenditures (i.e., with $X_t = 0$), the sales revenues of the firm ($\hat{Y}_t$) is \$21.87 million. With advertising expenditures of \$4 million (as in the first observation), $\hat{Y}_1 = 21.87 + 4.73(4) = \$40.79$ million. With advertising expenditures of \$8 million (as in the ninth observation year), $\hat{Y}_9 = 21.87 + 4.73(8) = \$59.71$ million. The estimated regression line could also be utilized to forecast that the firm's sales with advertising of, say, \$12 million would be $21.87 + 4.73(12) = \$78.63$ million. The *scatter of points* and regression line (*4-7*) are plotted in Fig. 4-1.

EXAMPLE 2. By extending Table 4.1 to find the values to fit into formula (*4-4*) for $s_{\hat{b}}$ [see Problem 4.2(*a*)], we get $s_{\hat{b}} = 0.61$. Therefore,

$$t = \frac{\hat{b}}{s_{\hat{b}}} = \frac{4.73}{0.61} = 7.74$$

Since this value of the t statistic exceeds the critical value of the t distribution (Table C.2) of 2.306 in the 0.05 probability column for $n - k = 10 - 2 = 8$ degrees of freedom, we conclude that $\hat{b}$ *is statistically significant at the 5 percent level. This means there is only a 5 percent probability that the true value of b is equal to zero* (i.e., that there is no relationship between X and Y). The test could also be conducted at the 1 percent level of significance by looking in the column headed 0.01 [see Problem 4.2(*b*)]. By further extending Table 4.1 to obtain the data to fit into formula (*4-6*) [see Problem 4.2(*c*)], we get $R^2 = 0.8821$. This means that the variation in advertising expenditures (X) explains 88.21 percent of the variation in sales (Y). Figure 4-1 shows the total, the explained, and the unexplained variation in Y for one observation point.

4.2 MULTIPLE REGRESSION ANALYSIS

With more than one independent (or explanatory) variable, we have *multiple regression*. The process of estimating the coefficients in multiple regression is in principle the same as for simple regression, but since the calculations are much more complex and time consuming, they are invariably done by computer. The computer also routinely provides the standard error of the coefficients, t statistics, R^2, and other statistics.

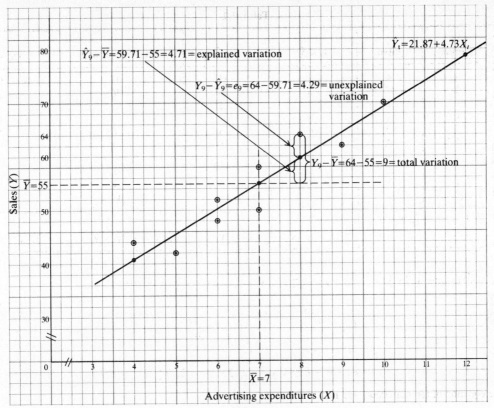

Fig. 4-1

All that is required is to be able to set up the regression, feed the data into the computer, and interpret the results.

As more relevant independent, or explanatory, variables are included in the regression, R^2 increases, but because there are fewer degrees of freedom, we use instead the *adjusted coefficient of determination* ($\overline{R}^2$), which is given by

$$\overline{R}^2 = 1 - (1 - R^2)\left(\frac{n-1}{n-k}\right) \qquad (4\text{-}8)$$

where n is the number of observations and k is the number of estimated coefficients.

We can also employ *analysis of variance* to test that not all regression coefficients are zero. This uses the *F statistic*, which is given by

$$F = \frac{\text{Explained variation}/(k-1)}{\text{Unexplained variation}/(n-k)} = \frac{R^2/(k-1)}{(1-R^2)/(n-k)} \qquad (4\text{-}9)$$

If the value of the F statistic exceeds the critical value of the F distribution (Table C.3 in Appendix C) at the 5 percent or 1 percent level of significance for $k - 1$ degrees of freedom for the numerator and $n - k$ for the denominator, we conclude that not all the regression coefficients are equal to zero.

EXAMPLE 3. Table 4.2 gives hypothetical data on the quantity demanded of a commodity (D), the price of the commodity (P), and consumers' income (Y) for the years 1976 to 1990. Demand theory postulates that D is inversely related to P and directly related to Y. Using the information in Table 4.3, we can write the following regression of D on P and Y:

$$D_t = 82.276 - 5.106P_t + 0.017Y_t \qquad \overline{R}^2 = 0.9424 \qquad F = 115.57 \qquad (4\text{-}10)$$

$$t \text{ statistic } \quad (-4.604) \quad\quad (2.545)$$

Table 4.2

Year	1976	1977	1978	1979	1980	1981	1982	1983	1984	1985	1986	1987	1988	1989	1990
$P(\$)$	9	8	9	8	7	6	6	8	5	5	5	3	4	3	4
$Y(\$)$	400	500	600	700	800	900	1,000	1,100	1,200	1,300	1,400	1,500	1,600	1,700	1,800
$D(Q)$	40	45	50	55	60	70	65	65	75	75	80	100	90	95	85

Table 4.3

```
SMPL 1-15
15 Observations
LS // Dependent variable is D
```

	Coefficient	Standard Error	t statistic
C	82.276	15.434	5.3310
P	−5.1061	1.4168	−3.6039
Y	0.0167	0.0066	2.5450

R squared	0.9506	Mean of dependent var	70.0000
Adjusted R squared	0.9424	SD of dependent var	18.1265
SE of regression	4.3497	Sum of squared resid	227.037
Durbin-Watson stat	1.8782	F statistic	115.566
Log likelihood	−41.662		

The above results indicate that for each dollar increase in price (P), the quantity demanded of the commodity (D) declines by 5.106 units, while for each \$100 increase in income (Y) D increases by 1.7 units. The critical value of the t distribution at the 0.05 level for $n - k = 15 - 3 = 12$ degrees of freedom (df) is 2.179 (from Table C.2 in Appendix C). Since this is smaller than the value of the t statistic below the coefficients in equation (*4-10*), we conclude that both slope coefficients are statistically significant at the 5 percent level. The value of $\bar{R}^2$ indicates that the variation in P and Y explains 94.24 percent of the variation in D. Finally, the critical value of the F distribution at the 0.05 level for $k - 1 = 3 - 1 = 2$ df for the numerator and $n - k = 15 - 3 = 12$ df for the denominator is 3.89 (from Table C.3). Since this is smaller than the value of the F statistic given above, we conclude that the coefficients of P and Y cannot both be equal to zero at the 5 percent level of significance.

Sometimes, the scatter of points or economic theory point to a nonlinear relationship. In that case, we can try to transform the nonlinear relationship into a linear one and continue to use the least-squares method to estimate the regression coefficients (see Problems 4.5 and 4.6).

4.3 PROBLEMS IN REGRESSION ANALYSIS

If two independent or explanatory variables in a regression are highly correlated, their estimated coefficients may be statistically insignificant even though R^2 may be very high. This is the problem of *multicollinearity* (see Problem 4.8). However, if the errors, or deviations of the observed points from the regression line, become larger or smaller (i.e., are not constant) for higher values of X (the independent variable), we face the problem of *heteroscedasticity*. This leads to biased or incorrect statistical tests (see Problems 4.9 and 4.10).

Finally, when consecutive deviations (errors) of the observed points from the regression line have the same sign or change sign frequently, we face the problem of *autocorrelation*. This exaggerates the value of the t statistic and may lead to the acceptance of a hypothesis that an estimated coefficient is statistically significant when, in fact, it is not. The presence of autocorrelation can be detected with the *Durbin-Watson statistic* (d) (which is also provided in printouts of computer-processed regression solutions).

EXAMPLE 4. In Table 4.3, $d = 1.8782$. Since this value exceeds the critical upper value $d_U = 1.54$ for $k' = 2$ (the number of independent variables in the regression) and $n = 15$ observations at the 5 percent level of significance (from Table C.4 in Appendix C), we do not face the problem of autocorrelation in our demand example. Had the value of the d statistic been between $d_L = 0.95$ and $d_U = 1.54$ (from Table C.4), the test would have been inconclusive. If the d statistic had been smaller than $d_L = 0.95$, we would have faced autocorrelation (see Problem 2.12). A figure showing heteroscedastic disturbances, or errors, and autocorrelation is shown in Fig. 4-2 in the answer to Problem 4-13.

Glossary

Adjusted coefficient of determination ($\overline{R}^2$)   The coefficient of determination adjusted for the reduction in degrees of freedom as more independent variables are included in the regression.

Analysis of variance   A test of the overall explanatory power of the regression, utilizing the F statistic.

Autocorrelation   The problem that can arise in regression analysis when consecutive errors have the same sign or change signs frequently; it leads to exaggerated values of the t statistic.

Coefficient of determination (R^2)   The proportion of the explained to the total variation in the dependent variable in regression analysis.

Durbin-Watson statistic (d)   The statistic used in the test for detecting autocorrelation.

F statistic   The ratio of the explained variance divided by $k - 1$ degrees of freedom to the unexplained variance divided by $n - k$ degrees of freedom, where k is the number of estimated parameters and n is the number of observations.

Heteroscedasticity   The problem that can arise in regression analysis when the error term is not constant; it leads to biased standard errors and incorrect statistical tests.

Least-squares method   A statistical technique for estimating a regression line that minimizes the sum of the squared vertical deviations, or errors, of the observed points from the regression line.

Multicollinearity   The problem in regression analysis that arises when two or more explanatory variables are highly correlated; it leads to exaggerated standard errors and biased statistical tests.

Multiple regression   A regression analysis with more than one independent or explanatory variable.

Regression analysis   A statistical technique for estimating the quantitative relationship between the economic variables that we seek to explain (the dependent variable) and one or more independent or explanatory variables.

Scatter of points   The plot of the observation points on a set of axes; also called *scatter diagram*.

Simple regression   A regression analysis with only one independent or explanatory variable.

Standard deviation, or error, of $\hat{b}(s_{\hat{b}})$ A measure of the dispersion in the distribution of $\hat{b}$.

t statistic   The ratio of the value of the estimated parameter to its standard deviation, or error.

Review Questions

1.   Regression analysis

   (*a*)   is a technique for estimating the relationship between a dependent variable and one or more independent or explanatory variables.

   (*b*)   is a technique for estimating the constant term and the slope coefficients of the linear relationship between the dependent and independent variable(s).

   (*c*)   utilizes the least-squares method.

   (*d*)   all of the above.

   Ans.   (*d*) See Section 2.1.

2.   The plot of the observation points on a graph is called

   (*a*)   a regression line.

   (*b*)   a scatter diagram.

   (*c*)   the least-squares technique.

   (*d*)   an estimated relationship.

   Ans.   (*b*) See Section 2.1 and Example 1.

3.   The statistical technique by which a regression line is estimated is called

   (*a*)   simple regression.

   (*b*)   multiple regression.

   (*c*)   the least-squares method.

   (*d*)   the *t* statistic.

   Ans.   (*c*) See Section 2.1.

4.   The least-squares method is used to estimate the regression line that

   (*a*)   maximizes the sum of the squared vertical deviations of the observations from the line.

   (*b*)   minimizes the sum of the vertical deviations of the observations from the line.

   (*c*)   minimizes the sum of the squared horizontal deviations of the observations from the line.

   (*d*)   minimizes the sum of the squared vertical deviations of the observations from the line.

   Ans.   (*d*) See Section 2.1 and Fig. 4-1.

5.   The standard error of estimate

   (*a*)   is the standard deviation of the distribution of the estimated coefficient.

   (*b*)   arises because different data samples will result in somewhat different estimated coefficients.

   (*c*)   is used to test for the statistical significance of the estimated coefficients.

   (*d*)   all of the above.

   Ans.   (*d*) See Section 2.1.

6.   The value of the *t* statistic is given by

   (*a*) $\hat{a}/\hat{b}$.

   (*b*) $\hat{a}/s_{\hat{b}}$.

   (*c*) $\hat{b}/s_{\hat{b}}$.

   (*d*) $s_{\hat{b}}/\hat{b}$.

   Ans.   (*c*) See Section 2.1.

7.   The degrees of freedom of the t distribution are

   (*a*) $n - 1$.

   (*b*) $n - k$.

   (*c*) $k - 1$.

   (*d*) n/k.

   Ans.   (*b*) See Section 2.1.

8.   The coefficient of determination measures the ratio of the

   (*a*)   explained to the total variation in Y.

   (*b*)   unexplained to the explained variation in Y.

   (*c*)   unexplained to the total variation in Y.

   (*d*)   total variation to the explained variation in Y.

   Ans.   (*a*) See Section 2.1.

9.   The adjusted coefficient of determination is used to take into consideration that as more independent or explanatory variables are included in the regression,

   (*a*) $n - k$ increases.

   (*b*)   the number of degrees of freedom declines.

   (*c*)   the ratio of the explained to the total variation in Y is expected to decline.

   (*d*)   the values of the estimated coefficients change.

   Ans.   (*b*) See Section 4.2.

10.   The F statistic

   (*a*)   is used to test the hypothesis that not all estimated coefficients are zero.

   (*b*)   is defined in terms of the $k - 1$ and $n - k$ degrees of freedom.

   (*c*)   can be calculated in terms of the coefficient of determination and the number of degrees of freedom.

   (*d*)   all of the above.

   Ans.   (*d*) See Section 4.2.

11.   Multicollinearity refers to the problem in regression analysis in which

   (*a*)   two or more independent variables are highly correlated.

   (*b*)   the deviations (error terms) of the observation points from the regression line are not constant.

   (*c*)   consecutive error terms are correlated.

   (*d*)   choices (*a*) and (*c*).

   Ans.   (*a*) See Section 4.3.

12.   Which of the following statements is false?

   (*a*)   The F statistic is used to test the overall performance of a regression.

   (*b*)   In regression analysis one can encounter the problems of multicollinearity, heteroscedasticity, and autocorrelation.

   (*c*)   The Durbin-Watson statistic is used to test for the presence of autocorrelation.

   (*d*)   None of the above.

   Ans.   (*d*) See Sections 2.7 and 2.8.

Solved Problems

SIMPLE REGRESSION ANALYSIS

4.1 (a) What is the purpose of regression analysis? (b) Using regression equation (4-7) in Example 1, estimate the value of Y for $X = \$5$ million, $X = \$10$ million, and $X = \$20$ million. (c) Why would you not be confident in the reliability of the estimated value of Y for $X = 20$?

(a) Regression analysis is a statistical technique for estimating the quantitative relationship between the economic variable that we seek to explain (the dependent variable, denoted by Y) and one or more independent or explanatory variables (denoted by X's). When there is only one independent variable, we have simple regression. With more than one independent variable, we have multiple regression. The regression equation is estimated by the least-squares method, which minimizes the sum of the squared vertical deviations of the observation points from the regression line.

(b) For $X = \$5$ million, $\hat{Y}_t = 21.87 + 4.73(5) = \$45.52$ million.
For $X = \$10$ million, $\hat{Y}_t = 21.87 + 4.73(10) = \$69.17$ million.
For $X = \$20$ million, $\hat{Y}_t = 21.87 + 4.73(20) = \$116.47$ million.

(c) We could not be confident in the reliability of the estimated value of Y for $X = \$20$ million because the advertising expenditure of $20 million is much larger than the advertising expenditure used to estimate the regression. That is, the regression equation can only be used to forecast sales for advertising expenditures that are within or very close to the range of values used in the estimation of the regression. For that reason, we often cannot have much confidence in the value of a (the constant term or vertical intercept), and so we do not usually test for its statistical significance.

4.2 (a) Extend Table 4.1 in Example 1 to calculate the value of $s_{\hat{b}}$. (b) Conduct the test of the statistical significance of $\hat{b}$ at the 1 percent level. (c) Extend Table 4.1 in Example 1 to calculate the total, the explained, and the unexplained variation in Y. (d) Show how to obtain the value of $R^2 = 0.8808$.

(a) Column (7) in Table 4.4 has been copied from the last column of Table 4.1. Thus,

$$s_{\hat{b}} = \sqrt{\frac{\sum e_t^2}{(n-k)\sum(X_t - \overline{X})^2}} = \sqrt{\frac{89.8746}{(10-2)(30)}} = \sqrt{0.3745} = 0.61$$

Table 4.4

Year (1)	X_t (2)	Y_t (3)	$\hat{Y}_t$ (4)	$Y_t - \hat{Y}_t = e_t$ (5)	$(Y_t - \hat{Y}_t)^2 = e_t^2$ (6)	$(X_t - \overline{X})^2$ (7)
1	4	44	40.79	3.21	10.3041	9
2	5	42	45.52	−3.52	12.3904	4
3	6	52	50.25	1.75	3.0625	1
4	6	48	50.25	−2.25	5.0625	1
5	7	50	54.98	−4.98	24.8004	0
6	8	60	59.71	0.29	0.0841	1
7	7	58	54.98	3.02	9.1204	0
8	9	62	64.44	−2.44	5.9536	4
9	8	64	59.71	4.29	18.4041	1
10	10	70	69.17	0.83	0.6889	9
$n = 10$	$\sum X_t = 70$ $\overline{X} = 7$	$\sum Y_t = 550$ $\overline{Y} = 55$			$\sum e_t^2 = 89.8746$	$\sum(X_t - \overline{X})^2 = 30$

Table 4.5

Year (t) (1)	Y_t (2)	$Y_t - \bar{Y}$ (3)	$(Y_t - \bar{Y})^2$ (4)	$\hat{Y}_t$ (5)	$\hat{Y}_t - \bar{Y}$ (6)	$(\hat{Y}_t - \bar{Y})^2$ (7)	$(Y_t - \hat{Y}_t)^2$ (8)
1	44	−11	121	40.79	−14.21	201.9241	10.3041
2	42	−13	169	45.52	−9.48	89.8704	12.3904
3	52	−3	9	50.25	−4.75	22.5625	3.0625
4	48	−7	49	50.25	−4.75	22.5625	5.0625
5	50	−5	25	54.98	−0.02	0.0004	24.8004
6	60	5	25	59.71	4.71	22.1841	0.0841
7	58	3	9	54.98	−0.02	0.0004	9.1204
8	62	7	49	64.44	9.44	89.1136	5.9536
9	64	9	81	59.71	4.71	22.1841	18.4041
10	70	15	225	69.17	14.17	200.7889	0.6889
$n = 10$	$\sum Y_t = 550$ $\bar{Y} = 55$		$\sum (Y_t - \bar{Y})^2 = 762$			$\sum (\hat{Y}_t - \bar{Y})^2 = 671.1910$	$\sum (Y_t - \hat{Y}_t)^2 = 89.8746$

(b)   To test the statistical significance of $\hat{b}$ at the 1 percent level, we look in the column headed 0.01 of the t distribution in Table C.2 for $n - k = 10 - 2 = 8$ degrees of freedom. The critical value we find is 3.355. Since the value of 7.74 for the t statistic that we found in Example 3 exceeds the critical value of the t distribution, we conclude that $\hat{b}$ is statistically significant at the 1 percent level also. It is more common, however, to conduct significance tests at the 5 percent level.

(c)   The last column of Table 4.5, which is the same as column (7) of Table 4.4, gives the unexplained variation in Y. The sum of the explained and unexplained variation in Y ($\$671.19 + \$89.87 = \$761.06$) is equal to the total variation in Y ($\$762$), except for rounding errors. Note that once we obtain two of the three values for the total, explained, and unexplained variation in Y, we can obtain the remaining value simply by subtraction.

(d)

$$R^2 = \frac{\text{Explained variation in } Y}{\text{Total variation in } Y} = \frac{\sum (\hat{Y}_t - \bar{Y})^2}{\sum (Y_t - \bar{Y})^2} = \frac{\$671.19}{\$762} = 0.8808$$

The square root of R^2 is the *coefficient of correlation* (r). This measures the covariation or degree of association that exists between variables X and Y. Thus, for our problem $r = \sqrt{R^2} = \sqrt{0.8808} = 0.94$. Here, r ranges in value from -1 (if all sample observation points fall on a negatively sloped straight line) to 1 (for perfect positive linear correlation). While regression analysis is based on the hypothesis that the variation in X causes the variation in Y, correlation simply measures the association between X and Y.

4.3   Following is the result of regressing D on P only, using the data in Table 4.2.

$$\hat{D}_t = 120.50 - 8.417P_t \qquad R^2 = 0.9240$$
$$(-12.572)$$

Explain how and why these results are biased.

In the simple regression of D on P, the value of $\hat{b} = -8.417$ (the coefficient of P in the above regression). This means that for each \$1 increase in the price of the commodity (P), the quantity demanded of the commodity (D) is estimated to decline by 8.417 units. This differs from the value of $\hat{b} = -5.106$ estimated in multiple regression equation (4-10) in Example 3. According to the latter estimate, each \$1 increase in P (while holding income, or Y, constant) is estimated to reduce D by only 5.106 units (a far smaller reduction in D than in the simple regression of D on P only).

The result of the simple regression is biased (i.e., it exaggerates the absolute value of the estimated $\hat{b}$ coefficient). The reason is that economic theory postulates that the quantity demanded of a commodity is a function of or depends on both the price of the commodity and consumers' income. Therefore, by including only the price of the commodity as an independent, or explanatory, variable in the regression, we obtain biased results. We would also obtain biased results if we regressed D on Y only.

MULTIPLE REGRESSION ANALYSIS AND FUNCTIONAL FORMS

4.4   Table 4.6 gives the price (P') of a commodity that is a substitute for the commodity examined in Problem 4.3 and Example 3. Table 4.7 then presents the results of regressing D on P, Y, and P'. (a) Write the equation of the regression of D on P, Y, and P', (b) interpret the results, and (c) compare them to those of equation (4-10). What overall conclusion can you reach with respect to the regression results of D on P, Y, and P'? (You will learn how to actually run a multiple regression by using the computer yourself in a course in statistics or econometrics. What we are interested in here is how to set up the regression analysis and how to interpret the results.)

Table 4.6

Year	1976	1977	1978	1979	1980	1981	1982	1983	1984	1985	1986	1987	1988	1989	1990
P' (\$)	10	14	12	13	11	15	16	17	22	19	20	23	18	24	21

Table 4.7

SMPL 1-15 15 Observations LS // Dependent variable is D			
	Coefficient	Standard Error	t statistic
C	79.106	19.782	3.9989
P	-4.9281	1.6111	-3.0589
Y	0.0159	0.0074	2.1456
P'	0.1748	0.6367	0.2745
R squared	0.9510	Mean of dependent var	70.0000
Adjusted R squared	0.9376	SD of dependent var	18.1265
SE of regression	4.5276	Sum of squared resid	225.492
Durbin-Watson stat	1.8181	F statistic	71.1328
Log likelihood	-41.611		

(a) $$D_t = 79.106 - 4.928P_t + 0.016Y_t + 0.175P'_t \qquad \bar{R}^2 = 0.9376 \qquad F = 71.13$$
$$(-3.059) \qquad (2.146) \quad (0.275)$$

(b) The critical value of the t distribution (from Table C.2 in Appendix C) at the 5 percent level of significance for $n - k = 15 - 4 = 11$ degrees of freedom is 2.201. Therefore, only the estimated coefficient of P_t is statistically significant at the 5 percent level. The estimated coefficient of Y_t is nearly significant, while the estimated coefficient of P'_t is very far from being significant. The regression explains 93.76 percent of the variation in D. Finally, the critical value of the F distribution (from Table C.3 in Appendix C) at the 5 percent level of significance for $k - 1 = 4 - 1 = 3$ degrees of freedom for the numerator and $n - k = 15 - 4 = 11$ degrees of freedom for the denominator is 3.59. Since the F statistic in the regression is 71.13, we conclude that not all regression coefficients are zero.

(c) The results of the regression of D on P, Y, and P' are inferior to those of regression (4-10) of D on P and Y only. The additional independent or explanatory variable (P') is statistically insignificant at the 5 percent level and $\bar{R}^2$ is smaller than for the regression of D on P and Y only. Therefore, we reach the overall conclusion that the regression of D on P and Y only [equation (4-10)] is superior to the regression of D on P, Y, and P' presented above.

4.5. The following regression results were obtained by first transforming all the variables in Table 4.2 into logarithms and then regressing the log of D on the log of P and the log of Y. What do the coefficient of the log P and the coefficient of the log Y represent? What is their usefulness?

$$\widehat{\log D_t} = 1.964 - 0.260 \log P_t + 0.391 \log Y_t \qquad \bar{R}^2 = 0.9668 \qquad F = 204.75$$
$$(-3.544) \qquad (6.641)$$

The coefficient of P in the regression of the log of D on the log of P and the log of Y measures the percentage decline in D for each 1 percent increase in P. However, the coefficient of Y measures the percentage increase in D for each 1 percent increase in Y. Thus, the coefficient of P now gives an estimate of the *price elasticity of demand* and the coefficient of Y gives an estimate of the *income elasticity of demand*. This is to be contrasted with the meaning of the estimated coefficients in regression (4-10), where the variables were not transformed into logs before running the regression, and where the coefficient of P measured $\Delta D/\Delta P$, while the coefficient of Y measured $\Delta D/\Delta Y$.

Since one of the primary purposes of regression analysis is to estimate elasticities and the *double-log regression* gives the elasticities directly, this is often the preferred form of the regression (more will be said on this in Chapters 5 and 6). Note also that the degree of statistical significance of the estimated coefficients (elasticities) and R^2 are also higher in the double-log regression than in the corresponding nonlog regression.

Table 4.8

Firm	1	2	3	4	5	6	7	8	9	10	11	12	13	14	15	16	17	18	19	20
Q	105	140	115	165	195	100	150	175	185	155	160	190	120	125	145	130	170	135	110	180
AC($)	12	6	11	9	16	13	5	11	13	7	8	14	9	9	5	8	9	7	12	10

4.6 Table 4.8 presents data on the quantity of output (Q) and the short-run average cost (AC) for a sample of 20 firms in an industry. The data were used to run a regression of AC on Q and Q', where $Q' = Q^2$. Using the regression results presented below, explain why the regression was run (*a*) on Q and Q' instead of on Q and Q^2 directly and (*b*) in this particular form (i.e., why wasn't AC regressed on Q only?).

$$\widehat{AC} = 85.101 - 1.084Q + 0.004Q' \qquad \bar{R}^2 = 0.9084 \qquad F = 95.25$$
$$(-13.236) \quad (13.525)$$

(*a*) The least-squares method is applicable only to estimate the coefficients of linear relationships. Thus, we had to transform the nonlinear (quadratic) function into a linear relationship before we could apply the least-squares method. This was accomplished by defining $Q^2 = Q'$ and then regressing AC on Q and Q' rather than on Q and Q^2.

(*b*) AC was regressed on Q and Q^2 (transformed to Q') because economic theory postulates that the AC curve of the firm is U-shaped, and a quadratic function of the form utilized is the simplest functional form that would result in a U-shaped curve. You can confirm this by simply assigning various values to Q and calculating the resulting values of AC. The excellent fit of the (transformed quadratic) function presented with Table 4.8 is evidence that the sample data do indeed indicate a U-shaped AC curve.

Note also that here the data consisted of one observation for each firm rather than data for the same firm over time. The former is called *cross-sectional data*, while the latter is referred to as *time-series data*. We can also conclude from the above that whenever economic theory or the scatter of observations points to a nonlinear relationship, we must first try to transform the nonlinear relationship into a linear one before we can apply the least-squares method to estimate the regression coefficients.

4.7 Table 4.9 gives the quantity of milk (in thousands of quarts) supplied by a firm per month (Q) at various prices in cents (P) over a 14-month period. Economic theory postulates that Q is a positive function of P. The firm faced a strike in some of its plants during the fifth, sixth, and seventh months. To test for a shift in the constant term, or intercept, during periods of strike as compared with periods of no strike, we defined a new variable (D) which assumed the value of 1 during the months of strike and the value of 0 during no-strike months. We then ran the regression of Q on P and D (treating D like any other variable, even though it assumes values of 1 or 0 only). Using the regression results presented below, (*a*) determine the value of the constant term during months of strike and no strike and (*b*) indicate the advantage of running a regression in this form rather than running one regression for the months of strike and another for the months of no strike.

$$\hat{Q} = -32.47 + 165.97P - 37.64D \qquad \bar{R}^2 = 0.98$$
$$(15.65) \ (-23.59)$$

Table 4.9

Month	1	2	3	4	5	6	7	8	9	10	11	12	13	14
Q	98	100	103	105	80	87	94	113	116	118	121	123	126	128
P	0.79	0.80	0.82	0.82	0.93	0.95	0.96	0.88	0.88	0.90	0.93	0.94	0.96	0.97
D	0	0	0	0	1	1	1	0	0	0	0	0	0	0

(a) During months of no strike (when $D = 0$), the constant term is -32.47 and the value of Q is estimated from $Q = -32.47 + 165.97P$. Since the coefficient of D is statistically significant at the 5 (and 1) percent level(s) of significance, the value of the constant during periods of strike is given by the sum of -32.47 plus the value of the coefficient of D in the regression. Thus, during periods of strike, the value of the constant term is $(-32.47) + (-37.64) = -70.11$, or lower than in periods of no strike. To estimate the value of $\hat{Q}$ during periods of strike, we then use the equation $\hat{Q} = -70.11 + 165.97P$. A variable such as D that can assume values of 0 or 1 only is called a *dummy variable*. Dummy variables can also be used to test for shifts in the slope coefficients between two periods and for seasonal effects (see Chapter 6).

(b) The advantage of running a regression in this form rather than running one regression for the months of strike and another for the months of no strike is that we conserve degrees of freedom. In fact, in this case, we could not even run a separate regression for the months of strike since the strike lasted only three months.

PROBLEMS IN REGRESSION ANALYSIS

4.8 Table 4.10 presents hypothetical data on consumption expenditures (C), disposable (i.e., after-tax) income (Y_d), and wealth (W), all in thousands of dollars, for a sample of 15 families in the United States. Economic theory postulates that C is a positive function of both Y_d and W. The results of regressing C on Y_d and W together and on Y_d and W separately are presented below. Indicate (a) the problem that these regression results show and (b) how this problem could be overcome or alleviated.

$$\hat{C} = 1.54 + 1.41Y_d - 0.15D \qquad R^2 = 0.994 \qquad \bar{R}^2 = 0.993$$
$$(1.94)\,(-0.83)$$
$$\hat{C} = 2.13 + 0.80Y_d \qquad R^2 = 0.994$$
$$(46.25)$$
$$\hat{C} = 2.92 + 0.19W \qquad R^2 = 0.992$$
$$(41.46)$$

Table 4.10

Family	1	2	3	4	5	6	7	8	9	10	11	12	13	14	15
C	32	11	15	17	16	13	18	20	14	17	41	17	33	20	18
Y_d	36	12	16	18	17	14	20	23	15	18	50	19	37	22	19
W	144	47	63	70	67	52	79	90	58	70	204	76	149	86	76

(a) Since neither slope coefficient is statistically significant in the multiple regression of C on Y_d and W (and the estimated coefficient of W even has the wrong sign), while R^2 and $\bar{R}^2$ are both very high, the multiple regression faces the problem of multicollinearity. That is, Y_d and W, the independent or explanatory variables in the regression, are highly correlated. This results in exaggerated standard errors of estimate and leads, therefore, to low values of the t statistics and to the conclusion that the coefficients are not statistically significant (even though the regression explains most of the variation in consumption). The conclusion is confirmed by the simple regressions of C on Y_d only and of C on W only. In both simple regressions, the estimated slope coefficients are statistically significant at the 5 and 1 percent levels.

(b) Serious multicollinearity can sometimes be overcome or reduced by (1) expanding the sample size (i.e., collecting more data), (2) utilizing *a priori* information (e.g., we may know from a previous study that $b_2 = 2b_1$), (3) transforming the functional relationship, and (4) dropping one of the highly collinear variables. Dropping a variable that theory tells us should be included in the model would lead, however, to specification bias, which is even more serious than the multicollinearity problem.

4.9 Explain (*a*) what heteroscedasticity is and why it is a problem, (*b*) how it can be detected, and (*c*) how it can be overcome.

(*a*) Heteroscedasticity arises in cross-sectional data when the error term is not constant, but varies with the size of one or more of the independent variables. This leads to biased standard errors and incorrect statistical tests.

(*b*) Heteroscedasticity can be detected by plotting the regression residuals against each independent or explanatory variable in the regression and determining, by inspection, if the errors increase or decrease with the values of the independent or explanatory variable. More sophisticated statistical tests are discussed in econometrics texts.

(*c*) Heteroscedasticity can be corrected by using the log of the variable that causes the problem in the regression or by running a *weighted least-squares regression*. To run a weighted least-squares regression, we first divide the dependent variable and all other independent variables by the variable that is responsible for the heteroscedasticity, and then run the regression using the transformed variables.

4.10 Table 4.11 presents data on investments (*I*) and sales (*S*), both in thousands of dollars, for a sample of 35 firms in an industry. Economic theory postulates that investment is a positive function of sales. Regressing *I* on *S* gives the results indicated in the first equation, (**A**) below, but the plot of the errors for this regression shows that they are larger for bigger firms than for smaller firms (i.e., there is heteroscedasticity). Therefore, a second regression, (**B**), is run with the results presented below. A plot of the errors indicates that heteroscedasticity is not present in regression **B**. (*a*) What type of regression is **B**? How was it run? (*b*) What are the values of the constant and slope coefficient when there is no heteroscedascity as compared with their values when heteroscedasticity is present?

$$\text{A: } \hat{I} = 21.637 + 0.079S \qquad R^2 = 0.94$$
$$\qquad\quad (28.50) \quad (22.00)$$

$$\text{B: } \widehat{I/S} = 0.074 + \frac{23.187}{S} \qquad R^2 = 98$$
$$\qquad\quad (20.41) \ (42.16)$$

Table 4.11

Investments							Sales
30.2	30.5	30.5	30.7	30.9	31.2	31.2	100
31.5	31.5	31.9	32.3	32.8	33.4	33.4	150
35.1	35.7	36.3	36.9	37.4	37.4	37.8	200
38.4	39.1	40.2	40.8	42.1	42.9	43.2	250
44.3	44.9	45.2	45.9	46.5	47.7	48.5	300

(*a*) Regression **B** is a weighted least-squares regression. It was run by first dividing each value of *I* and the constant term by the corresponding value of *S* and then running the regression on the transformed variables. Running a weighted least-squares regression can often overcome heteroscedasticity.

(*b*) The value of the constant term in the weighted least-squares regression, **B**, is 23.187 (instead of 21.637), and the slope coefficient associated with variable *S* is 0.074 (instead of 0.079). Thus, it is important to correctly interpret the results of a weighted least-squares regression.

4.11 Explain (*a*) what autocorrelation is and why it is a problem, (*b*) how it can be detected, and (*c*) how it can be overcome.

(*a*) Autocorrelation often arises in time-series data when consecutive errors have the same sign or change signs frequently. This leads to exaggerated *t* statistics, and an unreliable R^2 and *F* statistic.

(b) Autocorrelation can be detected by inspecting the plot of the errors or residuals against time or, more usually and precisely, by the Durbin-Watson test. The Durbin-Watson test is based on a comparison of the value of the Durbin-Watson statistic (d, usually given in printouts of computer-generated regression results) with the critical values of d from Table C.4 in Appendix C. The Durbin-Watson statistic (d) is given by

$$d = \frac{\sum\limits_{t=2}^{n} (e_t - e_{t-1})^2}{\sum\limits_{t=1}^{n} (e_t)^2} \tag{4-11}$$

where e_t and e_{t-1} refer, respectively, to the error term in period t and in the previous time period ($t - 1$). The value of d ranges from 0 to 4.

(c) Autocorrelation may be corrected by including a time trend or an important missing variable in the regression, using a nonlinear form, running the regression on first differences in the variables, or using more complex techniques.

4.12 Table 4.12 presents data on personal disposable (i.e., after-tax) income and personal consumption expenditures in the United States, both measured in billions of dollars, for the 18 years from 1962 to 1979. Economic theory postulates that real personal consumption expenditures in a given year (C_t) are primarily a linear function of real personal disposable income in the same year (Y_{d_t}). (a) Explain why the regression equation of C_t on Y_{d_t} indicates the presence of autocorrelation while the regression of ΔC_t on ΔY_{d_t} does not. (b) Describe how the regression equation of ΔC_t on ΔY_{d_t} was run.

$$\text{C: } \hat{C}_t = -11.40 + 0.93 Y_{d_t} \qquad R^2 = 0.999$$
$$(144.33) \qquad\qquad d = 0.75$$
$$\text{D: } \widehat{\Delta C}_t = 0.94 \Delta Y_{d_t} \qquad R^2 = 0.960$$
$$(37.79) \qquad\qquad d = 2.44$$

(a) The first regression, **C**, indicates the presence of autocorrelation at the 5 percent level of significance because $d = 0.75$, and this is smaller than the critical value of $d_L = 0.95$ for $k' = 1$ (the number of explanatory variables) and $n = 18$ (the number of observations) in Table C.4 in Appendix C. The second regression, **D**, however, does *not* indicate the presence of autocorrelation at the 5 percent level because $d = 2.24$, which exceeds the critical value of $d_U = 1.12$ for $k' = 1$ and $n = 18$ in Table C.4.

Table 4.12

Year	Income	Consumption
1962	383.9	355.2
1963	402.8	374.6
1964	437.0	400.4
1965	472.2	430.2
1966	510.4	464.8
1967	544.5	490.4
1968	588.1	535.9
1969	630.4	579.7
1970	685.9	618.8
1971	742.8	668.2
1972	801.3	733.0
1973	901.7	809.9
1974	984.6	889.6
1975	1,086.7	979.1
1976	1,184.5	1,089.9
1977	1,305.1	1,210.0
1978	1,458.4	1,350.8
1979	1,623.2	1,509.8

(b)   To run the regression for the change in consumption on the change in income, we calculate first differences for each variable and then run the regression using these transformed variables. Specifically, we subtract the second from the first value in each data column to obtain a new column of transformed data for each variable. By doing this, we lose one observation. But since the regression in terms of changes or first differences is usually run without a constant term (as was done here), the number of degrees of freedom is the same as before. While regression **D** overcomes the autocorrelation problem, its form is not as useful as that of regression **C**.

4.13   Draw a figure in four parts. In panels (a) and (b) show heteroscedastic disturbances or errors (in panel A show that the size of the errors increases with the size of the independent variable, X, and in panel (b) show that the size of the error decreases with the size of the independent variable). In panels (c) and (d) show autocorrelation (in panel (c) show positive autocorrelation and in panel (d) show negative autocorrelation).

See Fig. 4-2.

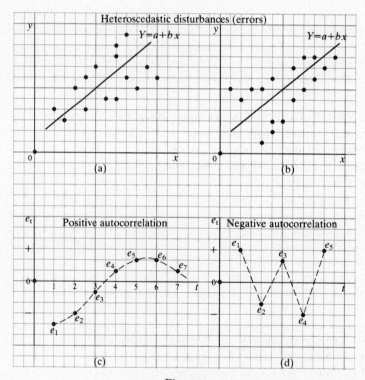

Fig. 4-2

Chapter 5

Demand Theory

5.1 THE DEMAND FOR A COMMODITY

One of the most important aspects of managerial economics is the analysis of demand. A firm would not be established or could not survive if a sufficient demand for its product did not exist or could not be created through advertising. The demand that a firm faces for the product it sells depends on the total market demand for the product, which in turn is a summation of the demand for the product of all the consumers in the market.

Consumer demand theory postulates that the quantity demanded of a commodity is a function of, or depends on, the price of the commodity, the consumer's income, the price of related (i.e., substitute and complementary) commodities, and the tastes of the consumer. In functional form, we can express this as

$$Q_{dx} = f(P_X, I, P_Y, T) \tag{5-1}$$

where Q_{dx} = the quantity demanded of commodity X by an individual per time period
   P_X = the unit price of commodity X
   I = the consumer's income
   P_Y = the price of related (i.e., substitute and complementary) commodities
   T = the tastes of the consumer

The quantity demanded of a commodity per time period increases with a reduction in its price, with an increase in the consumer's income, with an increase in the price of substitute commodities and a reduction in the price of complementary commodities, and with an increase in the consumer's taste for the commodity. The quantity demanded of the commodity declines with opposite changes, i.e., with an increase in price, a reduction in the consumer's income, etc.

For the purpose of analysis it is often useful to examine the relationship between the quantity demanded of a commodity and the price of the commodity only (i.e., independently of the other forces that affect demand). The inverse relationship between the price and quantity demanded of the commodity is called the *law of demand*, and the plot of the data (with price on the vertical axis and quantity on the horizontal axis) gives the *individual's demand curve*. An increase in the individual's income, in the price of substitute commodities, and in the taste for the commodity, as well as a reduction in the price of complementary commodities, will then shift the demand curve to the right, while opposite movements shift the demand curve to the left.

The *market demand curve* for a commodity is obtained by the horizontal summation of the demand curves of all the consumers in the market (see Example 1). Except in the case of monopoly (in which there is a single firm in the industry), the demand curve that a firm faces is a fraction of the market demand curve and depends on all the forces that affect individual and market demand for the commodity as well as on all other forces that are specific to the industry and firm (see Example 2).

EXAMPLE 1. The left panel of Fig. 5-1 shows the hypothetical demand curve for commodity X of an individual (d_X), while the right panel shows the corresponding market demand curve (D_X), on the assumption that there are 100 identical individuals in the market. Figure 5-1 shows that at $P_X = \$4$, $Q_{dx} = 4$ and $Q_{Dx} = 400$, while at $P_X = \$3$, $Q_{dx} = 6$ and $Q_{Dx} = 600$. The increase in Q_{dx} when P_X falls occurs because in consumption, the individual consumer substitutes commodity X for other commodities (which are now relatively more expensive). This is called the *substitution effect*. In addition, when P_x falls, a consumer can purchase more of X with a given amount of money income (i.e., the consumer's real income increases). This is called the *income effect*. The movement along a given demand curve resulting from a change in the commodity price is referred to as *a change in the quantity demanded*, while a shift in the demand curve resulting from a change in any of the factors that affect demand, other than the commodity price, is referred to as *a change in demand*.

61

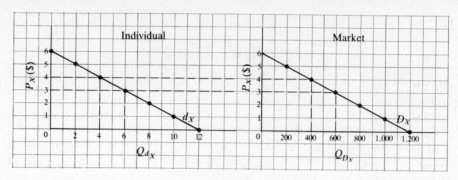

Fig. 5-1

EXAMPLE 2. The *demand function faced by a firm for a commodity* can be written as

$$Q_X = a_0 + a_1 P_X + a_2 N + a_3 I + a_4 P_y + a_5 T + \cdots \tag{5-2}$$

where Q_{dx} = the quantity demanded of commodity X faced by a firm, per time period
  P_X = price of commodity X
  N = number of consumers in the market
  I = consumers' income
  P_Y = price of related (substitute and complementary) commodities
  T = consumers' tastes

The a's represent the coefficients to be estimated by regression analysis (discussed in Chapter 4), and the dots at the end of equation (5-2) refer to the other determinants of demand that are specific to the particular firm in a given industry. These include price expectations, the level of advertising, the pricing and promotional policies of other firms in the industry, and the availability of credit [see Problem 5.2(b)].

  Q_X is postulated to increase with increasing numbers of people in the market, consumers' incomes, prices of substitutes, tastes for the commodity, expectations of higher prices for X in the future, and expenditures by the firm for advertising and to provide easier credit terms to consumers. Q_X is also expected to be higher the *lower* are P_X, the prices of complementary commodities, and competing firms' expenditures on advertising and for providing easier credit terms. By holding constant all the variables affecting Q_X other than P_X, we can derive the *demand curve for commodity X faced by the firm* (see Problem 5.5).

5.2 THE PRICE ELASTICITY OF DEMAND

The responsiveness (elasticity) in the quantity demanded of a commodity to a change in its price is very important to a firm. The *price elasticity of demand* (E_P) is measured by the percentage change in the quantity demanded of the commodity divided by the percentage change in the commodity's price, holding constant all other variables in the demand function. That is,

$$E_P = \frac{\Delta Q/Q}{\Delta P/P} = \frac{\Delta Q}{\Delta P} \cdot \frac{P}{Q} \tag{5-3}$$

where ΔQ and ΔP refer, respectively, to the change in quantity and the change in price. Note that the inverse of the slope of the demand curve (i.e., $\Delta Q/\Delta P$) is a component, but only a component, of the elasticity formula and that the value of $\Delta Q/\Delta P$ is negative because price and quantity move in opposite directions (i.e., when P rises, Q falls, and vice versa).

  Equation (5-3) gives *point price elasticity of demand*, or elasticity at a given point on the demand curve. More frequently in the real world, we measure *arc price elasticity of demand*, or price elasticity of demand between two points on the demand curve. If we used equation (5-3) to measure arc price elasticity of demand, however, we would get different results depending on whether the price rose or fell. To avoid this, we use the average of the two prices and the average of the quantities and express the formula for arc price elasticity of demand (E_P) as

$$E_P = \frac{\Delta Q}{\Delta P} \cdot \frac{(P_2 + P_1)/2}{(Q_2 + Q_1)/2} = \frac{Q_2 - Q_1}{P_2 - P_1} \cdot \frac{P_2 + P_1}{Q_2 + Q_1} \tag{5-4}$$

where the subscripts 1 and 2 refer to the original and to the new values, respectively, of price and quantity (see Example 3).

With a decline in price, the *total revenue* (TR) of the firm increases if demand is elastic (i.e., if $|E_P| > 1$, where $|E_P|$ is the absolute value of E_P); TR remains unchanged if demand is unitary elastic (i.e., if $|E_P| = 1$), and TR declines if demand is inelastic (i.e., if $|E_P| < 1$). The relationship among the firm's *marginal revenue* (MR), price (P), and price elasticity of demand (E_P) is given by equation (5-5) and can be shown graphically (see Example 4 and Fig. 5-3).

$$MR = P\left(1 + \frac{1}{E_P}\right) \tag{5-5}$$

The price elasticity of demand is larger, the closer the available substitutes for the commodity and the greater their number as well as the longer the time period allowed for consumers to respond to the change in price.

EXAMPLE 3. To find E_P at points A, B, C, F, G, H, and J on market demand curve D_X in Fig. 5-1 (repeated as Fig. 5-2 for ease of reference), we first note that $\Delta Q/\Delta P = -\frac{200}{1} = -200$. Therefore, at point A

$$E_P = \frac{\Delta Q}{\Delta P} \cdot \frac{P}{Q} = -200\left(\frac{P}{Q}\right) = -200\left(\frac{6}{0}\right) = -\infty$$

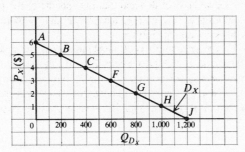

Fig. 5-2

Similarly, at point B on D_X, $E_P = -200(\frac{5}{200}) = -5$; at point C, $E_P = -200(\frac{4}{400}) = -2$; at point F, $E_P = -200(\frac{3}{600}) = -1$; at point G, $E_P = -200(\frac{2}{800}) = -1/2$; at point H, $E_P = -200(\frac{1}{1,000}) = -1/5$, and at point J, $E_P = -200(\frac{0}{1,200}) = 0$. Note that D_X is elastic (i.e., $|E_p| > 1$) above the midpoint, unitary elastic (i.e., $|E_p| = 1$) at the midpoint, and inelastic (i.e., $|E_p| < 1$) below the midpoint. This is always the case for linear demand curves.

If we used equation (5-3) to measure the arc price elasticity for a movement from point B to point C on D_X, we would get

$$E_P = \frac{\Delta Q}{\Delta P} \cdot \frac{P}{Q} = -200\left(\frac{5}{200}\right) = -5$$

However, for a movement from point C to point B, we would get

$$E_P = \frac{\Delta Q}{\Delta P} \cdot \frac{P}{Q} = -200\left(\frac{4}{400}\right) = -2$$

To avoid getting different results for a price decline and a price increase, we use equation (5-4) to measure arc E_P between points B and C, as follows:

$$E_P = \frac{Q_2 - Q_1}{P_2 - P_1} \cdot \frac{P_2 + P_1}{Q_2 + Q_1} = \frac{400 - 200}{4 - 5} \cdot \frac{4 + 5}{400 + 200} = \frac{(200)(9)}{(-1)(600)} = \frac{1,800}{-600} = -3$$

The price elasticity of demand can be measured for the individual's demand curve, the market demand curve, or the demand curve faced by a firm. In general, the demand curve faced by a firm is more elastic than the corresponding market demand curve because there are usually much better substitutes for the firm's product (from other firms in the industry) than for the industry's product.

EXAMPLE 4.   Suppose that a firm is a monopolist and faces the market demand curve for commodity X shown in Fig. 5-2. The monopolist's demand schedule is then given by the first two columns of Table 5.1. Column (3) gives the E_P

Table 5.1

P (1)	Q (2)	E_P (3)	TR $= P \cdot Q$ (4)	MR $= \Delta\text{TR}/\Delta Q$ (5)
$6	0	$-\infty$	$ 0	—
5	200	-5	1,000	5
4	400	-2	1,600	3
3	600	-1	1,800	1
2	800	$-\frac{1}{2}$	1,600	-1
1	1,000	$-\frac{1}{5}$	1,000	-3
0	1,200	0	0	-5

values found in Example 3. The monopolist's total revenue (TR), in column (4), is the product of price (P) times quantity (Q), while marginal revenue (MR), in column (5), is the change in total revenue per unit change in output.

Table 5.1 shows that a price decline leads to an increase in TR as long as D_X is price elastic; TR is at its maximum when D_X is unitary elastic and TR declines when D_X is inelastic. The relationship among E_P, TR, and MR is shown in Fig. 5-3. Note that since MR $= \Delta\text{TR}/\Delta Q$, the MR values in Table 5.1 are plotted *between* the levels of output in the bottom panel of Fig. 5-3.

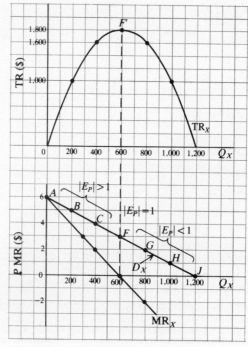

Fig. 5-3

The relationship among MR, P, and E_P shown in Fig. 5-3 is confirmed by the use of equation (5-5). Thus, at $P_X = \$4$, $E_P = -2$ and

$$\text{MR} = P\left[1 + \left(\frac{1}{E_P}\right)\right] = \$4\left[1 + \left(\frac{1}{-2}\right)\right] = \$4\left(\frac{1}{2}\right) = \$2$$

At $P = \$3$, $\text{MR} = \$3[1 + (\frac{1}{-1})] = 0$, and at $P = \$2$, $\text{MR} = \$2(-1) = -\$2$ (see Fig. 5-3). Note that with equation (5-5), we obtain MR *at* each level of output, while in Table 5.1 we found the values of MR *between* different levels of output.

5.3 THE INCOME ELASTICITY OF DEMAND

The responsiveness in the demand for a commodity to a change in consumers' income is measured by the *income elasticity of demand* (E_I). The point income elasticity of demand is given by

$$E_I = \frac{\Delta Q/Q}{\Delta I/I} = \frac{\Delta Q}{\Delta I} \cdot \frac{I}{Q} \tag{5-6}$$

where ΔQ and ΔI refer, respectively, to the change in quantity and the change in income. To avoid getting different results depending on whether income rises or falls, we usually measure *arc income elasticity of demand*, which is given by

$$E_I = \frac{\Delta Q}{\Delta I} \cdot \frac{(I_2 + I_1)/2}{(Q_2 + Q_1)/2} = \frac{Q_2 - Q_1}{I_2 - I_1} \cdot \frac{I_2 + I_1}{Q_2 + Q_1} \tag{5-7}$$

where the subscripts 1 and 2 refer, respectively, to the original and to the new levels of income and quantity.

Goods for which E_I is positive are called *normal goods*, while goods with negative E_I are called *inferior goods*. Most goods are normal. Some examples of inferior goods are flour, bologna, and pork and beans. Consumers purchase less of these when their income rises because they can then afford more expensive products. Normal goods are classified as necessities if E_I is between 0 and 1 and as luxuries if E_I exceeds 1. Examples of necessities are food, clothing, and housing. Examples of luxuries are champagne, vacations, and Ferraris. The concept of income elasticity of demand is very useful to a firm in estimating the demand for the product it sells and in forecasting future demand.

EXAMPLE 5. If the demand for commodity X is 400 units with $I = \$10,000$ and 600 units with $I = \$11,000$, arc E_I between the two levels of income is

$$E_I = \frac{Q_2 - Q_1}{I_2 - I_1} \cdot \frac{I_2 + I_1}{Q_2 + Q_1} = \frac{600 - 400}{\$11,000 - \$10,000} \cdot \frac{\$11,000 + \$10,000}{600 + 400} = \frac{200}{\$1,000} \cdot \frac{\$21,000}{1,000} = 4.2$$

Thus, commodity X is a normal good and a luxury.

5.4 THE CROSS-PRICE ELASTICITY OF DEMAND

The responsiveness in the demand for commodity X to a change in the price of commodity Y is measured by the *cross-price elasticity of demand* (E_{XY}). *Point cross-price elasticity of demand* is given by

$$E_{XY} = \frac{\Delta Q_X/Q_X}{\Delta P_Y/P_Y} = \frac{\Delta Q_X}{\Delta P_Y} \cdot \frac{P_Y}{Q_X} \tag{5-8}$$

where ΔQ_X and ΔP_Y refer, respectively, to the change in the quantity of commodity X and the change in the price of commodity Y. To avoid getting different results depending on whether P_Y rises or falls, we usually measure *arc cross-price elasticity of demand*, which is given by

$$E_{XY} = \frac{\Delta Q_X}{\Delta P_Y} \cdot \frac{(P_{Y_2} + P_{Y_1})/2}{(Q_{X_2} + Q_{X_1})/2} = \frac{Q_{X_2} - Q_{X_1}}{P_{Y_2} - P_{Y_1}} \cdot \frac{P_{Y_2} + P_{Y_1}}{Q_{X_2} + Q_{X_1}} \tag{5-9}$$

where the subscripts 1 and 2 refer, respectively, to the original and to the new levels of income and quantity.

Commodities X and Y are substitutes if E_{XY} is positive, complementary if E_{XY} is negative, and independent if E_{XY} is close to zero. Firms use the concept of E_{XY} to measure the effect of a change in the price of related commodities on the demand for the commodity that the firm sells. A high positive cross-price elasticity of demand is often used to define an industry since it indicates that the various commodities are very similar.

EXAMPLE 6. If the demand for commodity X is 400 units with $P_Y = \$1$ and 600 units with $P_Y = \$2$, arc E_{XY} between the two levels of P_Y is

$$E_{XY} = \frac{Q_{X_2} - Q_{X_1}}{P_{Y_2} - P_{Y_1}} \cdot \frac{P_{Y_2} + P_{Y_1}}{Q_{X_2} + Q_{X_1}} = \frac{600 - 400}{\$2 - \$1} \cdot \frac{\$2 + \$1}{600 + 400} = \frac{200}{\$1} \cdot \frac{\$3}{1,000} = 0.6$$

Thus, commodity Y is a substitute for commodity X.

5.5 USING ELASTICITIES IN MANAGERIAL DECISION MAKING

Analysis of the forces or variables that affect demand and reliable estimates of their quantitative effect on sales (elasticities) are essential in order for the firm to make the best operating decisions in the short run and to plan for its growth in the long run. As we have seen, a firm can usually set the price of the commodity it sells as well as decide on the level of its expenditures on advertising, product quality, and customer services. However, the firm has little or no control over the level and growth of consumers' incomes and price expectations or competitors' pricing decisions and expenditures on advertising, product quality, and customer services.

The firm can use the elasticity of demand of the variables under its control to determine the best policies that are open to the firm to maximize profits or the value of the firm. For example, if the demand for the firm's product is price inelastic, the firm will want to increase the product price since that would increase its total revenue and reduce its total costs (since consumers will purchase less of the commodity at a higher price), so that its profits would rise.

The elasticity of the firm's sales with respect to the variables beyond its control is also crucial to its ability to respond most effectively to competitors' policies and to plan the best growth strategy. For example, if the cross-price elasticity of demand for the firm's product is very high, the firm will need to respond quickly to a competitor's price reduction; otherwise the firm risks losing a great deal of its sales. Before lowering its price, however, the firm will need to weigh this risk against that of starting a price war. The firm may also want to plan to shift to the production of goods with a higher income elasticity of demand in order to benefit more from rising incomes in the future.

Thus, it is only by utilizing the elasticity of all the variables included in the demand function and examining their interaction that a firm can determine the best policies available to manipulate demand, to effectively respond to competitors' policies, and to plan its growth.

Glossary

Arc cross-price elasticity of demand The cross-price elasticity of demand for commodity X between two price levels of commodity Y; it is measured by $(Q_{X_2} - Q_{X_1})/(P_{Y_2} - P_{Y_1}) \cdot ((P_{Y_2} + P_{Y_1})/(Q_{X_2} + Q_{X_1}))$.

Arc income elasticity of demand The income elasticity of demand between two levels of income; it is measured by $(Q_2 - Q_1/I_2 - I_1) \cdot (I_2 + I_1/Q_2 + Q_1)$.

Arc price elasticity of demand The price elasticity of demand between two points on the demand curve; it is measured by $(Q_2 - Q_1/P_2 - P_1) \cdot (P_2 + P_1/Q_2 + Q_1)$.

Change in demand A shift in the demand curve of a commodity as a result of a change in consumers' incomes, prices of related commodities, consumers' tastes, or any other determinant of demand except commodity price.

Change in the quantity demanded The movement along a particular demand curve resulting from a change in the price of the commodity, while holding everything else constant.

Consumer demand theory   The study of the determinants of consumer demand for a commodity.

Cross-price elasticity of demand (E_{XY})   The percentage change in the demand for commodity X divided by the percentage change in the price of commodity Y, while holding constant all other variables in the demand function.

Demand curve faced by a firm   The graphical relationship between the price and the quantity demanded of a commodity that a firm faces.

Demand function faced by a firm   The relationship that specifies the determinants of the demand for a commodity faced by a firm; these include the price of the commodity, population size, consumers' incomes, prices of related commodities, and any other forces that are specific to the industry and firm.

Income effect   The increase in the quantity demanded of a commodity resulting only from the increase in real income that accompanies a price decline.

Income elasticity of demand (E_I)   The percentage change in the demand for a commodity divided by the percentage change in the consumer's income, while holding constant all the other variables in the demand function.

Individual's demand curve   The graphical relationship between the price and the quantity demanded of a commodity by an individual per time period.

Inferior goods   Goods the consumer purchases less of with an increase in income (so that E_I is negative).

Law of demand   The principle that the relationship between the price and the quantity demanded of a commodity per time period is inverse.

Marginal revenue (MR)   The change in total revenue per unit change in quantity sold.

Market demand curve   The graphical relationship between the price and the quantity demanded of a commodity per time period in the market as a whole; it is the summation of the demand curves of all the consumers in the market.

Normal goods   Goods the consumer purchases more of with an increase in income (so that E_I is positive).

Point cross-price elasticity of demand   The cross-price elasticity of demand for commodity X at a particular price of commodity Y; it is measured by $(\Delta Q_X / \Delta P_Y) \cdot (P_Y / Q_X)$.

Point income elasticity of demand   The income elasticity of demand at a particular level of income; it is measured by $(\Delta Q / \Delta I) \cdot (I / Q)$.

Point price elasticity of demand   The price elasticity of demand at a particular point on the demand curve; it is measured by $(\Delta Q / \Delta P) \cdot (P / Q)$.

Price elasticity of demand (E_P)   The percentage change in the quantity demanded of a commodity divided by the percentage change in its price, while holding constant all the other variables in the demand function.

Substitution effect   The increase in the quantity demanded of a commodity resulting only from the decline in its price and independent of the change in real income.

Total revenue (TR)   The price per unit of the commodity times the quantity sold.

Review Questions

1.   Analysis of demand is important in managerial economics because

   (*a*)   a firm would not be established if a sufficient demand for its product did not exist or could not be generated through advertising.

   (*b*)   a firm could not survive without a sufficient demand for its product.

   (*c*)   it affects the choice of the firm's production techniques and plans for future expansion.

   (*d*)   all of the above.

   Ans.   (*d*) See Section 5.1.

2.   In managerial economics we are primarily interested in

   (a)   the individual's demand curve.

   (b)   the market demand curve.

   (c)   the demand curve faced by the firm.

   (d)   all of the above.

   Ans.   (c) See Section 5.1.

3.   Which of the following forces does not directly affect an individual's demand for a commodity?

   (a)   The prices of the commodity and of related commodities

   (b)   The costs of producing the commodity

   (c)   The individual's income and tastes

   (d)   All of the above

   Ans.   (b) See Section 5.1.

4.   Which of the following statements is *false*?

   (a)   A firm's demand curve for a commodity depends on the market demand curve, which in turn depends on the number of consumers in the market.

   (b)   A decline in the price of a commodity leads to an increase in the demand for the commodity.

   (c)   A decline in the price of a commodity leads to a decrease in the demand for a substitute commodity.

   (d)   An increase in the advertising expenditures of a firm is likely to shift the demand curve of a competitive firm to the left.

   Ans.   (b) A decline in the price of a commodity leads to a decrease in the *quantity demanded*, not to a decrease in the demand for the commodity. See Section 5.1.

5.   The price elasticity of demand measures

   (a) $\Delta Q / \Delta P$.

   (b)   the percentage change in P divided by the percentage change in Q.

   (c)   the percentage change in Q divided by the percentage change in P.

   (d) $\Delta P / \Delta Q$.

   Ans.   (c) See Section 5.2.

6.   When demand is elastic, a decline in price leads to an increase in total revenue because

   (a)   the percentage increase in Q is larger than the percentage decline in P.

   (b)   the percentage increase in Q is smaller than the percentage decline in P.

   (c) $\Delta Q / \Delta P$ is larger than -1.

   (d)   none of the above.

   Ans.   (a) See Section 5.2.

7.   When demand is price inelastic, an increase in price leads to

   (a)   an increase in total revenue.

   (b)   a decline in total revenue.

   (c)   no change in total revenue.

   (d)   an increase or a decline in total revenue, but we cannot say which without additional information.

   Ans.   (a) The reason is that the decline in quantity is proportionately smaller than the increase in price. See Section 5.2.

8.   Which of the following statements is true?

   (a)   When demand is price elastic, MR is positive.

   (b)   When demand is unitary elastic, MR = 0.

   (c)   When demand is price inelastic, MR is negative.

   (d)   All of the above.

   Ans.   (d) See Section 5.2 and Fig. 5-3.

9.   Which of the following statements is false?

   (a)   The income elasticity of demand measures the percentage change in the demand for a commodity divided by the percentage change in income.

   (b)   A necessity is one for which E_I exceeds 1.

   (c)   A normal good is one for which E_I is positive.

   (d)   An inferior good is one for which E_I is negative.

   Ans.   (b) See Section 5.3.

10.   The cross-price elasticity of demand is measured by the percentage change in

   (a)   the demand for commodity X divided by the percentage change in P_X.

   (b)   the demand for commodity X divided by the percentage change in P_Y.

   (c) P_Y divided by the percentage change in the demand for commodity X.

   (d)   the demand for commodity X divided by the percentage change in income.

   Ans.   (b) See Section 5.4.

11.   Which of the following statements is false?

   (a)   When E_{XY} is positive, commodities X and Y are complements.

   (b)   When E_{XY} is close to zero, commodities X and Y are independent.

   (c)   A high E_{XY} indicates that commodities X and Y are in the same industry.

   (d)   Firms use E_{XY} to determine the effect on sales resulting from a change in the price of a related commodity.

   Ans.   (a) See Section 5.4.

12.   Which of the following statements is false?

   (a)   A firm can estimate the elasticity of demand for all the variables included in the demand function.

   (b)   A firm can use the elasticity of demand for the variables under its control to determine the best policies that are open to the firm.

   (c)   The elasticity of the firm's sales with respect to the variables outside the firm's control is crucial to the firm in responding most effectively to competitors' policies and for planning the best growth strategy.

   (d)   None of the above.

   Ans.   (d) See Section 5.5.

Solved Problems

THE DEMAND FOR A COMMODITY

5.1   (a) Why is the analysis of demand crucial in managerial economics? (b) On what does the demand function of an individual depend? (c) What is the law of demand? How can it be explained? (d) How is the market demand curve derived?

(a)   Demand is one of the most important aspects of managerial economics because a firm would not be estab-
      lished and could not survive if a sufficient demand for its product did not exist or could not be created
      through advertising. A firm could have the most efficient production techniques and the most effective
      management, but without a demand for its product that is sufficient to cover at least all production and
      selling costs over the long run, it simply could not survive. Indeed, many firms go out of business soon
      after being set up because their expectation of a sufficient demand for their products fails to materialize
      even with a great deal of advertising. Each year also sees many established and previously profitable firms
      close because consumers shifted their purchases to other firms and products. Demand is, thus, essential for
      the creation, survival, and profitability of a firm.

(b)   The demand for a commodity arises from consumers' willingness and ability (i.e., from their desire or need
      for the commodity backed by sufficient income) to purchase the commodity. Consumer demand theory
      postulates that the quantity demanded of a commodity is a function of, or depends on, the price of the
      commodity, consumers' income, the prices of related (i.e., complementary and substitute) commodities,
      and consumers' tastes.

(c)   The law of demand refers to the inverse relationship that exists between the price and the quantity demanded
      of a commodity per time period. The law of demand is explained by the substitution and the income effects.
      The substitution effect results when the price of a commodity falls and consumers substitute that commodity
      for other commodities which are now relatively more expensive. The income effect results when the price
      of a commodity falls and consumers can purchase more of the commodity because their *real* income is now
      higher. Most goods are *normal* in the sense that consumers purchase more of those goods when their income
      rises. Some inexpensive goods, such as potatoes and bologna, however, are *inferior* in the sense that
      consumers purchase less of those goods when their income rises.

(d)   The market demand curve for a commodity is obtained by the horizontal summation of the demand curves
      of all the consumers in the market. If all consumers were identical, the market demand curve would have
      the same shape as the individuals' demand curves, except that the quantity on the horizontal axis of the
      market demand curve would be a multiple of the quantity on the horizontal axis of the individuals' demand
      curves.

5.2   (a) What is the relationship between the demand curve that a firm faces for a commodity and the
           market demand curve for the commodity? (b) On what does the demand function that a firm faces for
           a commodity depend?

(a)   The demand that a firm faces for a commodity depends on the size of the market, or industry demand for
      the commodity, the form in which the industry is organized, and the number of firms in the industry. If the
      firm is the sole producer of a commodity for which there are no good substitutes (i.e., if the firm is a
      monopolist), the firm is or represents the industry and faces the industry or market demand for the
      commodity. At the opposite extreme is perfect competition. Here, a large number of firms produce a
      homogeneous (i.e., identical) product, and each firm is too small to affect the price of the commodity by
      its own actions. In such a case, each firm is a price taker and faces a horizontal demand curve for the
      commodity (i.e., the firm can sell any amount of the commodity at the given market price of the commodity).
          The vast majority of firms, however, operate under oligopoly or monopolistic competition. In oli-
      gopoly, there are only a few interdependent firms in the industry, producing either a homogeneous or a
      heterogeneous (i.e., differentiated) product. In monopolistic competition, there are many firms selling a
      heterogeneous product. Under all forms of market organization except perfect competition, the firm faces
      a negatively sloped demand curve for the commodity. Furthermore, except in the case of monopoly, the
      demand curve that a firm faces is a fraction of the market demand curve for the commodity.

(b)   The demand a firm faces for a commodity depends on all the forces that affect market demand for the
      commodity, as well as the forces that are specific to the industry and firm. The market forces include the
      price of the commodity, the number of consumers in the market, consumers' incomes, the prices of related
      (i.e., substitute and complementary) commodities, and consumers' tastes for the commodity. Among the
      forces that are specific to the industry and firm are consumers' expectations regarding the future price of
      the commodity, the firm's level of advertising and other promotional efforts, the pricing and promotional
      policies of other firms in the industry (especially in oligopoly), the availability of credit, and the type of
      commodity that the firm sells.

5.3 (*a*) What is meant by producers' goods? By a firm's derived demand for the inputs it uses in production? (*b*) Why is the demand for durable goods (both consumers' and producers') less stable than the demand for nondurable goods?

(*a*) Producers' goods refer to those goods (raw materials, semiprocessed materials, and equipment) that are used by the firm to produce the goods and services demanded by consumers (i.e., consumers' goods). Thus, the demand for producers' goods is a derived demand—derived from the demand for the commodities for which the inputs are used. The greater is the demand for the goods and services a firm sells, the greater is the firm's demand for the inputs or resources required to produce those goods and services.

(*b*) The demand for durable goods (automobiles, washing machines, refrigerators, capital equipment, and storable commodities) is less stable or more volatile than the demand for nondurable goods. This is so because the purchase of durable goods can be postponed by spending more on repairs and maintenance or by working off inventories until the economy improves, in the expectation of lower prices in future time periods. When the economy does improve, credit incentives are introduced, the lower prices materialize, and consumers and producers then greatly increase their demand for durable goods.

5.4 Given $Q_{dx} = 8 - P_X$, (*a*) derive the individual's demand schedule for commodity X and (*b*) plot it.

(*a*) By substituting various hypothetical values for P_X into the individual's demand function, we obtain the individual's demand schedule given in Table 5.2.

Table 5.2

P_X (\$)	8	7	6	5	4	3	2	1	0
Q_{dx}	0	1	2	3	4	5	6	7	8

(*b*) By plotting the individual's demand schedule given in Table 5.2 we obtain the individual's demand curve shown in Fig. 5-4.

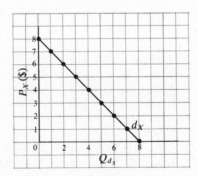

Fig. 5-4

5.5 Using the individual's demand schedule for commodity X in Problem 5.4, (*a*) derive the corresponding market demand schedule on the assumption that there are three identical individuals in the market, (*b*) derive the market demand curve for commodity X graphically from the three individuals' demand curves, (*c*) derive the market demand curve for commodity X on the assumption that there are 100 identical individuals in the market.

(*a*) The market demand schedule for commodity X is given in Table 5.3. It is obtained by summing the quantity demanded at each price by each of the three individuals in the market.

Table 5.3

P_X (\$)	8	7	6	5	4	3	2	1	0
Q_{dx} (1)	0	1	2	3	4	5	6	7	8
Q_{dx} (2)	0	1	2	3	4	5	6	7	8
Q_{dx} (3)	0	1	2	3	4	5	6	7	8
Q_{Dx}	0	3	6	9	12	15	18	21	24

(b) The market demand curve (D_X) in Fig. 5-5 is obtained from the lateral summation of the demand curve of each of the three individuals in the market. Thus, Fig. 5-5 shows the same information graphically that Table 5.3 shows numerically.

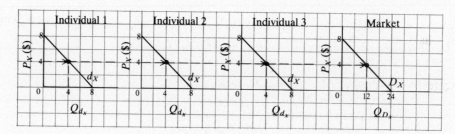

Fig. 5-5

(c) The demand curves for commodity X for one individual and for the market are shown in Fig. 5-6. Note that the market demand curve for commodity X has the same shape as the individual's demand curve, except that the quantity scale for the market demand curve is 100 times larger than the scale for the individual's demand curve because there are 100 identical individuals in the market.

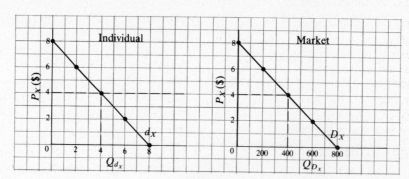

Fig. 5-6

5.6   Given the following estimated demand function for commodity X that a firm faces, explain how you would expect each of the variables included in the demand function to affect the demand for commodity X that the firm faces.

$$Q_X = f(P_X, N, I, T, P_Y, P_Z, E, A, A_c, C, C_c)$$

where P_X = price of commodity X

N = number of consumers in the market

I = consumers' income

T = consumers' taste for commodity X

P_Y = price of a commodity, Y, that is a substitute for commodity X

P_Z = price of a commodity, Z, that is complementary to commodity X

E = consumers' expectations of the future price of commodity X

A = advertising expenditures by the firm for commodity X

A_c = advertising expenditures by competitive firms, c

C = credit incentives by the firm

C_c = credit incentives by competitive firms

We expect Q_X to be directly related to N, I (if X is a normal good), T, P_Y, E (if consumers expect the future price of commodity X to be higher), A, and C. That is, Q_X is expected to be higher the *higher* the values of N, I, T, P_Y, E, A, C. Q_X is also expected to be higher, the *lower* the values of P_X, P_Z, E (if consumers expect the future price of commodity X to be higher), A_c, and C_c. By holding all variables except P_X constant, we can derive the demand schedule and the demand curve the firm faces for commodity X. The curve will be negatively sloped, thus reflecting the law of demand.

5.7 Suppose that William Berl, the manager of the Oldsmobile division of the General Motors Corporation, has estimated the following regression equation for Oldsmobiles:

$$Q_o = 90,000 - 200P_o + 3,000N + 100I + 50P_c - 2,000P_g + 5A$$

where Q_o = quantity demanded of Oldsmobiles per year

P_o = price of Oldsmobiles, in dollars

N = population of the United States, in millions

I = per capita disposable income, in dollars

P_c = price of Chevrolet automobiles, in dollars

P_g = real price of gasoline, in cents per gallon

A = advertising expenditures by Oldsmobile, in dollars per year

(a) Indicate the change in the number of Oldsmobiles purchased per year (Q_o) for each unit change in the independent, or explanatory, variables. (b) Find the value of Q_o if the average value of P_c = $10,000, N = 220 million, I = $12,000, P_c = $9,000, P_g = 100¢, and A = $200,000. (c) Derive the equation for the demand curve for Oldsmobiles, and (d) plot it.

(a)   The number of Oldsmobiles purchased per year (Q_o) increases by 3,000 units for each 1 million increase in population (N), by 100 units for each $1 increase in per capita disposable income (I), by 50 units for each $1 increase in the price of Chevrolets (P_c), and by 5 units for each $1 increase in advertising expenditures on Oldsmobiles (A). Q_o declines by 200 units for each $1 increase in the price of Oldsmobiles (P_o) and by 2,000 for each 1 cent increase in the price of gasoline (P_g).

(b)   To find the value of Q_o, we substitute the average value of the independent or explanatory variables into the estimated demand function. Thus, for P_o = $10,000, N = 220 million, I = $12,000, P_c = $9,000, P_g = 100¢, and A = $200,000, we have:

$$Q_o = 90,000 - 200(10,000) + 3,000(220) + 100(12,000) + 50(9,000) - 2,000(100) + 5(200,000)$$

$$= 90,000 - 2,000,000 + 660,000 + 1,200,000 + 450,000 - 200,000 + 1,000,000$$

$$= 1,200,000$$

(c)   To derive the equation for the demand curve for Oldsmobiles, we substitute into the estimated demand equation the average value of all the independent, or explanatory, variables given above, with the exception of P_o. Thus, the equation for the demand curve for Oldsmobiles is:

$$Q_o = 90,000 - 200 P_o + 3,000(220) + 100(12,000) + 50(9,000) - 2,000(100) + 5(200,000)$$

$$= 3,200,000 - 200 P_o$$

(d)   To derive the demand curve for Oldsmobiles (D_o), we substitute the hypothetical values of $12,000, $10,000, and $8,000 for P_o into the demand equation found in part (c). This gives, respectively, Q_o = 800,000, Q_o = 1,200,000, and Q_o = 1,600,000. Plotting these price-quantity values, we get the demand curve for Oldsmobiles, D_o, shown in Fig. 5-7.

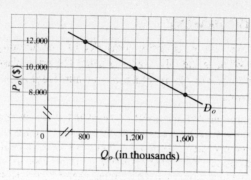

Fig. 5-7

5.8. Starting with the estimated demand function for Oldsmobiles given in Problem 5.7, assume that the average values of the independent variables change to $N = 240$ million, $I = \$14,000$, $P_c = \$10,000$, $P_g = 120¢$, and $A = \$300,000$. (a) Find the equation for the new demand curve for Oldsmobiles. (b) On the same set of axes, plot the new demand curve, D_o', and the demand curve, D_o, found in Problem 5.7(d). (c) What is the relationship between D_o and D_o'? What explains this relationship?

(a) To derive the equation for the new demand curve for Oldsmobiles we substitute the new average values for the independent or explanatory variables given in this problem into the estimated demand function given in Problem 5.7, and we get

$$Q_o = 90,000 - 200P_o + 3,000N + 100I + 50P_c - 2,000P_g + 5A$$
$$= 90,000 - 200P_o + 3,000(240) + 100(14,000) + 50(10,000) - 2,000(120) + 5(300,000)$$
$$= 3,970,000 - 200\,P_o$$

(b) To derive the new demand curve for Oldsmobiles, D_o', we substitute the hypothetical values of $\$12,000$, $\$10,000$, and $\$8,000$ for P_o into the equation for the new demand curve found in part (a). This gives, respectively, $Q_o' = 1,570,000$, $Q_o' = 1,970,000$, and $Q_o' = 2,370,000$. Plotting these price-quantity values, we get the new demand curve for Oldsmobiles, D_o', shown in Fig. 5-8. Figure 5-8 also shows D_o from Fig. 5-7.

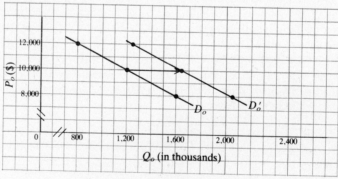

Fig. 5-8

(c) Since the constant term in the equation for the new demand curve found in part (a) of this problem (3,970,000) exceeds the constant term in the equation for the demand curve (3,200,000) found in part (c) of Problem 5.7, D_o' is to the right of D_o. That is, at each level of P_o, D_o' indicates a greater demand for Oldsmobiles than D_o. This results because the effect of the changes in all the forces that cause the demand curve to shift to the right (the increases in N, I, P_c, and A) exceeds the effect of the change in the force that causes the demand curve to shift to the left (the increase in P_g). Thus, D_o' is to the right of D_o.

THE PRICE ELASTICITY OF DEMAND

5.9 (*a*) Why is the responsiveness in the quantity demanded of a commodity to a change in its price very important to a firm? (*b*) What is the advantage of using the price elasticity rather than the slope of the demand curve, or its inverse, to measure the responsiveness in the quantity demanded of a commodity to a change in its price?

(*a*) The responsiveness in the quantity demanded of a commodity to a change in its price is very important to a firm because responsiveness determines whether the change in price will lead to an increase, a decline, or no change in the total revenue of the firm. A firm's pricing policies affect sales and thus also affect its production costs and its profitability. Hence, knowledge of the responsiveness in the quantity demanded of a commodity to a change in its price is essential to management in determining the best pricing policies for the firm.

(*b*) The responsiveness in the quantity demanded of a commodity to a change in its price could be measured by the inverse of the slope of the demand curve (i.e., by $\Delta Q/\Delta P$). Note that since price is plotted on the vertical axis and quantity on the horizontal axis, $\Delta Q/\Delta P$ is the inverse of the slope of the demand curve. The disadvantage of using $\Delta Q/\Delta P$ is that its value is expressed in terms of the units of measurement. Thus, simply changing prices from dollars to cents would reduce the value of $\Delta Q/\Delta P$ 100-fold. Furthermore, comparison of changes in quantity to changes in prices across commodities would be meaningless. In order to avoid these disadvantages, we use the price elasticity of demand rather than the inverse of the slope of the demand curve to measure the responsiveness in the quantity demanded of a commodity to a change in its price.

5.10 For the market demand curve in the right-hand panel of Fig. 5-6 (repeated for ease of reference as Fig. 5-9), find (*a*) the point price elasticity of demand at each dollar price and (*b*) the arc price elasticity of demand between consecutive dollar prices (i.e., between $P_X = \$8$ and $P_X = \$7$, $P_X = \$7$ and $P_X = \$6$, and so on).

(*a*) To find the point price elasticity of demand (E_P) at each price level, we apply the following formula, where $\Delta Q/\Delta P = -100$:

$$E_P = \frac{\Delta Q}{\Delta P} \cdot \frac{P}{Q} = -100\left(\frac{P}{Q}\right)$$

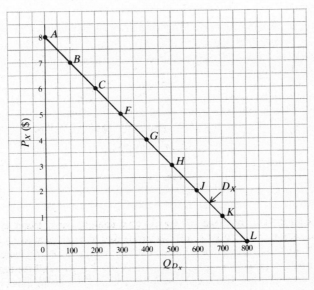

Fig. 5-9

$$\text{At } P = \$8, \quad E_P = -100(\tfrac{8}{0}) = \infty$$

$$\text{At } P = \$7, \quad E_P = -100(\tfrac{7}{100}) = -7$$

$$\text{At } P = \$6, \quad E_P = -100(\tfrac{6}{200}) = -3$$

$$\text{At } P = \$5, \quad E_P = -100(\tfrac{5}{300}) = -1.67$$

$$\text{At } P = \$4, \quad E_P = -100(\tfrac{4}{400}) = -1$$

$$\text{At } P = \$3, \quad E_P = -100(\tfrac{3}{500}) = -0.6$$

$$\text{At } P = \$2, \quad E_P = -100(\tfrac{2}{600}) = -0.33$$

$$\text{At } P = \$1, \quad E_P = -100(\tfrac{1}{700}) = -0.14$$

$$\text{At } P = \$0, \quad E_P = -100(\tfrac{0}{800}) = 0$$

(b) To find the arc price elasticity of demand (E_P) between consecutive price levels, we apply equation (5-4) where $\Delta Q/\Delta P = -100$, as in part (a), and the numbers 2 and 1 refer, respectively, to the new and original price and quantity. That is, arc price elasticity is found by using the following formula:

$$E_P = (-100)\frac{(P_2 + P_1)}{(Q_2 + Q_1)}$$

Thus, between points $P = \$8$ and $P = \$7$ (i.e., between points A and B on D_X), $E_P = -100(7 + 8)/(100 + 0) = -15$.

$$\text{Between points } B \text{ and } C, \quad E_P = -100(\tfrac{13}{300}) = -4.33$$

$$\text{Between points } C \text{ and } F, \quad E_P = -100(\tfrac{11}{500}) = -2.2$$

$$\text{Between points } F \text{ and } G, \quad E_P = -100(\tfrac{9}{700}) = -1.29$$

$$\text{Between points } G \text{ and } H, \quad E_P = -100(\tfrac{7}{900}) = -0.78$$

$$\text{Between points } H \text{ and } J, \quad E_P = -100(\tfrac{5}{1,100}) = -0.45$$

$$\text{Between points } J \text{ and } K, \quad E_P = -100(\tfrac{3}{1,300}) = -0.23$$

$$\text{Between points } K \text{ and } L, \quad E_P = -100(\tfrac{1}{1,500}) = -0.07$$

5.11 Using the Oldsmobile demand function (Q_o) estimated in Problem 5-7, calculate the price elasticity of demand (a) at $P_o = \$12,000$ and $Q_o = 800,000$, (b) at $P_o = \$10,000$ and $Q_o = 1,200,000$, (c) at $P_o = \$8,000$ and $Q_o = 1,600,000$, (d) between $P_o = \$12,000$ and $P_o = \$10,000$, and (e) between $P_o = \$10,000$ and $P_o = \$8,000$.

(a) In the regression equation in Problem 5-7, the estimated coefficient of P ($a_1 = -200$) gives the value of $\Delta Q_o/\Delta P_o$. Therefore, the formula for the point elasticity of demand can be rewritten as

$$E_P = a_1 \cdot \frac{P_o}{Q_o}$$

Thus, at $P_o = \$12,000$ and $Q_o = 800,000$, $E_P = -200(12,000/800,000) = -3$.

(b) At $P_o = \$10,000$ and $Q_o = 1,200,000$, $E_P = -200(10,000/1,200,000) = -1.67$.

(c) At $P_o = \$8,000$ and $Q_o = 1,600,000$, $E_P = -200(8,000/1,600,000) = -1$.

(d) To find the arc price elasticity of demand we use formula

$$E_P = a_1 \cdot \frac{P_2 + P_1}{Q_2 + Q_1}$$

Thus, between $P_o = \$12,000$ and $\$10,000$, $E_P = -200(22,000/2,000,000) = -2.2$.

(e) Between $P_o = \$10,000$ and $P_o = \$8,000$, $E_P = -200(18,000/2,800,000) = -1.29$.

5.12 The point price elasticity of demand can be obtained geometrically by dividing the price (P) of the commodity by $P - A$ at the point on the demand curve at which we want to find the elasticity, where A is the price at which the quantity demanded is zero (i.e., the price at which the demand curve crosses the vertical axis). For a curvilinear demand curve, we draw a tangent to the demand curve at the point at which we want to measure E_P and then proceed as if we were dealing with a linear demand curve. With the above in mind, find the price elasticity for D_X in Fig. 5-9 at $P_X = \$5$ graphically. Also show graphically that E_P would be the same if D_X were curvilinear but tangent to the linear D_X curve at $P_X = \$5$.

For linear demand curve D_X, E_P at $P_X = \$5$ is given by

$$E_P = \frac{P}{P - A} = \frac{\$5}{\$5 - \$8} = \frac{\$5}{-\$3} = -1.67$$

where P is the price of the commodity at which we want to find E_P, and A is the price of the commodity ($P_X = \$8$) at which $Q_X = 0$. This is the same as the value obtained in Problem 5.10(a) by the use of equation (5-3). The value of E_P at other points on D_X can be similarly obtained graphically. If the demand curve were curvilinear (D_X^* in Fig. 5-10) and tangent to D_X at $P_X = \$5$, $E_P = -1.67$ at $P_X = \$5$, as for D_X.

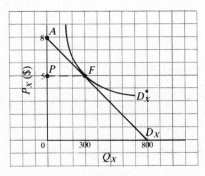

Fig. 5-10

5.13 Explain why the firm would never produce in the inelastic portion of its demand curve.

A firm would never produce in the inelastic portion of its demand curve because, by raising its price, the firm can increase its total revenue. Since, with an increase in price, the firm will sell fewer units of the commodity, it will also save on production costs. With total revenue increasing and total costs declining, the total profits of the firm will increase. Thus, the firm would never produce in the inelastic portion of its demand curve.

Another way to look at this is to remember (from Section 2.3) that in order to maximize profits, the firm should sell at the price at which marginal revenue equals marginal cost. Since marginal cost is positive, marginal revenue is also positive at the profit-maximizing price. But for marginal revenue to be positive, the firm should operate (i.e., charge a price that is) on the elastic portion of its demand curve.

5.14 For the demand curve in Figure 5-9, (a) construct a table similar to Table 5.1 in Example 4, showing the demand, total revenue, and marginal revenue schedules for commodity X. (b) Plot the demand, total revenue, and the marginal revenue schedules from part (a) in a figure similar to Fig. 5-3 in Example 4. Indicate on it the range over which demand is elastic, unitary elastic, and inelastic.

(a) The demand, total revenue, and marginal revenue schedules for demand curve D_X in Fig. 5-9 are given in Table 5.4.

(b) The demand, total revenue, and marginal revenue schedules of Table 5.4 are plotted in Fig. 5-11. D_X is price elastic at $P_X > \$4$, unitary elastic at $P_X = \$4$, and price inelastic at $P_X < \$4$. With a decline in P_X, TR increases and MR is positive when D_X is price elastic, TR is at its maximum and MR = 0 when D_X is unitary price elastic, and TR declines and MR is negative when D_X is price inelastic.

Table 5.4

P	Q	TR = $P \cdot Q$	MR = $\Delta TR / \Delta Q$
$8	0	$ 0	—
7	100	700	$ 7
6	200	1,200	5
5	300	1,500	3
4	400	1,600	1
3	500	1,500	−1
2	600	1,200	−3
1	700	700	−5
0	800	0	−7

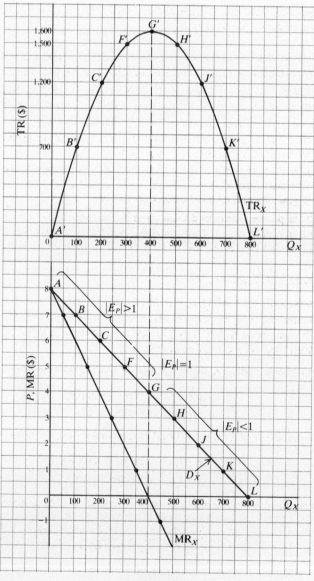

Fig. 5-11

5.15 Using equation (5-5) relating MR, P, and E_P, confirm the MR values at each P_X shown in Fig. 5-11.

Using the equation $MR = P(1 + 1/E_P)$ and the E_P values found in Problem 5.10(a), we get:

$$\text{At } P_X = \$8, \quad MR = \$8\left(1 + \frac{1}{\infty}\right) \quad = \$8$$

$$\text{At } P_X = \$7, \quad MR = \$7\left(1 - \frac{1}{7}\right) \quad = \$6$$

$$\text{At } P_X = \$6, \quad MR = \$6\left(1 - \frac{1}{3}\right) \quad = \$4$$

$$\text{At } P_X = \$5, \quad MR = \$5\left(1 - \frac{1}{1.67}\right) = \$2$$

$$\text{At } P_X = \$4, \quad MR = \$4\left(1 - \frac{1}{1}\right) \quad = 0$$

$$\text{At } P_X = \$3, \quad MR = \$3\left(1 - \frac{1}{0.6}\right) = \$2$$

Note that with equation (5-5), we obtain the values of MR *at* each level of output, while in Table 5.4 we found the MR values *between* different levels of output.

5.16 (a) Would you expect the price elasticity of demand to be higher for Oldsmobiles or for automobiles in general? Why? (b) Would you expect the price elasticity of demand for electricity for residential use to be higher or lower than for industrial use? Why? (c) Would you expect the price elasticity of demand for electricity to be higher or lower in the short run as compared with the long run? Why?

(a) We would expect the price elasticity of demand for Oldsmobiles to be much higher than the price elasticity of demand for automobiles in general because there are many good substitutes for Oldsmobiles, while few good substitutes are available for automobiles in general.

(b) We would expect the price elasticity of demand for electricity for residential use to be much greater than for industrial use because industrial users, using large amounts of electricity, could generate their own electricity. This is generally not feasible for residential users.

(c) We would expect the price elasticity of demand to be higher in the long run than in the short run because in the long run there is more time to learn about the availability of substitutes (such as gas ovens, solar energy, etc.) and to switch over to substitutes.

THE INCOME ELASTICITY OF DEMAND

5.17 If the demand for commodity X is 400 units at an income of \$10,000 and 500 units at an income of \$15,000, find the income elasticity of demand (a) for an increase in income from \$10,000 to \$15,000, (b) for a decline in income from \$15,000 to \$10,000, and (c) between the income levels of \$10,000 and \$15,000. (d) What type of good is commodity X?

(a) For an increase in income from \$10,000 to \$15,000, the point income elasticity of demand for commodity X is

$$E_I = \frac{\Delta Q}{\Delta I} \cdot \frac{I}{Q} = \frac{100}{\$5,000} \cdot \frac{\$10,000}{400} = 0.5$$

(b) For a decrease in income from \$15,000 to \$10,000, the point income elasticity of demand for commodity X is

$$E_I = \frac{\Delta Q}{\Delta I} \cdot \frac{I}{Q} = \frac{-100}{-\$5,000} \cdot \frac{\$15,000}{500} = 0.6$$

(c) The arc income elasticity of demand for commodity X between the income levels of \$10,000 and \$15,000 is

$$E_I = \frac{Q_2 - Q_1}{I_2 - I_1} \cdot \frac{I_2 + I_1}{Q_2 + Q_1} = \frac{100}{\$5,000} \cdot \frac{\$25,000}{900} = 0.56$$

This means that a 10 percent increase in consumers' incomes leads to an average increase of 5.6 percent in the demand for commodity X.

(d)   Since E_I is positive, commodity X is a normal good, but since E_I is smaller than 1, commodity X is a necessity. Note that E_I measures the shift in the demand curve at each price level.

5.18   Using the demand function for Oldsmobiles (Q_o) estimated in Problem 5.7, calculate the income elasticity of demand (a) at $I = \$12{,}000$ and $Q_o = 1{,}200{,}000$, (b) at $I = \$14{,}000$ and $Q_o = 1{,}400{,}000$, and (c) between $I = \$12{,}000$ and $I = \$14{,}000$. (d) What type of commodity are Oldsmobiles?

(a)   The estimated coefficient of I ($a_3 = 100$) in the regression equation for Q_o in Problem 5-7 gives the value of $\Delta Q_o | \Delta I |$. Therefore, the formula for the point income elasticity of demand can be rewritten as

$$E_I = a_3 \cdot \frac{I}{Q_o}$$

Thus, at $I = \$12{,}000$ and $Q_o = 1{,}200{,}000$, $E_I = 100(12{,}000/1{,}200{,}000) = 1$.

(b)   At $I = \$14{,}000$ and $Q_o = 1{,}400{,}000$, $E_I = 100(14{,}000/1{,}400{,}000) = 1$.

(c)   Since in this case E_I is the same for the price increase and the price decline, we can expect arc E_I to be the same also. This is not the usual situation. In the usual situation, we get different values for point E_I for an increase and a decline in income. To find arc income elasticity of demand we use the formula

$$E_I = a_3 \cdot \frac{I_2 + I_1}{Q_2 + Q_1}$$

Thus, between $I = \$12{,}000$ and $\$14{,}000$, $E_I = 100(26{,}000/2{,}600{,}000) = 1$.

(d)   Since $E_I = 1$, Oldsmobiles are a necessity, but they are right at the borderline between being a necessity and a luxury.

THE CROSS-PRICE ELASTICITY OF DEMAND

5.19   (a) Explain why commodities X and Y are substitutes if E_{XY} is positive, complementary if E_{XY} is negative, and independent if E_{XY} is zero. Give some examples of each set of commodities. (b) What are some of the uses of cross-price elasticity of demand?

(a)   An increase in P_Y causes Q_{D_Y} to fall (a movement along D_Y). If the demand for commodity X increases (i.e., D_X shifts to the right), it means that X is a substitute for Y. Since the increase in P_Y results in an increase in Q_X, E_{XY} is positive. Thus, a positive value for E_{XY} indicates that commodities X and Y are substitutes. Examples of substitute commodities are coffee and tea, coffee and cocoa, butter and margarine, hamburgers and hot dogs, Coca Cola and Pepsi, and electricity and gas. On the other hand, if E_{XY} is negative, commodities X and Y are complementary because an increase in P_Y leads to a reduction in (Q_Y and) Q_X. Examples of complementary commodities are coffee and sugar, coffee and cream, hamburgers and buns, hot dogs and mustard, and cars and gasoline. Finally, if E_{XY} is zero, commodities X and Y are independent because a change in the price of Y does not lead to a change in Q_X. This may be the case with books and beer, cars and candy, pencils and potatoes, and so on.

(b)   Firms use the concept of cross-price elasticity of demand to measure the effect of a change in the price of related commodities on the demand for the commodity that the firm sells. A high positive cross-price elasticity of demand is often used to define an industry since the high value indicates that the various firms in the industry produce very similar commodities. The cross-price elasticity concept is often used, also, by the courts to reach a decision in business antitrust cases.

5.20   If the demand for commodity X is 500 units at $P_Y = \$4$ and 400 units at $P_Y = \$6$, find E_{XY} for (a) an increase in P_Y from $\$4$ to $\$6$, (b) a decline in P_Y from $\$6$ to $\$4$, and (c) P_Y between $\$4$ and $\$6$. (d) Are commodities X and Y substitutes, complementary, or independent?

(a)   For an increase in P_Y from $\$4$ to $\$6$, the point E_{XY} is

$$E_{XY} = \frac{\Delta Q_X}{\Delta P_Y} \cdot \frac{P_Y}{Q_X} = \frac{-100}{\$2} \cdot \frac{\$4}{500} = -0.4$$

(b)   For a decrease in P_Y from $\$6$ to $\$4$, point E_{XY} is

$$E_{XY} = \frac{\Delta Q_X}{\Delta P_Y} \cdot \frac{P_Y}{Q_X} = \frac{100}{-\$2} \cdot \frac{\$6}{400} = -0.75$$

(c)   The arc E_{XY} for P_Y between \$4 and \$6 is

$$E_{XY} = \frac{Q_{X_2} - Q_{X_1}}{P_{Y_2} - P_{Y_1}} \cdot \frac{P_{Y_2} + P_{Y_1}}{Q_{X_2} + Q_{X_1}} = \frac{400 - 500}{\$6 - \$4} \cdot \frac{\$6 + \$4}{400 + 500} = \frac{-100}{\$2} \cdot \frac{\$10}{900} = -0.56$$

This means that a 10 percent increase in P_Y leads to an average decline of 5.6 percent in the demand for commodity X.

(d)   Since E_{XY} is negative, commodities X and Y are complementary.

5.21   Using the demand function for Oldsmobiles (Q_o) estimated in Problem 5.7, calculate the cross-price elasticity of demand for the price of Chevrolets (P_c) at P_c = \$9,000 and Q_o = 1,200,000 and at P_c = \$11,000 and Q_o = 1,300,000.

Since $a_4 = \dfrac{\Delta Q_o}{\Delta P_c}$, arc E_{oc} is equal to

$$E_{oc} = a_4 \cdot \frac{P_{c_2} + P_{c_1}}{Q_{o_2} + Q_{o_1}} = 50(20,000/2,500,000) = 0.4$$

This means that a 10 percent increase in P_c leads to an average rise in Q_o of 4 percent. Since E_{oc} is positive, Oldsmobiles and Chevrolets are substitutes.

USING ELASTICITIES IN MANAGERIAL DECISION MAKING

5.22   A firm selling commodity X, for which another firm's commodity Y may be a substitute, estimated that $E_P = -1$, $E_I = 2$, and $E_{XY} = 3$. Next year the firm would like to increase P_X by 5 percent. The firm expects that next year consumers' incomes (I) will increase by 4 percent and P_Y will fall by 2 percent. (a) If the sales of the firm are 1,000 units of X this year, how much of commodity X can the firm expect to sell next year? (b) What price should the firm charge for commodity X to keep its sales at 1,000 units?

(a)   Since $E_P = -1$, if the firm increased P_X by 5 percent, that change by itself would cause sales to change by −5 percent [= (−1)(5%)]. With $E_I = 2$, the forecasted increase in income of 4 percent would by itself result in an 8 percent [= (2)(4%)] increase in sales. Finally, since $E_{XY} = 3$, a *reduction* in P_Y by 2 percent would by itself result in a decline of 6 percent [= (3)(−2)] in sales. Therefore, the net effect of a 5 percent increase in P_X, a 4 percent increase in I, and a 2 percent reduction in P_Y would result in a net decline in the sales of the firm: −5% + 8% − 6% = −3%. Thus, sales of commodity X next year would be 1,000 − (1,000)(3%) = 1,000 − 30 = 970 units.

(b)   By themselves (i.e., without any increase in P_X), the increase in income and the reduction in P_Y would result in a 2 percent increase in sales. Thus, in order to keep sales unchanged, the firm can increase P_X only, which would by itself reduce sales. Since $E_P = -1$, the firm can increase P_X by 2 percent only in order to reduce sales by 2 percent so as to keep next year's sales unchanged at 1,000 units.

5.23   Using the demand function for Oldsmobiles (Q_o) estimated in Problem 5.7 (repeated below for ease of reference), calculate the elasticity of sales with respect to each variable in the demand function at P_o = \$10,000, N = 220 million, I = \$12,000, P_c = \$9,000, P_g = 100¢, and A = \$200,000.

$$Q_o = 90,000 - 200P_o + 3,000N + 100I + 50P_c - 2,000P_g + 5A$$

In Problem 5.7(b), we calculated that at the given values of the independent, or explanatory, variables Q_o = 1,200,000. Therefore, the elasticity of demand for Oldsmobiles with respect to P_o, N, I, P_c, P_g, and A is

$$E_P = a_1 \left(\frac{P_o}{Q_o} \right) = -200 \left(\frac{10,000}{1,200,000} \right) = -1.67 \qquad \text{[as in Problem 5.11(b)]}$$

$$E_N = a_2 \left(\frac{N}{Q_o} \right) = 3,000 \left(\frac{220}{1,200,000} \right) = 0.55$$

$$E_I = a_3 \left(\frac{I}{Q_o} \right) = 100 \left(\frac{12,000}{1,200,000} \right) = 1 \qquad \text{[as in Problem 5.18(a)]}$$

$$E_{oc} = a_4\left(\frac{P_c}{Q_o}\right) = 50\left(\frac{9,000}{1,200,000}\right) = 0.375$$

$$E_{og} = a_5\left(\frac{P_g}{Q_o}\right) = -2,000\left(\frac{100}{1,200,000}\right) = -0.167$$

$$E_A = a_6\left(\frac{A}{Q_o}\right) = 5\left(\frac{200,000}{1,200,000}\right) = 0.833$$

5.24 Using the estimated demand function and elasticities given in Problem 5.23, estimate sales if Oldsmobile increases P_o and A by 10 percent and the other variables increase as follows: N, by 2 percent; I, by 3 percent; P_c, by 8 percent; and P_g, by 5 percent.

If Oldsmobile increases P_o by 10 percent and its advertising by 10 percent and if, at the same time, N increases by 2 percent, I increases by 3 percent, P_c is increased by 8 percent, and P_g increases by 5 percent, sales of Oldsmobiles (Q_o') would be

$$Q_o' = Q_o + Q_o\left(\frac{\Delta P_o}{P_o}\right)E_P + Q_o\left(\frac{\Delta N}{N}\right)E_N + Q_o\left(\frac{\Delta I}{I}\right)E_I$$

$$+ Q_o\left(\frac{\Delta P_c}{P_c}\right)E_{oc} + Q_o\left(\frac{\Delta P_g}{P_g}\right)E_{og} + Q_o\left(\frac{\Delta A}{A}\right)E_A$$

$$= 1,200,000 + 1,200,000(10\%)(-1.67) + 1,200,000(2\%)(0.55)$$
$$+ 1,200,000(3\%)(1) + 1,200,000(8\%)(0.375)$$
$$+ 1,200,000(5\%)(-0.167) + 1,200,000(10\%)(0.833)$$
$$= 1,200,000 - 200,400 + 13,200 + 36,000 + 36,000 - 10,020 + 99,960$$
$$= 1,174,740$$

Chapter 6

Demand Estimation and Forecasting

6.1 MARKET RESEARCH APPROACHES

A firm's sales or demand can be estimated by market research approaches. These refer to consumer surveys, consumer clinics, and market experiments. *Consumer surveys* involve questioning a sample of consumers about how they would respond to particular changes in the price of the commodity and of related commodities, to changes in their incomes, and to changes in other determinants of demand. *Consumer clinics* are laboratory experiments in which participants are given a sum of money and asked to spend it in a simulated store to see how they react to changes in the commodity price, commodity packaging, displays, prices of competing commodities, and other factors affecting demand. In *market experiments*, the researcher changes the commodity price or other determinants of demand under experimental control (such as packaging and the amount and type of promotion) in a particular real-world store or stores and examines consumers' responses to the changes.

Since many economic decisions (such as businesses' plans to add to plant and equipment, and consumers' intentions of purchasing houses, automobiles, washing machines, refrigerators, and so on) are made well in advance of actual expenditures, surveys and opinion polls on the buying intentions of businesses and consumers can be used to forecast a firm's sales, or demand. These are often referred to as *qualitative forecasts*.

EXAMPLE 1. In 1962 University of Florida researchers conducted a market experiment in Grand Rapids, Michigan, to determine the price elasticity and cross-price elasticity of demand for three types of oranges: those from the Indian River district of Florida, those from the interior district of Florida, and those from California.[1] Nine supermarkets participated in the experiment, which involved changing the prices of the three types of oranges each day for 31 consecutive days and recording the quantity sold of each variety. The researchers found that the price elasticity of demand for the three types of oranges was, respectively, -3.07, -3.01, and -2.76. They also found that while the cross-price elasticity of demand was larger than 1 between the two types of Florida oranges, it was less than 0.20 between each type of Florida orange and the California ones. Thus, consumers regarded the two types of Florida oranges as close substitutes, but they did not view the California oranges in that way. This information can be used to forecast the demand for each type of orange, resulting from changes in prices and in other determinants of demand.

EXAMPLE 2. Some of the best-known published surveys that can be used to forecast economic activity in general and in particular sectors of the economy are surveys of business executives' plant and equipment expenditure plans (published in *Business Week* and in the *Survey of Current Business*), surveys of plans for inventory changes and sales expectations (conducted by the Department of Commerce, McGraw-Hill, the National Association of Purchasing Agents, and others), and surveys of consumer expenditure plans (conducted periodically by the Bureau of the Census and the Survey Research Center of the University of Michigan). For more specific forecasts of its own sales, a firm may rely on polls of its own executives and sales force or its own polls of consumer intentions.

6.2 TIME-SERIES ANALYSIS

One of the most frequently used methods of forecasting a firm's sales or demand is time-series analysis. *Time-series data* are data arranged chronologically by days, weeks, months, quarters, or years. Most economic time series exhibit a *secular trend* (long-run increases and decreases), *cyclical fluctuations* (the wavelike movement above and below the trend that appears every several years), *seasonal variation* (the fluctuations that regularly recur each year because of weather or social customs), and *irregular or random influences*

---

1. *Source:* M. B. Godwin, W. F. Chapman, and W. T. Hanley, "Competition between Florida and California Valencia Oranges in the Fruit Market," *Bulletin 704* (Gainsville, Florida: University of Florida, December 1965).

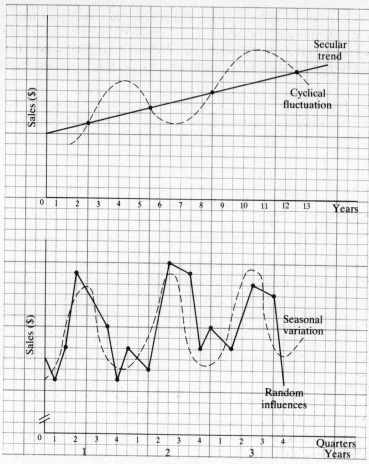

Fig. 6-1

arising from strikes, natural disasters, wars, or other unique events. While these components are shown separately for the time-series (sales) data in Fig. 6-1, they all operate at the same time in the real world.

The simplest form of *time-series analysis* is to forecast the past trend by fitting a straight line to the data (on the assumption that the past trend will continue in the future). The linear regression model will take the form of

$$S_t = S_0 + bt \qquad (6\text{-}1)$$

where S_t is the value of the time series in forecasting for period t, S_0 is the estimated value of the time series (the constant of the regression) in the base period (i.e., at time period $t = 0$), b is the absolute amount of growth per period, and t is the time period in which the time series is to be forecasted (see Example 3).

Sometimes, an exponential trend (showing a constant percentage change rather than a constant amount of change in each period) fits the data better. The exponential trend model can be specified as

$$S_t = S_0(1 + g)^t \qquad (6\text{-}2)$$

where g is the constant percentage growth rate to be estimated. To estimate g, we transform equation (6-2) into natural logarithms and run the following regression:

$$\ln S_t = \ln S_0 + t \ln (1 + g) \qquad (6\text{-}3)$$

Taking into consideration seasonal variation (when present) can significantly improve the trend forecast and can be done by the ratio-to-trend method. To do so, we simply find the average ratio by which the actual value of the time series differs from the corresponding estimated trend value in each period and then multiply the forecasted trend value by this ratio. (See Example 4.) An alternative is to use dummy variables.

EXAMPLE 3. Fitting a trend line to the electricity sales data (consumption in millions of kilowatt-hours) running from the first quarter of 1985 ($t = 1$) to the last quarter of 1988 ($t = 16$) given in Table 6.1 we get

$$S_t = 11.90 + 0.394t \qquad R^2 = 0.50$$
$$(4.00)$$

Table 6.1

Quarter	1985.1	1985.2	1985.3	1985.4	1986.1	1986.2	1986.3	1986.4
Quantity	11	15	12	14	12	17	13	16
Quarter	1987.1	1987.2	1987.3	1987.4	1988.1	1988.2	1988.3	1988.4
Quantity	14	18	15	17	15	20	16	19

The regression results indicate that electricity sales in the last quarter of 1984 (i.e., S_0) are estimated to be 11.90 million kwh and to increase at an average of 0.394 million kwh per quarter. The trend variable is statistically significant at better than the 1 percent level (from the t statistic below the estimated slope coefficient) and "explains" 50 percent of the variation in electricity consumption. Thus, based on the past trend, we can forecast electricity consumption (in million kwh) in the city to be

$$S_{17} = 11.90 + 0.394(17) = 18.60 \qquad \text{in the first quarter of 1989}$$
$$S_{18} = 11.90 + 0.394(18) = 18.99 \qquad \text{in the second quarter of 1989}$$
$$S_{19} = 11.90 + 0.394(19) = 19.39 \qquad \text{in the third quarter of 1989}$$
$$S_{20} = 11.90 + 0.394(20) = 19.78 \qquad \text{in the fourth quarter of 1989}$$

Similar results are obtained with an exponential trend (see Problem 6.6).

EXAMPLE 4. By incorporating the strong seasonal variation in the data in Table 6.1 (consumption in the second and fourth quarters of each year is consistently higher than in the first and third quarters) we can significantly improve the above forecast. To do this we first estimate, or forecast, electricity consumption in each quarter from 1985 to 1988 by substituting actual consumption into the above estimated equation. Then we find the ratio of actual to forecasted consumption in each quarter and calculate the average. This is shown in Table 6.2. Finally, we multiply the trend forecasts obtained in Example 3 by the average seasonal factors estimated in Table 6.2 (i.e., 0.887 for the first quarter, 1.165 for the second quarter, and so on) and get the following new forecasts based on both the linear trend and the seasonal adjustment:

$$S_{17} = 18.60(0.887) = 16.50 \qquad \text{in the first quarter of 1989}$$
$$S_{18} = 18.99(1.165) = 22.12 \qquad \text{in the second quarter of 1989}$$
$$S_{19} = 19.39(0.907) = 17.59 \qquad \text{in the third quarter of 1989}$$
$$S_{20} = 19.78(1.042) = 20.61 \qquad \text{in the fourth quarter of 1989}$$

Note that with the inclusion of the seasonal adjustment, the forecasted values for electricity sales seem to closely replicate the past seasonal pattern (i.e., they are higher in the second and fourth quarters than in the first and third quarters). Similar results are obtained by using dummy variables. (See Problem 6.7.)

Table 6.2

Quarter	Forecasted	Actual	Actual/Forecasted
1985.1	12.29	11.00	0.895
1986.1	13.87	12.00	0.865
1987.1	15.45	14.00	0.906
1988.1	17.02	15.00	0.881
			Average = 0.887
1985.2	12.69	15.00	1.182
1986.2	14.26	17.00	1.192
1987.2	15.84	18.00	1.136
1988.2	17.42	20.00	1.148
			Average = 1.165
1985.3	13.08	12.00	0.917
1986.3	14.66	13.00	0.887
1987.3	16.23	15.00	0.924
1988.3	17.81	16.00	0.898
			Average = 0.907
1985.4	13.48	14.00	1.039
1986.4	15.05	16.00	1.063
1987.4	16.63	17.00	1.022
1988.4	18.20	19.00	1.044
			Average = 1.042

6.3 SMOOTHING TECHNIQUES

Smoothing techniques can be used to forecast future values of a time series as some average of its past values when the series exhibits little trend or seasonal variation but a great deal of irregular or random variation. The simplest smoothing technique is the *moving average*. Here the forecasted value of a time series in a given period is equal to the average value of the series in a number of previous periods. For example, with a three-period moving average, the forecasted value of the time series for any period is given by the average value of the series in the previous three periods.

A better smoothing technique is *exponential smoothing*. Here the forecast for period $t + 1$ (i.e., F_{t+1}) is a weighted average of the actual and forecasted values of the time series in period t. The value of the time series at period t (i.e., A_t) is assigned a weight (w) between 0 and 1 inclusive, and the forecast for period t (i.e., F_t) is then assigned the weight of $1 - w$. The initial value of F_t is usually taken as the mean for the entire observed time series. The greater the value of w, the greater is the weight given to the value of the time series in period t as opposed to previous periods. The value of F_{t+1} is given by

$$F_{t+1} = wA_t + (1 - w)F_t \tag{6-4}$$

To determine which moving average or weight in exponential smoothing leads to a better forecast, we calculate the *root mean square error* (RMSE) of each forecast and utilize the forecast with the lowest RMSE. The formula for RMSE is

$$\text{RMSE} = \sqrt{\sum_{i=1}^{n}} \tag{6-5}$$

where Σ stands for "the sum of," "i is the index variable," A_t is the actual value of the time series in period t, F_t is the forecasted value, and n is the number of time periods or observations. The forecast difference (i.e., $A - F$) is squared in order to penalize larger errors proportionately more than smaller ones.

EXAMPLE 5.   Table 6.3 shows the calculation of a three-quarter and a five-quarter moving average for a firm's market share during eight quarters [columns (1) and (2)]. The forecast for the fourth quarter in column (3) is equal to the average of the values for the first three quarters in column (2). For the ninth quarter, the forecast is 19.67 with a three-quarter moving average and 20.6 with a five-quarter moving average.

The RMSEs are, respectively:

$$\text{RMSE} = \sqrt{\frac{39.4356}{5}} = 2.81 \quad \text{and} \quad \text{RMSE} = \sqrt{\frac{36.04}{3}} = 3.47$$

Since the three-quarter moving average forecast has the lower RMSE, we prefer it.

Table 6.3

Quarter (1)	Firm's Actual Market Share (A) (2)	Three-Quarter Moving Average Forecast (F) (3)	$A - F$ (4)	$(A - F)^2$ (5)	Five-Quarter Moving Average Forecast (F) (6)	$A - F$ (7)	$(A - F)^2$ (8)
1	20	—	—	—	—	—	—
2	22	—	—	—	—	—	—
3	23	—	—	—	—	—	—
4	24	21.67	2.33	5.4289	—	—	—
5	20	23.00	−3.00	9.0000	—	—	—
6	23	22.33	0.67	0.4489	21.8	1.2	1.44
7	19	22.33	−3.33	11.0889	22.4	−3.4	11.56
8	17	20.67	−3.67	13.4689	21.8	−4.8	23.04
9	—	19.67	—	—	20.6	—	—
Total	—	—	—	39.4356	—	—	36.04

EXAMPLE 6.   Table 6.4 shows the calculations used to obtain forecasts for the firm's market share data in Table 6.3 by exponential smoothing with $w = 0.3$ and $w = 0.5$. We let $F_1 = 21$ [the average of the values in column (2)] to get

Table 6.4

Quarter (1)	Firm's Actual Market Share (A) (2)	Forecast (F) with $w = 0.3$ (3)	$A - F$ (4)	$(A - F)^2$ (5)	Forecast (F) with $w = 0.5$ (6)	$A - F$ (7)	$(A - F)^2$ (8)
1	20	21.0	−1.0	1.00	21.0	−1.0	1.00
2	22	20.7	1.3	1.69	20.5	1.5	2.25
3	23	21.1	1.9	3.61	21.3	1.7	2.89
4	24	21.7	2.3	5.29	22.2	1.8	3.24
5	20	22.4	−2.4	5.76	23.1	−3.1	9.61
6	23	21.7	1.3	1.69	21.6	1.4	1.96
7	19	22.1	−3.1	9.61	22.3	−3.3	10.89
8	17	21.2	−4.2	17.64	20.7	−3.7	13.69
9	—	19.9	—	—	18.9	—	—
Total	—	—	—	46.29	—	—	45.53

88   DEMAND ESTIMATION AND FORECASTING   [CHAP. 6

the calculations started. Applying equation (6-4) to find the forecast for F_2 with $w = 0.3$ and $w = 0.5$, we get, respectively:

$$F_2 = 0.3(20) + (1 - 0.3)(21) = 20.7 \quad \text{and} \quad F_2 = 0.5(20) + (1 - 0.5)(21) = 20.5$$

Forecasts for the other quarters are similarly obtained. The RMSEs are, respectively,

$$\text{RMSE} = \sqrt{\frac{46.29}{8}} = 2.41 \quad \text{and} \quad \text{RMSE} = \sqrt{\frac{45.53}{8}} = 2.39$$

Therefore, we prefer the forecast of $F_9 = 18.9$ obtained by exponential smoothing with $w = 0.5$ to the forecast obtained with $w = 0.3$, and to the three-quarter and five-quarter moving average forecasts.

6.4 BAROMETRIC METHODS

Barometric forecasting relies on changes in *leading indicators* (time series that anticipate or lead changes in general economic activity) to forecast turning points (peaks and troughs) in business cycles. While our interest is primarily in leading indicators, some time series move in step, or coincide, with movements in general economic activity and are therefore called *coincident indicators*. Still others follow, or lag behind, movements in economic activity and are called *lagging indicators* (see Problem 6.11). Table 6.5 presents a list of the 12 best leading indicators (out of a much longer list available), together with their mean lead (−) time (in months) with respect to the actual cyclical peak or trough.

Table 6.5 also gives the *composite index*, a weighted average of the 12 leading indicators, with larger weights assigned to those indicators that do a better job of forecasting. The composite index smooths out

Table 6.5 Short List of 12 Leading Indicators

Indicators	Lead (−) in Months
Average work week of production workers, manufacturing	−7.3
Layoff rate, manufacturing	−8.6
New orders, consumer goods and materials, 1972 dollars	−6.7
Vendor performance, companies receiving slower deliveries	−7.3
Index of net business formation	−7.4
Contracts and orders, plant and equipment, 1972 dollars	−5.5
New building permits, private housing units	−10.9
Change in inventories on hand and on order, 1972 dollars	−5.6
Change in sensitive materials prices	−8.8
Stock prices, 500 common stocks	−7.0
Change in total liquid assets	−8.5
Money supply (M_2), 1972 dollars	−11.8
Composite index of the 12 leading indicators	−8.2

Source: U.S. Department of Commerce, Bureau of Economic Analysis, *Handbook of Cyclical Indicators* (Washington, D.C.: U.S. Government Printing Office, May 1977), pp. 174–191.

random variations and provides more reliable forecasts and fewer wrong signals than individual indicators. Another method of overcoming the difficulty arising when some of the 12 leading indicators move up and some move down is the *diffusion index*. This gives the percentage of the 12 leading indicators that are moving up. All these indicators are published monthly in *Business Conditions Digest* by the U.S. Department of Commerce. Three or four successive one-month declines in the composite index and a diffusion index of less than 50 percent are usually a prelude to a recession, (i.e., a slowing down) of economic activity.

Composite index of the 12 leading indicators (1967–1987)

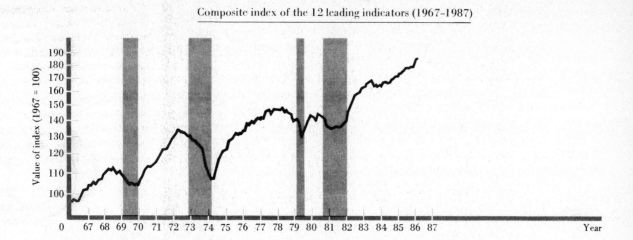

Diffusion index of the 12 leading indicators (1967–1987)

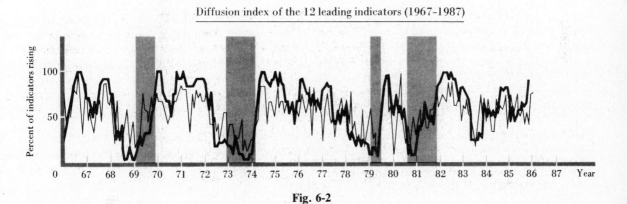

Fig. 6-2

EXAMPLE 7.   The top panel of Fig. 6-2 shows that the composite index of 12 leading indicators turned down prior to (i.e., led) the recessions of 1969–1970, 1973–1975, 1980, and 1981–1982 (the shaded regions in the figure). The bottom panel shows that the diffusion index for the leading indicators was generally below 50 percent in the months preceding recessions.

6.5 ECONOMETRIC METHODS

The most common method of estimating and forecasting firm's sales or demand is regression analysis. The first step is to specify the model, (i.e., to identify the determinants of sales or demand). The second step is to collect the data (over time or across different economic units at a given point in time) for the variables in the model. The third step is to determine the functional form. The simplest is the linear model. Here, the estimated slope coefficients measure the change in sales or demand per unit change in the independent or explanatory variables. An alternative specification is the logarithmic form, in which the estimated coefficients measure percentage changes, or elasticities. Both forms are often estimated, and the one that gives better results is usually reported. Finally, we must evaluate the regression results. That is, we check that the signs of the estimated coefficients conform to theory; conduct t tests on the statistical significance of the estimated coefficients; determine the proportion of the total variation in sales, or demand, that is "explained" by the model (R^2); and make sure that the regression results are free of econometric problems. (See Section 4.3.)

To forecast sales, or demand, we simply substitute the projected or forecasted values of the independent or explanatory variables into the estimated equation and then solve the equation. Forecasts obtained in this way are generally superior to forecasts obtained by other methods because regression analysis identifies the determinants of sales or demand and also provides an estimate of the magnitude of the forecast (not just whether sales or demand will rise or fall). Regression analysis can also incorporate trend analysis, seasonal adjustment, and leading indicators. Forecasts of more complex relationships such as gross national product (GNP) or sales of major sectors or industries are usually based on multiple- rather than single-equation models. These range from a few equations to hundreds. (See Problems 6.18 and 6.19.)

EXAMPLE 8. The following regression equation presents the estimated demand for air travel between the United States and Europe from 1965 to 1978 (numbers in parentheses are t values):[2]

$$\ln Q_t = 2.737 - 1.247 \ln P_t + 1.905 \ln \text{GNP}_t \qquad \bar{R}^2 = 0.97 \qquad D = W = 1.83$$
$$(-5.071) \qquad (7.286)$$

where Q_t = number of passengers per year traveling between the United States and Europe from 1965 to 1978, in thousands

P_t = average yearly air fare between New York and London, adjusted for inflation.

GNP_t = U.S. gross national product in each year, adjusted for inflation

Since the regression is run on the natural logs of the variables, the estimated coefficients represent demand elasticities. Thus, $E_P = -1.247$ and $E_I = 1.905$. The very high t values indicate that both estimated coefficients (elasticities) are statistically significant at better than the 1 percent level. Air fares and GNP "explain" 97 percent of the variation in the number of passengers flying between New York and London. Since both estimated slope coefficients have the correct sign and are statistically significant, there seems to be no multicollinearity problem. The high value of the Durbin-Watson statistic ($D = W$) indicates that there is no autocorrelation problem either.

EXAMPLE 9. Suppose that an airline estimated that 1979 air fares (adjusted for inflation) between New York and London (i.e., P_{t+1}) would be $550 and real GNP (i.e., GNP_{t+1}) would be $1,480. The natural log of 550 (i.e., $\ln 550$) is 6.310 and $\ln 1480$ is 7.300. Substituting these values into the regression we get

$$\ln Q_{t+1} = 2.737 - 1.247(6.310) + 1.905(7.300) = 8.775$$

The antilog of 8.775 is 6,470, i.e., a forecast of 6,470,000 passengers for 1979. The accuracy of this forecast depends on the accuracy of the estimated demand coefficients and of the estimated or forecasted values of the independent or explanatory variables in the demand equation.

Glossary

Barometric forecasting The method of forecasting turning points in business cycles by the use of leading economic indicators.

Coincident indicators Time series that move in step, or coincide, with movements in the level of general economic activity.

Composite index An index formed by a weighted average of the individual indicators.

Consumer clinics Laboratory experiments in which the participants are given a sum of money and asked to spend it in a simulated store to see how they react to changes in the commodity price and other determinants of demand.

Consumer surveys The questioning of a sample of consumers about how they would respond to particular changes in the price and other determinants of the demand for a commodity.

Cyclical fluctuations The major expansions and contractions in most economic time series that recur every number of years.

---

2. *Source:* J.M. Cigliano, "Price and Income Elasticities for Airline Travel: The North Atlantic Market," *Business Economics,* September 1980, pp. 17–21.

Diffusion index   An index that measures the percentage of the 12 leading indicators that are moving upward.

Exponential smoothing   A smoothing technique in which the forecast for a period is a *weighted* average of the actual and forecasted values of the time series in the previous period.

Irregular or random influences   The unpredictable variations in a data series resulting from wars, natural disasters, strikes, or other unforeseen events.

Lagging indicators   Time series that follow, or lag behind, movements in the level of general economic activity.

Leading economic indicators   Time series that tend to precede, or lead, changes in the level of general economic activity.

Market experiments   Attempts by the firm to estimate the demand for a commodity by changing price and other determinants of the demand for the commodity in the actual marketplace (i.e., in some stores).

Moving average   The smoothing technique in which the forecasted value of a time series in a given period is equal to the average value of the time series in a number of previous periods.

Qualitative forecasts   The estimation of the future value of a variable (such as the firm's sales) based on surveys and opinion polls of businesses' and consumers' buying intentions.

Root mean square error (RMSE)   The measure of the weighted average error of a forecast.

Seasonal variation   The regularly recurring fluctuations in economic activity that occur during each year because of weather and social customs.

Secular trend   The long-run increase or decrease in a data series.

Smoothing techniques   A method of naive forecasting in which future values of a time series are forecasted on the basis of some average of its past values only.

Time-series analysis   The technique of forecasting future values of a time series by examining past observations of the time-series data only.

Time-series data   The values of a variable arranged chronologically by days, weeks, months, quarters, or years.

Review Questions

1.   Which of the following is not a marketing research approach to demand estimation?

   (*a*)   Consumer clinics

   (*b*)   Regression analysis

   (*c*)   Market experiments

   (*d*)   Consumer surveys

   Ans.   (*b*) See Section 6.1.

2.   Consumer surveys refer to

   (*a*)   laboratory experiments in which the participants are given a sum of money and asked to spend it in a simulated store to see how they react to changes in the factors affecting demand.

   (*b*)   changes in the commodity price or other determinants of demand under the control of the firm, including control in a particular store or stores and examination of consumers' responses to the changes.

   (*c*)   questioning a sample of consumers about how they would respond to particular changes in the price of the commodity and of related commodities, to changes in their incomes, and to changes in other determinants of demand.

   (*d*)   any of the above.

   Ans.   (*c*) See Section 6.1.

3. Which of the following statements is false?

    (*a*) Qualitative forecasting is based on surveys and opinion polls of the buying intentions of businesses and consumers.

    (*b*) Surveys of plant and equipment expenditure plans of business executives are published in *Business Week* and in the *Survey of Current Business*.

    (*c*) Firms sometimes forecast their sales by polling consumers directly.

    (*d*) None of the above.

    Ans. (*d*) See Section 6.1 and Example 2.

4. Yearly sales data exhibit no

    (*a*) trend.

    (*b*) cyclical variation.

    (*c*) seasonal variation.

    (*d*) irregular variation.

    Ans. (*c*) See Section 6.2.

5. Time-series analysis

    (*a*) seeks to forecast a time series based on its past values only.

    (*b*) seeks to explain the underlying causes of the variation in the data.

    (*c*) can explain the irregular variation in the data.

    (*d*) all of the above.

    Ans. (*a*) See Section 6.2.

6. Which of the following statements is true with regard to time-series analysis?

    (*a*) The ratio-to-trend method is used to adjust the trend forecast for the seasonal variation in the data.

    (*b*) Sometimes an exponential trend fits time-series data better than a linear trend.

    (*c*) The seasonal variation in the data can be taken into consideration by using dummy variables.

    (*d*) All of the above.

    Ans. (*d*) See Section 6.2.

7. Smoothing techniques are useful methods of forecasting

    (*a*) the trend in a time series.

    (*b*) cyclical fluctuations.

    (*c*) the seasonal variation in a time series.

    (*d*) irregular or random influences in the data.

    Ans. (*d*) See Section 6.3.

8. Which of the following statements is false with regard to smoothing techniques?

    (*a*) The greater the number of periods used to calculate a moving average, the smaller will be the degree of smoothing in the time series.

    (*b*) Exponential smoothing usually gives better forecasts than moving averages.

    (*c*) The reliability of forecasts can be compared using the root mean square error.

    (*d*) None of the above.

    Ans. (*a*) See Section 6.3.

9. Which of the following statements is false with regard to barometric forecasting?

   (a) It relies on changes in leading indicators to forecast changes in the level of economic activity, just as changes in the mercury in a barometer are used to forecast changes in weather conditions.

   (b) Turning points in business cycles are usually forecasted with the composite and diffusion indexes of leading indicators.

   (c) A fall in the composite and diffusion indexes in a given month is used to predict a recession.

   (d) Barometric forecasting gives no indication of the magnitude of the forecasted change in the level of economic activity.

   Ans. (c) See Section 6.4.

10. In the process of estimating the demand for a commodity by regression analysis, the researcher needs to

   (a) determine the variables and equational form of the model.

   (b) collect the data on the variables of the model.

   (c) evaluate the regression results.

   (d) do all of the above.

   Ans. (d) See Section 6.5.

11. Which of the following statements is false with regard to the estimation of demand by regression analysis?

   (a) Specifying the model means identifying the variables in the model.

   (b) Time-series data are required.

   (c) Either a linear or a log demand equation can be estimated.

   (d) Evaluating the regression results involves determining, among other things, whether the estimated coefficients have the signs postulated by theory.

   Ans. (b) See Section 6.5.

12. Which of the following statements is false with regard to forecasting with econometric models?

   (a) It is accomplished by substituting into the estimated regression equation the estimated or forecasted values of the independent or explanatory variables and solving.

   (b) It usually provides better forecasts than other forecasting methods.

   (c) It cannot be combined with other forecasting methods.

   (d) It provides not only the direction of change in the variable to be forecasted, but also an estimate of the magnitude of the change.

   Ans. (c) See Section 6.5.

Solved Problems

MARKET RESEARCH APPROACHES TO DEMAND ESTIMATION

6.1 (a) What is meant by consumer surveys? How can they be used to estimate demand? (b) What are their advantages? (c) What are their disadvantages?

   (a) Consumer surveys involve questioning a sample of consumers about how they would respond to particular changes in the following: the price of the commodity and of related commodities, changes in their incomes, changes in advertising, credit incentives, and other determinants of demand. These surveys can be conducted by simply stopping people at a shopping center or by developing sophisticated questionnaires administered to a carefully constructed representative sample of consumers by trained interviewers.

(b)   The major advantages of estimating demand using consumer surveys are: (1) Surveys may be the only way to obtain information about consumers' possible responses to the introduction of a new commodity, changes in consumers' tastes and preferences, and consumers' expectations about future prices and business conditions. Survey results that show consumers are unaware of price differences between the firm's product and competing products may be a good indication that demand for the firm's product is price inelastic. (2) Consumer surveys can be made as simple or as elaborate as desired. (3) The researcher can ask specific questions pertaining to the demand for the product.

(c)   The major disadvantages of consumer surveys are: (1) Consumers may be unable or unwilling to provide reliable answers. For example, do you know by how much your monthly beer consumption would change if the price of beer rose by 10 cents per bottle? if the price of sodas fell by 5 cents? if your income rose by 20 percent? or if a beer producer doubled its advertising expenditures? Even if you tried to answer these questions as accurately as possible, your reaction might be entirely different if you were actually faced with any of the above situations. Sometimes consumers provide a response that they deem more socially acceptable rather than disclose their true preferences. (2) Depending on the size of the sample and the elaborateness of the analysis, consumer surveys can also be rather expensive.

6.2   (a) What is meant by consumer clinics? How can they be used to estimate demand? (b) What is their advantage? (c) What are their disadvantages?

(a)   Consumer clinics are laboratory experiments in which the participants are given a sum of money and asked to spend it in a simulated store to see how they react to changes in the commodity price, product packaging, displays, prices of competing products, and other factors affecting demand. Participants in the experiment can be selected so as to closely represent the socioeconomic characteristics of the market of interest.

(b)   By simulating how consumers behave in an actual market situation rather than simply asking them how they think they would behave, consumer clinics attempt to overcome the major disadvantage of consumer surveys.

(c)   The main disadvantages of consumer clinics are: (1) Participants know that they are in an artificial situation and that they are being observed, so they are not likely to act normally. For example, suspecting that the researchers might be interested in their reaction to price changes, participants are likely to show more sensitivity to price changes than in their everyday shopping. (2) The sample of participants must necessarily be small because of the high cost of running the experiment. However, inferring market behavior from the results of an experiment based on a very small sample can be dangerous.

6.3   (a) What is meant by market experiments? How can they be used to estimate demand? (b) What are their advantages? (c) What are their disadvantages?

(a)   Unlike consumer clinics, which are conducted under strict laboratory conditions, market experiments are conducted in the actual market place. There are many different ways of performing market experiments. One method is to select several markets with similar socioeconomic characteristics. The researcher then changes the commodity price in some markets or stores, the packaging in other markets or stores, and the amount and type of promotion in still other markets or stores, and records the responses (purchases) of consumers in the different markets. Alternatively, the researcher could change, one at a time, each of the determinants of demand under its control in a particular market over a period of time, and record consumers' responses.

(b)   The major advantages of estimating demand by market experiments are: (1) Consumers are in a real market situation and do not know that they are being observed. (2) The experiments can be conducted on a large scale, with some controls, so as to ensure the validity of the results.

(c)   The major disadvantages of using market experiments to estimate demand are: (1) In order to keep costs down, the experiment is likely to be conducted on too limited a scale and over too short a period of time, so that inferences about the entire market, over a more extended period of time, will be questionable. (2) Extraneous occurrences, such as a strike or unusually bad weather, may seriously bias the results of a market experiment. (3) Competitors could try to sabotage the experiment by also changing prices and other determinants of demand under their control, or they could monitor the experiment and gain very useful information that the firm would prefer not to disclose. (4) The firm may permanently lose customers in the process of raising prices in the market where it is experimenting with a high price.

6.4 (*a*) What is meant by forecasting? Why is it so important in the management of business firms and other enterprises? (*b*) What are qualitative forecasts? What is their rationale and usefulness? (*c*) What are the most important surveys of future economic activities? (*d*) Why and how do firms conduct opinion polls of future economic activities?

(*a*) Forecasting is the process of estimating a variable, such as the sales of the firm, at some future date. Forecasting is important to business firms, government, and not-for-profit organizations as a method of reducing the risk and uncertainty inherent in most managerial decisions.

(*b*) Qualitative forecasts estimate variables at some future date using the results of surveys and opinion polls of business and consumer spending intentions. The rationale is that many economic decisions are made well in advance of actual expenditures. For example, businesses usually plan to add to plant and equipment long before expenditures are actually incurred. Also, surveys and opinion polls are often used to make short-term forecasts when quantitative data are not available. Polls can also be very useful in supplementing quantitative forecasts, anticipating changes in consumer tastes or business expectations about future economic conditions, and forecasting the demand for a new product.

(*c*) Some of the best-known surveys are the ones conducted periodically on business executives' plant and equipment expenditure plans, plans for inventory changes, sales expectations, and on consumers' expenditure plans. In general, the record of these surveys has been rather good in forecasting actual expenditures.

(*d*) While the results of published surveys of expenditure plans of businesses, consumers, and governments are useful, the firm usually needs specific forecasts of its own sales. The firm can base its sales forecasts on polls of its top executives or outside experts, polls of its sales force in the field, or polls of a sample of consumers on their intentions to purchase some particular durable good, such as a house, an automobile, or a major appliance.

TIME-SERIES ANALYSIS

6.5 Draw a figure showing the linear trend and trend forecasts obtained in Example 3. On the same figure show also the trend forecasts adjusted for the seasonal variation obtained in Example 4.

See Fig. 6-3. The forecasts based only on the extension of the linear trend are shown by the dots on the dashed portion of the estimated trend line extended into 1989. On the other hand, the forecasts obtained by adjusting the trend forecasts to take into consideration the seasonal variation in the data are shown by the encircled points in the figure. The latter seem to closely replicate the past seasonal pattern in the data.

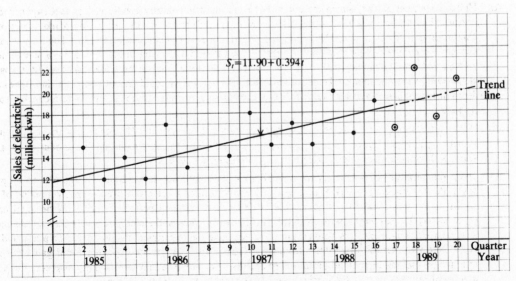

Fig. 6-3

6.6 (*a*) Fit an exponential trend to the data of Table 6.1. (*b*) Use the results to forecast electricity sales during each quarter of 1989. (*c*) Compare these forecasts with those obtained by using the estimated linear trend in Example 3.

(*a*) To run regression equation (*6-3*) we must first transform the data on electricity sales given in Table 6.1 into their natural logarithms. For example, the ln of 11 (the value in Table 6.1 for the first quarter of 1985) is 2.40 (obtained by simply entering the value of 11 into any full-function pocket calculator and pressing the "ln" key). Running regression (*6-3*), we get

$$\ln S_t = \ln S_0 + t \ln (1 + g)$$
$$= 2.4765 + 0.026t \qquad R^2 = 0.50$$
$$(4.06)$$

The fit is very similar to that found in Example 3. Since the estimated parameters are now based on the logarithms of the data, however, we must convert them into their antilogs in order to be able to interpret them in units of the original data. The antilog of $\ln S_0 = 2.4765$ is $S_0 = 11.90$ (obtained by simply entering the value of 2.4765 into any full-function pocket calculator and pressing the "e^x" key) and the antilog of $\ln (1 + g) = 0.026$ gives $(1 + g) = 1.026$. Substituting these values back into the above estimated regression equation, we have

$$S_t = 11.90(1.026)^t$$

where $S_0 = 11.90$ million kilowatt-hours is the estimated sales of electricity in the fourth quarter of 1984 (i.e., at $t = 0$) and the estimated growth rate is 1.026, or 2.6 percent per quarter.

(*b*) To forecast sales in any future quarter, we substitute the value of t for that quarter into the last equation above and solve for S_t. Thus,

$$S_{17} = 11.90(1.026)^{17} = 18.41 \qquad \text{in the first quarter of 1989}$$
$$S_{18} = 11.90(1.026)^{18} = 18.89 \qquad \text{in the second quarter of 1989}$$
$$S_{19} = 11.90(1.026)^{19} = 19.38 \qquad \text{in the third quarter of 1989}$$
$$S_{20} = 11.90(1.026)^{20} = 19.88 \qquad \text{in the fourth quarter of 1989}$$

(*c*) The forecasts obtained in part (*b*) are very similar to those obtained by using the fitted linear trend. Note that the forecasts obtained by the two methods differ by increasing amounts as the time series is forecasted further into the future. This is usually the case. In the real world, both the linear and the exponential trends are usually fitted to the data, and the one that gives the better results is then used in forecasting.

6.7 Using the data on electricity consumption given in Table 6.1 in Example 3, (*a*) run a linear regression with the trend variable and seasonal dummies (see Problem 4.7) as independent or explanatory variables. (*b*) Use the estimated regression equation to forecast electricity sales for each quarter of 1989 and (*c*) compare these forecasts with those obtained in Example 4.

(*a*) We take the last quarter as the base-period quarter and define dummy variable D_1 by a time series with 1 in the first quarter of each year and 0 in the other quarters, D_2 by a time series with 1 in the second quarter of each year and 0 in the other quarters, and D_3 by 1 in the third quarter of each year and 0 in the other quarters. We then obtain the following results by running a regression of electricity sales on the seasonal dummy variables and the linear time trend:

$$S_t = 12.75 - 2.375D_{1t} + 1.750D_{2t} - 2.125D_{3t} + 0.375t \qquad R^2 = 0.99$$
$$(-10.83) \quad (8.11) \qquad (-9.94) \quad (22.25)$$

Note that the estimated coefficients for the dummy variables and the trend variable are all statistically significant at better than the 1 percent level and that the regression "explains" 99 percent of the variation in electricity sales as compared with only 50 percent for the regression in Example 3.

(*b*) Utilizing the regression results obtained in part (*a*), we can forecast electricity sales for each quarter of 1989 to be:

$$S_{17} = 12.75 - 2.375 + 0.375(17) = 16.75 \quad \text{in the first quarter of 1989}$$

$$S_{18} = 12.75 + 1.750 + 0.375(18) = 21.25 \quad \text{in the second quarter of 1989}$$

$$S_{19} = 12.75 - 2.125 + 0.375(19) = 17.75 \quad \text{in the third quarter of 1989}$$

$$S_{20} = 12.75 \qquad\quad + 0.375(20) = 20.25 \quad \text{in the fourth quarter of 1989}$$

(c) These forecasted values are very similar to those obtained by the ratio-to-trend method in Example 4. Thus, in this case the two methods are good alternatives for taking into consideration the seasonal variation in the forecasts. It is important to remember, however, that these forecasts are based on the assumption that the past trend and seasonal patterns in the data will persist during 1989. If the pattern suddenly changes in a drastic manner, the forecasts are likely to be far off the mark. This is more likely the further into the future we attempt to forecast.

SMOOTHING TECHNIQUES

6.8   Using the index (with 1971 = 100) of new housing starts in a large metropolitan area in the table below, forecast the index for 1986, using a three-year and a five-year moving average. In which of the forecasts would we have more confidence?

Year	1976	1977	1978	1979	1980	1981	1982	1983	1984	1985
Index	132	127	120	75	87	125	92	134	128	140

The calculations needed to answer this problem are shown in Table 6.6. The RMSEs for the three-year and the five-year moving average forecasts are, respectively:

$$\text{RMSE} = \sqrt{\frac{5,692.76}{7}} = 28.52 \quad \text{and} \quad \text{RMSE} = \sqrt{\frac{3,034.32}{5}} = 24.63$$

Since RMSE for the five-year moving average forecast is smaller than for the three-year moving average forecast, we prefer the former forecast of 123.8 to the latter forecast of 134.0 for 1986.

6.9   Using the data in column (2) of Table 6.6 and the method of exponential smoothing, with $w = 0.3$ and $w = 0.5$, forecast (to one decimal place) the index of new housing starts for the year 1986. Which of the two forecasts is better?

Table 6.6

Year (1)	Index of New Housing Starts (A) (2)	Three-Year Moving Average Forecast (F) (3)	A − F (4)	(A − F)² (5)	Five-Year Moving Average Forecast (F) (6)	A − F (7)	(A − F)² (8)
1976	132	—	—	—	—	—	—
1977	127	—	—	—	—	—	—
1978	120	—	—	—	—	—	—
1979	75	126.3	−51.3	2,631.69	—	—	—
1980	87	107.3	−20.3	412.09	—	—	—
1981	125	94.0	31.0	961.00	108.2	16.8	282.24
1982	92	95.7	−3.7	13.69	106.8	−14.8	219.04
1983	134	101.3	32.7	1,069.29	99.8	34.2	1,169.64
1984	128	117.0	11.0	121.00	102.6	25.4	645.16
1985	140	118.0	22.0	484.00	113.2	26.8	718.24
1986	—	134.0	—	—	123.8	—	—
Total	—	—	—	5,692.76	—	—	3,034.32

The calculations needed to answer this problem are shown in Table 6.7. The forecasts in columns (3) and (6) of the table are obtained by applying equation (6-4) with $w = 0.3$ and $w = 0.5$, respectively. We let $F_{1976} = 116.0$ [the average value of column (2)] to get the calculations started in both cases. The RMSEs for the forecasts obtained with $w = 0.3$ and $w = 0.5$ are, respectively:

$$\text{RMSE} = \sqrt{\frac{5,430.64}{10}} = 23.30 \quad \text{and} \quad \text{RMSE} = \sqrt{\frac{5,560.73}{10}} = 23.70$$

Since the RMSE of the forecast of $F_{1986} = 124.1$, obtained by exponential smoothing with $w = 0.3$, is smaller than the RMSE for the forecast of $F_{1986} = 131.4$ obtained with $w = 0.5$, we prefer the former to the latter forecast. The forecast obtained by exponential smoothing with $w = 0.3$ is also superior to the three- and five-year moving average forecasts obtained in Problem 6.8.

Table 6.7

Year (1)	A (2)	F with $w = 0.3$ (3)	A − F (4)	$(A − F)^2$ (5)	F with $w = 0.5$ (6)	A − F (7)	$(A − F)^2$ (8)
1976	132	116.0	16.0	256.00	116.0	16.0	256.00
1977	127	120.8	6.2	38.44	124.0	3.0	9.00
1978	120	122.7	−2.7	7.29	125.5	−5.5	30.25
1979	75	121.9	−46.9	2,199.61	122.8	−47.8	2,284.84
1980	87	107.8	−20.8	432.64	98.9	−11.9	141.61
1981	125	101.6	23.4	547.56	93.0	32.0	1,024.00
1982	92	108.6	−16.6	275.56	109.0	−17.0	289.00
1983	134	103.6	30.4	924.16	100.5	33.5	1,122.25
1984	128	112.7	15.3	234.09	117.3	10.7	114.49
1985	140	117.3	22.7	515.29	122.7	17.3	299.29
1986	—	124.1	—	—	131.4	—	—
Total	—	—	—	5,430.64	—	—	5,570.73

BAROMETRIC METHODS

6.10 Draw a figure showing the positions of the leading, coincident, and lagging indicators relative to the peak and trough of a business cycle.

See Fig. 6-4. The figure shows that leading indicators precede business cycle peaks and troughs, coincident indicators move in step with business cycles, while lagging indicators follow, or lag behind, turning points in business cycles.

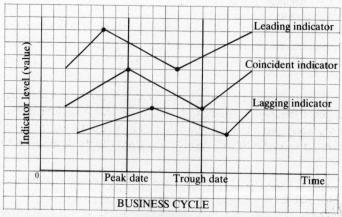

Fig. 6-4

6.11 Using the publication given at the bottom of Table 6.5 in Example 6, identify the short list of coincident and lagging indicators, and indicate their lead (−) or lag (+) time. Also indicate the lead or lag time for the composite indexes of the short list of coincident and lagging indicators.

   See Table 6.8. For the sake of comprehensiveness and comparison, Table 6.8 also includes the short list of leading indicators given in Table 6.5. From Table 6.8, it can be seen that the composite index of coincident indicators in fact leads the peaks and troughs in business cycles by about 1.2 months. The composite index of the lagging indicators lags behind the business cycle peaks and troughs by an average of 4.8 months.

Table 6.8 Short List of Leading, Coincident, and Lagging Indicators

Indicators	Lead (−) or Lag (+)
Leading indicators (12 series)	
Average work week of production workers, manufacturing	−7.3
Layoff rate, manufacturing	−8.6
New orders, consumer goods and materials, 1972 dollars	−6.7
Vendor performance, companies receiving slower deliveries	−7.3
Index of net business formation	−7.4
Contracts and orders, plant and equipment, 1972 dollars	−5.5
New building permits, private housing units	−10.9
Change in inventories on hand and on order, 1972 dollars	−5.6
Change in sensitive materials prices	−8.8
Stock prices, 500 common stocks	−7.0
Change in total liquid assets	−8.5
Money supply (M_2), 1972 dollars	−11.8
Roughly coincident indicators (4 series)	
Employees on nonagricultural payrolls	−0.3
Personal income, 1972 dollars	−0.6
Industrial production	−1.6
Manufacturing and trade sales, 1972 dollars	−2.3
Lagging indicators (6 series)	
Average duration of unemployment	+4.9
Manufacturing and trade inventories, 1972 dollars	+4.0
Labor cost per unit of output, manufacturing	+9.0
Average prime rate charged by banks	+7.1
Commercial and industrial loans outstanding	+3.9
Ratio, consumer installment debt to personal income	+5.6
Composite indexes	
Twelve leading indicators	−8.2
Four roughly coincident indicators	−1.2
Six lagging indicators	+4.8

Source: U.S. Department of Commerce, Bureau of Economic Analysis, *Handbook of Cyclical Indicators* (Washington, D.C.: U.S. Government Printing Office, May 1977), pp. 174–191.

6.12 Table 6.9 gives the monthly composite and diffusion indexes for the 12 leading indicators for 1986. (*a*) Did the changes in the indexes for the first part of 1986 correctly anticipate or forecast the moderate growth that in retrospect we know occurred in the latter part of the year? (*b*) Based on the changes in the indexes in the second half of 1986, what changes in the level of economic activity can you forecast for 1987?

(*a*) Since the composite index increased modestly from January to April 1986 and declined very slightly during May and June, and at the same time the diffusion index was 50 percent or more but never exceeded 75 percent, we would have forecasted moderate growth for the latter part of the year. This is in fact what occurred.

Table 6.9 Monthly Composite and Diffusion Indexes for the 12 Leading Indicators during 1986

Month	Composite Index	Diffusion Index
January	173.4	62.5
February	174.9	50.0
March	175.9	62.5
April	178.2	75.0
May	178.1	50.0
June	177.7	54.2
July	179.3	62.5
August	179.1	41.7
September	179.4	54.2
October	180.6	41.7
November	182.2	75.0
December	186.1	77.3

Source: U.S. Department of Commerce, Bureau of Economic Analysis, *Business Conditions Digest*, (Washington, D.C.: U.S. Government Printing office, January 1987), pp. 60, 74.

(b) With the continued modest rise (except in August 1986) in the composite index and with a diffusion index above 50 percent (except in August and October) but never above 77.3 percent, we can forecast moderate growth for the first part of 1987 as well. To be pointed out, however, is that barometric forecasting is only 80 to 90 percent accurate in forecasting turning points. It also does not provide any indication of the magnitude of the forecasted change in the level of economic activity. Thus, barometric forecasting is most useful when used in conjunction with econometric forecasting, which does give an estimate of the magnitude of the forecasted changes.

ECONOMETRIC METHODS

6.13 By using regression analysis, Houthakker and Taylor estimated the following demand equation for shoes in the United States over the period from 1929 to 1961:[3]

$$Q_t = 19.575 - 0.0923P_t + 0.0289X_t - 99.568C_t - 4.06D_t$$
$$(-1.7682) \qquad (9.3125) \quad (9.8964) \quad (3.50)$$
$$\bar{R}^2 = 0.857 \qquad D - W = 1.86$$

where Q_t = per capita personal consumption expenditures on shoes and other footwear during year t, in 1954 prices

P_t = relative price of shoes in year t, in 1954 prices

X_t = total per capita consumption expenditures during year t, in 1954 prices

C_t = per capita stock of automobiles in year t

D_t = dummy variable to separate pre- from post-World War II years; $D_t = 0$ for 1929–1941 and $D_t = 1$ for 1946–1961

and the numbers in parentheses are t values.

3. *Source:* H. S. Houthakker and L. D. Taylor, *Consumer Demand in the United States: Analyses and Projections* (Cambridge, Mass.: Harvard University Press, 1970), p. 66.

(a) Explain why the model was specified as indicated above. (b) In what way do variables Q_t and X_t differ from the usual specification of the demand model? Why do you think that Houthakker and Taylor used this specification? (c) What do the estimated coefficients measure? (d) How can the estimated slope coefficients be used to calculate demand elasticities?

(a) The researchers postulated that real per capita consumption expenditures on shoes in a given year were a function of, or depended on, the real, or relative, prices of shoes, real total personal consumption expenditures, and the stock of automobiles. The stock of automobiles was included as an explanatory variable because, presumably, the greater is the value of C_t, the less people walk and purchase shoes. The dummy variable was included to distinguish between nonwar years and war years.

(b) The dependent variable (Q_t) was expressed in real dollar terms rather than (as usual) in terms of physical units because of lack of data. For the same reasons, X_t was defined as total real per capita expenditures rather than real per capita income.

(c) The estimated coefficients measure the marginal change in the dependent variable (Q_t) per unit change in the independent, or explanatory, variables.

(d) The price elasticity of demand for shoes can be calculated by multiplying -0.0923 (the estimated coefficient of P_t) by the ratio of the average value of Q_t to the average value of P_t over the period of the analysis. Similarly, we can estimate the elasticity of Q_t with respect to X_t by multiplying 0.0289 (the estimated coefficient of X_t) by the ratio of the average value of Q_t to the average value of X_t. Finally, the elasticity of Q_t with respect to C_t is obtained by multiplying -99.568 (the estimated coefficient of C_t) by the ratio of the average value of Q_t to the average value of C_t.

6.14 For the estimated demand equation for shoes given in Problem 6.13, evaluate (a) the regression results in terms of the signs of the estimated coefficients, (b) the statistical significance of the estimated coefficients, (c) the proportion of the variation in Q_t "explained" by the model, and (d) the evidence for the presence or absence of autocorrelation.

(a) All the variables have the expected sign. That is, real expenditures on shoes are inversely related to the real price of shoes, the stock of automobiles, and the dummy variable, but directly related to total real per capita consumption expenditures. The negative value of the dummy variable indicates that, on the average, U.S. consumers walked less and spent less of their real income on shoes (a change in tastes) after World War II than before. Thus, in using regression results to estimate the real per capita expenditures on shoes for prewar years, the value of the constant would be 19.575 (the first coefficient in the estimated regression equation). However, for the postwar years, the constant to use would be $19.575 - 4.06 = 15.515$.

(b) Examining the t values reported below the estimated slope coefficients, we can determine that all coefficients are statistically significant at better than the 1 percent level, except for P_t, which is significant at the 10 percent level only (the t value for $n - k = 29 - 5 = 24$ degrees of freedom for the probability of 0.10 in Table C.2 in Appendix C is 1.711). This may, or may not, be due to multicollinearity.

(c) The adjusted coefficient of determination ($\overline{R}^2$) indicates that the explanatory variables as a group "explain" 86 percent of the variation in Q_t.

(d) Since the value of the Durbin-Watson ($D - W$) statistic exceeds the critical value of $d_U = 1.51$ with $n = 29$ (the number of observations) and $k' = 4$ (the number of explanatory variables in the regression) in Table C.4 in Appendix C, we can conclude that there is no evidence of autocorrelation.

6.15 In Fig. 6-5, E_1, E_2, E_3, and E_4 represent observed price-quantity points. Explain (a) why the solid line drawn through these points does not represent the demand for the commodity and (b) how a demand curve for the commodity can be derived by regression analysis.

(a) Observed price-quantity data points E_1, E_2, E_3, and E_4 result from the intersection of the corresponding unobserved (dashed) demand and supply curves D_1 and S_1, D_2 and S_2, D_3 and S_3, and D_4 and S_4. The solid line connecting observed points E_1, E_2, E_3, and E_4 joins points on different demand and supply curves for the commodity and therefore it does not represent the demand curve for the commodity. The inability to derive a demand curve by simply joining observed price-quantity points is called the *identification problem*. Over time or across different individuals or markets, the demand for the commodity shifts or differs because

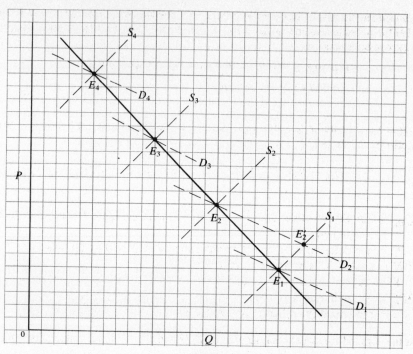

Fig. 6-5

of changes or differences in tastes, incomes, prices of related commodities, and so on. Similarly, over time or across different producers or markets, the supply curve shifts or is different because of changes or differences in technology, factor prices, and weather conditions (for agricultural commodities). It is by the intersection (equilibrium) of these different but unknown demand and supply curves that the different observed price-quantity points are generated.

(b) To derive a demand curve for the commodity, say D_2, we allow the supply to shift or to be different and use multiple regression analysis to correct for the forces that cause demand curve D_2 to shift or to be different. The estimated coefficient of the price variable in the demand equation gives the relationship between the quantity demanded of the commodity and the price of the commodity, or demand curve. Other demand curves (i.e., D_1, D_3, and D_4) result from holding constant at different levels, consumers' income, tastes, the prices of related commodities, and the other forces that cause the demand curve to shift.

6.16 Using the estimated regression equation given in Problem 6.13 for the demand for shoes in the United States, forecast the demand for shoes for (a) 1962 and (b) 1972 if the values of the independent or explanatory variables are those given in the following table.

Year	X	P	C
1962	1,646	20	0.4
1972	2,236	30	0.6

(a) By substituting the given values of the independent, or explanatory, variables and $D = 1$ (a nonwar year) for 1962 in the estimated demand equation, we get the following estimate of per capita personal consumption expenditures on shoes:

$$D_t = 19.575 - 0.0923(20) + 0.0289(1,646) - 99.568(0.4) - 4.06(1)$$

$$= \$21.41 \quad \text{at 1954 prices}$$

(b) By substituting the given values of the independent, or explanatory, variables and $D = 1$ (a nonwar year) for 1972 in the estimated demand equation, we get the following estimate of per capita personal consumption expenditures on shoes:

$$D_t = 19.575 - 0.0923(30) + 0.0289(2,236) - 99.568(0.6) - 4.06(1)$$

$$= \$17.63 \quad \text{at 1954 prices}$$

6.17 Following is an estimated regression equation for the demand for sweet potatoes in the United States for the period 1949 to 1972:[4]

$$Q_{D_s} = 7,609 - 1,606P_s + 59N + 947Y + 479P_w - 271t$$

where Q_{D_s} = quantity of sweet potatoes sold per year in the United States per thousand hundred-weight (cwt)

P_s = real dollar price of sweet potatoes per cwt received by farmers
N = total U.S. population, in millions
Y = real per capita personal disposable income, in thousands of dollars
P_w = real dollar price of white potatoes per cwt received by farmers
t = time trend ($t = 1$ for 1949, $t = 2$ for 1950, ... , $t = 24$ for 1972)

Forecast the demand for sweet potatoes for (a) 1972 and (b) 1973, using the values of the independent or explanatory variables given in the following table:

Year	P_s	N	Y	P_w
1972	4.10	208.78	3.19	2.41
1973	4.00	210.90	3.55	2.40

(a) By substituting the given values of the independent or explanatory variables and $t = 24$ for 1972 in the estimated demand equation, we get the quantity demanded (sales) of sweet potatoes in the United States in 1972, i.e.,

$$Q_{D_s} = 7,609 - 1,606(4.10) + 59(208.78) + 947(3.19) + 479(2.41) - 271(24)$$

$$= 11,013.74 \text{ thousand cwt (11.01 million cwt)}$$

(b) By substituting the given values of the independent or explanatory variables and $t = 25$ for 1973 in the estimated demand equation, we get the quantity demanded (sales) of sweet potatoes in the United States in 1973 of:

$$Q_{D_s} = 7,609 - 1,606(4.00) + 59(210.90) + 947(3.55) + 479(2.40) - 271(25)$$

$$= 11,364.55 \text{ thousand cwt (11.36 million cwt)}$$

cwt is a standard abbreviation for agricultural commodites.

6.18 The following is a very simple three-equation model of the national economy:

$$C_t = a_1 + b_1 \text{ GNP}_t + u_{1_t} \qquad (1)$$

$$I_t = a_2 + b_2 \pi_{t-1} + u_{2_t} \qquad (2)$$

$$\text{GNP}_t = C_t + I_t + G_t \qquad (3)$$

4. *Source:* Ronald A. Schrimper and Gene A. Mathia, "Reservation and Market Demands for Sweet Potatoes at the Farm Level," *American Journal of Agricultural Economics*, Vol. 57, February 1975.

where C = consumption expenditures
GNP_t = gross national product in year t
I = investment
π = profits
G = government expenditures
u = stochastic disturbance
t = current year
$t - 1$ = previous year

Equation (*1*) postulates that consumption expenditures in year t (C_t) are a linear function of GNP in the same year (i.e., GNP_t). Equation (*2*) postulates that investment in year t (I_t) is a linear function of profits in the previous year (i.e., π_{t-1}). Finally, equation (*3*) defines GNP in year t as the sum of consumption expenditures, investment, and government expenditures in the same year. (*a*) Indicate which are the variables we seek to explain or predict and which are those we must be given in order to solve the model. (*b*) Explain the general difference between equations (*1*) and (*2*), on the one hand, and equation (*3*), on the other. (*c*) How can the above model be used in forecasting?

(*a*)   The variables that we seek to explain or predict are C_t, I_t, and GNP_t [i.e., the variables to the left of the equals signs in equations (*1*), (*2*), and (*3*)]. These are called *endogenous variables*. The variables π_{t-1} and G_t, however, must be given and fed into the model in order to solve it (i.e., in order to find the value of the endogenous variables). These are called *exogenous variables*. When endogenous variables also appear to the right of the equals signs, as in the above model, the meaning is that they both affect and are in turn affected by the other variables in the model (i.e., they are simultaneously determined).

(*b*)   Equations (*1*) and (*2*) seek to explain the relationship between the particular endogenous variable and the other variables in the system. They are called *structural (behavioral) equations*. However, equation (*3*) is a *definitional equation* or an *identity* and is always true by definition. Note that equation (*3*) has no parameters or coefficients to be estimated. We will see that, given the values of the exogenous variables (π_{t-1} and G_t), we can solve the system and estimate the values of the endogenous variables. A change in the value of an exogenous variable will directly affect the endogenous variable in the equation in which it appears and indirectly affect the other endogenous variables in the system. For example, an increase in π_{t-1} leads to a rise in I_t directly [equation (*2*)]. The induced increase in I_t then leads to an increase in GNP_t and, through it, in C_t as well.

(*c*)   To forecast the values of the endogenous variables for a specific period, we substitute, into the estimated model the predicted or estimated values of the exogenous variables for that period. We then solve for the endogenous variables. To do this, however, we must first express each equation in the model in terms of the exogenous variables only. These equations are called *reduced-form equations*. (See Problem 6.19.)

6.19   Derive the reduced-form equation for GNP_t, using the model in Problem 6.18.

To derive the reduced-form equation for GNP_t, we begin by substituting equation (*1*) into equation (*3*) and we get

$$GNP_t = a_1 + b_1\,GNP_t + I_t + G_t \tag{4}$$

By then substituting equation (*2*) into equation (*4*), we get

$$GNP_t = a_1 + b_1 GNP_t + a_2 + b_2 \pi_{t-1} + G_t \tag{5}$$

Collecting the GNP_t terms on the left of the equals sign in equation (*5*) and isolating GNP_t, we have

$$GNP_t(1 - b_1) = a_1 + a_2 + b_2 \pi_{t-1} + G_t \tag{6}$$

Dividing both sides of equation (*6*) by $1 - b_1$, we finally obtain

$$GNP_t = \frac{a_1 + a_2}{1 - b_1} + \frac{b_2 \pi_{t-1}}{1 - b_1} + \frac{G_t}{1 - b_1} \tag{7}$$

Equation (7) is the reduced-form equation for GNP_t because GNP_t is expressed in terms of π_{t-1} and G_t only (the exogenous variables of the model). By inserting into equation (7) the value of π_t (which is known in year $t + 1$) and the predicted value of G_{t+1}, we obtain the forecasted value for GNP_{t+1}. The reduced-form equations for C_t and I_t can be similarly obtained. The accuracy of these forecasts depends on the accuracy with which the coefficients of the model have been estimated and on the accuracy with which the value of G_{t+1} is predicted or forecasted.

Chapter 7

Production Theory and Estimation

7.1 THE PRODUCTION FUNCTION

Production refers to the transformation of inputs or resources into outputs of goods and services. *Inputs* can be broadly classified into labor (including entrepreneurial talent), capital, and land or natural resources. *Fixed inputs* are those that cannot be readily changed during the time period under consideration. *Variable inputs* are those that can be varied easily and on short notice. The time period during which at least one input is fixed is called the *short run*. If all inputs are variable, we are in the *long run*.

A *production function* is an equation, table, or graph showing the maximum output of a commodity that a firm can produce per period of time with each set of inputs. Inputs and outputs are usually measured in physical rather than monetary units. Technology is assumed to remain constant during the period of the analysis. The general equation of the production function of a firm using labor (L) and capital (K) to produce a good or service (Q) can be written as

$$Q = f(L, K) \tag{7-1}$$

EXAMPLE 1. Table 7.1 gives a hypothetical production function, which shows the outputs (the Q's) that the firm can produce with various combinations of labor (L) and capital (K). The table shows that by using one unit of labor ($1L$) and one unit of capital ($1K$), the firm would produce 1 unit of output ($1Q$). With $2L$ and $1K$, output is $4Q$; with $3L$ and $1K$, output is $9Q$; with $3L$ and $2K$, output is $15Q$; with $4L$ and $2K$, output is $16Q$; and so on.

Table 7.1

Capital (K)	Output (Q)					
6	6	14	16	20	24	25
5	9	15	20	24	26	24
4	9	15	20	24	24	20
3	7	16	18	20	20	18
2	4	12	15	16	15	12
K 1	1	4	9	12	12	9
	1	2	3	4	5	6
L	Labor (L) $\longrightarrow$					

EXAMPLE 2. The production function of Table 7.1 is shown in the top panel of Fig. 7-1, where the height of the bars refers to the maximum output that the firm can produce with each combination of labor and capital shown on the axes. If we assume that inputs and outputs are continuously or infinitesimally divisible (rather than being measured in discrete units), we would have the continuous production surface shown in the bottom panel of Fig. 7-1. This indicates that by increasing L with K_1 of capital the firm produces the output shown by the height of cross section K_1AB (with base parallel to the labor axis). Increasing L with K_2, we have cross section K_2CD. Increasing K with L_1, we have cross section L_1EF (with base parallel to the capital axis).

7.2 PRODUCTION WITH ONE VARIABLE INPUT

By changing the quantity used of one input while holding constant the quantity used of another (so that we are in the short run), we generate the *total product* (TP) of the variable input. We then use TP to derive the marginal and average products. The *marginal product* (MP) is the change in total product per unit change in the variable input used. The *average product* (AP) equals total product divided by the quantity used of the variable input. *Output elasticity* measures the percentage change in output, or total product, divided by

106

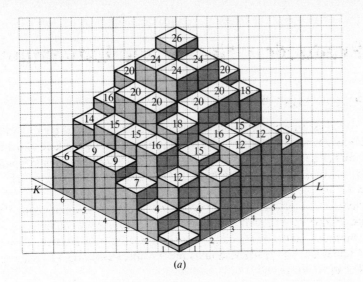

(a)

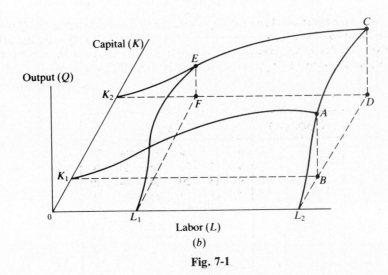

(b)

Fig. 7-1

the percentage change in the variable input used. If the variable input is labor, we have

$$MP_L = \frac{\Delta TP}{\Delta L} \qquad (7\text{-}2)$$

$$AP_L = \frac{TP}{L} \qquad (7\text{-}3)$$

$$E_L = \frac{\%\Delta Q}{\%\Delta L} \qquad (7\text{-}4)$$

Rewriting equation (7-4) in a more explicit form and rearranging, we get

$$E_L = \frac{\Delta Q/Q}{\Delta L/L} = \frac{\Delta Q/\Delta L}{Q/L} = \frac{MP_L}{AP_L} \qquad (7\text{-}5)$$

In the short run, we have the *law of diminishing returns*. It postulates that, after a point, the marginal product of a variable input declines. We can also define the *stages of production*. *Stage I* covers the range of increasing average product of the variable input. *Stage II* covers the range from the point of maximum average product of the variable input to the point at which the marginal product of the input is zero. *Stage III* covers the range of negative marginal product of the variable input. (See Example 4.)

EXAMPLE 3. With capital held constant at $K = 1$ and labor increasing from $L = 0$ to $L = 6$, we have the total product given in the last row in Table 7.1, which is reproduced in column (2) of Table 7.2. Note that adding the sixth unit of labor leads to a decline in TP as workers start getting in each other's way. From the TP schedule, we derive the MP_L and AP_L schedules [columns (3) and (4)] and, from them, the E_L schedule [column (5)].

EXAMPLE 4. The TP, MP_L, and AP_L schedules of Table 7.2 are plotted in Fig. 7-2. Note that each value of MP_L is plotted halfway between the quantities of labor used. Past $2.5L$, the MP_L curve declines (i.e., the law of diminishing returns begins to operate). The MP_L curve intercepts the AP_L curve at its highest point. The AP_L curve rises when the MP_L is above it, and falls when the MP_L curve is below it. The bottom panel of Figure 7-2 also shows the stages of production for labor. A rational producer (firm) would produce only in stage II, where MP_L is positive but declining. [See Problem 7.5(b).]

Table 7.2   Total, Marginal, and Average Product of Labor, and Output Elasticity

L (1)	TP (2)	$MP_L = \Delta TP/\Delta L$ (3)	$AP_L = TP/L$ (4)	$E_L = MP_L/AP_L$ (5)
0	0	—	—	—
1	1	1	1	1
2	4	3	2	1.5
3	9	5	3	1.67
4	12	3	3	1
5	12	0	2.4	0
6	9	−3	1.5	−2

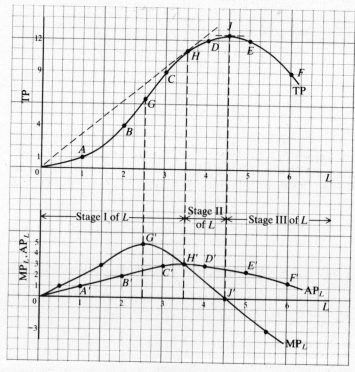

Fig. 7-2

7.3 OPTIMAL USE OF THE VARIABLE INPUT

The *marginal revenue product* (MRP) of a variable input equals the marginal product (MP) of the input times the marginal revenue (MR) received from the sale of the extra output produced. If the variable input is labor (L) and the commodity price (P) is constant (so that MR $= P$), we have

$$\text{MRP}_L = (\text{MP}_L)(\text{MR}) = (\text{MP}_L)(P) \tag{7-6}$$

The *marginal resource cost* (MRC) of a variable input, is equal to the increase in total costs that results from hiring an additional unit of the variable input. If the variable input is labor and the wage rate (w) is constant, we have

$$\text{MRC}_L = \frac{\Delta \text{TC}}{\Delta L} = w \tag{7-7}$$

As long as MRP exceeds MRC, it pays for the firm to expand the use of the variable input because by doing so it adds more to its total revenue than to its total costs (so that the firm's total profits rise). The firm should not hire those units of the variable input for which MRP falls short of MRC. Thus, the optimal use of the variable input (i.e., the quantity at which the firm maximizes profits) is at MRP = MRC. If the variable input is labor and the wage rate is constant, the firm should hire labor until

$$\text{MRP}_L = w \tag{7-8}$$

EXAMPLE 5. Column (2) in Table 7.3 gives the marginal product of labor as read off from the MP_L curve in stage II, in the bottom panel of Figure 7-2. The fractional units of labor are based on the assumption that the firm can hire

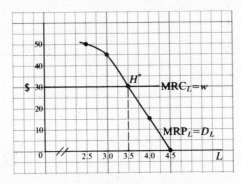

Fig. 7-3

labor for half a day at a time. Column (3) gives $P = \text{MR} = \$10$. Column (4) gives MRP_L, which is equal to $(\text{MP}_L)(\text{MR})$. Column (5) gives $\text{MRC}_L = w = \$30$ for each half day of work. In order to maximize profits the firm should hire 3.5L, at which $\text{MRP}_L = \text{MRC}_L = w$. This is shown at point H^* in Figure 7-3. Note that $\text{MRP}_L = D_L$ represents the firm's demand curve for labor.

Table 7.3

L (1)	MP_L (2)	$P = \text{MR}$ (3)	$\text{MRP}_L = (\text{MP}_L)(\text{MR})$ (4)	$\text{MRC}_L = \Delta\text{TC}/\Delta L = w$ (5)
2.5	5	$10	$50	$30
3.0	4.5	10	45	30
3.5	3	10	30	30
4.0	1.5	10	15	30
4.5	0	10	0	30

7.4 PRODUCTION WITH TWO VARIABLE INPUTS

The production function with two variable inputs can be depicted graphically with isoquants. An *isoquant* shows the various combinations of two inputs (say, labor and capital) that a firm can use to produce a specific level of output. A higher isoquant refers to a larger output, while a lower isoquant refers to a smaller output. A firm would never operate on the positively sloped portion of an isoquant because the firm could produce the same output with less labor and capital (see Example 6). *Ridge lines* separate the relevant (i.e., negatively sloped) from the irrelevant (or positively sloped) portions of the isoquants. The absolute value of the slope of the isoquant is called the *marginal rate of technical substitution* (MRTS). MRTS = MP_L/MP_K and diminishes as we move down an isoquant, so that the isoquant is convex to the origin. The smaller the degree of curvature of an isoquant, the greater is the degree of substitutability of inputs in production.

EXAMPLE 6. In Table 7.1, we saw that 9 units of output can be produced with $3L$ and $1K$, $6L$ and $1K$, $1L$ and $4K$, or $1L$ and $5K$. These are shown by isoquant $9Q$ in Fig. 7-4. The figure also shows the isoquants for $15Q$, $20Q$, and $24Q$. The firm would never produce $9Q$ with $6L$ and $1K$ (point T) because it could produce $9Q$ with $3L$ and $1K$ (point S). Similarly, the firm would not produce $9Q$ with $1L$ and $5K$ (point M) because it could produce $9Q$ with $1L$ and $4K$ (point N). Thus, only the negatively sloped portion of the isoquants between the ridge lines is relevant. The firm can move from point N to point R on isoquant $9Q$ by substituting $0.5L$ for $2K$. Thus, the absolute slope or MRTS of isoquant $9Q$ between points N and R is $2K/0.5L = 4$. The MRTS at point R is $\frac{4}{3}$ (the absolute value of the slope of the tangent to the isoquant at point R). Note that as we move down an isoquant its absolute slope or MRTS diminishes so that the isoquant is convex to the origin.

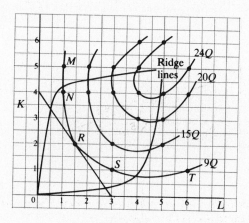

Fig. 7-4

7.5 OPTIMAL COMBINATION OF INPUTS

To determine the optimal combination of labor (L) and capital (K) for the firm to use, we also need an *isocost line*. This shows the various combinations of L and K that the firm can hire or rent at given input prices (w and r) and total cost (C). That is

$$C = wL + rK \qquad (7\text{-}9)$$

By subtracting wL from both sides of equation (7-9) and then dividing by r, we get

$$K = \frac{C}{r} - \frac{w}{r}L \qquad (7\text{-}10)$$

where C/r is the vertical intercept of the isocost line and $-w/r$ is its slope.

The optimal combination of inputs used to minimize costs or maximize output is given at the tangency point of an isoquant and an isocost. At the tangency point, the (absolute) slope of the isoquant (MRTS = MP_L/MP_K) is equal to the (absolute) slope of the isocost line (w/r). That is

$$\text{MRTS} = \frac{MP_L}{MP_K} = \frac{w}{r} \qquad\qquad (7\text{-}11)$$

By cross multiplying, we get

$$\frac{MP_L}{w} = \frac{MP_K}{r} \qquad\qquad (7\text{-}12)$$

That is, to minimize costs or maximize output, the marginal product per dollar spent on labor should be equal to the marginal product per dollar spent on capital.

Finally, to maximize profits a firm should produce the profit-maximizing level of output with the optimal (least-cost) input combination. This occurs when the firm employs each input until the marginal revenue product of the input equals the marginal resource cost of hiring the input. With constant input prices, this condition becomes

$$MRP_L = (MP_L)(MR) = w \qquad\qquad (7\text{-}13)$$

$$MRP_K = (MP_K)(MR) = r \qquad\qquad (7\text{-}14)$$

EXAMPLE 7. If $C = \$12$, $w = \$4$ and $r = \$3$, the firm could either hire $3L$ or rent $4K$, or any combination of L and K shown on isocost line AB in Fig. 7-5. The equation of the isocost line is then

$$K = 4 - \frac{4}{3}L$$

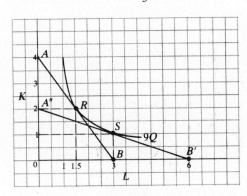

Fig. 7-5

and the firm must give up $\frac{4}{3}K$ for each additional unit of L it wants to hire. The lowest cost of producing $9Q$ is given by point R, where isoquant $9Q$ is tangent to isocost line AB and

$$\text{MRTS} = \frac{w}{r} = \frac{4}{3}$$

Thus, the firm should use $1.5L$ and $2K$ at a total cost of $C = \$12$. If w declined from $w = \$4$ to $w = \$2$, while r increased from $r = \$3$ to $r = \$6$ and C remained at $\$12$, the new isocost line would be $A''B'$ (see Fig. 7-5). The firm would then substitute L for K in production until it reached the new optimal input combination at point S. By changing total costs or expenditures while holding input prices constant, the firm can define different but parallel isocost lines. By joining tangency points of isoquants with isocosts the firm defines its *expansion path* [see Problem 7.17(a)]. By hiring labor and renting capital until

$$MRP_L = w = \$4 \qquad \text{and} \qquad MRP_K = r = \$3$$

the firm will produce the profit-maximizing level of output with the optimal input combination [see Problem 7.20(b)].

7.6 RETURNS TO SCALE AND EMPIRICAL PRODUCTION FUNCTIONS

If the quantity of all inputs used in production is increased by a given proportion (so that we are in the long run), we have *constant returns to scale* if output increases in the same proportion as the increase in inputs, *increasing returns to scale* if output increases by a greater proportion than the increase in inputs, and *decreasing returns to scale* if output increases by a smaller proportion than the increase in inputs (see Example 8). Increasing returns to scale arise because, as the scale of operation increases, a greater division of labor and specialization can take place and more specialized and productive machinery can be used. Decreasing returns to scale arise primarily because, as the scale of operation increases, it becomes more difficult to manage the firm effectively and to coordinate its various operations and divisions.

The most commonly used production function is the *Cobb-Douglas* of the form

$$Q = AK^a L^b \tag{7-15}$$

where Q, K, and L refer, respectively, to the quantities of output, capital, and labor, and A, a, and b are the parameters to be estimated. Parameters a and b represent, respectively, the output elasticities of capital and labor (E_K and E_L). If $a + b = 1$ we have constant returns to scale, if $a + b > 1$ we have increasing returns to scale, and if $a + b < 1$ we have decreasing returns to scale. To estimate the Cobb-Douglas production function by regression analysis, we must first transform it:

$$\ln Q = \ln A + a \ln K + b \ln L \tag{7-16}$$

EXAMPLE 8. The left panel of Fig. 7-6 shows that doubling inputs from $3L$ and $3K$ to $6L$ and $6K$ doubles output from 100 (point A) to 200 (point B). Thus, $OA = AB$ along ray OE, and we have constant returns to scale. The middle panel shows that output triples by doubling inputs. Thus, $OA < AC$ (i.e., the isoquants come closer together) and we have increasing returns to scale. The right panel shows decreasing returns to scale. Here, output changes proportionately less than labor and capital, and $OA > AD$. Empirical estimates of the Cobb-Douglas production function indicate that most industries exhibit near-constant returns to scale (see Problem 7.23).

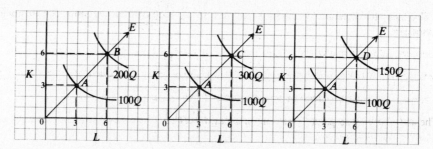

Fig. 7-6

Glossary

Average product (AP) The total product divided by the quantity of the variable input used.

Cobb-Douglas production function A production function of the form $Q = AK^a L^b$, where Q, K, and L are physical units of output, labor, and capital, and A, a, and b are the parameters to be estimated empirically.

Constant returns to scale The case in which output changes in the same proportion as inputs.

Decreasing returns to scale The case in which output changes by a smaller proportion than inputs.

Expansion path The line joining tangency points of isoquants and isocosts (with input prices held constant) that shows optimal input combinations.

Fixed inputs Inputs that cannot be changed readily during the time period under consideration.

Increasing returns to scale The case in which output changes by a larger proportion than inputs.

Inputs Resources used in the production of goods and services.

Isocost line   The line showing the various combinations of two inputs that the firm can hire with a given total cost outlay.

Isoquant   A curve showing the various combinations of two inputs that can be used to produce a specific level of output.

Law of diminishing returns   The principle that after a point, the marginal product of a variable input declines.

Long run   The time period during which all inputs are variable.

Marginal product (MP)   The change in total product per unit change in the variable input used.

Marginal rate of technical substitution (MRTS)   The absolute value of the slope of the isoquant. It equals the ratio of the marginal products of the two inputs.

Marginal resource cost (MRC)   The increase in total cost that results form hiring an additional unit of the variable input.

Marginal revenue product (MRP)   The marginal product of the variable input times the marginal revenue from the sale of the extra output produced.

Output elasticity   The percentage change in output or total product divided by the percentage change in the variable input used.

Production   The transformation of inputs or resources into outputs of goods and services.

Production function   An equation, table, or graph that shows the maximum output that a firm can produce per period of time with each set of inputs.

Ridge lines   The lines that separate the relevant (i.e., negatively sloped) from the irrelevant (or positively sloped) portions of the isoquant.

Short run   The time period during which at least one input is fixed.

Stages of production   The relationship between the marginal and average products of an input.

Stage I   The range of increasing average product of the variable input.

Stage II   The range from the point of maximum average product of the variable input to the point at which the marginal product of the input is zero.

Stage III   The range of negative marginal product of the variable input.

Total product (TP)   The output produced by using different quantities of an input with fixed quantities of other input(s).

Variable inputs   Inputs that can be varied easily and on very short notice.

Review Questions

1.   Which of the following statements is false?

   (a)   Production refers to the transformation of inputs or resources into outputs of goods and services.

   (b)   Variable inputs are those that can be varied easily and on very short notice.

   (c)   Using two variable inputs with a fixed input refers to the long run.

   (d)   A production function is an equation, table, or graph that shows the maximum output that a firm can produce per period of time with each set of inputs.

   Ans.   (c) See Section 7.1.

2. Which of the following terms refers to the short run?

    (a) Total product

    (b) Marginal product

    (c) Average product

    (d) All of the above

    Ans.   (d) See Section 7.2.

3. Which of the following statements about the output elasticity of labor is false?

    (a) It is equal to the percentage change in output or total product divided by the percentage change in the quantity labor used.

    (b) It is equal to the ratio of MP_L to AP_L.

    (c) It can never be negative.

    (d) It is smaller than 1 in stage II of production for labor.

    Ans.   (c) See Section 7.2 and Examples 3 and 4.

4. Which of the following statements is true?

    (a) Stage I for labor covers the range over which MP_L is rising.

    (b) Stage II for labor covers the range over which MP_L is declining.

    (c) Stage III for labor covers the range over which MP_L is negative.

    (d) All of the above.

    Ans.   (d) See Section 7.2 and Example 4.

5. Which of the following statements is false?

    (a) The rational producer produces in the range of increasing returns.

    (b) The MP_L curve goes through the highest point of the AP_L curve.

    (c) The AP_L curve rises as long as the MP_L is above it and falls as long as the MP_L curve is below it.

    (d) None of the above.

    Ans.   (a) See Section 7.2 and Example 4.

6. Which of the following statements is true?

    (a) MRP_L equals MP_L times MR.

    (b) MRC_L equals the increase in total costs that result from hiring an additional unit of labor.

    (c) When the commodity price (P) is constant, $MR = P$, and when the wage rate (w) is constant, $MRC_L = w$.

    (d) All of the above.

    Ans.   (d) See Section 7.3.

7. In order to maximize profits, the rational producer should hire labor as long as

    (a) $MRP_L = w$.

    (b) $MRP_L > w$.

    (c) $MRP_L < w$.

    (d) Any of the above.

    Ans.   (a) See Section 7.3.

8.   In their relevant range, isoquants are

(*a*)   negatively sloped.

(*b*)   convex to the origin.

(*c*)   nonintersecting.

(*d*)   all of the above.

Ans.   (*d*) See Section 7.4 and Example 6.

9.   Which of the following statements with regard to isoquants is false?

(*a*)   MRTS measures the quantity of an input that a firm can give up by increasing the quantity of another input by one unit and still remain on the same isoquant.

(*b*) MP_L or MP_K is negative in the positively sloped range of an isoquant.

(*c*)   The convexity of an isoquant reflects increasing MRTS.

(*d*)   The slope of an isoquant is given by the ratio of the marginal productivity of the inputs.

Ans.   (*c*) The convexity of an isoquant reflects diminishing MRTS. See Section 7.4 and Example 6.

10.   Which of the following statements is false?

(*a*)   The vertical intercept of isocost line $A''B'$ in Fig. 7-5 is $\$12/\$6 = 2K$.

(*b*)   The absolute slope of isocost line $A''B'$ in Fig. 7-5 is $\$2/\$6 = \frac{1}{3}$.

(*c*)   At point S in Fig. 7-5, MRTS $= MP_L/MP_K = \frac{1}{3}$.

(*d*)   At point S, K/L is greater than at point R.

Ans.   (*d*) See Section 7.5 and Fig. 7-5.

11.   If output less than doubles when all inputs are doubled, we have

(*a*)   diminishing returns.

(*b*)   decreasing returns to scale.

(*c*)   increasing returns to scale.

(*d*)   constant returns to scale.

Ans.   (*b*) See Section 7.6 and Example 8.

12.   Which of the following statements with respect to a Cobb-Douglas production function is true?

(*a*) MP_K and MP_L depend on the quantity used of both K and L.

(*b*)   The exponent of each input refers to its output elasticity.

(*c*)   We must first transform it into its logarithmic form if we wish to estimate it.

(*d*)   All of the above.

Ans.   (*d*) See Section 7.6.

Solved Problems

THE PRODUCTION FUNCTION

7.1   (a) What is meant by production? By inputs? (b) What is meant by fixed inputs, variable inputs, short run, long run? (c) How long is the time period of the long run?

  (a)   Production refers to the physical transformation of resources into outputs of goods and services. Inputs are the resources that the firm transforms into outputs of good and services. The broad categories of inputs are labor (including entrepreneurship), capital, and land or raw materials.

  (b)   Fixed inputs are those that cannot be changed readily during the period of the analysis except, perhaps, at such a great expense to the firm as to make their change impractical. Variable inputs, on the other hand, are those that can be changed readily by the firm and on short notice. The short run is the time period during which at least one input is fixed. The long run is the time period that is long enough to allow the firm to change all inputs.

  (c)   The time period of the long run differs in different industries. In some cases, such as the setting up or expanding of a duplicating (photocopying) business, the long run may be only a few weeks or months. In others, such as the building of a new steel plant, the long run may be several years. It all depends on the time period required by the firm to conveniently change all inputs.

7.2   (a) What is the basic production decision facing a firm? What is required in order for the firm to make such decisions? (b) What is a production function? What is its usefulness in the analysis of the firm's production?

  (a)   The basic production decision facing the firm is how much of the commodity or service to produce and how much labor, capital, and other resources or inputs to use to produce that output most efficiently. To answer these questions, the firm requires engineering or technological data on production possibilities (the so-called production function), as well as economic data on input and output prices.

  (b)   A production function is a table, graph, or equation showing the maximum output of a commodity that a firm can produce per period of time with each set of inputs. Thus, a production function provides the framework for the analysis of production by the firm. It summarizes the technological production possibilities available to the firm and provides the basis for the determination of the most efficient combination of inputs in production.

7.3   Assume that $L_1 = 1$ and $L_2 = 6$, while $K_1 = 1$ and $K_2 = 4$ in the bottom panel of Fig. 7-1 in Example 2. Using Table 7.1, in Example 1, indicate the number of units of output to which the following refer: (a) FE, (b) BA, and (c) DC.

  (a)   In the bottom panel of Fig. 7-1 in Example 2, we see that FE is the output (Q) that results when the firm uses $L = 1$ and $K = 4$. In Table 7.1 in Example 1, we see that with $L = 1$ and $K = 4$, $Q = 9$ units.

  (b)   In the bottom panel of Fig. 7-1 in Example 2, we see that BA is the output (Q) that results when the firm uses $L = 6$ and $K = 1$. In Table 7.1 in Example 1, we see that with $L = 6$ and $K = 1$, $Q = 9$.

  (c)   In the bottom panel of Fig. 7-1 in Example 2, we see that DC is the output (Q) that results when the firm uses $L = 6$ and $K = 4$. In Table 7.1 in Example 1, we see that with $L = 6$ and $K = 4$, $Q = 20$.

PRODUCTION WITH ONE VARIABLE INPUT

7.4   (a) What is the relationship between the marginal product and the average product curves of labor? (b) Explain the reason for this relationship. (c) Give an example of the relationship between average product and marginal product in terms of changes in a student's grade point average.

(a) The MP_L curve reaches its maximum point sooner than the AP_L curve. As long as the AP_L curve is rising, the MP_L curve is above it. When the AP_L curve is falling, the MP_L curve is below it, and when the AP_L curve is highest, the MP_L curve intersects the AP_L curve.

(b) The reason for the relationship between MP_L and AP_L is that for AP_L to rise, MP_L must be greater than the average to ''pull'' up the average. For AP_L to fall, MP_L must be lower than the average to ''pull'' down the average. For the average product to be at its maximum (i.e., neither rising nor falling) the marginal product must be equal to the average product (see the slope of line OH in Fig. 7-2 in Example 4).

(c) To increase a cumulative average test score, the student must receive a grade on the next (marginal) test that exceeds the previous average. With a lower grade on the next test, the student's cumulative average will fall. If the grade on the next test equals the previous average, the cumulative average will remain unchanged.

7.5   (a) How is the law of diminishing returns reflected in the shape of the total product curve? (b) What is the relationship between diminishing returns and the stages of production?

(a) The law of diminishing returns refers to the range over which the marginal product of the variable input declines. This corresponds to the portion of the total product curve from the point of inflection onward (i.e., from the point at which the total product curve begins to increase at a decreasing rate). Diminishing returns continue as the total product curve reaches its maximum point (so that the marginal product of the variable input is zero) and then declines (so that the marginal product curve of the variable input is negative).

(b) Diminishing returns appear over part of stage I for the variable input and in all of stages II (where the marginal product of the variable input is declining but positive) and III (where the marginal product of the variable input is declining and negative). A negative marginal product means that the firm could produce more output by using less of the variable input!

    While not shown in Fig. 7-2 in Example 4, stage I of labor (the variable input) corresponds to stage III of capital (the fixed input), where MP_K is declining and negative. Since MP_L is negative in stage III of labor and MP_K is negative in stage I of labor (which corresponds to stage III of capital), the rational producer would produce only in stage II of labor and capital, where both MP_L and MP_K are positive and declining.

7.6   If the total product curve increases at a decreasing rate from the very beginning (i.e., from the point at which the variable input is zero), what would be the shape of the corresponding marginal and average product curves?

    If the total product curve increases at a decreasing rate from the very beginning (i.e., from the origin), its slope, or marginal product of the variable input, would decline from the very beginning. That is, we would have no range of increasing marginal product. Similarly, the average product curve of the variable input would also lack a rising portion and would decline from the very beginning. This type of production function is often encountered in the empirical estimation of production functions (see Section 7.6). For this type of production function, the slope of a ray from the origin to any point on the total product curve, or average product, is also smaller than the slope of the total product curve at that point. Thus, the average product curve of the variable input is not only declining over its entire range but is also below the marginal product curve for each quantity of the variable input used. The student should draw such curves.

7.7   (a) Using the data in Table 7.1, construct a table similar to Table 7.2, showing the total product, the marginal product, and the average product of labor as well as the output elasticity of labor when capital is kept constant at 2 units rather than at 1 unit. (b) Using the results in part (a), draw a figure similar to Fig. 7-2, showing the total, marginal, and average products of labor. (c) How do the results in parts (a) and (b) differ from those in Table 7.2 and Fig. 7-2 in Examples 3 and 4?

(a) See Table 7.4.

(b) See Fig. 7-7.

Table 7.4

L (1)	TP (2)	$MP_L = \Delta TP/\Delta L$ (3)	$AP_L = TP/L$ (4)	$E_L = MP_L/AP_L$ (5)
0	0	—	—	—
1	4	4	4	1
2	12	8	6	1.33
3	15	3	5	0.6
4	16	1	4	0.25
5	15	−1	3	−0.33
6	12	−3	2	−1.5

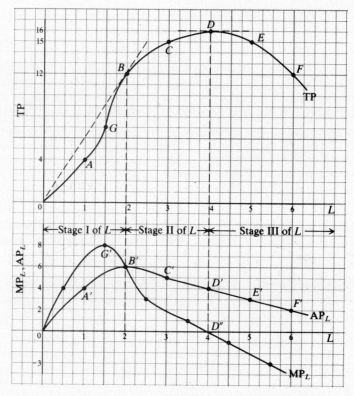

Fig. 7-7

(c) When capital is fixed at 2 units rather than at 1 unit, MP_L and AP_L are both greater than when capital is held constant at 1 unit. This is reasonable. Having more capital to work with, each unit of labor is more productive, so that both MP_L and AP_L are higher and diminishing returns set in later (i.e., after more units of labor have been used).

7.8 (a) Using the data in Table 7.1, construct a table similar to Table 7.2, showing the total product, marginal product, and average product of capital as well as the output elasticity of capital when labor is kept constant at 1 unit. (b) Using the results in part (a), draw a figure similar to Fig. 7-2, showing the total, marginal, and average products of capital. (c) How much capital would a rational producer use?

(a) See Table 7.5

Table 7.5

K (1)	TP (2)	$MP_K = \Delta TP / \Delta K$ (3)	$AP_K = TP/K$ (4)	$E_K = MP_K/AP_K$ (5)
0	0	—	—	—
1	1	1	1	1
2	4	3	2	1.5
3	7	3	2.33	1.29
4	9	2	2.25	0.89
5	9	0	1.8	0
6	6	−3	1	−3

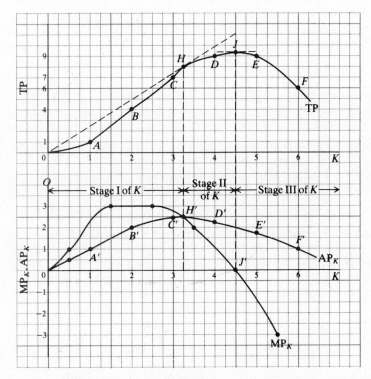

Fig. 7-8

(b) See Fig. 7-8.

(c) The rational producer would use between $3.25K$ and $4.5K$ (i.e., production would take place in stage II of capital, which is also stage II of labor), where the marginal product of K and L are diminishing but positive. Precisely how much capital and labor the producer would use depends on the prices of capital, labor, and output.

OPTIMAL USE OF THE VARIABLE INPUT

7.9   (a) Explain the meaning of the marginal revenue product of an input and how it is calculated. Why does the marginal revenue product of an input decline as more units of the input are used? (b) Explain the meaning of the marginal resource cost. When is this equal to the input price? (c) What is the principle that specifies the optimal use of a variable input?

(a) The marginal revenue product of an input is equal to the marginal product of the input times the marginal revenue generated by the sale of the extra output produced. The marginal revenue product of a variable input declines because the rational producer always produces in stage II of production, where the marginal product of the input is positive but declining. If the marginal revenue from the sale of the extra product also declines (this occurs if the firm must lower the price on all units of the commodity to sell the extra output produced), then the marginal revenue product of the input will decline even more rapidly.

(b) The marginal resource cost of a variable input refers to the increase in a firm's total costs that results from hiring an additional unit of the variable input. Only if the firm is small and can hire additional units of the variable input at a given (constant) market price will the marginal resource cost remain constant and be equal to the market price of the input. If, in order to hire more units of the variable input, the firm must pay higher prices for the input, the marginal resource cost of the input will differ from (i.e., will be higher than) the input price.

(c) The optimal use of the variable input (i.e., the point at which the firm maximizes profits) is at MRP = MRC for the input. As long as MRP exceeds MRC, it pays for the firm to expand the use of the variable input because by doing so the firm adds more to its total revenue than to its total costs (so that the firm's total profits rise). However, the firm should not hire any units of the variable inputs for which MRP falls short of MRC.

7.10 The Offtrack Betting Corporation (OTBC) is contemplating opening an office in a particular neighborhood. OTBC estimates that the total number of bets placed per day in the new office will depend on the number of clerks hired, as indicated in the following table. If the price of each bet is $10 and each clerk hired must be paid a wage of $50 per day, how many clerks should OTBC hire?

Workers hired	0	1	2	3	4	5
Total product	0	20	35	45	50	50

OTBC should hire clerks as long as their marginal revenue product (MRP) exceeds their marginal resource cost (MRC), and until the MRP = MRC. We can find the MRP and MRC for each clerk (L) by constructing a table analogous to Table 7.3 in Example 5, as shown in Table 7.6.

Table 7.6

Number of Workers (L) (1)	TP (2)	MP_L (3)	$MR = P$ (4)	$MRP_L = (3) \times (4)$ (5)	$MRC_L = w$ (6)
0	0	—	$10	—	$50
1	20	20	10	$200	50
2	35	15	10	150	50
3	45	10	10	100	50
4	50	5	10	50	50
5	50	0	10	0	50

Since OTBC can hire additional clerks at the given daily wage (w) of $50, MRC = w = $50 [column (6) in Table 7.6]. OTBC's total profits will be at their maximum when it hires four clerks, at which MRP = MRC = w = $50.

7.11 (a) Find the marginal revenue product of clerks for the data in Problem 7.10, using the change in total revenue resulting from the employment of each additional clerk, and show that the number of workers OTBC should hire is the same as the figure obtained in Problem 7.10. (b) Show the result of part (a) graphically. What does the MRP_L curve represent?

(a) We can find the marginal revenue product of each additional clerk hired by calculating the change in total revenue of OTBC that results from the hiring of each additional clerk. This is shown in Table 7.7.

Since OTBC can hire additional clerks at the given daily wage (w) of $50, MRC $= w =$ $50 [column (6) in Table 7.7], the firm's total profits will be at their maximum when it hires four workers, so that MRP $=$ MRC $= w =$ $50. The result is the same as that obtained in Problem 7.10, where MRP was obtained by multiplying the MP of clerks by the MR, or P, of the bets, rather than by using the change in total revenue per additional clerk hired, as was done in Table 7.7.

Table 7.7

Number of Clerks (L) (1)	TP (2)	P (3)	TR $=$ (TP)(P) (4)	MRP$_L$ $= \Delta$TR$/\Delta L$ (5)	MRC$_L$ $= w$ (6)
0	0	$10	$ 0	—	$50
1	20	10	200	$200	50
2	35	10	350	150	50
3	45	10	450	100	50
4	50	10	500	50	50
5	50	10	500	0	50

(b) See Fig. 7-9. Note that the MRP$_L$ values are plotted at the midpoint of each additional clerk hired. The MRP$_L$ represents the demand for clerks (D_L) by OTBC.

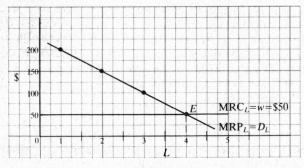

Fig. 7-9

PRODUCTION WITH TWO VARIABLE INPUTS

7.12 (a) Do isoquants refer to the short run or to the long run? Why? (b) Indicate in what way isoquants are similar to and different from indifference curves. (c) Explain why isoquants cannot intersect.

(a) Isoquants can refer to the short or the long run. If the two inputs measured on the axes of an isoquant diagram are the only inputs used in production, then the isoquant refers to the long run, since both inputs are variable. However, if there are other fixed inputs as well as the two variable inputs used in the drawing, then we are still in the short run. Unless it is otherwise indicated, however, isoquants refer to the long run.

(b) Both indifference curves and isoquants are negatively sloped (within their relevant ranges) and convex to the origin, and they do not intersect. However, while an indifference curve shows the various combinations of two commodities that provide the consumer with equal satisfaction (measured ordinally, that is, hierarchically), an isoquant shows the various combinations of two inputs that give the same level of output (measured cardinally, that is, in actual units of the commodity).

(c) The meaning of intersecting isoquants would be that two different levels of output of the same commodity could be produced with the identical input combination (i.e., at the point where the two isoquants intersect). This is impossible under our assumption that the most efficient production techniques are used at all times.

7.13   (*a*) What is the slope of the isoquants at the point at which they are intersected by the bottom, or right-hand, ridge line? By the top, or left-hand, ridge line? (*b*) Using isoquant 24*Q* in Fig. 7-4, explain why the marginal product of labor is negative to the right of the bottom ridge line and the marginal product of capital is negative to the left of the top ridge line. (*c*) To what stages of production do the positively sloped portions of the isoquants refer? the negatively sloped portion?

(*a*)   The bottom, or right-hand, ridge line joins points at which the isoquants have zero slope (i.e., they are horizontal). The top, or left-hand, ridge line joins points where the isoquants have infinite slope (i.e., they are vertical). Thus, isoquants are negatively sloped between the ridge lines and positively sloped outside the ridge lines.

(*b*)   Starting from the point at which the firm uses 5*L* and 4*K* on isoquant 24*Q*, if the firm used more labor and the same quantity of capital, the firm would fall back to a lower isoquant (see Fig. 7-4). Thus, the MP_L is negative. This means that in order to remain on isoquant 24*Q*, the firm must also increase the quantity of capital used (see points 6*L* and 5*K* on isoquant 24*Q* in Fig. 7-4). Starting from the point at which the firm uses 4*L* and 5*K* on isoquant 24*Q*, if the firm used more capital and the same quantity of labor, the firm would fall back to a lower isoquant (see Fig. 7-4). Thus, the MP_K is negative. This means that in order to remain on isoquant 24*Q*, the firm must also increase the quantity of labor used (see points 5*L* and 6*K* on isoquant 24*Q* in Fig. 7-4).

(*c*)   Since MP_L is negative to the right of the bottom ridge line, the positively sloped range of the isoquants to the right of that line refers to production stage III for labor. However, since MP_K is negative to the left of the top ridge line, the positively sloped range of the isoquants to the left of that line refers to production stage III for capital (which corresponds to production stage I for labor). Thus, the negatively sloped portions of the isoquants between the ridge lines refer to production stage II for labor and capital, and MP_L and MP_K are positive but declining.

7.14   (*a*) Determine MRTS between points *R* and *S* on isoquant 9*Q* in Fig. 7-4. What is MRTS at point *S*? (*b*) Prove that MRTS = MP_L/MP_K. (*c*) Explain why MRTS declines as we move down an isoquant. What is the characteristic of isoquants that results from diminishing MRTS?

(*a*)   The firm can move from point *R* to point *S* by reducing the quantity of capital used by 1 unit and increasing the quantity of labor used by 1.5 units. Thus, MRTS = $1K/1.5L = \frac{2}{3}$, or 0.66. At point *S*, MRTS = $\frac{1}{3}$, or 0.33, and is given by the absolute slope of the tangent to isoquant 9*Q* at point *S*.

(*b*)   We can prove that MRTS = MP_L/MP_K by remembering that all points on an isoquant refer to the same level of output. Thus, for movement down a given isoquant, the gain in output resulting from the use of more labor must be equal to the loss in output resulting from the use of less capital. Specifically, the increase in the quantity of labor used (ΔL) times the marginal product of labor (MP_L) must equal the reduction in the amount of capital used ($-\Delta K$) times the marginal product of capital (MP_K). That is

$$(\Delta L)(MP_L) = -(\Delta K)(MP_K)$$

so that

$$\frac{MP_L}{MP_K} = \frac{-\Delta K}{\Delta L} = \text{MRTS}$$

(*c*)   As the firm moves down an isoquant and uses more labor and less capital, MP_L declines and MP_K increases (since the firm is in stage II of production for both labor and capital). MP_L also declines because the firm uses less capital. MP_K also increases because the firm uses more labor. With MP_L declining and MP_K rising, MP_L/MP_K = MRTS declines as the firm moves down the isoquant. Declining MRTS is reflected in the convex shape of the isoquant.

7.15   (*a*) What does the shape of an isoquant show? Why is this very important in managerial economics? (*b*) Draw isoquants for labor and capital, assuming that they are perfect substitutes. (*c*) Draw isoquants for labor and capital, assuming that they are perfect complements.

(*a*)   The shape of an isoquant shows the degree or ease with which one input can be substituted for another in production. On the one hand, the smaller the curvature of the isoquant, the greater is the degree, or ease, with which one input can be substituted for the other in production. On the other hand, the greater is the curvature of the isoquant, the smaller is the degree, or ease, with which one input can be substituted for the other in production. To be able to easily substitute one input for another when the price of the latter increases is extremely important to the firm in order to keep production costs down.

(b) See Fig. 7-10. When labor and capital are perfect substitutes the rate at which labor can be substituted for capital in production (i.e., the absolute slope of the isoquant or MRTS) is constant. For example, in Fig. 7-10, $2L$ can be substituted for $1K$ regardless of the amount of production the isoquant represents. In fact, point A on the labor axis shows that the level of output indicated by the middle isoquant can be produced with labor alone (i.e., without any capital). Similarly, point B on the capital axis indicates that the same level of output can be produced with capital only (i.e., without any labor). Examples of perfect input substitutability are oil and gas used to operate some heating furnaces, energy and time in a drying process, and fish meal and soybeans to provide protein in a feed mix.

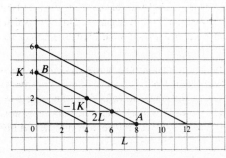

Fig. 7-10

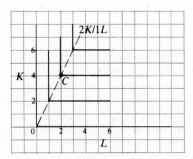

Fig. 7-11

(c) See Fig. 7-11. When labor and capital are perfect complements, they must be used in a fixed proportion in production ($2K/1L$ in Fig. 7-11) and there is zero substitutability between labor and capital. For example, starting at point C on the middle isoquant in Fig. 7-11, output remains unchanged if only the quantity of labor is increased (i.e., $MP_L = 0$ along the horizontal portion of the isoquant). Similarly, output remains unchanged if only the quantity of capital is increased (i.e., $MP_K = 0$ along the vertical portion of the isoquant). Output can be increased only by increasing both the quantity of labor and the quantity of capital in the proportion $2K/1L$. Examples of perfect complementary inputs are certain chemical processes that require basic elements (chemicals) to be combined in specified fixed proportions, engines and bodies for automobiles, two wheels and a frame for bicycles, and so on. In these cases, inputs can only be used in the fixed proportion specified (i.e., there is no possibility of substituting one input for another in production).

While perfect substitutability and perfect complementarity of inputs in production are possible, in most cases isoquants exhibit some curvature (i.e., inputs are imperfect substitutes), as shown in Fig. 7-4. This means that in the usual production situation, labor can be substituted for capital to some degree. The ability to substitute one input for another in production is extremely important in keeping production costs down when the price of one input increases relative to the price of another.

OPTIMAL COMBINATION OF INPUTS

7.16 On the same set of axes draw the isocost for $C = \$100$ and $w = r = \$10$, another for $C = \$140$ and $w = r = \$10$, and a third for $C = \$100$ but $w = \$5$ and $r = \$10$.

See Fig. 7-12. With $C = \$100$ and $w = r = \$10$, we have isocost line AB with vertical intercept $C/r = \$100/\$10 = 10K$ and absolute slope $w/r = \$10/\$10 = 1$. With $C = \$140$ and $w = r = \$10$, we have isocost line $A'B'$, which is parallel to isocost line AB (because $w/r = 1$ for both) but is higher (because $C = \$140$ rather than $C = \$100$). Finally, with $C = \$100$ and $w = \$5$ and $r = \$10$, we have isocost line AB'', which has the same vertical intercept as isocost line AB (because $C = \$100$ and $r = \$10$ are the same as for isocost AB), but has the absolute slope of $w/r = \$5/\$10 = \frac{1}{2}$, which is half that of isocost line AB.

124   PRODUCTION THEORY AND ESTIMATION   [CHAP. 7

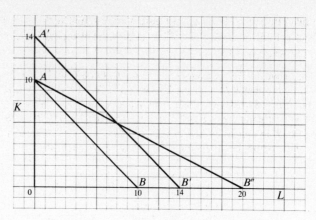

Fig. 7-12

7.17 (a) Using isocost lines AB and $A'B'$ in Fig. 7-12, draw a figure with isoquants showing that the optimal input combination needed to produce both 10 units and 14 units of output takes place at $K/L = 1$. On the same figure draw the expansion path of the firm. (b) Show that the firm could produce $10Q$ at $C = \$140$ but this would not represent the optimal input combination.

(a) See Fig. 7-13. The optimal input combination to produce $10Q$ is shown by point T, where isoquant $10Q$ is tangent to isocost line AB and the firm uses $5L$ and $5K$, so that $K/L = 1$. The optimal input combination to produce $14Q$ is shown by point U, where isoquant $14Q$ is tangent to isocost $A'B'$ and the firm uses $7L$ and $7K$, so that $K/L = 1$. At the tangency points, the absolute slopes of the isoquants (MRTS = MP_L/MP_K) equal the absolute slopes of the isocost lines (w/r), so that $MP_L/w = MP_K/r$. By joining the tangency points of isoquants with isocost lines (i.e., points of optimal input combinations) we get the expansion path of the firm (see Fig. 7-13). Note that the expansion path of the firm is a straight line through the origin. This is usually the case in the empirical estimation of production functions.

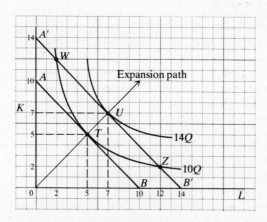

Fig. 7-13

(b) The firm could produce $10Q$ at point W by using $2L$ and $12K$ on isocost $A'B'$ (i.e., with $C = \$140$). But this would not represent the optimal input combination because the absolute slope of isoquant $10Q$ at point W (MRTS) exceeds the absolute slope of isocost line $A'B'$ ($w/r = 1$). The firm could also produce $10Q$ at point Z by using $12L$ and $2K$ on isocost $A'B'$. But this also would not represent the optimal input combination because the absolute slope of isoquant $10Q$ at point Z is smaller than the absolute slope of isocost line $A'B'$. Only at point T in Fig. 7-13 (i.e., by using $5K$ and $5L$) would MRTS = w/r and the firm be using the optimal (i.e., least-cost) input combination to produce $10Q$ (with $C = \$100$).

7.18 Starting at point T in Fig. 7-13, draw a figure showing that with $r = \$10$ but $w = \$5$, the firm could produce $10Q$ at a total cost of $\$70$. What is K/L at the new input combination? Why does K/L change when the wage rate falls?

In Fig. 7-14, isoquant $10Q$ is tangent to isocost AB (with $C = \$100$ and $w/r = \$10/\$10 = 1$) at point T by using $5K$ and $5L$, so that $K/L = 1$ (as in Fig. 7-13). With $r = \$10$ but $w = \$5$, the absolute slope of the isocost becomes $w/r = \$5/\$10 = \frac{1}{2}$. We can then reach isoquant $10Q$ with isocost $A''B'$ (with $C = \$70$ and $w/r = \$5/\$10 = \frac{1}{2}$) at point S by using $8L$ and $3K$, so that $K/L = \frac{3}{8}$. Note that as the wage rate falls, the firm will substitute L for K in production (so that L/K increases, which means that K/L falls) in order to minimize the cost (i.e., use the optimal combination of L and K) to produce $10Q$.

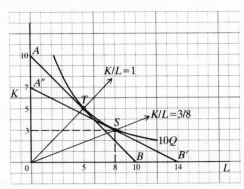

Fig. 7-14

7.19 Suppose that the marginal product of the last worker employed by a firm is 60 units of output per day, and the daily wage that the firm must pay is $\$30$, while the marginal product of the last machine rented by the firm is 80 units of output per day, and the daily rental price of the machine is $\$20$. (a) Why is this firm not maximizing output or minimizing costs in the long run? (b) How can the firm maximize output or minimize costs?

(a) The firm is not maximizing output or minimizing costs (i.e., the firm is not using the optimal input combination) because $MP_L/w = 60/\$30 = 2$ is not equal to $MP_K/r = 80/\$20 = 4$.

(b) The firm can maximize output or minimize costs by hiring fewer workers and renting more machines. Since the firm produces in stage II of production for both labor and capital, as the firm employs fewer workers, the marginal product of the last remaining worker rises. However, as the firm rents more machines, the marginal product of the last machine rented declines. This process should continue until $MP_L/w = MP_K/r$. One such point of output maximization or cost minimization might be where:

$$\frac{MP_L}{w} = \frac{90}{\$30} = \frac{MP_K}{r} = \frac{60}{\$20} = 3$$

7.20 (a) Explain how a firm should combine inputs in order to minimize the cost of producing a given level of output or to maximize the output that the firm can produce with a given cost outlay or expenditure. (b) What is the condition for profit maximization? How is this related to the condition for cost minimization?

(a) To minimize the cost of producing a given level of output, the firm must seek the lowest isocost with which it can reach the given isoquant. This occurs at the tangency point of an isocost with the given isoquant. To maximize output for a given cost outlay or expenditure, the firm must seek the highest isoquant it can reach with the given isocost line. This occurs at the tangency point of an isoquant with the given isocost. Thus, in order to minimize the cost of producing a given level of output or to maximize the output with a given cost outlay, or expenditure, the firm must produce at the point at which an isoquant is tangent to an isocost. At the tangency point, the absolute slope of the isoquant ($MRTS = MP_L/MP_K$) is tangent to the absolute slope of the isocost (w/r), so that $\mathrm{MP}_L/w = \mathrm{MP}_K/r$. That is, the marginal product per dollar spent on labor should be the same as the marginal product per dollar spent on capital.

(b) In order to maximize profits a firm should use each input until the marginal revenue product (MRP) of the input is equal to the marginal resource cost (MRC) of the input. But MRP = (MP)(MR) and MRC = p (price of the input, when the input price is constant). Thus the firm should hire labor and rent capital until

$$\mathrm{MRP}_L = (\mathrm{MP}_L)(\mathrm{MR}) = w \quad \text{and} \quad \mathrm{MRP}_K = (\mathrm{MP}_K)(\mathrm{MR}) = r$$

Dividing the first equation by the second gives the condition for the optimal combination of inputs:

$$\frac{\mathrm{MP}_L}{\mathrm{MP}_K} = \frac{w}{r} \quad \text{or} \quad \frac{\mathrm{MP}_L}{w} = \frac{\mathrm{MP}_K}{r}$$

There is an optimal input combination for each level of output (see points T and U in Fig. 7-13), but only at the point at which MRP of each input equals the input price will the firm maximize profits. That is, to maximize profits the firm must produce the profit-maximizing level of output with the optimal input combination. By using each input until its marginal revenue product equals its price, however, both conditions will be met at the same time. That is, the firm will produce the best or profit-maximizing level of output with the optimal input combination.

RETURNS TO SCALE AND EMPIRICAL PRODUCTION FUNCTIONS

7.21 Using the data in Table 7.1, indicate whether we have constant, increasing, or decreasing returns to scale when the firm increases the quantity of labor and capital used from (a) $2L$ and $1K$ to $4L$ and $2K$, (b) $2L$ and $2K$ to $3L$ and $3K$, (c) $2L$ and $2K$ to $4L$ and $4K$, and (d) $3L$ and $3K$ to $6L$ and $6K$.

(a) Doubling (i.e., increasing by 100 percent) the quantity of labor and capital used from $2L$ and $1K$ to $4L$ and $2K$ leads to an increase in output from 4 to 16 units (i.e., by 400 percent). Thus, we have increasing returns to scale in this range of the production function.

(b) With $2L$ and $2K$, output is 12 units. With $3L$ and $3K$ (i.e., with a 50 percent increase in inputs), output increases to 18 units (a 50 percent increase). Thus, we have constant returns to scale in this range of the production function.

(c) Doubling the quantity of labor and capital used from $2L$ and $2K$ to $4L$ and $4K$ leads to a doubling of output also—from $12Q$ to $24Q$. Thus, we also have constant returns to scale in this range of the production function.

(d) Doubling (i.e., increasing by 100 percent) the quantity of labor and capital used from $3L$ and $3K$ to $6L$ and $6K$ leads to an increase in output from 18 to 25 units (a 39 percent increase). Thus, we have decreasing returns to scale in this range of the production function.

7.22 If an estimated Cobb-Douglas production function is $Q = 10K^{0.5}L^{0.7}$, (a) what are the output elasticities of capital and labor? If the firm increases by 10 percent either the quantity of capital used or the quantity of labor used, by how much would output increase? (b) What type of returns to scale does this production function indicate? If the firm increases, at the same time, both the quantity of capital and the quantity of labor used by 10 percent, by how much would output increase? (c) Do increasing returns to scale occur only at low levels of output and decreasing returns to scale only at high levels of output? Why, do you think, do most industries in the United States exhibit near-constant returns to scale?

(a) The output elasticity of capital (E_K) is given by the exponent of K in the estimated production function. Thus, $E_K = a = 0.5$. Similarly, the output elasticity of labor (E_L) is given by the exponent of L in the estimated production function. Thus, $E_L = b = 0.7$. If the firm increases the quantity of capital used in production by 10 percent, but keeps the quantity of labor used constant, output increases by 5 percent. However, if the firm increases the quantity of labor used in production by 10 percent, but keeps the quantity of capital used constant, output increases by 7 percent. Thus, the estimated production function exhibits positive but diminishing returns to both capital and labor.

(b) Since $a + b = 0.5 + 0.7 = 1.2$ and exceeds 1.0, the estimated production function exhibits increasing returns to scale. Thus, if the firm increases the quantities used of both capital and labor by 10 percent, its output would increase by 12 percent.

(c)   In the real world, the forces for increasing and decreasing returns to scale often operate side by side at all or most levels of output, with the former usually overwhelming the latter at low levels of output, and the latter overwhelming the former at very high levels of output. In the United States most industries seem to operate at near-constant returns to scale, where the forces for increasing and decreasing returns to scale are more or less in balance.

7.23   Table 7.8 gives the estimated output elasticities of capital [column (1)], production workers [column (2)], and nonproduction workers [column (3)] for 18 manufacturing industries in the United States for the year 1957. (a) Specify the form in which the Cobb-Douglas production function was estimated.

Table 7.8

Industry	Output Elasticity of			Returns to Scale (1) + (2) + (3)
	Capital (1)	Production Workers (2)	Nonproduction Workers (3)	
Furniture	0.205	0.802	0.102	1.110
Chemicals	0.200	0.553	0.336	1.089
Printing	0.459	0.045	0.574	1.078
Food and beverages	0.555	0.439	0.076	1.070
Rubber and plastics	0.481	1.033	−0.458	1.056
Instruments	0.205	0.819	0.020	1.044
Lumber	0.392	0.504	0.145	1.041
Apparel	0.128	0.437	0.477	1.041
Leather	0.076	0.441	0.523	1.040
Stone, clay, etc.	0.632	0.032	0.366	1.030
Fabricated metals	0.151	0.512	0.364	1.027
Electrical machinery	0.368	0.429	0.229	1.026
Transport equipment	0.234	0.749	0.041	1.024
Nonelectrical machinery	0.404	0.228	0.389	1.021
Textiles	0.121	0.549	0.334	1.004
Paper and pulp	0.420	0.367	0.197	0.984
Primary metals	0.371	0.077	0.509	0.957
Petroleum	0.308	0.546	0.093	0.947

Source: J. Moroney, "Cobb-Douglas Production Functions and Returns to Scale in U.S. Manufacturing Industry," *Western Economic Journal*, December 1967, pp. 39–51.

(b) Indicate by how much the output of furniture would increase on the average by increasing the quantity of capital, production workers, and nonproduction workers by 1 percent, first one at a time and then all together. (c) What is the range of returns to scale in the 18 industries studied? Why do we then say that most industries exhibit near-constant returns to scale?

(a)   The form in which the Cobb-Douglas was estimated to get the results reported in Table 7.8 is

$$\ln Q = \ln A + a \ln K + b \ln L + c \ln L'$$

where L refers to production workers and L' to nonproduction workers.

(b)   From the data in the first row of Table 7.8, we see that by increasing, one at a time, the quantity of capital, and the numbers of production and nonproduction workers by 1 percent, we increase the output of furniture by 0.205 percent, 0.802 percent, and 0.102 percent, respectively. Increasing all three inputs at the same time by 1 percent leads to a rise in $Q = a + b + c = 0.205 + 0.802 + 0.102 = 1.11$ percent. This means that we have slightly increasing returns to scale in furniture production.

(c)   The returns to scale reported in Table 7.8 range from 1.11 (slightly increasing) for furniture to 0.947
      (slightly decreasing) for petroleum. Since they are fairly close to 1, we conclude that most industries in the
      United States seem to exhibit near-constant returns to scale.

7.24 (a) What types of data are required to estimate the Cobb-Douglas production function? (b) What are
      some possible difficulties that may arise in estimating it?

(a)   The Cobb-Douglas production function can be estimated either from data for a single firm, industry, or
      nation over time (i.e., using time-series analysis), or for a number of firms, industries, or nations at one
      point in time (i.e., using cross-sectional data).

(b)   Some of the difficulties that may arise in estimating Cobb-Douglas production functions are as follows:

      1. If the firm produces a number of different products, output may have to be measured in monetary rather
          than in physical units. In time-series analysis, this will require deflating the value of output by a price
          index. In cross-sectional analysis, adjustments will be necessary for price differences of firms and
          industries located in different regions.

      2. Only the capital consumed in the production of the output should be counted, ideally. Since machinery
          and equipment are of different types and ages (vintages) and productiveness, however, the total stock
          of capital in existence must be used instead.

      3. In time-series analysis we must usually include a time trend to take into consideration technological
          changes over time, while in cross-sectional analysis we must be sure that all firms or industries utilize
          the same technology (the best available).

Chapter 8

Cost Theory and Estimation

8.1 THE NATURE OF COSTS

Economic costs include explicit and implicit costs. *Explicit costs* are the actual expenditures of the firm to purchase or hire inputs. *Implicit costs* refer to the value of the inputs owned and used by the firm in its own production activity. The value of these inputs is imputed or estimated by what they could earn in their best alternative use (see Problem 8.1). The firm must pay each input (whether owned or purchased) a price equal to what the same inputs could earn in their best alternative use. This is the *alternative or opportunity cost theory*. Economic or opportunity costs must be distinguished from *accounting costs*, which refer only to the firm's actual expenditures, or explicit costs, incurred for purchased or hired inputs. Accounting or historical costs are important for financial reporting by the firm and for tax purposes. For managerial decision-making purposes, however, economic or opportunity costs are the *relevant cost* concepts to use.

We must also distinguish between marginal and incremental costs. *Marginal cost* refers to the change in total cost for a one-unit change in output. *Incremental cost* is a broader concept and refers to the change in total costs that results from implementing a particular management decision, such as the introduction of a new product line. The costs that are not affected by the decision are irrelevant and are called *sunk costs*.

EXAMPLE 1. Suppose that John Smith, an accountant working for an accounting firm and earning $50,000 per year, is contemplating opening his own accounting office. To do so, he would have to give up his present job and use as his office a store that he owns and rents out for $15,000 per year. Smith estimates that he would earn an income of $100,000 for the year and incur $40,000 of out-of-pocket expenses to hire a secretary, rent office equipment, and pay utility costs and taxes. Should Smith open his own accounting office? The answer is no because his total economic costs of $105,000 (explicit costs of $40,000 plus the implicit costs of $65,000) exceed his total earnings of $100,000.

8.2 SHORT-RUN COST FUNCTIONS

In the short run, some of the firm's inputs are fixed and some are variable, and this leads to fixed and variable costs. *Total fixed costs* (TFC) are the total obligations of the firm per time period for all fixed inputs. *Total variable costs* (TVC) are the total obligations of the firm for all variable inputs. *Total costs* (TC) equal total fixed costs plus total variable costs. That is,

$$TC = TFC + TVC \qquad (8\text{-}1)$$

Within the limits imposed by the given plant and equipment, the firm can vary its output in the short run by varying the quantity of the variable inputs used. This gives rise to the TFC, TVC, and TC schedules or functions. These show the minimum costs (explicit plus implicit) of producing various levels of output. From the total cost curves we can derive the per unit cost curves. *Average fixed cost* (AFC) equals total fixed costs divided by the level of output (Q). *Average variable cost* (AVC) equals total variable costs divided by output. *Average total cost* (ATC) equals total cost divided by output. ATC also equals AFC plus AVC. *Marginal cost* (MC) is the change in TC or TVC per unit change in output. That is,

$$AFC = \frac{TFC}{Q} \qquad (8\text{-}2)$$

$$AVC = \frac{TVC}{Q} \qquad (8\text{-}3)$$

$$ATC = \frac{TC}{Q} = AFC + AVC \qquad (8\text{-}4)$$

$$MC = \frac{\Delta TC}{\Delta Q} = \frac{\Delta TVC}{\Delta Q} \qquad (8\text{-}5)$$

Table 8.1   Total and Per Unit Cost Schedules

Q (1)	TFC (2)	TVC (3)	TC (4)	AFC (5)	AVC (6)	ATC (7)	MC (8)
0	$120	$ 0	$120	—	—	—	—
1	120	60	180	$120	$60	$180	$60
2	120	80	200	60	40	100	20
3	120	90	210	40	30	70	10
4	120	104	224	30	26	56	14
5	120	140	260	24	28	52	36
6	120	210	330	20	35	55	70

EXAMPLE 2.   Table 8.1 gives the hypothetical short-run total and per unit cost schedules of a firm. These are plotted in Figure 8-1. From column (2) of the table we see that TFC are $120 regardless of the level of output. TVC [column (3)] is zero when output is zero and rises as output rises. At point H' (the point of inflection in the top panel of Fig. 8-1), the law of diminishing returns begins to operate, and the TVC curve faces up or increases at a growing rate. The TC curve has the same shape as the TVC curve but is $120 (the TFC) above it at each output level. MC is plotted halfway between the various levels of output in the bottom panel of Fig. 8-1. The AVC, ATC, and MC curves are U-shaped. AFC is equal to the vertical distance between the ATC and AVC curves. Graphically, AVC is the slope of a ray from the origin to the TVC curve, ATC is the slope of a ray from the origin to the TC curve, and the MC is the slope of the TC or TVC curve. Note that the MC curve reaches its minimum at a lower level of output than, and intercepts from below, the AVC and ATC curves at their lowest point. The U-shape of the AVC and MC curves can be explained, respectively, from the inverted U-shape of the AP and MP curves (see Problem 8.4).

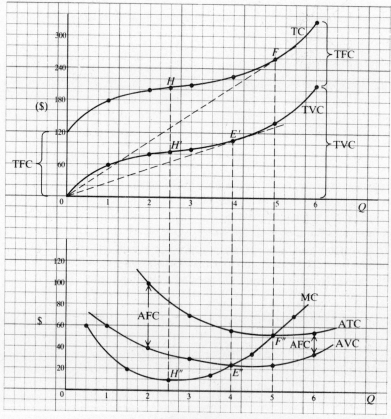

Fig. 8-1

8.3 LONG-RUN COST FUNCTIONS

The long run is the time period during which all inputs and costs are variable (i.e., the firm faces no fixed inputs or costs). The firm's *long-run total cost* (LTC) curve is derived from the firm's expansion path and shows the minimum long-run total costs of producing various levels of output. From the LTC curve we can then derive the firm's *long-run average cost* (LAC) and *long-run marginal cost* (LMC) curves. LAC is equal to LTC divided by output (Q) and is given by the slope of a ray from the origin to the LTC curve. That is,

$$LAC = \frac{LTC}{Q} \tag{8-6}$$

whereas LMC measures the change in LTC per unit change in output and is given by the slope of the LTC curve. That is,

$$LMC = \frac{\Delta LTC}{\Delta Q} \tag{8-7}$$

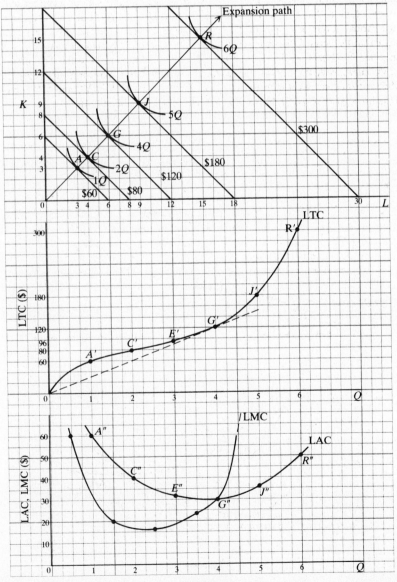

Fig. 8-2

132   COST THEORY AND ESTIMATION   [CHAP. 8

EXAMPLE 3. The top panel of Fig. 8-2 shows the expansion path of the firm. Point A shows that the optimal combination of inputs to produce one unit of output ($1Q$) is three units of labor ($3L$) and three units of capital ($3K$). If the wage of labor (w) is $10 per unit and the rental price of capital (r) is also $10 per unit, the minimum total cost of producing $1Q$ is $60. This is shown as point A' on the long-run total cost (LTC) curve in the middle panel. Other points on the LTC curve are similarly obtained. [At point E' on the LTC curve the firm uses $4.8L$ and $4.8K$ to produce $3Q$, the isoquant for $3Q$ (and, hence, E') are not shown in order not to clutter the figure.] Note that the LTC curve starts at the origin because there are no fixed costs in the long run. The LAC to produce $1Q$ is obtained by dividing the LTC of $60 (point A' on the LTC curve in the middle panel) by 1. This is plotted as point A'' in the bottom panel. Note that the LAC curve declines up to point G'' ($4Q$) because of increasing returns to scale and rises thereafter because of decreasing returns to scale. For an increase in output from 0 to $1Q$, LTC increases from $0 to $60. Therefore, LMC is $60 and is plotted at $0.5Q$ (i.e., halfway between $0Q$ and $1Q$) in the bottom panel. The LMC curve intersects the LAC curve from below at the lowest point (G'') on the LAC curve.

8.4 PLANT SIZE AND ECONOMIES OF SCALE

The long-run average cost (LAC) curve is the tangent or "envelope" to the short-run average cost (SAC) curves and shows the lowest average cost of producing each level of output when the firm can build any scale of plant. If the firm can build only a few scales of plants, its LAC curve will not be smooth as in the bottom panel of Fig. 8-2 but will have kinks at the points where the SAC curves cross (see Example 4). The firm operates in the short run and plans for the long run (the *planning horizon*). Declining LACs reflect increasing returns to scale. These arise because as the scale of operation increases, a greater division of labor and greater specialization can take place, and more specialized and productive machinery can be used (technological reasons). Furthermore, large firms can receive quantity discounts by purchasing raw material in bulk, can usually borrow at lower rates than small firms, and can achieve economies in their promotional efforts (financial reasons). However, rising LAC reflects decreasing returns to scale. These arise because, as the scale of operation increases, effective management of the firm becomes ever more difficult [see Problem 8.11(d)]. In the real world, the LAC curve is often found to have a nearly flat bottom and to be L-shaped rather than U-shaped.

EXAMPLE 4. If the firm can build only the four scales of plant given by SAC_1, SAC_2, SAC_3, and SAC_4 in Fig. 8-3, the LAC curve of the firm is $A''B*C''E*G''J*R''$. This shows that the minimum LAC of producing $1Q$ is $60 and arises when the firm operates plant 1 at point A''. The firm can produce $1.5Q$ at LAC = $55 by utilizing either plant 1 or plant 2 at point $B*$. To produce $2Q$, the firm will utilize plant 2 at point C'' ($40) rather than plant 1 at point $C*$ (the lowest point on SAC_1, which refers to the average cost of $53). If the firm could build many more scales of plant, the kinks at points $B*$, $E*$, and $J*$ would become less pronounced and at the limit would disappear, thus giving a smooth LAC curve (as in the bottom panel of Fig. 8-2).

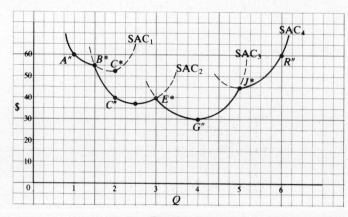

Fig. 8-3

8.5 COST-VOLUME-PROFIT ANALYSIS AND OPERATING LEVERAGE

Cost-volume-profit (or break-even) analysis examines the relationship among total revenue, total costs, and total profits of the firm at various levels of output. This technique is often used by business executives to determine the sales volume required for the firm in order to break even, as well as to determine the total profits and losses at other sales levels. The analysis utilizes a chart in which the total revenue (TR) and the total cost (TC) curves are represented by straight lines, and the break-even output (Q_B) is determined at their intersection (see Example 5). Q_B can also be determined algebraically by

$$Q_B = \frac{\text{TFC}}{P - \text{AVC}} \tag{8-8}$$

where TFC refers to total fixed costs, P refers to price, and AVC to average variable costs. The denominator in equation (8-8), i.e., $P - \text{AVC}$, is called the *contribution margin per unit* because it represents the portion of the selling price that can be applied to cover the fixed costs of the firm and to provide for profits. The target output (Q_T) to earn a specific target profit (π_T) is then given by

$$Q_T = \frac{\text{TFC} + \pi_T}{P - \text{AVC}} \tag{8-9}$$

The ratio of the firm's total fixed costs to total variable costs is called its *operating leverage*. When a firm becomes more highly leveraged, its total fixed costs increase, its average variable costs decline, its break-even output is larger, and its profitability becomes more variable. The *degree of operating leverage* (DOL), or sales elasticity of profits, measures the percentage change in the firm's total profits resulting from a one-percentage-point change in the firm's output or sales and can be obtained from

$$\text{DOL} = \frac{Q(P - \text{AVC})}{Q(P - \text{AVC}) - \text{TFC}} \tag{8-10}$$

Linear cost-volume-profit analysis is applicable only if prices and average variable costs are constant.

EXAMPLE 5. In Fig. 8-4, the slope of the TR curve refers to $P = \$20$, the price at which the firm can sell its output. TFC = \$300 (the vertical intercept of the TC curve) and AVC = \$10 (the slope of the TC curve). The firm breaks even (with TR = TC = \$600) at $Q = 30$ (point B in the figure). The firm has losses at smaller outputs and profits at higher outputs. Algebraically,

$$Q_B = \frac{\text{TFC}}{P - \text{AVC}} = \frac{\$300}{\$20 - \$10} = 30$$

The contribution margin per unit (i.e., $P - \text{AVC}$) is \$10.

The target output (Q_T) to earn the target profit of $\pi_T = \$100$ is

$$Q_T = \frac{\text{TFC} + \pi_T}{P - \text{AVC}} = \frac{\$300 + \$100}{\$20 - \$10} = 40$$

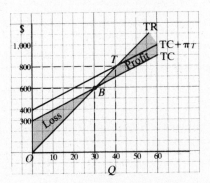

Fig. 8-4

This is shown at the intersection of the TR and TC + π_T curves in Fig. 8-4. At $Q = 50$ on the TC curve,

$$\text{DOL} = \frac{Q\,(P - \text{AVC})}{Q\,(P - \text{AVC}) - \text{TFC}} = \frac{50\,(\$20 - \$10)}{50\,(\$20 - \$10) - \$300} = \frac{\$500}{\$200} = 2.5$$

DOL increases as the firm becomes more highly leveraged (i.e., more capital intensive) and as it moves closer to the break-even output (see Problem 8.15). The effect of an increase in P can be shown by increasing the slope of the TR curve; an increase in TFC, by an increase in the vertical intercept of the TC curve; and an increase in AVC, by an increase in the slope of the TC curve. The chart will then show the change in Q_B and the profits or losses at other output or sales levels (see Problem 8.14).

8.6 EMPIRICAL ESTIMATION OF COST FUNCTIONS

The firm's short-run cost functions are usually estimated by regression analysis, whereby total variable costs are regressed on output, input prices, and other operating conditions, for the time period within which the size of the plant is fixed. To do this, opportunity costs must be extracted from the available accounting cost data. Costs must be correctly apportioned to the various products produced and matched to output over time. The period of time for the estimation must be chosen, and costs must be deflated to correct for inflation. While economic theory postulates an S-shaped (cubic) TVC curve, a linear approximation often gives a better empirical fit for the observed range of outputs (see Problem 8.21).

Since the type of product that the firm produces and the technology it uses are likely to change in the long run, the long-run average cost curve is estimated by cross-sectional regression analysis (i.e., with cost-quantity data for a number of firms at a given point in time). Since firms in different geographic areas are likely to pay different prices for their inputs, input prices must be included, together with output, as independent explanatory variables in the regression. The different accounting practices of the firms in the sample must be reconciled, and we must ensure that the firms are operating the optimal scale of plant at the optimal level of output (i.e., at the point on the SAC curve of the firm that forms part of its LAC curve). Empirical studies indicate that the LAC curve is L-shaped (see Problem 8.13).

The LAC curve can also be estimated by the *engineering technique* and the *survival technique*. The first method estimates the LAC curve by determining the optimal input combinations necessary to produce various levels of output, given input prices and the available technology. The survival technique determines the existence of increasing, decreasing, or constant returns to scale depending on whether the share of industry output coming from large firms (as compared with the share of industry output coming from small firms) increases, decreases, or remains the same over time.

Glossary

Accounting costs   Historical explicit costs.

Alternative or opportunity cost theory   The theory that postulates that the cost to the firm of using a purchased or owned input is equal to what the input could earn in its best alternative use.

Average fixed cost (AFC)   Total fixed costs divided by output.

Average total cost (ATC)   Total costs divided by output. Also equals AFC + AVC.

Average variable cost (AVC)   Total variable costs divided by output.

Contribution margin per unit   The excess of the selling price of the product over the average variable costs of the firm (i.e., $P - \text{AVC}$) that can be applied to cover the fixed costs of the firm and to provide profits.

Cost-volume-profit or break-even analysis   A method that uses the total revenue and total cost functions of a firm to estimate the output at which the firm breaks even or earns a target profit.

Degree of operating leverage (DOL)   The percentage change in the firm's profits divided by the percentage change in output or sales; the sales elasticity of profits.

Economic costs   The sum of explicit and implicit costs.

Engineering technique   The method of estimating the long-run average cost curve of the firm from a determination of the optimal input combinations necessary to produce various levels of output, given input prices and the present technology.

Explicit costs   The actual expenditures of the firm to hire or purchase inputs.

Implicit costs   The value of the inputs (as determined by their best alternative use) that are owned and used by the firm.

Incremental cost   The total increase in costs for implementing a particular managerial decision.

Marginal cost (MC)   The change in total costs or total variable costs per unit change in output.

Operating leverage   The ratio of the firm's total fixed costs to its total variable costs.

Planning horizon   The period of time of the long run, when the firm can build any desired scale of plant.

Relevant costs   The costs that should be considered in making a managerial decision; economic or opportunity costs.

Sunk costs   The costs that are not affected by a particular managerial decision.

Survival technique   The method of determining the existence of increasing, decreasing, or constant returns to scale depending on whether the share of industry output coming from large firms (as compared with the share of industry output coming from small firms) increases, decreases, or remains the same over time.

Total costs (TC)   Total fixed costs plus total variable costs.

Total fixed costs (TFC)   The total obligations of the firm per time period for all the fixed inputs the firm uses.

Total variable costs (TVC)   The total obligations of the firm per time period for all the variable inputs the firm uses.

Review Questions

1.   Economic costs include

   (*a*)   explicit costs.

   (*b*)   implicit costs.

   (*c*)   opportunity costs.

   (*d*)   all of the above.

   Ans.   (*d*) See Section 8.1 and Example 1.

2.   The costs to implement a managerial strategy are called

   (*a*)   marginal costs.

   (*b*)   incremental costs.

   (*c*)   sunk costs.

   (*d*)   explicit costs.

   Ans.   (*b*) See Section 8.1 and Example 1.

3.   Which of the following statements is false?

   (*a*)   Economic costs are sometimes equal to accounting costs.

   (*b*)   Accounting profits can correspond to economic losses.

   (*c*)   Accounting profits are positive if economic losses exceed implicit costs.

   (*d*)   Accounting costs equal economic costs if implicit costs are zero.

   Ans.   (*c*) See Section 8.1 and Example 1.

4.   When the law of diminishing returns begins to operate, the TVC curve begins to

    (*a*)   fall at an increasing rate.

    (*b*)   rise at a decreasing rate.

    (*c*)   fall at a decreasing rate.

    (*d*)   rise at an increasing rate.

    Ans.   (*b*) See Example 1 and Fig. 8-1.

5.   At the point where a straight line from the origin is tangent to the TC curve, ATC

    (*a*)   is at its minimum.

    (*b*)   equals MC.

    (*c*)   equals AVC plus AFC.

    (*d*)   is all of the above.

    Ans.   (*d*) See Section 8.2 and Fig. 8-1.

6.   Which of the following statements is false?

    (*a*)   The expansion path shows the minimum cost of producing various levels of output.

    (*b*)   The LTC curve shows the optimal input combination needed to produce each level of output.

    (*c*)   The LAC curve declines as long as the LMC curve is below it.

    (*d*)   The LAC curve is U-shaped because of the law of diminishing returns.

    Ans.   (*c*) See Section 8.3 and Fig. 8-2.

7.   The LAC curve is at its minimum when

    (*a*)   a ray from the origin is tangent to the LTC curve.

    (*b*)   the slope of the LTC curve is minimum.

    (*c*)   the slope of the expansion path is 1.

    (*d*)   all of the above.

    Ans.   (*a*) See Section 8.3 and Fig. 8-2.

8.   The LAC curve is

    (*a*)   intersected by the LMC curve from below at its lowest point.

    (*b*)   the envelope to the SAC curves.

    (*c*)   often L-shaped and has a flat bottom in the real world.

    (*d*)   all of the above.

    Ans.   (*d*) See Sections 8.3 and 8.4.

9.   Decreasing returns to scale arise because

    (*a*)   of division of labor.

    (*b*)   as the scale of operation increases, effective management of the firm becomes more difficult.

    (*c*)   of the use of more specialized machinery.

    (*d*)   of bulk purchases of raw materials.

    Ans.   (*b*) See Section 8.4.

10.   Cost-volume-profit analysis can be used to determine

    (*a*)   the break-even output.

    (*b*)   the target output the firm needs in order to earn a target profit.

    (*c*)   the effect of increasing the operating leverage of the firm.

    (*d*)   all of the above.

    Ans.   (*d*) See Section 8.5.

11.   Which of the following statements is false?

    (*a*)   Cost-volume-profit analysis can be used only when P and AVC are constant.

    (*b*)   Operating leverage refers to the ratio of the firm's fixed-to-variable costs.

    (*c*)   DOL refers to the profit elasticity of sales.

    (*d*)   If the firm becomes less highly leveraged, its DOL decreases.

    Ans.   (*c*) DOL refers to the *sales* elasticity of profit; see Section 8.5.

12.   Which of the following statements is false?

    (*a*)   The short-run total variable cost curve is estimated by time-series regression analysis.

    (*b*)   Short-run cost curves can also be estimated by use of engineering studies or survival techniques.

    (*c*)   The most common method of estimating the long-run average cost curve is by cross-sectional regression analysis.

    (*d*)   Empirical studies seem to indicate that short-run and long-run marginal costs are constant over the observed range of outputs.

    Ans. (*b*) See Section 8.6.

Solved Problems

THE NATURE OF COSTS

8.1   (*a*) What is meant by implicit costs? Why must implicit costs be included among the costs of production? Give some examples of implicit costs. (*b*) What is the distinction between economic costs and accounting costs? (*c*) Which are important for calculating the economic profits of the firm?

    (*a*)   Implicit costs refer to the value of the inputs owned and used by a firm in its own production activity. Even though the firm does not incur any actual expenditures when using these inputs, they are not free, since the firm could sell or rent them out to other firms. The amount for which the firm could sell or rent out these owned inputs to other firms represents a cost of production for the firm owning and using them. Implicit costs include the highest wage that the entrepreneur could earn in the best alternative employment (say, in managing another firm for somebody else), the highest return that the firm could receive from investing its capital in the most rewarding alternative use, or from renting its land and buildings to the highest bidder rather than using them itself.

    (*b*)   Economic costs refer to alternative or opportunity costs. These include not only the explicit or out-of-pocket expenditures of the firm to purchase or hire inputs but also the implicit costs or the value (imputed from their best alternative use) of inputs owned and used by the firm in its production processes. Accounting costs, however, are the historical explicit costs of the firm. These are used for the firm's financial reporting to stockholders and for tax purposes. For managerial decision making, however, the firm must use economic costs.

(c) Profits equal total revenue minus total costs. But costs refer to the economic rather than the accounting costs. That is, in calculating profits, the firm must include among its costs not only the explicit, or accounting, costs but also its implicit costs. Thus, it is quite possible that accounting profits might actually involve economic losses for the firm.

8.2 (a) What is the distinction between marginal cost and incremental costs? (b) How are sunk costs treated in managerial decision making? Why?

(a) Marginal cost is the change in total costs per unit change in output. Incremental costs refer to the total increase in costs resulting from the implementation of a particular managerial decision, such as the introduction of a new product, entrance into a new market, improvement in the quality of the firm's product. While the two concepts are related, incremental costs are a broader concept than marginal cost and may involve no increase, or a large increase, in output (if, for example, the firm simply wishes to change the quality, but not the quantity, of its output).

(b) Sunk costs are those costs that are incurred regardless of the current managerial decisions of the firm. Thus, sunk costs are entirely irrelevant in determining the best course of action by the firm in the present period. For example, it pays for the firm to produce an output even if a loss results, as long as the loss is smaller than the sunk costs. The reason is that if the firm decided not to produce the output, it would incur the larger loss equal to its sunk costs.

8.3 Angela Bates, who works in a duplicating (photocopying) establishment for $20,000 per year, decides to open a small duplicating place of her own. She runs the operation by herself without hired help and invests no money of her own. She rents the premises for $15,000 per year and the machines for $25,000 per year. She spends $10,000 per year on supplies (paper, ink, envelopes), electricity, telephone, and so on. During the year her gross earnings are $75,000. (a) How much are the explicit costs of this business? (b) How much are the implicit costs? (c) Should Bates remain in business after the year, if she has no strong preference between working for herself and working for others in a similar capacity?

(a) The explicit costs are $15,000 + $25,000 + $10,000 = $50,000.

(b) The implicit costs are equal to the forgone earnings of $20,000 in the previous occupation.

(c) The total costs are equal to the explicit costs of $50,000 plus the implicit costs of $20,000 or $70,000. Since the total earnings, or revenues, are $75,000, Bates earns an economic profit of $5,000 for the year. Thus, it pays for her to remain in business.

SHORT-RUN COST FUNCTIONS

8.4 (a) Identify the most important fixed and variable costs of a firm. (b) Why do cost curves show the minimum cost of producing various levels of output? (c) What costs are included in cost functions? (d) What assumption is made with regard to input prices in defining a firm's cost functions? What happens if the assumption does not hold?

(a) Fixed costs include interest payments on borrowed capital, rental expenditures on leased plant and equipment (or depreciation associated with the passage of time on owned plant and equipment), property taxes, and those salaries (such as for top management) that are fixed by contract and must be paid over the life of the contract whether the firm produces or not. Variable costs include payments for raw materials, fuels, depreciation associated with the use of the plant and equipment, most labor costs, and excise taxes.

(b) Cost curves show the minimum costs of producing various levels of output because the curves are derived from the optimal or least-cost input combinations needed to produce each level of output (as explained in Section 7.3).

(c) In defining the firm's cost functions, all inputs are valued at their opportunity cost, which includes both explicit and implicit costs.

(d) Input prices are assumed to remain constant regardless of the quantity demanded of each input by the firm. The shape of the cost curves, therefore, reflects only the operation of the law of diminishing returns. If input prices increase when the firm demands a greater quantity of the inputs to expand output, all of the firm's cost curves shift up. If input prices decline, the firm's cost curves shift down.

8.5 Given the following total cost schedule of a firm, (a) derive the firm's total fixed cost and total variable cost schedules, and from them derive the average fixed cost, average variable cost, average total cost, and marginal cost schedules. (b) Plot all the schedules of part (a) on a figure similar to Fig. 8-1.

Q	0	1	2	3	4	5	6
TC	$60	90	100	105	116	135	180

(a) At $Q = 0$, TC = TFC = \$60. The TVC schedule of the firm is obtained by subtracting TFC = \$60 from the TC value at each level of output. AFC = TFC/Q; AVC = TVC/Q; ATC = TC/Q; MC = ΔTVC/ΔQ = ΔTC/ΔQ. All of these schedules are given in Table 8.2.

(b) See Fig. 8-5.

Table 8.2

Q (1)	TFC (2)	TVC (3)	TC (4)	AFC (5)	AVC (6)	ATC (7)	MC (8)
0	$60	$ 0	$ 60	—	—	—	—
1	60	30	90	$60	$30	$90	$30
2	60	40	100	30	20	50	10
3	60	45	105	20	15	35	5
4	60	56	116	15	14	29	11
5	60	75	135	12	15	27	19
6	60	120	180	10	20	30	45

8.6 (a) Why does the ATC curve reach its lowest point at a higher level of output than the AVC curve?
(b) Why does the MC curve intersect the AVC and ATC curves from below at their lowest points?
(c) How can the AFC, AVC, ATC, and MC curves be derived geometrically?

(a) The ATC curve reaches its lowest point at a higher level of output than the AVC curve because for a short period the decline in AFC exceeds the rise in AVC.

(b) The MC curve intersects the AVC and the ATC curves from below at their lowest points because for AVC and ATC to decline MC must be lower in value than they are, and for AVC and ATC to rise, MC must be higher. At the lowest point of the AVC and ATC curves, AVC and ATC are neither rising nor declining and so MC must equal them.

(c) AFC, AVC, and ATC at each level of output (Q) equals the slope of a ray from the origin to the TFC, TVC, and TC curves, respectively, while MC at each level of Q equals the slope of the TVC or TC curves at that Q.

8.7 Assuming that labor is the only variable input and the wage rate is constant, explain the reason for the U-shape of the (a) AVC curve and (b) MC curve.

(a) With labor as the only variable input, TVC for the output level (Q) equals the wage rate (w) times the quantity of labor (L) used. Thus:

$$\text{AVC} = \frac{\text{TVC}}{Q} = \frac{wL}{Q} = \frac{w}{Q/L} = \frac{w}{\text{AP}_L}$$

Since the average physical product of labor (AP_L or Q/L) usually first rises, reaches a maximum, and then falls (see Section 7.2) with w constant, it follows that the AVC curve first falls, reaches a minimum, and

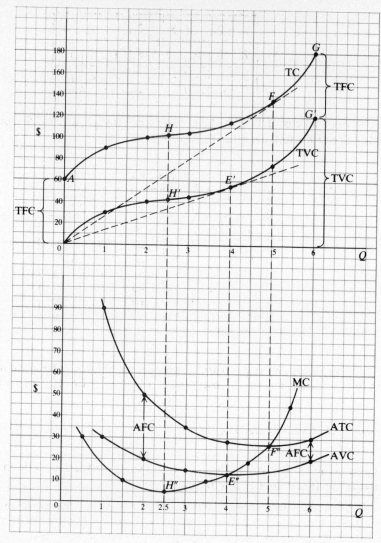

Fig. 8-5

then rises. Since the AVC curve is U-shaped, the ATC curve is also U-shaped. The ATC curve continues to fall after the AVC curve begins to rise as long as the decline in AFC exceeds the rise in AVC.

(b) The U-shape of the MC curve can be explained as follows:

$$MC = \frac{\Delta TVC}{\Delta Q} = \frac{\Delta(wL)}{\Delta Q} = \frac{w(\Delta L)}{\Delta Q} = \frac{w}{\Delta Q/\Delta L} = \frac{w}{MP_L}$$

Since the marginal product of labor (MP_L or $\Delta Q/\Delta L$) first rises, reaches a maximum, and then falls, it follows that the MC curve first falls, reaches a minimum, and then rises. Thus, the rising portion of the MC curve reflects the operation of the law of diminishing returns.

LONG-RUN COST FUNCTIONS

8.8 The following table shows the optimal combinations of labor (L) and capital (K) a firm must use in order to produce various levels of output, given a wage rate (w) of $5 and a rental price of capital (r) of $5. Derive the firm's long-run total, average, and marginal cost schedules.

L	0	2	3	3.3	4	6	12
K	0	2	3	3.3	4	6	12
Q	0	1	2	3	4	5	6

The long-run total cost (LTC), the long-run average cost (LAC), and the long-run marginal cost (LMC) schedules of the firm are given in Table 8.3.

Table 8.3

L	K	Q	LTC	LAC	LMC
0	0	0	$ 0		
2	2	1	20	$20	$20
3	3	2	30	15	10
3.3	3.3	3	33	11	3
4	4	4	40	10	7
6	6	5	60	12	20
12	12	6	120	20	60

The LTC of producing any level of output is obtained by adding the product of the optimal quantity of each input used times the input price. For example, the LTC of $20 to produce $1Q$ is obtained by

$$(2L)(\$5) + (2K)(\$5) = \$20$$

LAC = LTC/Q and LMC = ΔLTC/ΔQ.

8.9 Draw a figure similar to Fig. 8-2 in Example 3, showing the expansion path, the LTC curve, and the LMC curve of the firm described in Problem 8.8.

See Fig. 8-6. The top panel of the figure shows the expansion path of the firm. The path gives the optimal input combination to produce each level of output. (The isocost for $33 and the optimal combination of 3.3L and 3.3K to produce $3Q$ are not shown in order not to clutter the figure.) The middle panel shows the firm's LTC curve. This gives the minimum LTC to produce each level of output. The LTC curve starts at the origin because LTC = 0 when Q = 0 (i.e., there are no fixed costs in the long run).

The LAC curve in the bottom panel declines up to Q = 4 because of increasing returns to scale and rises thereafter because of decreasing returns to scale. This contrasts with the U-shape of the short-run average cost curve, which is based on the law of diminishing returns. The LAC curve declines as long as the LMC curve is below it and rises when the LMC curve is above it. Thus, the LMC curve intersects the LAC curve from below at the lowest point of LAC.

8.10 Electrical utility companies usually operate their most modern and efficient equipment around the clock and use their older and less efficient equipment only to meet periods of peak demand for electricity. (*a*) What does this imply for the short-run marginal cost of these firms? (*b*) Why do these firms not replace all of their older equipment with newer equipment in the long run?

(*a*) In order to expand output in the short run to meet peak electricity demand, electrical utility companies bring into operation older and less efficient equipment, causing their short-run marginal costs to rise sharply.

(*b*) New generating equipment would have to be run around the clock or nearly so for its average fixed costs to be sufficiently low to make its average total cost lower than for older equipment. To meet only peak demand, older and fully depreciated equipment is cheaper.

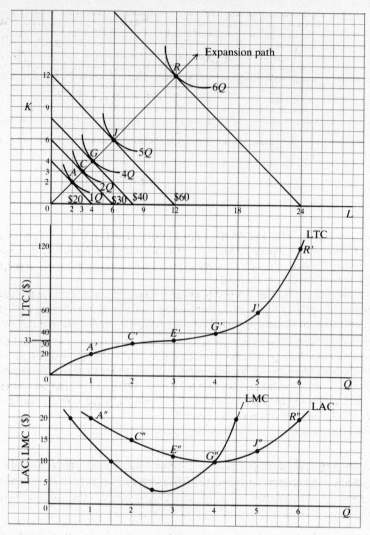

Fig. 8-6

PLANT SIZE AND ECONOMIES OF SCALE

8.11 (*a*) Redraw the LAC curve in the bottom panel of Fig. 8-6 as a dashed curve and superimpose on it short-run average cost (SAC) curves showing that plant 1 is the best plant for output levels between $1Q$ and $1.5Q$, plant 2 is the best plant for output levels between $1.5Q$ and $3Q$, plant 3 is the best plant for output levels between $3Q$ and $5Q$, and plant 4 is the best plant for output levels between $5Q$ and $6Q$. (*b*) What would be the LAC of the firm if the four plants in the figure in part (*a*) were the only plants that the firm could build in the long run? Under what conditions would the LAC curve of the firm be the smooth dashed LAC curve? Why is the long run referred to as the "planning horizon" of the firm? (*c*) At what output level in the figure in part (*a*) would the firm operate at the lowest point on the SAC curve? At what point on its SAC curve would the firm operate at lower levels of output? at higher levels of output?

(*a*) See Fig. 8-7.

(*b*) If the four plants shown in Fig. 8-7 are the only plants that the firm can build in the long run, the LAC curve of the firm would be $A''B*C''E*G''J*R''$. The LAC curve of the firm would be the smooth dashed

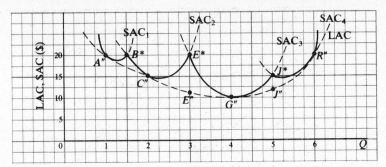

Fig. 8-7

LAC curve (i.e., $A''C''E''G''J''R''$) only if the firm could build a very large or an infinite number of plants in the long run. Each point on the LAC curve would then be formed by the tangency of the SAC curve that represents the most appropriate plant to produce for that specific level of output. The LAC curve would then be the "envelope" for the SAC curves.

The long run is often referred to as the planning horizon because in the long run the firm can build the plant that minimizes the cost of producing any anticipated level of output. Once the plant has been built, the firm operates in the short run. Thus, the firm plans for the long run and operates in the short run.

(c) The firm operates at the lowest point on the SAC curve only at $Q = 4$ (point G'' on SAC$_3$ in Fig. 8-7). At outputs smaller than $Q = 4$, the firm operates on the declining portion of the relevant SAC curve, while at outputs larger than $Q = 4$ the firm operates on the rising portion of the appropriate SAC curve (see Fig. 8-7). Note that if the firm is uncertain about the level of demand and production in the future, it may want to build a more flexible plant for the *range* of anticipated outputs, rather than the optimal plant for producing a *particular* level of output at an even lower cost.

8.12 (a) Explain why a declining LAC curve implies increasing returns to scale and a rising LAC curve implies decreasing returns to scale. (b) What are the technological reasons for increasing returns to scale? How do they operate? (c) What are the financial reasons for increasing returns to scale? (d) Explain the reason for decreasing returns to scale.

(a) Economies of scale refer to the situation in which output grows proportionately faster than the use of inputs. Suppose, on the one hand, output more than doubles with a doubling of inputs. With input prices constant, LAC declines. Thus, declining LAC implies increasing returns to scale. On the other hand, decreasing returns to scale refers to the situation in which output grows proportionately less than the use of inputs. With input prices constant, LAC rises. Thus, a rising LAC implies decreasing returns to scale.

(b) At the technological level, economies of scale arise because as the scale of operation increases, a greater division of labor and greater specialization can take place, and more specialized and productive machinery can be used. Specifically, in a large-scale operation, each worker can be assigned to perform a repetitive task rather than numerous different ones. This results in increased proficiency and the avoidance of the time lost in moving from one machine to another. At higher scales of operation, more specialized and productive machinery can also be used. For example, using a conveyor belt to unload a small truck may not be justified, but it greatly increases efficiency in unloading a whole train or ship. Furthermore, some physical properties of equipment and machinery also lead to increasing returns to scale. For example, doubling the diameter of a pipeline more than doubles the flow without doubling costs, doubling the weight of a ship more than doubles its capacity to transport cargo without doubling costs, and so on. Thus, per unit costs decline. Firms also need fewer supervisors, fewer spare parts, and smaller inventories per unit of output as the scale of operation increases.

(c) Because of bulk purchases, larger firms are more likely than smaller firms to receive quantity discounts in purchasing raw materials and other intermediate (i.e., semiprocessed) inputs. Large firms can usually place bonds and stocks more favorably and receive bank loans at lower interest rates than smaller firms. Large firms can also achieve economies of scale or decreasing costs in advertising and other promotional efforts.

(d) Decreasing returns to scale arise primarily because, as the scale of operations increases, effective management of the firm and coordination of its various operations and divisions become ever more difficult. The number of meetings, the paper work, the telephone bills, etc., increase more than proportionately to the increase in the scale of operations, and it becomes increasingly difficult for those in top management to ensure that their directives and guidelines are being properly carried out by their subordinates. Thus, efficiency decreases and cost per unit tends to rise.

8.13 (a) Draw a figure showing one LAC curve that is U-shaped, one that is L-shaped, and one that is constantly declining. (b) Under what conditions would each of these LAC curves prevail?

(a) See Fig. 8-8.

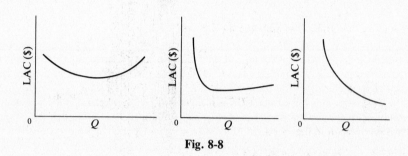

Fig. 8-8

(b) The U-shaped LAC curve in the left-hand panel of Fig. 8-8 arises when increasing returns to scale prevail at low levels of output and decreasing returns to scale prevail at high levels of output. The lowest point on the LAC curve occurs at the output level at which the forces of increasing and decreasing returns to scale just balance each other. The L-shaped LAC curve in the middle panel arises when economies of scale are rather quickly exhausted, and constant or near-constant returns to scale prevail over a considerable range of outputs. This situation is often encountered in the real world. In industries characterized by this situation, small firms coexist with much larger ones. To be noted, however, is that the inability to observe rising LAC in the real world may occur because firms avoid expanding output when LAC begins to rise rapidly.

The right-hand panel shows an LAC curve that declines continuously as the firm expands output, to the point at which a single firm could satisfy the total market for the product or service more efficiently than two or more firms. These cases are usually referred to as "natural monopolies" and often arise in the provision of electricity, public transportation, etc. (public utilities). In such cases the local government often allows a single firm to supply the service to the entire market but subjects the firm to regulation (i.e., regulates the price, or rate, charged for the service).

8.14 Draw a figure showing the LTC curve for constant returns to scale. On a separate panel show the corresponding LAC and LMC curves. On still another panel show the LAC and LMC curves and two SAC curves.

With constant returns to scale the LTC curve is a straight line through the origin. This is shown in the left-hand panel of Fig. 8-9. Since the LTC curve is a straight line through the origin, LAC = LMC and equals the

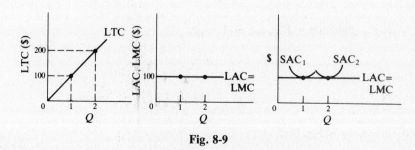

Fig. 8-9

constant slope of the LTC curve. This is shown on the middle panel of the figure. Finally, since the LAC curve is horizontal, the SAC curves are tangent to the LAC curve at the lowest point on the SAC curves (see the right-hand panel of the figure).

COST-VOLUME-PROFIT ANALYSIS

8.15 For the firm in Example 5 for which TFC = $300, P = $20, and AVC = $10, determine the break-even output and the output that would lead to a total profit (π_T) of $100, and draw a chart showing your results if (a) the total fixed costs of the firm decline to TFC′ = $200, (b) TFC = $300, but average variable costs decline to AVC′ = $5, (c) TFC = $300, AVC = $10, but the firm raises its price to P^* = $15.

(a) With TFC′ = $200, P = $20, and AVC = $10

$$Q_{B'} = \frac{TFC'}{P - AVC} = \frac{\$200}{\$20 - \$10} = 20$$

$$Q_{T'} = \frac{TFC' + \pi_T}{P - AVC} = \frac{\$200 + \$100}{\$20 - \$10} = 30$$

These are shown in Fig. 8-10.

(b) With TFC = $300, P = $20, and AVC′ = $5

$$Q_{B''} = \frac{TFC}{P - AVC'} = \frac{\$300}{\$20 - \$5} = 20$$

$$Q_{T''} = \frac{TFC + \pi_T}{P - AVC'} = \frac{\$300 + \$100}{\$20 - \$5} = 26.7$$

These are shown in Fig. 8-11.

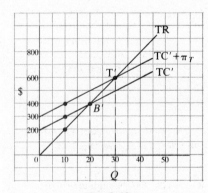

Fig. 8-10

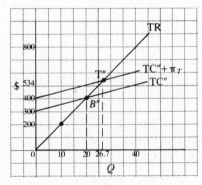

Fig. 8-11

(c) With TFC = $300, P^* = $30, and AVC = $20

$$Q_{B*} = \frac{TFC}{P^* - AVC} = \frac{\$300}{\$30 - \$10} = 15$$

$$Q_{T*} = \frac{TFC + \pi_T}{P^* - AVC} = \frac{\$300 + \$100}{\$30 - \$10} = 20$$

These are shown in Fig. 8-12.

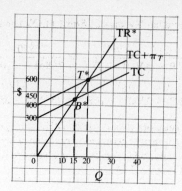

Fig. 8-12

8.16 Two firms in the same industry sell their product at $P = \$20$ per unit but in one firm TFC = $40 and AVC = $10 while in the other TFC$'$ = $90 and AVC$'$ = $5. (a) Determine the break-even output of each firm; why is the break-even output of the second firm larger than that of the first firm? (b) Find the degree of operating leverage for each firm at $Q = 7$ and at $Q = 8$. Why is the degree of operating leverage greater for the second than for the first firm? Why is the degree of operating leverage greater at $Q = 7$ than at $Q = 8$?

(a) The break-even output for the first firm (Q_B) and the second firm ($Q_{B'}$) are

$$Q_B = \frac{\text{TFC}}{P - \text{AVC}} = \frac{\$40}{\$20 - \$10} = 4$$

$$Q_{B'} = \frac{\text{TFC}'}{P - \text{AVC}'} = \frac{\$90}{\$20 - \$5} = 6$$

These are shown in Fig. 8-13.

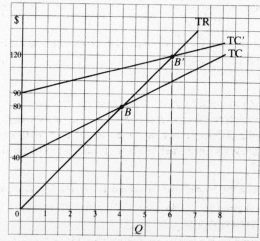

Fig. 8-13

The break-even output of the second firm (i.e., the more highly leveraged firm) is larger than that of the first firm because the second firm has larger overhead costs. Thus, it takes a greater level of output for the second firm to cover its larger overhead costs.

(b) At $Q = 7$, the degrees of operating leverage of firm 1 (DOL) and firm 2 (DOL') are

$$\text{DOL} = \frac{Q(P - \text{AVC})}{Q(P - \text{AVC}) - \text{TFC}} = \frac{7(\$20 - \$10)}{7(\$20 - \$10) - \$40} = \frac{\$70}{\$30} = 2.33$$

$$\text{DOL}' = \frac{Q(P - \text{AVC}')}{Q(P - \text{AVC}') - \text{TFC}'} = \frac{7(\$20 - \$5)}{7(\$20 - \$5) - \$90} = \frac{\$105}{\$15} = 7$$

Thus, the more highly leveraged firm has a higher DOL (i.e., greater variability of profits) than the less highly leveraged firm. The reason for this is that firm 2 has a larger contribution margin per unit (i.e., $P - \text{AVC}$) than firm 1. Graphically, this is reflected in a larger difference between the slopes of TR and TC' than between the slopes of TR and TC. At $Q = 8$,

$$\text{DOL} = \frac{Q(P - \text{AVC})}{Q(P - \text{AVC}) - \text{TFC}} = \frac{8(\$20 - \$10)}{8(\$20 - \$10) - \$40} = \frac{\$80}{\$40} = 2$$

$$\text{DOL}' = \frac{Q(P - \text{AVC})}{Q(P - \text{AVC}) - \text{TFC}} = \frac{8(\$20 - \$5)}{8(\$20 - \$5) - \$90} = \frac{\$120}{\$30} = 4$$

Thus, the larger is the level of output, the smaller are DOL and DOL'. The reason for this is that the farther we are from the break-even point the smaller is the percentage change in profits (since the level of profits is higher—see the next problem).

8.17 From the definition of the degree of operating leverage, derive equation (8-10).

The degree of operating leverage (DOL) measures the responsiveness or sensitivity in the firm's total profits (π) to a change in its output or sales (Q). This is nothing else than the sales elasticity of profit and is defined as the percentage change in profit divided by the percentage change in output or sales. That is,

$$\text{DOL} = \frac{\%\Delta\pi}{\%\Delta Q} = \frac{\Delta\pi/\pi}{\Delta Q/Q} = \frac{\Delta\pi}{\Delta Q} \cdot \frac{Q}{\pi}$$

But $\pi = Q(P - \text{AVC}) - \text{TFC}$ and $\Delta\pi = \Delta Q(P - \text{AVC})$. Substituting these values into equation (8-10), we get

$$\text{DOL} = \frac{\Delta Q(P - \text{AVC})Q}{\Delta Q[Q(P - \text{AVC}) - \text{TFC}]} = \frac{Q(P - \text{AVC})}{Q(P - \text{AVC}) - \text{TFC}} \qquad (8\text{-}11)$$

The numerator in equation (8-10) is the total contribution to fixed costs and profits of all units sold by the firm, and the denominator is total (economic) profit.

8.18 If the total revenue (TR) and total cost (TC) curves of the firm are as shown in Fig. 2-3, indicate (a) the outputs (Q) at which the firm breaks even and (b) the output at which the firm earns a profit (π) of $4. (c) What is the difference between the optimization analysis examined in Section 2.3 and the cost-volume-profit analysis examined in Section 8.5? (d) When is a cost-benefit-analysis chart as in Fig. 2-3 appropriate?

(a) The firm breaks even at the output levels at which TR = TC. These are at $Q = 1\frac{1}{4}$ and $3\frac{1}{2}$.

(b) The firm earns a total profit (π) of $4 at $Q = 2\frac{1}{2}$. This is the maximum profit. That is, at $Q = 2\frac{1}{2}$, TR exceeds TC by the greatest amount.

(c) The difference between the optimization analysis examined in Section 2.3 and the cost-volume-profit analysis examined in Section 8.5 is in the objective of the analysis. In optimization analysis the objective is to determine the optimum price and output of the firm. In cost-volume-profit analysis the objective is to determine the output level at which the firm breaks even or earns a desired target profit.

(d) A cost-volume-profit analysis chart as in Fig. 2-3 is appropriate when price and average variable costs are not constant, so that the TR and TC functions are curves rather than straight lines. This is referred to as nonlinear cost-volume-profit analysis.

EMPIRICAL ESTIMATION OF COST FUNCTIONS

8.19 (*a*) Why is knowledge of short-run cost functions essential in managerial decision making? (*b*) What is the most common method of estimating the short-run cost function of the firm? (*c*) Why is the total variable cost estimated instead of the total cost function? (*d*) How does the shape of the estimated total variable cost curve compare to that postulated by economic theory? How can the two be reconciled?

(*a*) Knowledge of short-run cost functions is essential to the firm in determining the optimal level of output and the price to charge.

(*b*) The most common method of estimating the firm's short-run cost functions is by regressing total variable costs on output, input prices, and a few other operating variables during the time period for which the size of the plant is fixed.

(*c*) The total variable cost rather than the total cost function is usually estimated because of the difficulty of allocating fixed costs to the various products produced by the firm. The firm's total cost function can then be obtained by simply adding the best estimate possible of the fixed costs to the total variable costs. The firm's average variable and marginal cost functions can be easily obtained from the total variable cost function, as indicated in Section 8.2.

(*d*) While economic theory postulates an S-shaped (cubic) TVC curve, a linear approximation often gives a better empirical fit for the observed range of outputs. One possible explanation for this is that the firm brings more of its fixed capital (perhaps machinery) into operation when it hires more labor, so that the capital-labor ratio and the firm's marginal cost remain constant even in the short run (the estimated TVC curve is a straight line).

8.20 What are the most important problems a firm faces in estimating its total variable cost curve?

The firm faces the following problems in the empirical estimation of short-run cost functions:

Opportunity costs must be extracted from the available accounting cost data. That is, each input used in production must be valued at its opportunity cost, which is based on what the input could earn in its best alternative use, rather than on the actual expenditures for the input.

Not only must costs be correctly apportioned to the various products produced by the firm but care must also be exercised to match cost to output over time (i.e., to allocate costs to the period in which the output is produced rather than to the period when the costs were incurred). For example, while a firm may postpone all but emergency maintenance until a period of slack production, these maintenance costs must be allocated to the earlier production periods.

The period of time for the estimation must be long enough to allow for sufficient variation in output and costs, but not long enough for the firm to change plant size (since the firm would then no longer be operating in the short run).

Since output is usually measured in physical units (e.g., number of automobiles of a particular type produced per time period) while costs are measured in monetary units, the various costs must be deflated by the appropriate price index to correct for inflation.

8.21 A researcher regresses monthly data for a firm's total variable costs (TVC), on its output (Q), and the wage rates paid by it (w) over the past two years (after deflating TVC and w by their respective price index) and obtains:

$$\text{TVC} = 79.7 + 4.0Q + 2.15w \qquad \bar{R}^2 = 0.96 \qquad D\text{-}W = 2.1$$
$$(2.9) \quad (4.2) \quad (3.7)$$

(The figures in parentheses are t values.) (*a*) If $w = \$20$, derive the firm's TVC, AVC, and MC functions. (*b*) Plot the firm's TVC, AVC, and MC curves. How do the shapes of these curves differ from those postulated by production theory? (*c*) Was the researcher correct in fitting a linear TVC function? Why?

(a) Substituting $w = \$20$ into the estimated regression equation we get

$$TVC = a + bQ + cw$$
$$= 79.7 + 4Q + 2.15(\$20)$$
$$= 120 + 4Q$$

Thus, the TVC function is a straight line with a vertical intercept of $120 and a slope of $4. Note that the estimated parameter $a = 79.7$. (The constant in the estimated regression cannot be interpreted as representing the fixed costs of the firm since the researcher estimated the TVC function. Specifically, $Q = 0$ is usually so far removed from the actual observed data points on the TVC curve that no economic significance can be attached to the estimated parameter a.) The AVC function is

$$AVC = \frac{TVC}{Q} = \frac{120}{Q} + 4$$

The MC function is the slope of the TVC curve. That is,

$$MC = b = 4$$

(b) See Fig. 8-14. The top panel of the figure shows the TVC curve of the firm, and the bottom panel shows the corresponding AVC and MC curves. The dashed cubic TVC′ curve in the top panel is the TVC curve

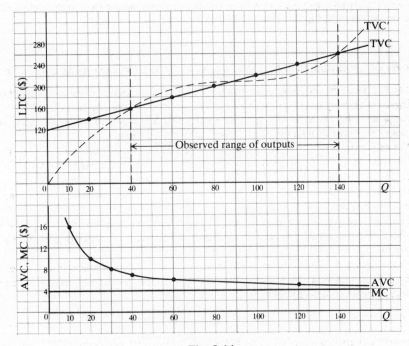

Fig. 8-14

postulated by production theory. In the bottom panel the AVC curve declines rapidly and gets closer and closer to the horizontal MC curve at MC = $4 (as compared to the U-shape of the AVC and MC curves postulated by production theory).

(c) Based on the excellent results obtained, the researcher seems to have made the correct decision in fitting a linear TVC function to the data. All estimated coefficients are statistically significant at better than the 1 percent level, the regression "explains" 96 percent of the variation in TVC, and the Durbin-Watson D-W statistic indicates the absence of autocorrelation. The linear form often gives a very good fit in the empirical estimation of the TVC function.

8.22 (a) Why is knowledge of the long-run average cost curve essential in managerial decision making? (b) What is the most common method of estimating the long-run average cost function of the firm? (c) What are the most important estimation problems faced? (d) How does the shape of the estimated long-run average cost curve compare to that postulated by economic theory? How can the two be reconciled?

(a)   Knowledge of the long-run average cost function is essential in planning for the optimal scale of plant for the firm to build in the long run.

(b)   The most common method of estimating the long-run average cost curve of the firm is to regress average costs on output and input prices for a number of firms at a given point in time (i.e., by cross-sectional regression analysis). The reason for preferring cross-sectional to time-series regression analysis is that in the long run the type of product the firm produces and the technology it uses are likely to change, and these will define points on *different* LAC curves rather than points on a given LAC curve.

(c)   One serious problem that arises in estimating the LAC curve by cross-sectional regression analysis is the need to reconcile the different accounting and operational practices of the different firms in the sample. The researcher must also ensure that each firm is operating the optimal scale of plant at the optimal level of output (i.e., at the point on its SAC curve that forms part of its LAC curve). Otherwise, the estimated LAC curve will exaggerate the degree of economies or diseconomies of scale present.

(d)   Estimated long-run average cost curves seem to indicate sharply increasing returns to scale (falling LAC curve) at low levels of output followed by near-constant returns to scale at higher levels of output (i.e., the LAC curve seems to be L-shaped or nearly so, as in the middle panel of Fig. 8-8). This does not necessarily disprove the U-shaped LAC curve postulated by economic theory. It may simply be a reflection of the unwillingness of firms to expand when they see their LAC turn upward.

8.23   Redraw Fig. 8-7 and show on it that if firm 1 (with plant SAC_1) produces to the left of point A'', firm 2 produces to the left of point C'', firm 3 produces at point G'', and firm 4 produces to the right of point R'', the estimated long-run average cost curve of the firm will overestimate both economies and diseconomies of scale.

If the four firms are producing at points A^*, D^*, G'', and R^*, respectively, instead of at points A'', C'', G'', and R'', we would be estimating the dashed LAC^* curve in Fig. 8-15 instead of the solid LAC curve. The dashed LAC^* curve overestimates the degree of both the economies and diseconomies of scale (i.e., its U-shape is more pronounced than that of the correct LAC curve).

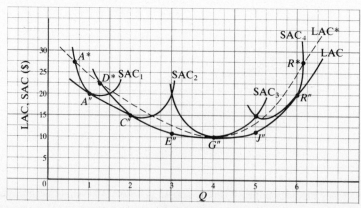

Fig. 8-15

8.24   What are the advantages and disadvantages of estimating the long-run average cost curve by (a) the engineering technique and (b) the survival technique?

(a)   The advantages of the engineering technique of estimating the long-run average cost curve are as follows: It permits estimation of the LAC curve for new products or technologies when historical data are not available; it is based on the present technology, thus avoiding mixing present technology and old technology; it avoids the problem that arises in using different input prices in different geographical regions; and it avoids the difficult cost-allocation and input-valuation accounting problems that plague regression estimation.

The disadvantages of the engineering technique arise because it deals only with the technical aspects of production and does not consider administrative, financing, and marketing costs; it deals with production under ideal rather than actual real-world conditions; and it is based on current technology, which may soon become obsolete.

(b) The main advantage of the survival technique in estimating the long-run average cost curve, or better, the presence of economies or diseconomies of scale, is that it is very simple to understand and apply.

Its main disadvantages are that (1) it implicitly assumes a highly competitive form of market structure in which survival depends only on economic efficiency and (2) it does not allow us to measure the *degree* of economies or diseconomies of scale.

Chapter 9

Linear Programming

9.1 THE BASIC CONCEPTS

Linear programming is a mathematical technique for solving constrained maximization and minimization problems when there is more than one constraint and both the objective function to be optimized and the constraints faced are linear (i.e., can be represented by straight lines). A basic assumption of linear programming is that commodities can be produced with only a limited number of input combinations. With two inputs, capitol and labor each input combination, or capitol-labor ratio, is called a *production process* and can be represented by a straight line ray from the origin in input space. By joining points of equal output on the rays, or processes, we define the isoquant for the particular output level of the commodity. Isoquants are made up of straight line segments and have kinks (rather than being smooth as in Chapter 7). By superimposing on the figure the linear constraints on production, we define the *feasible region*, i.e., the area of attainable input combinations. A point on an isoquant that is not on a ray, or process, can be reached by the appropriate combination of the two adjacent processes. The best or *optimal solution* is at the point where the feasible region reaches the highest isoquant.

EXAMPLE 1. Figure 9-1(*a*) shows production process 1, using $K/L = 3$; process 2, using $K/L = 1$; and process 3, using $K/L = \frac{1}{3}$, which a firm can use to produce a particular commodity, where K is capital and L is labor, as in previous chapters. Part (*b*) shows that 100 units of output (100*Q*) can be produced with 2*L* and 6*K* (point *A*), 3*L* and 3*K* (point *B*), or 6*L* and 2*K* (point *C*). Joining these points we get the isoquant *ABC* for 100*Q*. Since we also assume constant returns to scale, using twice as much *L* and *K* along each production process (ray) results in twice as much output. Joining such points we get the isoquant *DEF* for 200*Q*. If the firm faced only one constraint, such as isocost line *GH* in part (*c*), the feasible region, that is, the area of attainable input combinations, would be represented by shaded triangle *OJN*. The best or optimal solution is at point *E*, where the feasible region reaches the isoquant for 200*Q* (the highest possible) with process 2 by using 6*L* and 6*K*. Panel (*d*) extends the analysis to the case in which the firm faces no cost constraint but has available only 5*L* and 9*K* per period. The feasible region is then given by the shaded area *ORST*. The optimal solution, or maximum output, is given by point *S* (200*Q*), where the firm produces 100*Q* with process 1 (*OA*) and 100*Q* with process 2 (*OB* = *AS*).

9.2 PROCEDURE FOR FORMULATING AND SOLVING LINEAR PROGRAMMING PROBLEMS

The function to be optimized in linear programming is called the *objective function*. This usually refers to profit maximization or cost minimization. In linear programming problems, constraints are given by inequalities (called *inequality constraints*). The reason is that the firm often can use up to, but not more than, specified quantities of some inputs, or the firm must meet some minimum requirements. In addition, there are *nonnegativity constraints* on the solution to indicate that the firm cannot produce a negative output or use a negative quantity of any input. The varying quantities of each product to be produced in order to maximize profits, or inputs to be used to minimize costs, are called *decision variables*.

The steps used in solving a linear programming problem are the following:

1. Express the objective function of the problem as an equation and the constraints as inequalities.
2. Graph the inequality constraints and define the feasible region.
3. Graph the objective function as a series of isoprofit (i.e., equal profit) or isocost lines, one for each level of profit or cost, respectively.
4. Find the optimal solution (i.e., the values of the decision variables) at the extreme point or corner of the feasible region that touches the highest isoprofit line or the lowest isocost line.

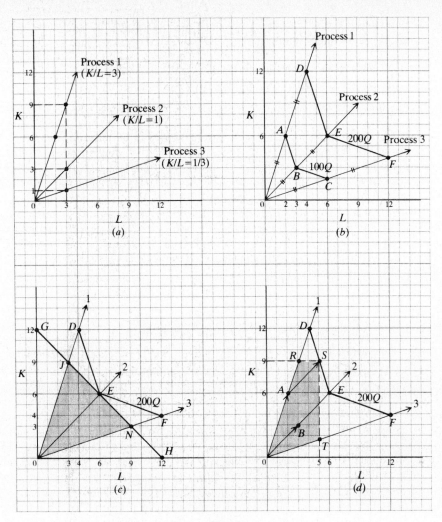

Fig. 9-1

9.3   LINEAR PROGRAMMING: PROFIT MAXIMIZATION

Most firms produce more than one product, and the problem is to determine the output mix that maximizes the total profits of the firm subject to the many constraints on inputs that the firm usually faces. The contribution to the firm's profits made by each unit of the product is equal to the selling price of the product minus its average variable cost. This is the amount available to the firm to cover its overhead (fixed) costs and to provide for profits. Since the total fixed costs of the firm are constant by definition, when the firm produces the product mix that maximizes the total contribution to profits, it will also maximize its total profits. Constrained profit-maximization problems can be formulated and solved by linear programming by following the steps outlined in the previous section.

EXAMPLE 2.   Suppose that a firm produces products X and Y using three inputs: A, B, and C. The production of each unit of X requires $1A$, $3B$, and $1C$. Each unit of Y requires $0.5A$, $3B$, and $3C$. The firm can use no more than $8A$, $30B$, and $24C$ per time period. The contribution that each unit of the product makes to overhead costs and profits is \$4 for product X and \$3 for product Y. We can determine the quantity of products X and Y (i.e., Q_X and Q_Y) that the firm should produce in order to maximize its total profits, as follows:

1. Formulate the linear programming problem by expressing the objective function as an equation and the constraints as inequalities. When we do this we get:

$$
\begin{array}{lll}
\text{Maximize:} & \pi = \$4Q_X + \$3Q_Y & \text{(objective function)} \\
\text{Subject to:} & 1Q_X + 0.5Q_Y \leq 8 & \text{(input } A \text{ constraint)} \\
& 3Q_X + 3Q_Y \leq 30 & \text{(input } B \text{ constraint)} \\
& 1Q_X + 3Q_Y \leq 24 & \text{(input } C \text{ constraint)} \\
& Q_Y \geq 0 & \text{(nonnegativity constraint)}
\end{array}
$$

The A constraint indicates that $1A$ (required to produce each unit of X) times Q_X plus $0.5A$ (to produce each unit of Y) times Q_Y must be equal to or less than the $8A$ available to the firm. The constraints imposed by inputs B and C are similarly obtained.

2. Treating the inequality constraint for input A as an equation and graphing it, we get the constraint line in Fig. 9-2(a). Since the firm can use up to but not more than 8 units of input A, the constraint imposed by input A is satisfied at every point on or to the left of the constraint line (the shaded area). Treating all inequality constraints as equations and graphing them, we get feasible region $ODEFG$ (the shaded area) in Fig. 9-2(b), which satisfies all the constraints simultaneously.

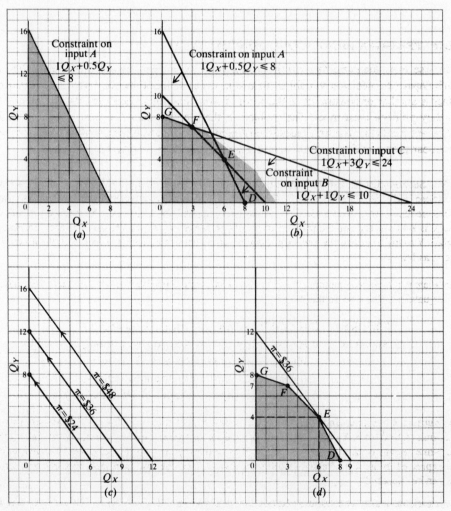

Fig. 9-2

3. Solving the objective function for Q_Y, we get

$$Q_Y = \frac{\pi}{3} - \frac{4Q_X}{3}$$

Figure 9-2(c) gives the isoprofit lines for $\pi = \$24$, $\$36$, and $\$48$, each with slope of $-\frac{4}{3}$ (the profit contribution ratio).

4. Figure 9-2(d) combines parts (b) and (c) and shows that the feasible region touches the highest isoprofit line at point E ($6X$ and $4Y$), at which π is at its maximum:

$$\pi = \$4(6) + \$3(4) = \$36$$

Since point E is formed by the intersection of the constraint lines for inputs A and B and is below the constraint line for input C, inputs A and B are fully utilized (i.e., they are *binding constraints*), while input C is not fully utilized (i.e., it is a *slack variable*) at the optimal solution.

Problems with more than two decision variables are beyond the scope of the graphical approach but can be solved algebraically (see Problem 9.8). Computers can quickly solve these problems by comparing the values of the objective function at the various corners of the feasible region and picking the extreme point or corner solution that maximizes the objective function. This method of solution is the *simplex method*, and it utilizes the extreme-point theorem. [The case of multiple solutions is examined in Problem 9.9(b).]

9.4 LINEAR PROGRAMMING: COST MINIMIZATION

Firms usually use more than one input to produce a good or service, and a crucial choice they face is how much of each input (the decision variables) to use in order to minimize the costs of production. Usually, firms also face a number of constraints in the form of some minimum requirements that they or the good or service that they produce must meet. The problem is then to determine the input mix that minimizes costs subject to the constraints that the firm faces. Constrained cost-minimization problems can be formulated and solved with linear programming by following the steps outlined in Section 9.2.

EXAMPLE 3.   Suppose that raising chickens requires that they be fed a minimum daily requirement of basic nutrients A, B, and R. These have been established at $11A$, $14B$, and $18R$. A chicken farmer can use feed grains X and Y to meet these nutritional requirements. Feed grain X contains $0.5A$, $1B$, and $3R$. Feed grain Y contains $1A$, $1B$, and $1R$. The price of grain X is \$400 per ton and the price of grain Y is \$600 per ton. In order to determine the amount of feed grain X and feed grain Y to use to satisfy the minimum daily requirements of nutrients A, B, and R at the lowest possible cost, we can proceed as follows:

1. Formulate the linear programming problem by expressing the objective function as an equation and the constraints as inequalities. When we do this we get

$$
\begin{aligned}
\text{Minimize:} \quad & C = \$400\,Q_X + \$600\,Q_Y && \text{(objective function)} \\
\text{Subject to:} \quad & 0.5Q_X + 1Q_Y \geq 11 && \text{(nutrient } A \text{ constraint)} \\
& 1Q_X + 1Q_Y \geq 14 && \text{(nutrient } B \text{ constraint)} \\
& 3Q_X + 1Q_Y \geq 18 && \text{(nutrient } R \text{ constraint)} \\
& Q_X, Q_Y \geq 0 && \text{(nonnegativity constraint)}
\end{aligned}
$$

The nutrient A constraint indicates that $0.5A$ (found in each unit of feed grain X) times Q_X plus $1A$ (found in each unit of feed grain Y) times Q_Y must be equal to *or larger than* the $11A$ minimum daily requirement that the farmer wants to satisfy. The other inequality constraints are similarly obtained. The inequality constraints are expressed in the form "equal to or larger than," since the minimum daily requirements must be fulfilled but can be exceeded.

2. Treat each inequality constraint as an equation and plot it. All points on or *above* the constraint line satisfy the particular inequality constraint. The feasible region is then given by the shaded area above *DEFG* in

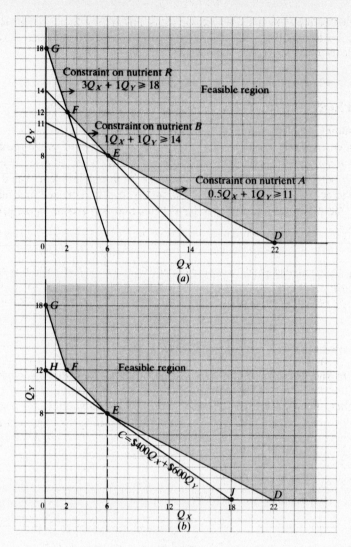

Fig. 9-3

Fig. 9-3(a). All points within the feasible region simultaneously satisfy all the inequality and nonnegativity constraints of the problem.

3. Solve the objective function for Q_Y. When we do this, we get

$$Q_Y = \frac{C}{600} - \frac{400}{600} Q_X$$

This gives a series of parallel isocost lines (one for each level of costs) with absolute slope of \$400/\$600 or $\frac{2}{3}$ (the ratio of the price of grain X to the price of grain Y).

4. Find the optimal solution at the extreme point or corner of the feasible region that touches the lowest isocost line. This is point E ($6X$, $8Y$) in Fig. 9-3(b), where the feasible region touches isocost line HJ (the lowest that reaches the feasible region). Thus, the lowest cost at which the farmer can satisfy all the nutritional requirements is

$$C = \$400(6) + \$600(8) = \$7,200$$

Note that point E is formed by the intersection of the constraint lines for nutrient A and nutrient B but is above the constraint line for nutrient R. This means that the minimum daily requirements for nutrients A and B are just met, while the minimum requirement for nutrient R is more than met.

9.5 THE DUAL PROBLEM AND SHADOW PRICES

Every linear programming problem, called the *primal problem*, has a corresponding or symmetrical problem called the *dual problem*. A profit-maximization primal problem has a cost-minimization dual problem, and vice versa. The solution of a dual problem yields the *shadow prices*. They give the change in the value of the objective function per unit change in each constraint in the primal problem. The dual problem is formulated directly from the corresponding primal problem and solved as indicated in Example 4. According to the *duality theorem*, the optimal value of the objective function is the same in the primal and in the corresponding dual problems.

EXAMPLE 4. Using the constrained profit-maximization problem in Example 2, which is repeated in the left-hand column of Table 9.1, we formulate the corresponding dual problem in the right-hand column, where V_A, V_B, and V_C are, respectively, the shadow prices of inputs A, B, and C, and C is the total cost that the firm minimizes.

Table 9.1

Original Primal Profit-Maximization Problem	Corresponding Dual Cost-Minimization Problem
Maximize: $\pi = \$4Q_X + \$3Q_Y$ (objective function) Subject to: $1Q_X + 0.5Q_Y \leq 8$ (input A constraint) $3Q_X + 3Q_Y \leq 30$ (input B constraint) $1Q_X + 3Q_Y \leq 24$ (input C constraint) $Q_X, Q_Y \geq 0$ (nonnegatively constraint)	Minimize: $C = 8V_A + 30V_B + 24V_C$ Subject to: $1V_A + 3V_B + 1V_C \geq \$4$ $0.5V_A + 3V_B + 3V_C \geq \$3$ $V_A, V_B, V_C \geq 0$

The dual objective function is given by the sum of the shadow price of each input times the quantity of the input available to the firm. We have a constraint for each of the two decision variables (Q_X and Q_Y) in the primal problem. Each constraint postulates that the sum of the shadow price of each input times the quantity of the input required to produce one unit of each product must be equal to or larger than the profit contribution of a unit of the product. Note that the direction of the inequality constraints in the dual problem is opposite to that of the corresponding primal problem and that the shadow prices cannot be negative. Since we know from the primal problem that input C is a slack variable, we set $V_C = 0$; then, treating the constraints as equations and subtracting the second constraint from the first we get

$$\begin{array}{r} 1.0V_A + 3V_B = \$4 \\ \underline{0.5V_A + 3V_B = \$3} \\ 0.5V_A \quad\quad\;\; = \$1 \end{array}$$

This gives values of $V_A = \$2.00$, $V_B = \$0.67$, and $C = 8(\$2.00) + 30(\$0.67) + 24(\$0) = \$36.00$. Thus, the minimum cost of producing $6X$ and $4Y$ (from the primal solution of Example 2) equals the maximum profit of $\pi = \$36.00$ in the primal solution. The values of $V_A = \$2.00$ and $V_B = \$0.67$ mean that each unit of input A contributes $\$2.00$ to the firm's profits, and each unit of input B contributes $\$0.67$, so that it would pay for the firm to acquire more of each input if the price of the input is smaller than its profit contribution. (For the formulation and solution of the dual of the primal cost-minimization problem in Example 3, see Problem 9.21.)

Glossary

Binding constraint   A variable that is fully utilized at a particular point.

Decision variables   The quantities of inputs or output that the firm can vary in order to optimize the objective function.

Dual problem   The inverse of the primal linear programming problem.

Duality theorem   Postulates that the optimal value of the primal objective function is equal to the optimal value of the dual objective function.

Feasible region   The area that includes all the solutions that are possible with the given constraints.

Inequality constraints   Limitations on the use of some inputs or some minimum requirements that must be met.

Linear programming   A mathematical technique for solving constrained maximization and minimization problems when there are many constraints and the objective function to be optimized, as well as the constraints faced, are linear.

Nonnegativity constraints   Limits that preclude negative values for the solution in a linear programming problem.

Objective function   The function to be optimized in linear programming.

Optimal solution   The best of the feasible solutions.

Primal problem   The original maximization (e.g., profit) or minimization (e.g., cost) linear programming problem.

Production processes   The various capital-labor ratios that a firm can use to produce a commodity; each process is depicted by a ray from the origin in input space.

Shadow price   The marginal valuation of an input or output of a firm.

Simplex method   A mathematical technique for solving linear programming problems.

Slack variable   A variable that is not fully utilized at a particular point.

Review Questions

1.   Linear programming

   (a)   is a mathematical technique for solving constrained optimization problems.
   (b)   assumes that the function to be optimized, as well as the constraints faced, are linear.
   (c)   can be used when the firm faces many constraints.
   (d)   all of the above.

   Ans.   (d) See Section 9.1.

2.   Linear programming cannot be used when

   (a)   commodity prices are constant.
   (b)   input prices are constant.
   (c)   there are strong economies of scale in production.
   (d)   commodities can be produced with a limited number of input combinations.

   Ans.   (c) See Section 9.1.

3. The greater the number of processes with which a commodity can be produced,

   (*a*) the fewer are the number of kinks on the isoquants.

   (*b*) the smoother are the isoquants.

   (*c*) the more useful is linear programming.

   (*d*) all of the above.

   Ans. (*b*) See Example 1 and Fig. 9-1.

4. If a firm produces a commodity with different combinations of two inputs that are subject to no quantitative restrictions, the firm faces

   (*a*) zero constraints.

   (*b*) one constraint.

   (*c*) two constraints.

   (*d*) we cannot say without additional information.

   Ans. (*b*) See Section 9.1 and Example 1.

5. In linear programming we optimize

   (*a*) an objective function subject to the inequality constraints.

   (*b*) an inequality constraint subject to the objective function.

   (*c*) an objective constraint subject to the inequality functions.

   (*d*) the feasible region that can be reached with the objective function.

   Ans. (*a*) See Section 9.2.

6. The area showing all possible solutions in the face of existing constraints is called the

   (*a*) primal region.

   (*b*) dual region.

   (*c*) feasible region.

   (*d*) optimal region.

   Ans. (*c*) See Section 9.2.

7. If the slope of the isoprofit line in Fig. 9-2(*d*) had been -1, the optimal solution would have been

   (*a*) 6X and 4Y only.

   (*b*) 3X and 7Y only.

   (*c*) all combinations of X and Y along EF.

   (*d*) 9X and 12Y.

   Ans. (*c*) See Fig. 9-2(*d*).

8. At the optimal solution point, E, in Fig. 9-2(*d*), the firm uses

   (*a*) all units of input A available to it.

   (*b*) all units of input B available to it.

   (*c*) less than the total number of units of input C available to it.

   (*d*) all of the above.

   Ans. (*d*) See Example 2.

9.   If the slope of the isocost line in Fig. 9-3(b) had been −3, the optimal solution would have been

     (a)   22X and 0Y.

     (b)   6X and 8Y.

     (c)   all combinations of X and Y along EF.

     (d)   all combinations of X and Y along FG.

     Ans.   (c) See Fig. 9-3(b).

10.   The amount of nutrient R provided at the optimal solution point, E, in Fig. 9-3(b), is

     (a)   26 units.

     (b)   22 units.

     (c)   18 units.

     (d)   8 units.

     Ans.   (a) From the constraint on nutrient R, we can calculate that the inputs of 6X and 8Y at point E provide $6(3) + 8(1) = 26$ units of nutrient R.

11.   Which of the following statements is false?

     (a)   The dual of profit maximization is cost minimization.

     (b)   The dual of cost minimization is profit maximization.

     (c)   Cost minimization is the dual of reaching the lowest possible isocost line.

     (d)   Reaching the highest isoprofit line possible is the dual of reaching the lowest possible isocost line.

     Ans.   (c) See Section 9.5.

12.   Shadow price refers to

     (a)   the change in the value of the constraint per unit change in the objective function.

     (b)   the change in the value of the objective function per unit change in any one of the constraints.

     (c)   the change in the value of the primal solution per unit change in the dual solution.

     (d)   any of the above.

     Ans.   (b) See Section 9.5.

Solved Problems

THE BASIC CONCEPTS

9.1   (a) In what way does linear programming differ from the optimization techniques examined in Chapter 2? (b) Why is the assumption of linearity important in linear programming? Is this assumption usually satisfied in the real world? (c) What types of problems can linear programming be used to solve?

     (a)   Linear programming is similar to the optimization techniques examined in Chapter 2. That is, they are both used to solve constrained profit-maximization and cost-minimization problems. However, while the objective function that the firm seeks to optimize, as well as the constraints that the firm faces, can be linear or nonlinear in optimization problems in general, they must be linear in linear programming. The assumption of linearity allows the firm to solve optimization problems subject to many different constraints that would be difficult or impossible to solve with other more general optimization techniques.

     (b)   The assumption of linearity in linear programming means that input and output prices are constant, returns to scale are constant, and the commodity can be produced with only a few production processes. With these assumptions, average and marginal costs are equal and constant, profit per unit is constant, and isoquants are formed by linear segments between the input combinations with which a given quantity of the commodity can be produced. The assumption of linearity is often satisfied in the real world within the relevant or usual range of outputs of the firm.

(c)   Linear programming can be and has been used to solve a wide variety of constrained optimization problems when the firm faces many constraints and both the objective function the firm seeks to optimize and the constraints it faces are linear (i.e., can be represented by straight lines). Optimization in linear programming refers either to profit maximization or cost minimization.

9.2   (a) In what way do the isoquants in linear programming differ from those of traditional production theory? (b) How can you determine the number of processes required to reach the optimal solution in linear programming?

(a)   The isoquants in linear programming are not the smooth curves described by production theory in Chapter 7, but instead have kinks at the points at which they intersect each production process. Smooth isoquants imply that a particular amount of a commodity can be produced with an infinite number of combinations of the two inputs. The kinks in the isoquants in linear programming refer to the limited number of production processes that the firm can use to produce the commodity. The greater the number of processes available to produce the particular commodity, the less pronounced are these kinks and the more closely the isoquants approach the smooth curves assumed in production theory.

(b)   To reach the optimal solution, a firm will require *no more* processes than the number of constraints that the firm faces. Sometimes fewer processes will do. For example, if the amounts of the two inputs available to the firm happen to fall on the ray for a particular production process, then only one production process is necessary (the one on which the input constraints fall) for the firm to reach the optimal solution (i.e., the maximum output subject to the input constraints it faces).

9.3   A firm uses three different processes in production: process 1 with $K/L = 2.5$, process 2 with $K/L = 1$, and process 3 with $K/L = 0.4$. Fifty units of output ($50Q$) can be produced with $2L$ and $5K$, $3L$ and $3K$, or $5L$ and $2K$, and the firm operates under constant returns to scale. The wage rate (w) of labor is $27 per day (the unit of labor) and the rental price of capital (r) is $18 per day. If the firm cannot incur expenses of more than $270 per day, determine the maximum daily output of the firm and the production process that it will use.

The three production processes as well as the isoquants for $50Q$ and $100Q$ are shown in Fig. 9-4(a). Note also that corresponding segments on the isoquant for $50Q$ and $100Q$ are parallel. For the maximum expenditures of $270 per day and $w = \$27$ and $r = \$18$, the isocost line is GH, in part (b) of the figure, with absolute slope of $w/r = \$27/\$18 = 1.5$. The feasible region is then the shaded area OJN. That is, the firm can purchase any

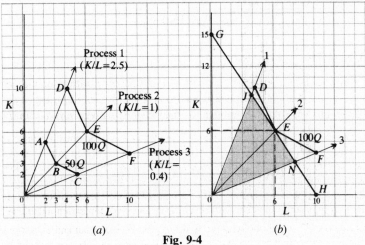

(a)   (b)

Fig. 9-4

combination of labor and capital on or below isocost line *GH*, but since no production process is available that is more capital intensive than process 1 (i.e., with a K/L higher than 2.5) or less capital intensive than process 3 (i.e., with K/L smaller than 0.4), the feasible region is restricted to the shaded area *OJN*. The optimal solution is given by point *E*, at which the firm uses $6L$ and $6K$ with process 2 and reaches the isoquant for $100Q$.

9.4   (*a*) Starting with the solution to Problem 9.3, suppose that the wage rate rises from \$27 to \$30 and the rental price of capital declines from \$18 to \$15. What would be the maximum output that the firm could produce with expenditures of \$270 per day? Draw a figure showing your answer. Which process would the firm utilize to produce $100Q$? What would happen if w rose above \$30 and r fell below \$15? (*b*) Between what w/r ratios would the firm use $6L$ and $6K$ to produce $100Q$? (*c*) If the firm could not hire more than 8 workers per day or rent more than 5 units of capital per day, what is the maximum output that the firm could produce? What process or processes would the firm have to use in order to reach this output level? How many units of labor and capital would the firm use in each process if it used more than one process?

(*a*) If w rose from \$27 to \$30 and r declined from \$18 to \$15, the firm could hire either 9 units of labor (from \$270/\$30) or 18 units of capital, or any combination of L and K that would keep expenditures at \$270. The isocost of the firm would then be $G'H'$, shown in Fig. 9-5(*a*). The maximum output that the firm could produce with isocost $G'H'$ is $100Q$ per day. Since isocost $G'H'$ coincides with segment *DE* of the isoquant for $100Q$, the firm could produce this output at point *E* with process 2 by using $6L$ and $6K$ (as in Problem 9.3); at point *D*, with process 1 by using $4L$ and $10K$, or by any combination of L and K along *DE*. If w rose above \$30 and r fell below \$15, the firm would use only process 1 to produce $100Q$.

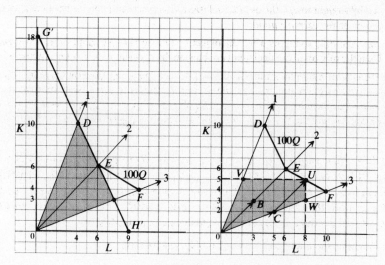

Fig. 9-5

(*b*) As long as w/r exceeds $\frac{1}{2}$ [the absolute slope of *EF* in Fig. 9-5(*a*)] and is less than 2 [the absolute slope of *DE* in Fig. 9-5(*a*)], the firm will continue to produce $100Q$ at point *E* by using only process 2 with $6L$ and $6K$.

(*c*) If the firm could not hire more than 8 workers or rent more than 5 units of capital per day, the feasible region would be the shaded area *OVUW* in Fig. 9-5(*b*). The maximum output of the firm would still be 100 units as shown by point *U* on the isoquant for $100Q$. The firm would use $5L$ and $2K$ to produce $50Q$ (*OC*) with process 3 and use the remaining $3L$ and $3K$ to produce the other $50Q$ (*OB* = *CU*) with process 2. *OC* and *OB* are called vectors. Thus, the above is an example of vector analysis, and vector *OU* (not shown) is equal to the sum of vectors *OC* and *OB*.

9.5 Determine how much of the output of $100Q$ would be produced with each process in Fig. 9-5(b) if point U were (a) one-quarter of the way from point E along line segment EF; (b) halfway between points E and D on ED. (c) From your results in parts (a) and (b) of the problem, deduce a general rule for determining the proportion of total output produced by two adjacent processes, using the distance that the production point is from each process.

(a) If point U were one-quarter of the distance from point E along EF, the firm would produce $1 - \frac{1}{4} = \frac{3}{4}$ of $100Q$, or 75 units, of the commodity with production process 2 and the remaining 25 units of the commodity with process 3. You can draw in the answer in part (b) of the figure.

(b) If point U had been halfway between points E and D on ED, the firm would produce $50Q$ with process 1 and $50Q$ with process 2 [see Fig. 9-5 (b)].

(c) To reach any point on an isoquant between two adjacent production processes, we utilize the process to which the point is closer, in proportion to 1 minus the distance of the point from the process (ray). The amount of each input that is used in each process is then proportional to the output produced by each process.

LINEAR PROGRAMMING: PROFIT MAXIMIZATION

9.6 (a) Why do only the corners of the feasible solution need to be examined in solving a linear programming problem? (b) Under what conditions is it possible to have multiple solutions? (c) Does the presence of multiple solutions invalidate the extreme-point theorem? (See 9.2, step 4.)

(a) Since the objective function and the constraints of a linear programming problem are linear (i.e., can be represented by straight lines), the optimal solution will always be at one of the corners of the feasible region. This is known as the *extreme point*.

(b) We will have multiple solutions when the objective function has the same slope as a segment of the feasible region. Then the mix of all the decision variables on the segment will result in the maximum level of profits.

(c) Even in the case of multiple optimal solutions, the extreme-point theorem holds up. The reason is that the segment of the feasible region that has the same slope as the objective function (and thus leads to multiple optimal solutions) includes the two corners defining the segment. Thus, in the multiple-solution case, too, we need examine only the corners of the feasible region to determine an optimal solution.

9.7 A firm uses labor (L), capital (K), and raw materials (R) to produce products X and Y. Product X gives a profit of $20 per unit, and product Y gives a profit of $30 per unit. To produce each unit of X, the firm uses 1L, 0.5K, and no R. To produce each unit of Y the firm uses 1L, 1K, and 1R. The firm cannot use more than 6L, 4K, and 3R per time period. Find the quantity of products X and Y that the firm should produce in order to maximize its total profits.

We can formulate the linear programming problem as follows:

$$\text{Maximize:} \quad \pi = \$20Q_X + \$30Q_Y \quad (\text{objective function})$$
$$\text{Subject to:} \quad 1Q_X + 1Q_Y \leq 6 \quad (\text{input } L \text{ constraint})$$
$$0.5Q_X + 1Q_Y \leq 4 \quad (\text{input } K \text{ constraint})$$
$$1Q_Y \leq 3 \quad (\text{input } R \text{ constraint})$$
$$Q_X, \; Q_Y \geq 0 \quad (\text{nonnegativity constraint})$$

Treating each inequality constraint as an equation and plotting it, we get feasible region *ODEFG* in Fig. 9-6(a). The isoprofit lines for $\pi = \$120$, $\$140$, and $\$150$ are plotted in Fig. 9-6(b). Superimposing the isoprofit lines in part (b) of the figure on the feasible region in part (a), we get the optimal solution at corner point E in Fig. 9-6(c). At optimal point E, the firm produces 4X and 2Y and maximizes its total profits at

$$\pi = \$20(4) + \$30(2) = \$140$$

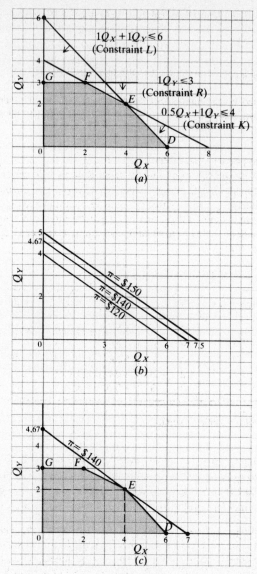

Fig. 9-6

9.8 Solve Problem 9.7 algebraically.

We can solve the linear programming problem algebraically by identifying (algebraically) the corners of the feasible region and then comparing the profits at each corner. Since each corner is formed by the intersection of two constraint lines, the coordinates of the intersection point (i.e., the values of Q_X and Q_Y at the corner) can be found by solving simultaneously the equations of the two intersecting lines.

In Fig. 9-6(a), we can see that since corner point D is formed by the intersection of the constraint line for input L with the horizontal axis, Q_X at corner point D is obtained by substituting $Q_Y = 0$ into the equation for constraint L. That is, substituting $Q_Y = 0$ into $1Q_X + 1Q_Y = 6$ we get $Q_X = 6$. Thus, at point D, $Q_Y = 0$ and $Q_X = 6$.

Corner point E is formed by the intersection of the constraint lines for inputs L and K [see Fig. 9-6(a)], which are, respectively:

$$1.0Q_X + 1Q_Y = 6 \quad \text{and} \quad 0.5Q_X + 1Q_Y = 4$$

Subtracting the second equation from the first, we have

$$1.0Q_X + 1Q_Y = 6$$
$$0.5Q_X + 1Q_Y = 4$$
$$\overline{0.5Q_X \qquad\quad = 2}$$

so that $Q_X = 4$. Substituting $Q_X = 4$ into the first of the two equations, we get $Q_Y = 2$. Thus, at point E, $Q_X = 4$ and $Q_Y = 2$.

Corner point F is formed by the intersection of the constraint lines for inputs K and R. The equation for constraint R is $Q_Y = 3$. Substituting $Q_Y = 3$ into the equation for the constraint for input K, we have

$$0.5Q_X + 1(3) = 4$$

Therefore, $Q_X = 2$. Thus, at point F, $Q_X = 3$ and $Q_Y = 3$.

Since corner point G is on the constraint line for input R on the vertical axis (along which $Q_X = 0$), we substitute $Q_X = 0$ into the constraint equation for input R and get $Q_Y = 3$. Also, at the origin $Q_X = Q_Y = 0$.

By substituting the values of Q_X and Q_Y (the decision variables) at each corner of the feasible region into the objective function, we can determine the firm's profit or total profit contribution (π) at each corner. These are shown in Table 9.2. The optimal or profit-maximizing point is at corner E, at which $\pi = \$140$ [the same as the graphical solution in Fig. 9-6(c)].

Table 9.2

Corner Point	Q_X	Q_Y	$\$20Q_X + \$30Q_Y$	Profit
O	0	0	$\$20(0) + \$30(0)$	$\$\ 0$
D	6	0	$\$20(6) + \$30(0)$	120
E^*	4	2	$\$20(4) + \$30(2)$	140
F	2	3	$\$20(2) + \$30(3)$	130
G	0	3	$\$20(0) + \$30(3)$	90

*Profit-maximizing point.

9.9 (*a*) Which are the binding constraints at the optimal solution in Problem 9-7? Which is the slack input? What is the unused quantity of the slack input? (*b*) What must the profit contribution per unit of products X and Y be in order to have multiple solutions along the segment of the feasible region formed by the constraint line for capital input? Draw a figure showing this case.

(*a*) Since the optimal solution is at corner point E, which is formed by the intersection of the constraint lines for inputs L and K but is below the constraint line for input R, the constraints imposed on inputs L and K are binding, while the constraint imposed on input R is not binding (i.e., input R is a slack input). Each unit of product X requires no units of input R, while each unit of product Y requires 1 unit of input R, and at optimum point E $(4X, 2Y)$, the amount used of input R is 2. Since 3 units of input R are available, 1 unit of input R is not used (i.e., is idle) at E.

(*b*) The constraint line for input K has an absolute slope of 0.5. Therefore, the profit contribution of each unit of product X would have to be half that of each unit of product Y in order for the isoprofit line to coincide with the constraint line for input K and have optimal solutions along segment EF of the feasible region (see Fig. 9-7).

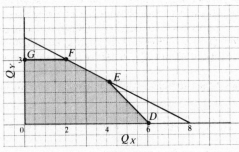

Fig. 9-7

9.10 The Dependable Washing Machine Company manufactures two types of washing machine: type X, on which it earns a profit of $40 per unit; and type Y, on which it earns a profit of $30 per unit. In order to produce each unit of machine X the company uses one unit of input A, one unit of input B, and no units of input C. To produce each unit of machine Y the company uses one unit each of inputs A and C, and half a unit of input B. The firm can use only 12 units of input A and 10 units of inputs B and C per time period. Determine how many machines of type X and how many of type Y the firm should produce in order to maximize its total profits.

The problem can be formulated as follows:

$$\begin{aligned}
\text{Maximize:} \quad & \pi = \$40Q_X + \$30Q_Y && \text{(objective function)} \\
\text{Subject to:} \quad & 1Q_X + 1Q_Y \le 12 && \text{(input } A \text{ constraint)} \\
& 1Q_X + 0.5Q_Y \le 10 && \text{(input } B \text{ constraint)} \\
& 1Q_Y \le 10 && \text{(input } C \text{ constraint)} \\
& Q_X, Q_Y \ge 0 && \text{(nonnegativity constraint)}
\end{aligned}$$

Treating each inequality constraint as an equation and plotting it, we get feasible region *ODEFG* in Fig. 9-8 (*a*). Superimposing the isoprofit lines for $\pi = \$360$, $\$440$, and $\$480$ on the feasible region in part (*b*) of the figure, we get the optimal solution at corner point *E*, at which 8*X* and 4*Y* are produced, and the total profits of the firm are maximized at $\pi = \$40(8) + \$30(4) = \$440$.

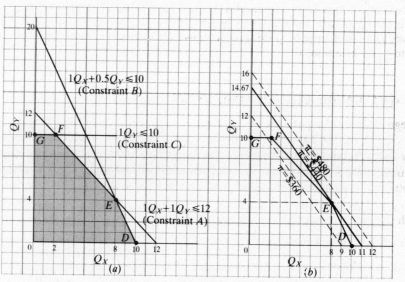

Fig. 9-8

9.11 In Problem 9.10, (*a*) determine how much of each input the firm uses to produce the product mix that maximizes total profits. (*b*) If the profit per unit of product X remains constant at $40, how much can profit per unit of product Y vary without necessitating that the firm change its product mix in order to continue to maximize profits?

(*a*) At profit-maximizing point *E*, the firm produces 8*X* and 4*Y*. Since each unit of X and Y requires one unit of input A, 8*A* are used in the production of X and 4*A* in the production of Y. Since a total of 12*A* are used in the production of X and Y, and this is equal to the total quantity of input A available to the firm per unit of time, input A is a binding constraint at the optimal point.

Since each unit of X requires 1*B*, while each unit of Y requires 0.5*B*, 8*B* are used in the production of X and 2*B* in the production of Y. Since a total of 10*B* are used in the production of X and Y, and this is equal to the total quantity of input B available to the firm per unit of time, input B is also a binding constraint at the optimal point.

Input C is used only in the production of Y. Since $1C$ is used in the production of each unit of Y, and $4Y$ are produced at the optimum point, only 4 of the 10 units of input C are used, i.e., 6 units are idle and input C is a slack variable.

(b) If the profit on each unit of machine X remains constant at \$40, the profit on each unit of machine Y can vary between \$80 (so that the absolute slope of the isoprofit line would be 2, the same as the absolute slope of the constraint line for input B) and \$40 (so that the absolute slope of the isoprofit line would have the same absolute slope of 1 as the constraint line for input A) without necessitating that the firm change its product mix in order to maximize its total profits.

9.12 Suppose that a fourth constraint in the form $1Q_X + 1Q_Y \geq 20$ were added to the profit-maximization linear programming problem examined in Problem 9.11. Would you be able to solve the problem? Why?

If a fourth constraint in the form of $1Q_X + 1Q_Y \geq 20$ were added to the linear programming problem examined in Problem 9.11, there would no longer be an optimal solution to the problem. The reason for this is that by treating such an inequality constraint as an equation and graphing it, we would get a line that crosses the axes at $Q_X = Q_Y = 20$. Since this constraint requires that $1Q_X + 1Q_Y$ be equal to or *larger* than 20, the constraint is satisfied at all points on or *above* the constraint line. The feasible region would then be given by all points on or inside the area *ODEFG* and on and above the new constraint line that crosses the axes at $Q_X = Q_Y = 20$ (see Fig. 9-8). Since the two areas of the feasible region have no point in common, they cannot be reached by a single objective function (isoprofit line). Hence, the problem has no optimal solution. This condition is referred to as *degeneracy*. In large linear programming problems, it is often difficult or impossible to know in advance whether degeneracy exists. The computer program is run, and if no solution that satisfies all the constraints simultaneously is found, degeneracy exists. Some of the constraints of the problem will then have to be changed in order to get an optimal solution.

LINEAR PROGRAMMING: COST MINIMIZATION

9.13 The Oregon Mining Company operates two mines, A and B. It costs the company \$3,000 per day to operate mine A and \$2,000 per day to operate mine B. Each mine produces ores of high, medium, and low qualities. Mine A produces 2 tons of high-grade ore, 1 ton of medium-grade ore, and 0.5 ton of low-grade ore per day. Mine B produces 1 ton of each grade of ore per day. The company has contracted to provide local smelters with a minimum of 14 tons of high-grade ore, 10 tons of medium-grade ore, and 6 tons of low-grade ore per month. Determine graphically the minimum cost at which the company can meet its contractual obligations.

This problem can be formulated as follows:

Minimize:	$C = \$3,000A + \$2,000B$		(objective function)
Subject to:	$2A + 1B$	≥ 14	(high-grade ore constraint)
	$1A + 1B$	≥ 10	(medium-grade ore constraint)
	$0.5A + 1B$	≥ 6	(low-grade ore constraint)
	A, B	≥ 0	(nonnegativity constraint)

Treating each inequality constraint as an equation and plotting it, we get feasible region *DEFG* in Fig. 9-9(a). Figure 9-9(b) shows that *HJ* is the lowest isocost line that allows the company to reach the feasible region. The absolute slope of cost line *HJ* is $\frac{3}{2}$, which is the ratio of the cost of operating mine A to the cost of operating mine B. The company minimizes costs by operating mine A for 4 days per month and mine B for six days per month (point *E*) at a cost of

$$C = \$3,000(4) + \$2,000(6) = \$24,000.$$

9.14 For Problem 9.13 and Fig. 9-9, determine (a) the level of the company's costs at the other corners of the feasible region, (b) which of the company's obligations are just met at the optimal point and which are more than met, and (c) the number of days that the company should run each mine in order

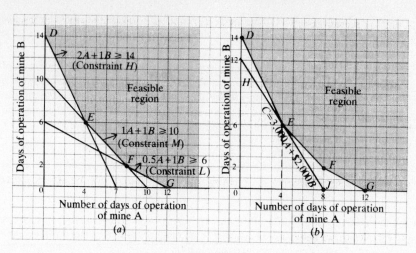

Fig. 9-9

to minimize the cost of meeting its contractual obligations if the cost of running mine B increased to $3,000 per day.

(a) At corner point D (0, 14): $C = \$3,000(0) + \$2,000(14) = \$28,000$
At corner point F (8, 2): $C = \$3,000(8) + \$2,000(2) = \$28,000$
At corner point G (12, 0): $C = \$3,000(12) + \$2,000(0) = \$36,000$

(b) Since optimal point E is formed by the intersection of the constraint lines for the high- and medium-grade ores, but is above the constraint line for the low-grade ore, the minimum monthly requirements for the high- and medium-grade ores are just met, while the minimum requirement for the low-grade ore is more than met.

(c) If the cost of running mine B increased to $3,000 per day (so that the ratio of the cost of running mine A to the cost of running mine B is 1), the lowest isocost line that reaches the feasible region would coincide with segment EF of the feasible region. In that case, all the combinations of days of operation of mines A and B along segment EF would result in the same minimum cost of meeting the contractual obligations of the company. Using point E for the calculations, we get

$$C = \$3,000(4) + \$3,000(6) = \$30,000$$

9.15 Show how you would solve Problem 9.13 algebraically.

Treating the first inequality constraint of Problem 9.13 as an equation and setting $A = 0$, we get

$$2(0) + 1B = 14$$

Thus, we define corner point D at $A = 0$ and $B = 14$, at which

$$C = \$3,000(0) + \$2,000(14) = \$28,000$$

Treating the first and second constraints as equations and subtracting the second constraint from the first, we get

$$2A + 1B = 14$$
$$1A + 1B = 10$$
$$\overline{1A \qquad = 4}$$

Therefore, $B = 6$. Defining corner point E at $A = 4$ and $B = 6$, we get

$$C = \$3,000(4) + \$2,000(6) = \$24,000$$

Treating the second and the third constraints as equations and subtracting the third constraint from the second, we get

$$
\begin{aligned}
1.0A + 1B &= 10 \\
0.5A + 1B &= 6 \\
\hline
0.5A \phantom{{}+ 1B} &= 4
\end{aligned}
$$

Therefore, $A = 8$ and $B = 2$. Defining corner point F at $A = 8$ and $B = 2$, we have

$$ C = \$3,000(8) + \$2,000(2) = \$28,000 $$

Finally, treating the third constraint as an equation and setting $B = 0$, we get

$$ 0.5A + 1(0) = 6 $$

so that $A = 12$. Thus, we define corner point G as $(0, 12)$, at which

$$ C = \$3,000(12) + \$2,000(0) = \$36,000 $$

Therefore, the firm minimizes the cost of fulfilling its contractual obligations at corner point E by operating mine A for 4 days per month and mine B for 6 days per month at a cost of $24,000. This is the same result as the one obtained graphically in Problem 9.13.

9.16 For Problem 9.13, determine how much (i.e., what proportion) of the contractual agreement is met by the output of mine A and how much by mine B.

At optimal point E, $A = 4$, and each day that mine A is operated it supplies 2 tons of high-grade ore, 1 ton of medium-grade ore, and 0.5 ton of low-grade ore. Thus, in the 4 days that mine A is operated, it supplies 8 tons of high-grade ore, 4 tons of medium-grade ore, and 2 tons of low-grade ore. At optimal point E, $B = 6$, and each day that mine B is operated, it supplies 1 ton of each grade of ore. Thus, in the 6 days that mine B is operated, it supplies 6 tons of each grade of ore.

Therefore, mine A supplies 8 tons and mine B supplies the remaining 6 tons of the 14 tons of high-grade ore that the company agreed to supply. Mine A supplies 4 tons and mine B supplies the remaining 6 tons of the 10 tons of medium-grade ore that the company agreed to supply. Mine A supplies 2 tons and mine B supplies 6 tons of low-grade ore per month as compared with the 6 tons under contract.

9.17 (a) In what way is the definition of the feasible region in a cost-minimization linear programming problem different from that in a profit-maximization problem? (b) What would happen if we added a fourth constraint in Fig. 9-9(a) that would be met by all points on or above a straight line connecting points D and G?

(a) In a cost-minimization linear programming problem the inequality constraints are expressed in the form of "equal to or greater than." Thus, the feasible region is given by all points on or above the constraint lines for the problem. This means that the constraints of the problem in the form of minimum product requirements must be met but can be exceeded.

In profit-maximization linear programming problems, by contrast, the inequality constraints are expressed in the form of "equal to or smaller than" and the feasible region is represented by all points on or below the constraint lines of the problem. This means that the constraints of the problem in the form of availability of inputs can be reached but cannot be exceeded.

(b) If, in Fig. 9-9(a), we added a fourth constraint that would be met by all points on or above a straight line from point D to point G, the feasible region would be all points on or above the new constraint line, and the other three constraints in the problem would be irrelevant.

THE DUAL PROBLEM AND SHADOW PRICES

9.18 (a) Why is the solution of the dual problem useful? (b) What is the usefulness of shadow prices to the firm in a profit-maximization problem? (c) What is the usefulness of shadow prices to the firm in a cost-minimization problem? (d) What is meant by duality theory?

(a) The solution of the dual problem is useful because (1) it may be easier to obtain the optimal values of the decision variables of the primal problem from the solution of the corresponding dual problem and (2) the solution of the dual problem gives the imputed value, or marginal valuation, of the inputs (the constraints in the profit-maximization problem) to the firm or the imputed or marginal cost of the decision variables (the constraints in the cost-minimization primal problem).

(b) The shadow prices in the profit-maximization problem are the imputed values, or marginal valuations, of each input to the firm. These are important for determining how much of each input the firm should acquire in order to minimize costs. A firm should increase the use of an input as long as the marginal value, or shadow price, of the input exceeds the cost of acquiring the input. If the shadow price of the input is zero, the firm has a surplus of the input (i.e., the input is a slack variable in the corresponding primal problem).

(c) The shadow prices in a cost-minimization primal problem are the imputed or marginal costs of each decision variable of the firm. These are important for determining how much of each decision variable to supply in order to maximize profits. A firm should supply more of a decision variable if the profit generated by an extra unit of the decision variable is greater than the cost of supplying it.

(d) Duality theory postulates that the optimal value of the primal objective function equals the optimal value of the dual objective function. It also postulates that the primal and dual problems will give the same values of the decision variables in the primal objective function and their respective optimal points.

9.19 For Problem 9.7, (a) formulate the dual problem and (b) solve it.

(a) Defining V_L, V_K, and V_R as the shadow prices of L, K, and R, respectively, and C as the total costs of the firm, we can formulate the dual of Problem 9.7 as follows:

$$
\begin{aligned}
\text{Minimize:} \quad & C = 6V_L + 4V_K + 3V_R \\
\text{Subject to:} \quad & 1V_L + 0.5V_K \quad\quad\;\; \geq \$20 \\
& 1V_L + 1V_K + 1V_R \geq \$30 \\
& V_L, V_K, V_R \geq 0
\end{aligned}
$$

(b) To solve the dual problem we follow the same general steps used in solving the primal problem. That is, we find the values of the decision variables (V_L, V_K, and V_R) at each corner and choose the corner with the lowest value of C. Since we have three decision variables, necessitating a three-dimensional figure (which is awkward and difficult to draw and interpret), we solve the problem algebraically. The algebraic solution is simplified because we know from the solution of the primal problem that input R is a slack variable. We set $V_R = 0$ then, treating the constraints as equations and subtracting the first constraint from the second, we get the solution of the dual problem:

$$
\begin{aligned}
1V_L + 1.0V_K &= \$30 \\
1V_L + 0.5V_K &= \$20 \\
\hline
0.5V_K &= \$10
\end{aligned}
$$

so that $V_K = \$20$. Substituting $V_K = \$20$ into the first equation, we get $V_L = \$10$ and

$$ C = 6(\$10) + 4(\$20) + 3(\$0) = \$140 $$

This minimum total cost is equal to the maximum total profits (i.e., $\pi = \$140$) obtained from the solution of the primal problem, as postulated by duality theory.

9.20 For Problem 9.10, (a) formulate the dual problem and (b) solve it. (c) Indicate how the shadow prices could have been obtained from the primal solution.

(a) Defining V_A, V_B, and V_C as the shadow prices of A, B, and C, respectively, and C as the total cost of the firm, we can formulate the dual of Problem 9.10 as follows:

$$\text{Minimize:} \quad C = 12V_A + 10V_B + 10V_C$$
$$\text{Subject to:} \quad 1V_A + 1V_B \geq \$40$$
$$1V_A + 0.5V_B + 1V_C \geq \$30$$
$$V_A, V_B, V_C \geq 0$$

(b) We know from the solution of the primal problem that input C is a slack variable, so that $V_C = 0$. Hence, treating the constraints as equations and subtracting the second constraint from the first, we get the solution of the dual problem:

$$1V_A + 1.0V_B = \$40$$
$$1V_A + 0.5V_B = \$30$$
$$\overline{\qquad 0.5V_B = \$30}$$

so that $V_B = \$20$, $V_A = \$20$ and

$$C = 12(\$20) + 10(\$20) + 10(\$0) = \$440$$

which is the same as the maximum $\pi = \$440$ found in Problem 9.10.

(c) V_A and V_B could also have been obtained by relaxing the constraints for inputs A and B by one unit and calculating the increase in the total profit in the primal solution. Relaxing the input A constraint from 12 to 13 units, and solving the simultaneous constraint equations for inputs A and B, we get

$$1Q_X + 1.0Q_Y = 13$$
$$1Q_X + 0.5Q_Y = 10$$
$$\overline{\qquad 0.5Q_Y = 3}$$

so that $Q_Y = 6$ and $Q_X = 7$. Substituting these values into the π function in Problem 9.10, we get

$$\pi = \$40(7) + \$30(6) = \$460$$

This is $20 above the previous level of π. Therefore, $V_A = \$20$, the same as in the dual solution. Following the same procedure for input B, we would get $V_B = \$20$ also. In general, however, V_A and V_B are obtained from the dual, as indicated in part (b).

9.21 For Example 3, (a) formulate the dual problem and (b) solve it. (c) Indicate how the shadow prices could have been obtained from the primal solution.

(a) Defining V_A, V_B, and V_R as the imputed values (marginal cost), or shadow prices, of nutrients A, B, and R, respectively, in the primal problem, and as the imputed values, or costs, of the fixed amounts of nutrients A, B, and R that the farmer must provide, we can formulate the following dual profit-maximization problem:

$$\text{Maximize:} \quad \pi = 11V_A + 14V_B + 18V_R$$
$$\text{Subject to:} \quad 0.5V_A + 1V_B + 3V_R \geq \$400$$
$$1V_A + 1V_B + 1V_R \geq \$600$$
$$V_A, V_B, V_R \geq 0$$

Note that the direction of the inequality constraints in the dual problem is opposite that of the corresponding primal problem and that the shadow prices cannot be negative.

(b) We know from the solution of the primal problem that nutrient R is a slack variable (so that $V_R = 0$). Thus, treating the constraints as equations and subtracting the first constraint from the second, we get the solution of the dual problem:

$$1.0V_A + 1V_B = \$600$$
$$0.5V_A + 1V_B = \$400$$
$$\overline{\quad 0.5V_A = \$200}$$

so that $V_A = \$400$, $V_B = \$200$, and

$$\pi = 11(\$400) + 14(\$200) + 18(\$0) = \$7,200$$

This is the maximum total profit (π) and is equal to the minimum total cost (C) found in the primal problem.

(c) V_A and V_B could have been obtained by relaxing the constraints for nutrients A and B by one unit, and calculating the increase in total cost in the primal solution. Relaxing the nutrient A constraint from 11 to 12 units, and solving the simultaneous constraint equations for nutrients A and B, we get

$$1.0Q_X + 1Q_Y = 14$$
$$\underline{0.5Q_X + 1Q_Y = 12}$$
$$0.5Q_X \qquad\; = 2$$

so that $Q_X = 4$ and $Q_Y = 10$, and

$$C = \$400(4) + \$600(10) = \$7,600$$

This is $400 above the previous level of C. Therefore, $V_A = \$400$ (the same as in the dual solution). Following the same procedure for nutrient B, we would get $V_B = \$200$.

9.22 For Problem 9.13, (a) formulate the dual problem and (b) solve it. (c) Indicate how the firm could use the information to plan capacity expansion.

(a) Defining V_H, V_M, and V_L as the shadow prices of the high-grade, medium-grade, and low-grade ores, respectively, and π as the total imputed value, or cost, of the fixed quantities of the various grades of ore that the firm must provide, we can formulate the following dual profit-maximization problem:

$$\text{Maximize:} \quad \pi = 14V_H + 10V_M + 6V_L$$
$$\text{Subject to:} \quad 2V_H + 1V_M + 0.5V_L \leq \$3,000$$
$$1V_H + 1V_M + \quad 1V_L \leq \$2,000$$
$$V_H, V_M, V_L \geq 0$$

(b) We know from the solution of the primal problem that the low-grade ore is a slack variable (so that $V_L = 0$). Thus, treating the constants as equations and subtracting the second constraint from the first, we get the solution of the dual problem:

$$2V_H + 1V_M = \$3,000$$
$$\underline{1V_H + 1V_M = \$2,000}$$
$$1V_H \qquad\;\; = \$1,000$$

so that $V_M = \$1,000$ also and

$$\pi = 14(\$1,000) + 10(\$1,000) + 6(\$0) = \$24,000$$

which is equal to the value of C in the corresponding primal problem.

(c) If the expected return (profit) from supplying one additional ton of the high-grade and medium-grade ores exceeds $1,000, the firm would gain by expanding its level of operations so as to be able to supply more of these two grades. If the opposite is the case, the firm's profits would rise due to the reduction of its scale of operation.

Chapter 10

Market Structure

10.1 MARKET STRUCTURE AND DEGREE OF COMPETITION

The process by which price and output are determined in the real world is strongly affected by the structure of the market. A *market* consists of all the potential buyers and sellers of a particular product. *Market structure* refers to the competitive environment in which the buyers and sellers of a product operate. Four different types of market structure are usually identified: perfect competition at one extreme, monopoly at the opposite extreme, and monopolistic competition and oligopoly in between.

Perfect competition is the form of market organization in which (1) there are many buyers and sellers of a product, each too small to affect the price of the product; (2) the product is identical, or homogeneous; (3) there is perfect mobility of resources; and (4) economic agents have perfect knowledge of market conditions. *Monopoly* is the form of market organization in which a single firm sells a product for which there are no close substitutes. Entry into the industry is very difficult or impossible (as evidenced by the fact that there is but a single firm in the industry). *Monopolistic competition* refers to the case in which there are many sellers of a differentiated product and entry into or exit from the industry is rather easy in the long run. *Oligopoly* is the case in which there are few sellers of a homogeneous or differentiated product. While entry into the industry is possible, it is not easy (as evidenced by the limited number of firms in the industry). The conditions of monopoly, monopolistic competition, and oligopoly are often referred to as *imperfect competition* to distinguish them from perfect competition.

10.2 PERFECT COMPETITION

In a perfectly competitive market, the market price of a product is determined at the intersection of the market demand curve and market supply curve of the product. The perfectly competitive firm is then a *price taker* and can sell any quantity of the commodity at that price (see Problem 10.4). The best level of output of a firm in the short run is given at the point at which price (P) or marginal revenue (MR) equals marginal cost (MC). This is true as long as P exceeds the average variable cost (AVC) of the firm. If, at the best level of output, P is smaller than the average total cost (ATC) but is larger than the average variable cost (AVC), the firm incurs a loss, but its loss would be even greater if it stopped producing. The *shut-down point* for the firm is at $P = $ AVC. The rising portion of the firm's MC curve that is above the AVC curve then represents the *competitive firm's short-run supply curve* (see Example 1). In the long run, the firm will build the optimal scale of plant to produce the best level of output. The existence of profits will also attract more firms into the industry, while losses will cause some firms to leave it. This proceeds until the long-run equilibrium point is reached, at which all firms produce at the P that equals the lowest point on the long-run average cost (LAC) curve, and all firms break even (see Example 2).

EXAMPLE 1. In Fig. 10-1, the per-unit cost curves are those of Fig. 8-1 and d is the infinitely elastic demand curve faced by the perfectly competitive firm when the market price of the product is $90. Since the firm can sell any quantity of the product at $P = 90, the change in total revenue per unit change in output, or MR, also equals $90. With $P = 90, the best level of output of the firm is 6 units and is given by point E, where $P = $ MR $= $ MC $= $90. At $Q = 6$, ATC $= $55; therefore, the firm earns a profit of $EA = $35 per unit and ($35)(6) = $210 in total. If $P = $36 instead, the firm would face demand curve d'. The best level of output of the firm is then 4.5 units and is given by point E', at which $P' = $ MR' $= $ MC $= $36. At $Q = 4.5$, ATC $= $53; therefore, the firm incurs a loss of $FE' = $17 per unit and ($17)(4.5) = $76.50 in total. If the firm went out of business, however, it would incur the greater loss of $FA' = $26 per unit (the average fixed cost) and ($26)(4.5) = $117 in total (the total fixed costs of the firm). If $P = $ AVC $= $26 (point H in the figure), the total loss of the firm equals its total fixed costs whether the firm produces or not. Thus, point H is the firm's shut-down point. Since the firm always produces at $P = $ MR $= $ MC (as long as $P > $ AVC), the rising portion of the MC curve represents the short-run supply curve of the firm. If input prices are constant, the market supply

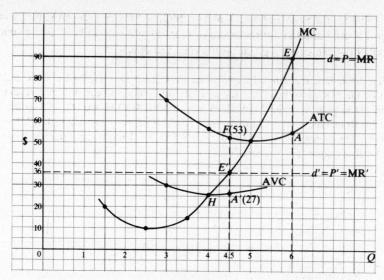

Fig. 10-1

curve of the product is obtained by the horizontal summation of the individual firms' supply curves. Thus, the market supply curve in Fig. 10-1 is obtained on the assumption that there are 100 firms in the market identical to the one shown in Fig. 10-2.

EXAMPLE 2.   Figure 10-2 shows that when a perfectly competitive market is in long-run equilibrium at $P = \$40$, the best level of output of the perfectly competitive firm is 8 units and is given by point E, at which $P = \mathrm{MR} = \mathrm{LMC} = \mathrm{lowest\ LAC} = \$40$. Because of free or easy entry into and exit from the competitive market, all profits and losses are eliminated, and all firms break even. The firm operates the scale of plant given by the short-run average total cost (SATC) curve shown in Fig. 10-2 at point E (its lowest point), so that short-run marginal cost (SMC) equals LMC also. If a firm has more productive resources or inputs and lower LAC, the more productive resources will be able, by threatening to leave, to extract higher rewards (payments) from their employer to fully compensate them for their higher productivity. As a result, the lowest LAC will be the same for all competitive firms when they are in long-run equilibrium.

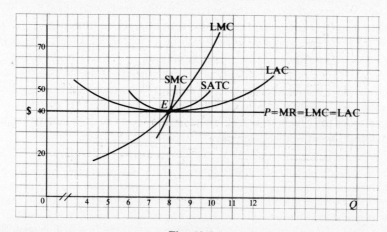

Fig. 10-2

10.3 MONOPOLY

Monopoly is the form of market organization in which a single firm sells a product for which there are no close substitutes. Thus, the monopolist faces a market demand curve for the product that is negatively sloped, and $\mathrm{MR} < P$. Monopoly can arise from several causes [see Problem 10.9(a)]. In the short run, the best level of output of a monopolist is at the point at which MR = MC, as long as $P >$ AVC (see Example 3). In the long run, the monopolist can build the optimal scale of plant to produce the best level of output. Because of blocked entry, a monopolist can earn long-run profits (see Example 4).

EXAMPLE 3.   In Fig. 10-3, D is the demand curve faced by a monopolist and MR is the corresponding marginal revenue curve. Note that the MR curve has twice the absolute slope of the D curve. The best level of output of the monopolist in the short run is given by point E, at which MR = MC. At $Q = 400$, $P = \$8$ (point A on the D curve) and ATC = \$6 (point F), so that the monopolist maximizes profits at $AF = \$2$ per unit and $AFCB = \$800$ in total (the shaded area in the figure). The monopolist would break even if $P =$ ATC and would minimize losses if $P <$ ATC but $P >$ AVC at the best level of output (see Problem 10.10).

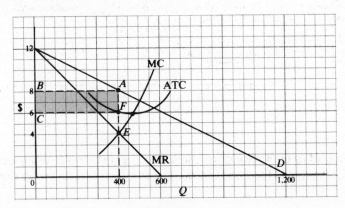

Fig. 10-3

EXAMPLE 4.   In Fig. 10-4, the best level of output of the monopolist in the long run is 500 units and is given by point E', at which $P =$ LMC. At $Q = 500$, $P = \$7$ (point A' on the D curve) and the monopolist operates the optimal scale of plant at point F', where SATC = LAC = \$4. Thus, the monopolist earns a long-run profit of $A'F' = \$3$ per unit and $A'F'B'C' = \$1,500$ in total. Because of blocked entry, the monopolist does not usually produce at the lowest point on its LAC curve (see Fig. 10-4) and can continue to earn profits in the long run.

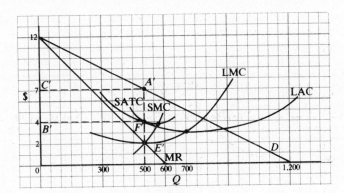

Fig. 10-4

10.4 MONOPOLISTIC COMPETITION

Monopolistic competition is the form of market organization in which there are many sellers of a *differentiated product* and entry into and exit from the industry is rather easy in the long run. Thus, the demand curve facing a monopolistic competitor is negatively sloped but highly price elastic. The best level of output in the short run is given at the point at which MR = MC, provided that $P >$ AVC. As in other forms of market organization, the firm under monopolistic competition can earn profits, break even, or incur losses in the short run. If firms earn profits, more firms enter the market in the long run. This shifts the demand curve facing each firm to the left (as its market share declines) until all firms break even. Since the demand curve facing a monopolistic competitor is negatively sloped, price and LAC are somewhat higher than under perfect competition. Thus, each firm operates with excess capacity, and this allows more firms (overcrowding) to exist in the market. A monopolistically competitive firm can increase the degree of product variation as well as its selling expenses in an effort to increase the demand for its product and make the demand less elastic. The optimal level of these efforts is given by the point at which MR = MC.

EXAMPLE 5. In Fig. 10-5, D is the highly price-elastic demand curve faced by a typical monopolistic competitor, and MR is the corresponding marginal revenue curve. The best level of output of the firm in the short run is 8 units and is given by point E, at which MR = MC. At $Q = 8$, $P = \$8$ (point A on the demand curve) and ATC = \$6 (point F), so that the monopolistic competitor maximizes profits of $AF = \$2$ per unit and $AFCB = \$16$ in total (the shaded area in the figure). The monopolistic competitor would break even if $P = $ ATC and would minimize losses if $P < $ ATC, as long as $P > $ AVC at the best level of output (see Problem 10.15). Note that Fig. 10-5 is very similar to Fig. 10-3, except that the D curve is more price elastic for the monopolistic competitor than for the monopolist.

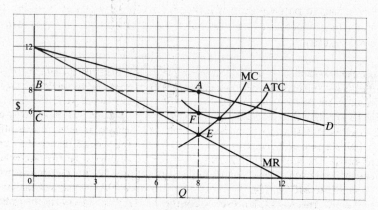

Fig. 10-5

EXAMPLE 6. Since the typical or representative monopolistically competitive firm earns a profit in the short run, more firms enter the market in the long run. This causes the demand curve of the typical firm to shift down to D' in Fig. 10-6 (as its market share declines), so as to be tangent to the LAC curve at the output level of 6 units, at which MR' = LMC (point E'). At $Q = 6$, $P = $ LAC $= $ SATC $= \$6$ (point A') and the firm breaks even in the long run. This compares to $Q = 9$, at which $P = $ LAC $= $ SATC $= \$5$ (point E^*) if the market had been organized along perfectly competitive lines. The slightly higher price and LAC under monopolistic competition ($P = \$6$ as compared to $P = \$5$ under perfect competition) is due to product differentiation (i.e., the cost of providing consumers with a variety of products rather than

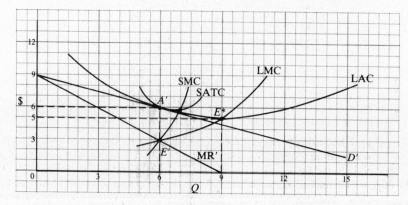

Fig. 10-6

a single undifferentiated product). The difference between $Q = 9$ and $Q = 6$ can be taken as a measure of excess capacity under monopolistic competition, and this allows many more firms (overcrowding) to exist in the market. For some serious criticisms leveled against the theory of monopolistic competition, see Problem 10.17.

10.5 OLIGOPOLY

Oligopoly is the form of market organization in which there are few sellers of a homogeneous or differentiated product, and entry into or exit from the industry is difficult but possible (see Problem 10.19). Oligopoly is the most prevalent form of market organization in the manufacturing sector of industrial countries, including the United States. The degree of prevalence can be measured by concentration ratios (see Problem 10.20). The distinguishing characteristics of oligopoly are the interdependence and rivalry among the firms in the industry. There are many models of oligopoly, each based on the particular behavioral response of competitors. *The kinked demand curve model* seeks to explain the price rigidity often encountered in oligopolistic markets (see Example 7). *The centralized cartel model* can lead to the monopoly solution (see Problem 10.23). Another oligolistic model is the one of *price leadership* by the dominant firm (see Example 8). In the short run, an oligopolist continues to produce even if it incurs a loss, as long as $P > $ AVC. In the long run, an oligopolist is not likely to produce at the lowest point on its LAC curve and can earn profits because of restricted entry into the industry.

EXAMPLE 7. The kinked demand curve model postulates that the demand curve facing an oligopolist has a kink at the prevailing price, and is much more elastic for price increases than for price cuts on the assumption that competitors do not match price increases but do match price cuts. In Fig. 10-7, the demand curve facing the oligopolist is D, or the line segments described by points ABC, and has a kink at the prevailing price of $10 and quantity of 30 units (point B). Note that the curve is much more elastic above than below point B. The marginal revenue curve is MR, which is described by points $AGHJ$; AG is the segment corresponding to the AB portion of the demand curve and HJ corresponds to the BC portion of the demand curve. The kink at point B on the demand curve causes the GH discontinuity in the marginal revenue curve. The oligopolists' marginal cost curve can shift anywhere within the discontinuous or vertical portion of the MR curve (i.e., from MC to MC' in Fig. 10-7) without inducing the oligopolist to change the prevailing price of $10 and its output of 30 units. This model, however, rationalizes rather than explains price rigidity, and the existence of the kink has been questioned. (See Problem 10.22.)

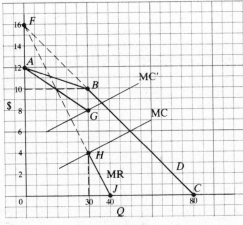

Fig. 10-7

EXAMPLE 8. Under price leadership by the dominant firm, the latter sets the industry price that maximizes its own total profits, allows the other firms in the industry to sell all they want at that price, and then comes in to fill the market. This is shown in Fig. 10-8. In the figure, D_T (line $ABCFG$) is the total market demand curve for the homogeneous product sold in the oligopolistic market and curve ΣMC_F is the horizontal summation of the marginal cost curves of the follower firms in the industry. Since the follower firms behave as perfect competitors, they produce where price (set by the leader) equals MC_F. Then $D_T - \Sigma MC_F = D_L$ is the demand curve faced by the leader or dominant firm. For example,

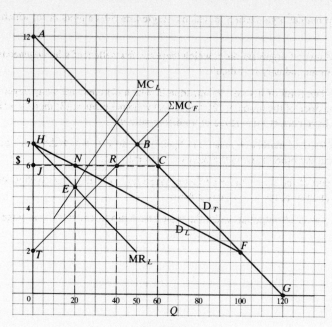

Fig. 10-8

if the leader sets $P = \$7$, the followers supply $HB = 50$ units of the product, leaving nothing to be supplied by the leader. This gives the vertical intercept (point H) on D_L. If the leader sets $P = \$6$, $\Sigma MC_F = JR = 40$ units, leaving $RC = JN = 20$ units to be supplied by the leader (point N on D_L). At $P = \$2$, $MC_F = 0$ (point T) and the leader would face the total quantity demanded in the market (point F). Thus, the demand curve faced by the leader is D_L (line $HNFG$) and its marginal revenue curve is MR_L. If the marginal cost curve of the leader is MC_L, the leader will set $P = \$6$ (given by point N on D_L, which is directly above the point where $MC_L = MR_L$) in order to maximize its total profits. At $P = \$6$, the followers will supply $JR = 40$ units (see the figure) and the leader fills the market by selling $RC = 20$ units. We could also have price leadership by the low-cost firm. (See Problem 10.24.)

Glossary

Centralized cartel   A formal agreement among oligopolists to set the monopoly price, allocate output among member firms, and share profits.

Competitive firm's short-run supply curve   The rising portion of the firm's short-run marginal cost curve above its average variable cost curve.

Differentiated products   Products that are similar, but not identical, and that satisfy the same basic need.

Imperfect competition   Monopoly, monopolistic competition, and oligopoly.

Kinked demand curve model   The model that seeks to explain price rigidity by postulating a demand curve with a kink at the prevailing price.

Market   All the actual and potential buyers and sellers of a particular product.

Market structure   The competitive environment in which the buyers and sellers of the product operate.

Monopolistic competition   The form of market organization in which there are many sellers of a differentiated product and entry into or exit from the industry is rather easy in the long run.

Monopoly   The form of market organization in which a single firm sells a product for which there are no close substitutes.

Oligopoly   The form of market organization in which there are few sellers of a homogeneous or differentiated product and entry into or exit from the industry is difficult.

Perfect competition   The form of market organization in which (1) there are many buyers and sellers of a product, each too small to affect the price of the product; (2) the product is homogeneous; (3) there is perfect mobility of resources; and (4) economic agents have perfect knowledge of market conditions.

Price leadership   The form of market collusion in oligopolistic firms in which the firm that serves as the price leader initiates a price change and the other firms in the industry soon match it.

Price taker   The situation of the seller under perfect competition: each firm has no effect on the price of the product it sells and can sell any quantity at the given market price.

Shut-down point   The level of output at which the price of the product equals the average variable cost of the firm.

Review Questions

1.   Which of the following industries most closely approximates the perfectly competitive model?

   (a)   Automobile
   (b)   Cigarette
   (c)   Newspaper
   (d)   Wheat farming

   Ans.   (*d*) In the first three choices the market has few sellers, the product is differentiated, and vast amounts of capital are needed in order to enter the industry. These conditions are not true in wheat farming.

2.   The best, or optimum, level of output for a perfectly competitive firm is given by the point at which

   (a)   MR equals ATC.
   (b)   MR equals MC.
   (c)   MR exceeds MC by the greatest amount.
   (d)   MR equals *P*.

   Ans.   (*b*) See points *E* and *E′* in Fig. 10-1.

3.   At the best, or optimum, short-run level of output, the firm

   (a)   maximizes total profits.
   (b)   minimizes total losses.
   (c)   either maximizes total profits or minimizes total losses.
   (d)   maximizes profits per unit.

   Ans.   (*c*) Whether the firm maximizes total profits or minimizes total losses in the short run depends on whether *P* exceeds ATC or falls short of ATC at the best level of output.

4.   The short-run supply curve of the perfectly competitive firm is given by the rising portion of the MC curve above

    (*a*)   the shut-down point.

    (*b*)   the break-even point.

    (*c*)   the ATC curve.

    (*d*)   all of the above.

    Ans.   (*a*) See Fig. 10-1.

5.   When the perfectly competitive firm and industry are in long-run equilibrium

    (*a*) $P = \text{MR} = \text{SMC} = \text{LMC}$.

    (*b*) $P = \text{MR} = \text{SAC} = \text{LAC}$.

    (*c*) $P = \text{MR} = $ lowest point on the LAC curve.

    (*d*)   all of the above.

    Ans.   (*d*) See point E in Fig. 10-2.

6.   When the perfectly competitive firm, but not the industry, is in long-run equilibrium

    (*a*) $P = \text{MR} = \text{SMC} = \text{SAC}$.

    (*b*) $P = \text{MR} = \text{LMC} = \text{LAC}$.

    (*c*) $P = \text{MR} = \text{SMC} = \text{LMC} = \text{SAC} = \text{LAC}$.

    (*d*) $P = \text{MR} = \text{SMC} = \text{LMC} = \text{SAC} = $ lowest point on the LAC curve.

    Ans.   (*c*) See Fig. 10-2 and Problems 10.7 and 10.8.

7.   In the short run, a monopolist

    (*a*)   earns a profit.

    (*b*)   breaks even.

    (*c*)   incurs losses.

    (*d*)   any of the above.

    Ans.   (*d*) See Section 10.3.

8.   If a monopolist incurs losses in the short run, then in the long run

    (*a*)   the firm will go out of business.

    (*b*)   the firm will stay in business.

    (*c*)   the firm will break even.

    (*d*)   any of the above is possible.

    Ans.   (*d*) See Section 10.3.

9.   Which of the following statements is false with respect to a monopolistically competitive firm?

    (*a*)   It is one of many sellers of a differentiated product.

    (*b*)   It can earn profits, break even, or incur losses in the short run.

    (*c*)   It can produce at the lowest point on its LAC curve in the long run.

    (*d*)   It breaks even in the long run.

    Ans.   (*c*) See Section 10.4.

10.   The distinguishing characteristic of oligopoly is

    (*a*)   the interdependence among the firms in the industry.

    (*b*)   the inelastic demand for the industry product.

    (*c*)   the existence of barriers to entry into the industry.

    (*d*)   all of the above.

    Ans.   (*a*) See Section 10.5.

11.   The kinked demand curve model

    (*a*)   seeks to explain the price rigidity often found in oligopolistic markets.

    (*b*)   implies that oligopolists recognize their interdependence.

    (*c*)   does not imply collusion on the part of the oligopolists.

    (*d*)   all of the above.

    Ans.   (*d*) See Section 10.5 and Example 7.

12.   In the case of price leadership by the dominant firm, all firms in the purely oligopolistic industry will produce their best level of output

    (*a*)   always.

    (*b*)   never.

    (*c*)   sometimes.

    (*d*)   often.

    Ans.   (*a*) This is so because the dominant firm will set the industry price at which it maximizes its total profits and all the other firms in the industry will behave as perfect competitors and produce at $P = \Sigma MC$.

Solved Problems

MARKET STRUCTURE AND DEGREE OF COMPETITION

10.1.   Identify the characteristics in terms of which the four types of market structure are defined.

    The characteristics in terms of which perfect competition, monopoly, monopolistic competition, and oligopoly are defined and distinguished from one another are (1) the number and size of buyers and sellers of the product in the market, (2) the type of product bought and sold (i.e., standardized, or homogeneous, as contrasted to differentiated), (3) the degree of mobility of resources (i.e., the ease with which firms can enter or exit the market), (4) the degree of knowledge that economic agents (i.e., firms, suppliers of inputs, and consumers) have of prices, costs, and demand and supply conditions.

10.2   (*a*) What four different types of market organization are usually identified? (*b*) Why do we identify these four types of market organization? (*c*) Why do we study the two extreme forms of market organization first?

    (*a*)   The four different types of market organization usually identified are perfect competition, monopolistic competition, oligopoly, and monopoly. All but the first form fall into the realm of imperfect competition.

    (*b*)   We identify these four types of market organization in order to systematize and organize their analysis. In the real world, however, such a sharp distinction does not, in fact, exist. In the real world firms often exhibit elements of more than one market form, and so it may be difficult to classify them into any one of the above market categories.

(c) We look first at the two extreme forms of market organization (i.e., perfect competition and monopoly) because historically, these are the models that were first developed. More importantly, their development is fuller and more satisfactory. The monopolistic competition and oligopoly models, though more realistic in terms of the actual forms of business organization in our economy (and, in general, in most other industrial economies), are not very satisfactory and leave much to be desired from a theoretical point of view.

PERFECT COMPETITION

10.3 Explain in detail exactly what is meant by each of the four component parts of the definition of perfect competition given in Section 10.1.

(a) According to the first part of the definition of perfect competition, there are a large number of sellers and buyers of the product, but they are individually too small in relation to the market to be able to affect the price of the product by their own actions. This means that a change in the output of a single firm will not *perceptibly* affect the market price of the product. Similarly, each buyer of the product is too small to be able to extract from the seller such things as quantity discounts and special credit terms.

(b) The product of each firm in the market is homogeneous, identical, or perfectly standardized. An example of this might be grade A winter wheat. As a result buyers cannot distinguish the output of one firm from that of another, and so are indifferent as to the particular firm from which they buy. This refers not only to the physical characteristics of the product but also to the "environment" (such as the pleasantness of the seller, selling location, etc.) in which the purchase is made.

(c) There is perfect mobility of resources. That is, workers and other inputs can easily move geographically from one job to another, and respond very quickly to monetary incentives. No input required in the production of the product is monopolized by its owners or producers. In the long run, firms can enter or leave the industry without much difficulty. That is, there are no patents or copyrights, "vast amounts" of capital are not required to enter the industry, and already established firms do not have any long-lasting cost advantage over new entrants because of experience or size.

(d) Consumers, resource owners, and firms in the market have perfect knowledge of present and future prices, costs, and economic opportunity in general. Thus, consumers will not pay a higher price than necessary for the product. Price differences are quickly eliminated, and a single price prevails throughout the market for the product. Resources are sold to the highest bidder. With perfect knowledge of present and future prices and costs, producers know exactly how much to produce.

10.4 (a) Plot the following market demand (QD) and market supply (QS) schedules for a product in a perfectly competitive market. Determine the equilibrium price and the equilibrium quantity, and show the demand curve faced by a perfectly competitive firm in this market. Why is the marginal revenue of the firm equal to the price of the product? (b) What would happen if the product price were $120 to begin with? $50 to begin with? (c) Show graphically what would happen if the market demand curve shifted to the right by 200 units but remained parallel to the original demand curve. On the same figure show what would happen if subsequently the market supply curve also shifted to the right by 200 units but remained parallel to the original supply curve.

P($)	120	90	36	26
QD	150	600	870	920
QS	650	600	450	400

(a) See Fig. 10-9. Figure 10-9(a) shows that the equilibrium price is at P = $90 and the equilibrium quantity is at Q = 600. These are determined at the intersection of the market demand curve and the market supply curve at point E. Part (b) shows the demand curve d faced by a firm in a perfectly competitive market. This is horizontal or infinitely elastic (i.e., the firm is a price taker), indicating that the firm can sell any quantity of the product at P = $90. Since P is constant, the marginal revenue (MR), that is, the change in the total

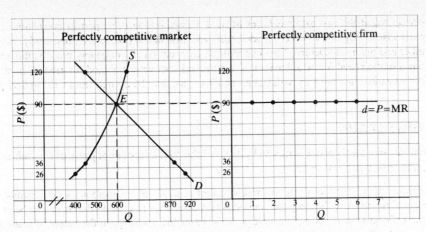

Fig. 10-9

revenue that the firm receives from selling each additional unit of the product, is equal to the price of the product. That is, $d = P = MR = \$90$.

(b) In Fig. 10-9(a) we can see that at $P = \$120$, QS > QD and P falls toward \$90 (the equilibrium price). As P falls, QD increases and QS declines until $P = \$90$ is reached at point E, where QD = QS. However, at $P = \$50$, QD > QS and P rises toward \$90. As P rises, QD declines and QS increases until $P = \$90$ is reached at point E, where QD = QS. Thus, $P = \$90$ is the equilibrium price in the sense that any divergence from it sets in motion automatic forces that push P toward \$90.

(c) Figure 10-10 shows that with D', the equilibrium price is at $P = \$120$ and the equilibrium quantity is at $Q = 650$ (point E'). With S', the equilibrium price is at $P = \$60$ and the equilibrium quantity is at $Q = 750$ (point E^* in the figure). Finally, with D' and S', the equilibrium price is at $P = \$90$ and the equilibrium quantity is at $Q = 800$ (point E'').

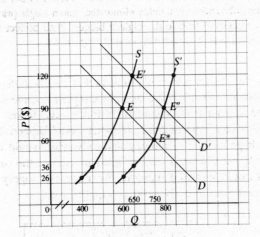

Fig. 10-10

10.5 Given the short-run cost curves shown in Fig. 10-11 for a firm in a perfectly competitive market, find the firm's best level of output and its total profits if the equilibrium market price is (a) \$18, (b) \$13, (c) \$9, (d) \$5, and (e) \$3.

(a) When $P = \$18$, the best or optimum level of output is 7,000 units (point A). The firm earns a profit of AN = \$4 per unit and \$28,000 in total. This is the maximum total profit that the firm can earn at this price.

(b) When $P = \$13$, the best level of output is 6,000 units (point B), and the firm breaks even.

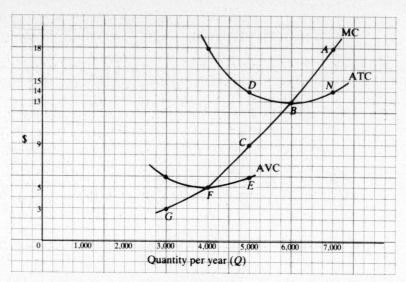

Fig. 10-11

(c) When $P = \$9$, the best level of output is 5,000 units (point C). At this level of output the firm incurs a loss of $DC = \$5$ per unit and \$25,000 in total. If the firm went out of business, however, it would incur a total loss equal to its TFC of \$40,000 (obtained by multiplying the AFC of $DE = \$8$ per unit by the 5,000 units). Thus, the firm would minimize its total losses in the short run by staying in business.

(d) When $P = \$5$, the best level of output is 4,000 units (point F). However, since $P = $ AVC, and thus TR $= $ TVC $= \$20,000$, the firm is indifferent whether it produces or not. In either case, the firm would incur a short-run total loss equal to its TFC of \$40,000. Point F is thus the shut-down point.

(e) Since at $P = \$3$, P is smaller than the AVC, the TR of \$9,000 does not even cover the TVC of \$18,000. Therefore, the firm would incur a total loss equal to its TFC of \$40,000 *plus* the \$9,000 by which the TVC exceeds the TR (i.e., $\$18,000 - \$9,000 = \$9,000$). Thus, it pays for the firm to shut down and minimize its total losses at \$40,000 (its TFC) over the period of the short run.

10.6 (a) Draw the supply curve for the perfectly competitive firm of Problem 10.5. Also draw the industry short-run supply curve on the assumptions that there are 100 identical firms in the industry and that factor prices remain unchanged as industry output expands (and thus more factors are used) and (b) explain the graph of part (a). (c) What quantity of the service will be supplied by each firm and the industry at a price of \$9? at \$18? at prices below \$5?

(a) See Fig. 10-12.

(b) The firm's short-run supply curve is given by the rising portion of its MC curve above its AVC curve. If the supplies of inputs to the industry are perfectly elastic (that is, if the prices of the factors of production remain the same regardless of the quantity of factors demanded per unit of time by the industry), then the market or industry short-run supply curve is obtained by the horizontal summation of the MC curves (over their respective AVC curves) of all the firms in the industry. Note that when a single firm expands its output (and demands more factors), factor prices can reasonably be expected to remain unchanged. However, when all firms together expand output (and demand more factors), factor prices are likely to rise.

(c) If the short-run market price for the service is \$9, each of the 100 identical firms in the industry will produce and sell 5,000 units of the output (point C) and the total for the industry will be 500,000 units. At $P = $ \$18, each firm produces and sells 7,000 units and the industry total is 700,000 units. No output of the service is produced at prices below \$5 per unit (i.e., below the shut-down point, the supply curves coincide with the price axis).

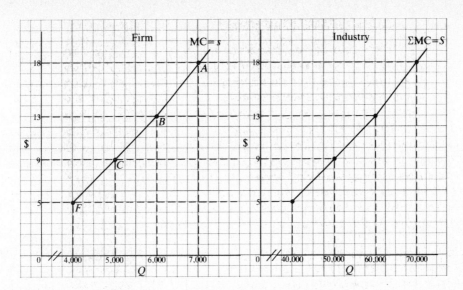

Fig. 10-12

10.7 Suppose that Fig. 10-13 refers to a perfectly competitive firm with scale of plant SAC_1 and that the short-run market equilibrium price is $16. (*a*) What output will this firm produce and sell in the short run? Is the firm making a profit or incurring a loss at this level of output? (*b*) Discuss the adjustment process for this firm in the long run, *if only this firm* and no other in the industry adjusted in the long run.

    (*a*) The best or optimum level of output for this firm in the short run is given by the point at which $P = SMC_1$. At this level of output (400 units), the firm earns a profit of $4 per unit and $1,600 in total.

    (*b*) If only this firm adjusts in the long run (a simplifying and unrealistic assumption for a perfectly competitive market), the firm will produce at $P = SMC_3 = LMC$. The firm will build the scale of plant indicated by SAC_3 and will produce and sell 800 units of output. The firm will earn a profit of $5 per unit and $4,000 in total. Note that since we are dealing with a perfectly competitive firm, we can safely assume that if only this firm expands its output, the effect on the equilibrium price will be imperceptible.

10.8 (*a*) Explain the long-run adjustment process for the firm and the market in Fig. 10-13 in Problem 10.7. (*b*) What implicit assumption about factor prices was made in the solution to part (*a*)? What would happen if input prices increased as more firms entered the market and demanded more inputs?

    (*a*) In the long run, all firms in the market will adjust their scale of plant and their level of output, and more firms will enter the market, attracted by the short-run profits. This will increase the industry supply of the

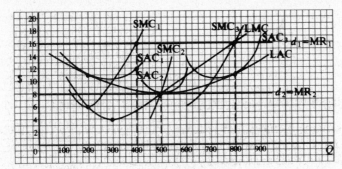

Fig. 10-13

product and thus cause a fall in the equilibrium price to $8 (see Fig. 10-13). At this price, $P = MR_2 = SMC_2 = LMC = SAC_2 = LAC$. Each firm produces 500 units of output (if they all have the same cost curves) and receives only a "normal return" (equal to the implicit opportunity cost) on its owned factors. If firms were incurring short-run losses to begin with, the exact opposite would occur. In any event when all firms are in long-run equilibrium, they all produce at the lowest point on their LAC curve, they all break even, and they all spend little if anything on sales promotion.

(b) In the solution to part (a), the implicit assumption was made that factor prices remained unchanged as more firms entered the industry and industry output was expanded. If, as more firms enter the market and demand more inputs, input prices increase, all of the firms' cost curves shift up, so that when the perfectly competitive industry is in long-run equilibrium, $P = LMC = $ lowest LAC, but the lowest LAC is now higher than when input prices were assumed to be constant.

MONOPOLY

10.9 Indicate (a) the possible sources of monopoly, (b) the extent of its occurrence in the United States today, and (c) the limitations on its market power.

(a) The firm may control the entire supply of the raw materials required to produce the product. For example, until World War II, Alcoa controlled almost every source of bauxite (the raw material necessary to produce aluminum) in the United States and thus had a monopoly in the production of aluminum in the United States.

The firm may own a patent or copyright that precludes other firms from producing the same product. For example, when cellophane was first introduced, Du Pont had monopoly power over cellophane production because of patents the company held. A monopoly may be established by a government franchise. In that case, the firm is set up as the sole producer and distributor of the product, subject to government regulation.

In some industries, increasing returns to scale may operate over such a wide range of outputs as to leave only one firm producing the product. These situations are called "natural monopolies" and are fairly common in the areas of public utilities and tranportation. In these cases the government usually allows the monopolist to operate, subject to government regulation. For example, electricity rates in New York City are set so as to leave the supplier, Con Edison, with only a "normal rate of return" (say 10 percent) on its investment.

(b) Aside from regulated monopolies, cases of pure monopoly in the United States have been rare in the past and are forbidden today by antitrust laws. Even so, the monopoly model is often useful in explaining observed business behavior in cases approximating pure monopoly, and also gives insights into the operation of other types of imperfectly competitive markets (i.e., monopolistic competition and oligopoly).

(c) A monopolist does not have unlimited market power. The monopolist faces indirect competition for consumers' dollars from all other products on the market. Furthermore, though there are no close substitutes for the product sold by the monopolist, substitutes may nevertheless exist. For example, even when Alcoa had monopoly power in the production and sale of aluminum in the United States, aluminum faced competition from steel, plastic, copper, and other materials. Fear of government prosecution and the threat of potential competition also act as checks on the monopolist's market power. In general, all monopoly power based on barriers to entry is subject to decay in the long run, except that based on government franchise.

10.10 Referring to Fig. 10-3, which shows output price and output determination for the monopolist, suppose that the average fixed cost of the monopolist increases by $4 and that its AVC is $5 less than the new ATC at the best level of output. Draw a figure showing the best level of output and price, the amount of profit or loss per unit and in total, and whether it pays for the monopolist to produce or not.

See Fig. 10-14. The figure shows that an increase in average fixed costs shifts the ATC curve up by $4 but does not change the MC curve. Since the D and MR curves are also unchanged, the best level of output for the monopolist remains at 400 units (given by point E, at which MR = MC) and the price remains at $8 (point A on the D curve). Since ATC = $10 now (point F'), the monopolist incurs a loss of $F'A = $2 per unit and $F'AB'C' = $800 in total. The monopolist, however, minimizes losses by staying in business. By going out of

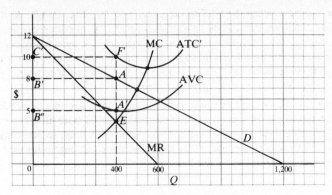

Fig. 10-14

business the monopolist would incur the larger loss of $F'A'$ = \$5 per unit (equal to AFC) and $F'A'B''C'$ = \$2,000 in total (equal to its total fixed costs).

10.11 Explain why the monopolist would never produce on the inelastic portion of the demand curve.

A monopolist produces at the point at which MR = MC, just the same as a perfect competitor. Since MC is positive, MR must also be positive at the best level of output. But for MR to be positive, the demand curve faced by the monopolist must be elastic. Another way of saying this is that only when the demand curve is elastic will a reduction in the product price result in an increase in TR so that MR will be positive. Thus, a monopolist will never operate in the inelastic portion of the demand curve.

10.12 Starting with Fig. 10-3, show graphically that the rising portion of the MC curve above the AVC curve does not represent the monopolist's short-run supply curve.

See Fig. 10-15. In the figure, D^* is a demand curve alternative to (and less price elastic than) D, and its associated MR* curve crosses the MC curve at point E (the same point at which the MR curve crosses it). Note that the MR* curve is halfway between the D^* curve and the vertical or price axis (as it should be).

Since the MR and MR* curves cross the MC curve at point E, the best level of output is 400 units in either

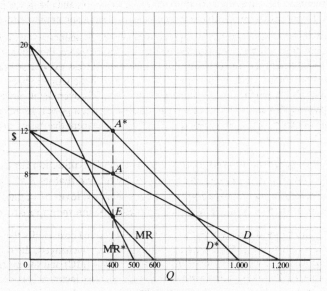

Fig. 10-15

case, even though the price (P) is \$8 (point A) with demand curve D but \$12 (point A^*) with demand curve D^*. Thus, the same quantity (400 units) could be supplied at different prices depending on the price elasticity of demand. In general, the less price elastic the demand curve is, the higher will be the price of the commodity.

Since there is no unique relationship between the price of a commodity and the quantity supplied under monopoly, we cannot derive the supply curve from the rising portion of the monopolist's MC curve above the AVC curve, as we can for a perfectly competitive firm.

10.13 Referring to Fig. 10-4, which shows the monopolist's long-run equilibrium, draw a figure (a) showing that the monopolist would break even if costs rose sufficiently in the long run and (b) showing the change in demand that would result in the monopolist's producing at the lowest point on its LAC curve.

(a) See Fig. 10-16. In the figure, the D and MR curves are the same as those in Fig. 10-4, but all the cost curves are higher. The reason is that in the long run there are no fixed costs, and an increase in costs shifts all cost curves upward. The best level of output of the monopolist is 400 units and is given by point E'' at which MR = SMC′ = LMC′. At $Q = 400$, P = SAC = LAC = \$8, and the monopolist breaks even.

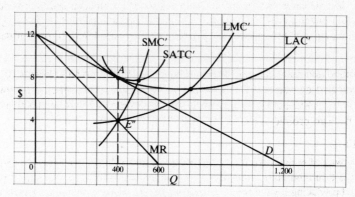

Fig. 10-16

(b) See Fig. 10-17. In the figure, the LAC and LMC curves are the same as those in Fig. 10-4, but the D' and MR′ curves are higher. Since the MR′ curve intercepts the LAC curve at its lowest point, the monopolist produces at that point (i.e., at point E^*, at which $Q = 700$ and MR′ = LMC). Since P = \$10 (point A^* on the D' curve) while LAC = \$3, the monopolist earns a profit of A^*E^* = \$7 per unit and $A^*E^*B^*C^*$ = \$4,900 in total.

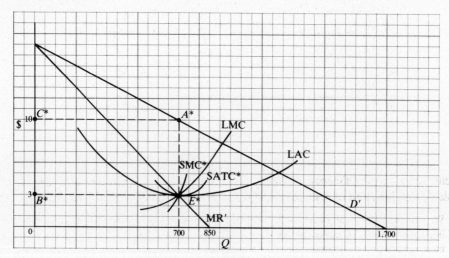

Fig. 10-17

MONOPOLISTIC COMPETITION

10.14 (*a*) Define monopolistic competition and give a few examples of it. (*b*) Identify the competitive and monopolistic elements in monopolistic competition. (*c*) Why is it difficult or impossible to define the market demand curve, the market supply curve, and the equilibrium price under monopolistic competition?

(*a*) Monopolistic competition refers to the market organization in which there are many sellers of a differentiated product. Monopolistic competition is very common in the retail and service sectors of our economy. Examples of monopolistic competition are the numerous barber shops, gasoline stations, grocery stores, liquor stores, and drug stores located close to one another.

(*b*) The competitive element results from the presence in a monopolistically competitive market (as in a perfectly competitive market) of so many firms that the activities of each have no perceptible effect on the other firms in the market. Furthermore, firms can enter or leave the market without much difficulty in the long run. The monopolistic element results because the many firms in the market sell a differentiated rather than a homogeneous product.

(*c*) Since, under monopolistic competition, each firm produces a somewhat different product, we cannot define the market demand curve and the market supply curve of the product, and we do not have a single equilibrium price but rather a cluster of prices, each for the different product produced by each firm. Thus, the graphical analysis of monopolistic competition must be confined to the typical or representative firm.

10.15 (*a*) On the demand and marginal revenue curves in Fig. 10-5, draw an alternative ATC curve showing that at the best level of output of 8 units, the monopolistically competitive firm incurs a loss of $2 per unit, but $P >$ AVC by $2. (*b*) What is the total profit or loss of the firm at the best level of output? Will the firm produce or not? Why?

(*a*) See Fig. 10-18.

(*b*) At the best level of output of 8 units, the firm incurs a total loss of $16 per time period. However, since $P >$ AVC, the firm minimizes its total losses by continuing to produce in the short run. Specifically, if the firm stopped producing it would incur a total loss of $32 (equal to the $4 average fixed cost at $Q = 8$ units times the output of 8 units) as compared to a total loss of $16 by continuing to produce.

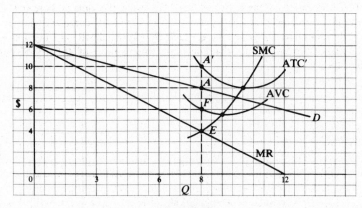

Fig. 10-18

10.16 Discuss the long-run efficiency implications of monopolistic competition with respect to (*a*) utilization of plant, (*b*) allocation of resources, and (*c*) advertising and product differentiation.

(*a*) When a monopolistically competitive market is in long-run equilibrium, the demand curve facing each firm is tangent to its LAC curve (so that each firm breaks even). Since the demand curve is negatively sloped, the tangency point will always occur to the left of the lowest point on the firm's LAC curve. Thus, the firm underutilizes a smaller-than-optimum scale of plant when in long-run equilibrium. This allows the existence of more firms in the industry than otherwise. An example of this is the "overcrowding" of gasoline stations, barber shops, grocery stores, etc., with each business idle much of the time.

(b) When the monopolistically competitive market is in long-run equilibrium, the price charged by each firm exceeds the LMC of the last unit produced. Therefore, resources are underallocated to the firms in the market and misallocated in the economy. This misallocation of resources is not large, however, because the demand curve facing the monopolistically competitive firm, though negatively sloped, is highly elastic.

(c) Though some advertising is useful (since it informs consumers), the amount of advertising undertaken by monopolistically competitive firms may be excessive. This only adds to costs and prices. Similarly, some product differentiation is beneficial since it gives the consumer a greater range of choices. However, an excessive number of brands, styles, designs, etc., only serves to confuse the consumer and adds to costs and prices.

10.17 Give the reasons why the theory of monopolistic competition has fallen somewhat into disrepute in recent years.

The theory of monopolistic competition has fallen somewhat into disrepute recently because:

(1) It may be difficult to define the market and determine the firms and products to include in it. For example, should moist paper tissues be included with other paper tissues or with soaps? Are toothpaste, dental floss, toothpicks, and water picks part of the same market or product group?

(2) In markets in which there are many small sellers, the demand curve facing monopolistic competitors is nearly horizontal, so that the model of perfect competition is appropriate to use.

(3) In markets in which there are strong brand preferences, the product usually turns out to have only a few sellers, so that oligopoly is the relevant model.

(4) Even in markets in which there are many small sellers of a good or service (say, gasoline stations) a change in price by one of them affects nearby stations significantly and evokes a response. In such cases, the oligopoly model is the more appropriate model to use.

Despite these serious criticisms, however, the monopolistic competition model provides some important insights, such as its emphasis on product differentiation and selling exenses, that are applicable to oligopolistic markets.

OLIGOPOLY

10.18 (a) Define oligopoly. (b) What is the single most important characteristic of oligopolistic markets? (c) To what problem does this characteristic lead? (d) What does oligopoly theory achieve?

(a) Oligopoly is the form of market organization in which there are few sellers of a product. If there are only two sellers we have a duopoly. If the product is homogeneous (e.g., steel, cement, copper), we have a pure oligopoly. If the product is differentiated (e.g., automobiles, cigarettes), we have a differentiated oligopoly. Oligopoly is the most prevalent form of market organization in the manufacturing sector of modern economies.

(b) The interdependence of the firms in an oligopolistic industry is the single most important characteristic setting oligopoly apart from other market structures. This interdependence is the natural result of limited numbers. That is, since there are few firms in an oligopolistic industry, when one of them lowers its price, undertakes a successful advertising campaign, or introduces a better model, the demand curve faced by other oligopolists will shift down. Therefore, the other oligopolists react.

(c) There are many different reaction patterns for the other oligopolists to the actions of the first, and unless and until we assume a specific reaction pattern, we cannot define the demand curve faced by the first oligopolist. As a result, we have an indeterminate solution. But even if we assume a particular reaction pattern so that we may have a determinate solution, this is only one of many possible solutions.

(d) Because of the situation outlined in part (c), we do not have a general theory of oligopoly. All we have are many specific cases and models. These models accomplish three things: (1) they show clearly the nature of oligopolistic interdependence, (2) they point out the gaps that a satisfactory theory of oligopoly must fill, and (3) they give some indication of how difficult this branch of microeconomics really is.

10.19 Identify and discuss the most important factors that give rise to oligopoly and, in the long run, also act as barriers to entry into oligopolistic industries.

The most important factors that give rise to oligopoly and act as barriers to entry are these:

(1) Economies of scale may operate over a scale of outputs sufficiently large to leave only a few firms as suppliers of the entire market.

(2) Huge capital investments and specialized inputs are usually required to enter an oligopolistic industry (say automobiles, aluminum, steel, and similar industries) and this acts as an important natural barrier to entry.

(3) Because of their patent ownership, a few firms may have the exclusive right to produce a commodity or to use a particular production process.

(4) Established firms may have a loyal customer following based on product quality and service that new firms would find very difficult to match.

(5) A few firms may own or control the entire supply of a raw material required in the production of the product.

(6) The government may give a franchise to only a few firms to operate in the market.

10.20 (a) What is meant by concentration ratios? What is their usefulness? (b) What are some of the most serious limitations in using concentration ratios as a measure of the degree of competition in an oligopolistic industry?

(a) Concentration ratios give the percentage of total industry sales of the 4, 8, and 20 largest firms in the industry, and so measure the degree by which an industry is dominated by a few large firms.

(b) Some of the most serious limitations in using concentration ratios to measure the degree of competition in an industry are these:

(1) In industries in which imports are significant, concentration ratios may greatly overestimate the relative importance of the largest firms in the industry. For example, since automobile imports are about 25 percent of the domestic market in the United States, the real four-firm concentration ratio in the automobile industry is not 92 percent but 69 percent (i.e., 92 percent times 0.75).

(2) Concentration ratios refer to the nation as whole, while the relevant market may be local. For example, the four-firm concentration ratio for the cement industry is 31 percent, but because of very high transportation costs, only two or three firms may actually compete in many local market.

(3) How broadly or narrowly a product is defined is also very important. For example, concentration ratios in the computer industry as a whole are higher than in the industry's personal computer segment.

(4) Concentration ratios do not give any indication of the number of potential entrants into the market and of the degree of actual and potential competition in the industry. Vigorous competition can also take place among few sellers. In short, concentration ratios provide only one dimension of the degree of competition in the market, and while useful, they must be used with great caution.

10.21 Assuming that an oligopolistic firm, presently selling its product at a price of $8, faced $Q = 360 - 40P$ as its relevent demand function for price increases, and $Q' = 120 - 10P$ for price reductions (in both cases P is measured in dollars). (a) Draw the demand curve facing this oligopolist, give an explanation for the shape of the curve, and derive the marginal revenue curve; on the same set of axes also sketch the set of cost schedules given in the following table. (b) If the oligopolist's cost schedules are given by MC and AC, find how much profit this oligopolist earns. (c) If the oligopolist's cost schedules change to MC' and AC', find the new best level of output, the price at which this output is sold, and the new level of profits for this oligopolist.

Q	MC ($)	AC ($)	MC' ($)	AC' ($)
20	3	4.50	4	5.50
30	4	4.00	5	5.00
40	5	4.50	6	5.50

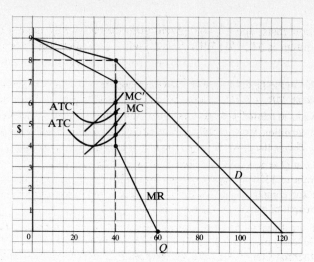

Fig. 10-19

(a)   See Fig. 10-19. The shape of D in Fig. 10-19 can be explained by assuming that if the oligopolistic firm raises its price from the prevailing level of $8, the other oligopolists in the market will not raise theirs, so that the firm will lose a great deal of its sales to rivals and the firm's demand curve will be very elastic. If the firm lowers its price, others will also lower theirs, so our oligopolist retains more or less only its own share of the market and its demand curve becomes less elastic.

(b)   With cost curves MC and AC, the oligopolist makes a profit of $3.50 per unit on each of the 40 units it sells and thus earns a total profit of $140.

(c)   If the oligopolist's cost curves shift up to MC' and ATC', its best level of output remains at 40 units per time period (since the MC' curve still intersects the discontinuous or vertical portion of the MR curve) and the firm will continue to sell at the price of $8. But now the oligopolist's profit is only $2.50 per unit and $100 in total. (Note that there is also a wide range over which the oligopolist's demand curve, with its kink at $8, can shift and result only in a change in the oligopolist's equilibrium quantity but not in the equilibrium price.)

10.22   (a) What does the kinked demand curve, or Sweezy model, accomplish? (b) What would happen if the new and higher MC curve (e.g., the MC' curve in Fig. 10-19) intersected the MR curve to the left of and above its vertical or discontinuous portion? (c) Why is the oligopolist in general reluctant to lower its price even when justified by demand and cost considerations? (d) Do oligopolists recognize their interdependence in the kinked demand curve model? Do they collude?

(a)   The kinked demand curve model can *rationalize* price rigidity in oligopolistic markets in the face of widespread changes in cost conditions. The model is of no use, however, in explaining how the prevailing price was determined in the first place.

(b)   If a new and higher MC curve intersects the MR curve to the left of and above its vertical or discontinuous portion, this and other firms would want to increase prices. An orderly price increase might then occur through price leadership.

(c)   Oligopolists are, in general, reluctant to lower prices for fear of starting a price war. Therefore, firms prefer to compete on the basis of quality, product design, advertising, and service.

(d)   In the kinked demand curve model, firms recognize their mutual dependence, but act without collusion.

10.23   Assume that (1) the 10 identical firms in a purely oligopolistic industry form a centralized cartel, (2) the total market demand function facing the cartel is given by $Q = 240 - 10P$, where P is expressed in dollars, (3) each firm's MC is given by $0.10Q$ for $Q > 4$ units, and factor prices remain constant. Determine (a) the best level of output and price for this cartel, (b) how the cartel can minimize production costs, and (c) how much profit the cartel will make if the ATC for each firm at the best level of output is $12. (d) Why do we study cartel models if cartels are illegal in the United States today?

(a) See Fig. 10-20. In the figure we see that the best level of output for this cartel is 80 units and is given by the point at which MR = Σ MC. The cartel will set the price at $16. This is the monopoly solution.

(b) If the cartel wants to minimize costs of production, it will set a quota of 8 units of production for each firm (given by the condition $MC_1 = MC_2 = \cdots MC_{10} = MR = \$8$, where the subscripts refer to the firms in the cartel). This is the same as the solution for the multiplant monopolist.

(c) If ATC = $12 at $Q = 8$, each firm will earn a profit of $4 per unit and $32 in total. The cartel as a whole will earn a profit of $320. In this case, each firm will very likely share equally in the cartel's profits. In more realistic and complicated cases, it may not be so easy to decide how to share the cartel's profits. The bargaining strength of each firm will then become important.

(d) Even if cartels are illegal in the United States, cartel models give some indication of how a tightly organized oligopolistic industry might operate. The best-known *international* cartel today is OPEC (Organization of Petroleum Exporting Countries). Note that the greater the number of firms in the cartel, the easier it is for members to cheat on each other and thus cause the collapse of the collusive agreement.

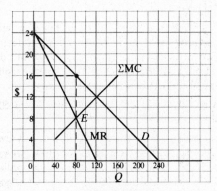

Fig. 10-20

10.24 Suppose that only one high-cost firm (firm 1) and one low-cost firm (firm 2) are selling a homogeneous product and that they tacitly agree to share the market equally. If D in Fig. 10-21 is the total market demand curve for the product, then $D_1 = D_2$ is the half-share demand curve of firms 1 and 2 and $MR_1 = MR_2$ is the correpsonding marginal revenue curve. Determine what each firm wants to do and what it actually does.

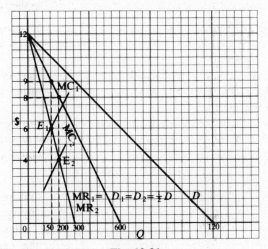

Fig. 10-21

See Fig. 10-21. In the figure, we see that firm 1 wants to sell 150 units of the product at a price of $9 (given by point E_1, at which $MC_1 = MR_1$) while firm 2 wants to sell 200 units of the product at a price of $8 (given by point E_2, at which $MC_2 = MR_2$). Since the product is homogeneous, however, firm 1 will have to follow firm 2 and also sell at the price of $8. Thus, only firm 2 (i.e., the price leader) will usually be producing and selling its best level of output.

10.25 Assume that (1) in a purely oligopolistic industry there is one dominant firm, which acts as the price leader, and there are 10 identical follower firms; (2) the total market demand function for the commodity is $D = 240 - 10P$, where P is in dollars; and (3) the MC function for the dominant firm is $0.20Q$ for $Q > 10$ units, while the MC function for each of the small firms is $1Q$ for $Q > 4$ units, and the AVC for each of the small firms is $4 at $Q = 4$. (a) On the same set of axes sketch D_T, the supply curve of all the follower firms combined, the demand curve of the dominant firm, its marginal revenue curve, and its marginal cost curve. (b) What price will the dominant firm set? How much will all the follower firms together and the dominant firm sell at that price? (c) What do the cartel and price leadership models have in common?

(a) See Fig. 10-22. In the figure, the ΣMC_F curve represents the supply curve of all the follower firms together. This is so because the followers behave as perfect competitors or price takers. Since the AVC of each follower is $4 at 4 units of output, the followers will supply nothing at prices below $4 per unit. By subtracting ΣMC_F from D_T at each price, we get the demand curve faced by the leader or dominant firm (D_L). This is given by $HNMFG$. Note that since followers supply nothing at prices below $4, the demand curve of the leader coincides with the market demand curve for segment FG.

(b) The leader will set the price of $10, at which it can sell its best level of output of 40 units (given by point E, at which $MR_L = MC_L$). Since each follower can sell all it wants to at this price, each faces an infinitely elastic demand curve (which coincides with its marginal revenue curve) at the price of $10. Each follower produces at $P = \Sigma MC_F = \$10$, and all the followers combined produce 100 units (point R on the ΣMC_F curve), leaving 40 units (segment $RC = JN$) to be sold by the dominant firm (shown by point N on its demand curve). To find the amount of profit, we need the value of ATC at the best level of output for each firm.

(c) In the cartel and price leadership models, the oligopolists recognize their mutual dependence and act collusively. The collusion is perfect in the cartel models and imperfect in price leadership models.

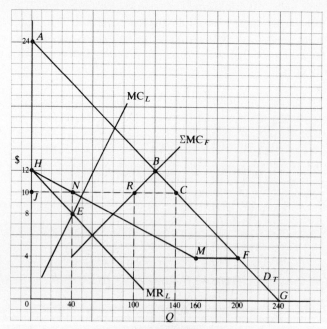

Fig. 10-22

10.26 What are the possible (*a*) harmful and (*b*) beneficial effects of oligopoly in the long run?

    (*a*)   In the long run, oligopoly may lead to the following harmful effects:

        (1)   As in monopoly, price usually exceeds LAC in oligopolistic markets.

        (2)   The oligopolist will usually not produce at the lowest point on its LAC curve.

        (3) $P >$ LMC, so that there is an underallocation of the economy's resources to the firms in an oligopolistic industry.

        (4)   When oligopolists produce a differentiated product, too much may be spent on advertising and model changes.

    (*b*)   For technological reasons (economies of scale), many products (such as automobiles, steel, aluminum) cannot possibly be produced under conditions of perfect competition because their costs of production would be prohibitive. In addition, oligopolists spend a great deal of their profits on research and development, and many economists believe that this leads to much faster technological advance and higher standards of living than if the industry were organized along perfectly competitive lines. Finally, some advertising is useful since it informs consumers, and some product differentiation has the economic value of satisfying the differing tastes of consumers.

Chapter 11

Pricing Practices

11.1 PRICING OF MULTIPLE PRODUCTS WITH INTERDEPENDENT DEMANDS

Optimal pricing and output decisions by a multiproduct firm require that the firm consider demand and production interrelationships. *Demand interrelationships* (substitutability and complementarity) among the products that the firm produces are reflected in the marginal revenue functions. For a two-product (A and B) firm the marginal revenue (MR) functions of the firm are:

$$MR_A = \frac{\Delta TR_A}{\Delta Q_A} + \frac{\Delta TR_B}{\Delta Q_A} \qquad (11\text{-}1)$$

$$MR_B = \frac{\Delta TR_B}{\Delta Q_B} + \frac{\Delta TR_A}{\Delta Q_B} \qquad (11\text{-}2)$$

where TR is total revenue and Q is the quantity of output. The second term in equations $(11\text{-}1)$ and $(11\text{-}2)$ is positive if products A and B are complements, and negative if A and B are substitutes (see Problem 11.1).

Firms produce more than one product in order to make fuller use of their plant and production capacities. The firm will introduce new products (or different varieties of existing products) in order of their profitability until $MR_A = MR_B = MR_C$, where product C is the least profitable product. Prices P_A, P_B, and P_C are then determined from their respective demand curves (see Problem 11.2).

11.2 PRICING AND OUTPUTS OF JOINTLY PRODUCED PRODUCTS

When products are jointly produced in fixed proportions, there is no rational way of allocating the cost of producing the entire "production package" to the individual products in the package. The best level of output will then be at the point at which the total marginal revenue, MR_T (obtained by vertically summing the marginal revenue curves of all the jointly produced products) equals the marginal cost (MC) of the joint production package. Prices are then determined from the demand curves of the respective products. A firm will not, however, *sell* any unit of a jointly produced product for which the marginal revenue is negative (see Example 1).

The optimal output of products that are jointly produced in variable proportions is given at the tangency point of the isorevenue (i.e., equal revenue) line and the product transformation (or total cost) curve that leads to the overall maximum profits for the firm (see Problems 11.6 and 11.7).

EXAMPLE 1. In both parts of Fig. 11-1, D_A and MR_A and D_B and MR_B refer, respectively, to the demand and marginal revenue curves of products A and B, which are jointly produced in fixed proportions. Products A and B can be thought of as beef and hides, which are produced in the ratio of one-to-one in slaughtering each cow. The total marginal revenue (MR_T) curve is obtained from the vertical summation of the MR_A and MR_B curves because the firm receives marginal revenues from the sale of both products. Note that for $Q > 45$, for which $MR_B < 0$, $MR_T = MR_A$. When the marginal cost of the jointly produced package is MC [see Fig. 11-1(a)], the best level of output is 40 units and is given by point E, at which $MR_T = MC$. At $Q = 40$, $P_A = \$11$ on D_A and $P_B = \$5$ on D_B. However, with MC' [see Fig. 11-1(b)], the best level of output of the production package is 60 units (given by point E', at which $MR_T = MC'$). At $Q = 60$, $P_{A'} = \$9$ on D_A, but since $MR_B < 0$ for $Q > 45$, the firm sells only 45 units of product B at $P_{B'} = \$4.50$ (for which TR_B is the maximum and $MR_B = 0$) and disposes of (i.e., keeps off the market) the remaining 15 units of product B.

11.3 PRICE DISCRIMINATION

Price discrimination refers to the charging of different prices for different quantities of a product, at different times, to different customer groups, or in different markets, when these price differences are not justified by cost differences. Three conditions must be met for a firm to be able to practice price discrimination: (1) the

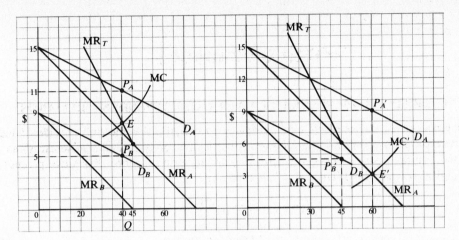

Fig. 11-1

firm must have some market power, (2) the price elasticities of demand for the product in different markets must differ, and (3) the markets must be separable or be able to be segmented. *First-degree price discrimination* involves selling each unit of the product separately and charging the highest price possible for each unit sold. By practicing first-degree price discrimination, the firm can extract from consumers all of the *consumers' surplus* (the difference between what consumers are willing to pay for a product and what they actually pay for it). *Second-degree price discrimination* refers to the charging of a uniform price per unit for a specific quantity or block of the product, a lower price per unit for an additional quantity or block of the product, and so on. By doing this, the firm can extract part, but not all, of the consumers' surplus (see Problem 11.9). *Third-degree price discrimination* refers to the charging of different prices for the same product in different markets until the marginal revenue of the last unit of the product sold in each market equals the marginal cost of the product. This involves selling the product at a higher price in the market with the less elastic demand (see Example 2).

EXAMPLE 2. Figure 11-2 shows third-degree price discrimination by a firm that sells a product in two different markets. Figure 11-2(a) shows D_1 and MR_1 (the demand and marginal revenue curves faced by the firm in market 1), part (b) shows D_2 and MR_2, and part (c) shows D and MR (the total demand and marginal revenue curves for the two markets combined). $D = \Sigma D_{1+2}$, and $MR = \Sigma MR_{1+2}$, by horizontal summation. The best level of output of the firm is 90 units and is given by point E in part (c), at which $MR = MC = \$2$. The firm sells 50 units of the product in market 1 and 40 units in market 2, so that $MR_1 = MR_2 = MR = MC = \$2$ (see points E_1, E_2, and E). For $Q_1 = 50$, $P_1 = \$7$ (on D_1) in market 1, and for $Q_2 = 40$, $P_2 = \$4$ (on D_2) in market 2. With an average total cost of \$3 per unit for $Q = 90$, the firm earns a profit of \$4 per unit and \$200 in total in market 1, and \$1 per unit and \$40 in total in

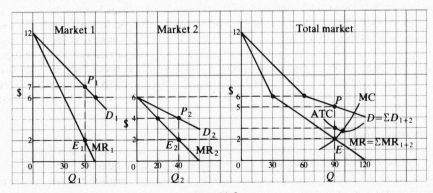

Fig. 11-2

market 2, for an overall total profit of $240 in both markets. In the absence of price discrimination, $Q = 90$, $P = \$5$ [see part (c)], so that profits are $2 per unit and $180 in total.

11.4 TRANSFER PRICING

The rapid rise of the modern large-scale enterprise has been accompanied by decentralization and the establishment of semiautonomous profit centers in order to contain rising communication and organizational costs. This also gave rise to the need for *transfer pricing*, or the need to determine the price of intermediate products produced by one semiautonomous division of the firm and sold to another semiautonomous division of the same firm. Appropriate transfer pricing is essential in determining the optimal output of each division and of the firm as a whole, in evaluating divisional performance, and in determining divisional rewards. For simplicity, we assume here that the firm has only two divisions—a production division and a marketing division—and that one unit of the intermediate product is required to produce each unit of the final product.

In the absence of an external market for the intermediate product, the transfer price for the intermediate product is given by the marginal cost of the production division at the best level of output of the intermediate product (see Example 3). When a perfectly competitive external market for the intermediate product exists, the transfer price is given by the external competitive price of the intermediate product (see Example 4). When an imperfectly competitive external market exists for the intermediate product, the product's (internal) transfer price is given at its best total level of output at which the net marginal revenue of the marketing division equals the marginal cost of the production division; the price on the external market is given on the external demand curve (see Problem 11.16).

EXAMPLE 3. In Fig. 11-3, the marginal cost of the firm (MC) is equal to the vertical summation of MC_p and MC_m, the marginal cost curves of the firm's production and marketing divisions, respectively. D_m is the external demand for the final product faced by the firm's marketing division, and MR_m is the corresponding marginal revenue curve. The firm's best level of output of the final product is 30 units and is given by point E_m, at which $MR_m = MC$, so that $P_m = \$9$. Since the production of each unit of the final product requires one unit of the intermediate product, the transfer price for the intermediate product, P_t, is set equal to MC_p at $Q_p = 30$. Thus, $P_t = \$4$. Since the intermediate-product demand and marginal revenue curves faced by the firm's production division equal D_p and MC_p (i.e., with $D_p = MR_p = P_t = MC_p = \$4$) at $Q_p = 30$ (see point E_p), $Q_p = 30$ is the best level of output of the intermediate product for the production division.

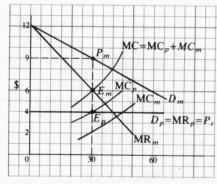

Fig. 11-3

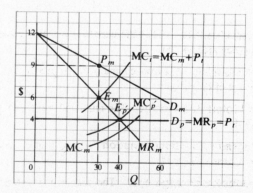

Fig. 11-4

EXAMPLE 4. Figure 11-4 is identical to Fig. 11-3, except that $MC_{p'}$ is lower than MC_p. At the perfectly competitive external price of $P_t = \$4$ for the intermediate product, the production division of the firm faces $D_p = MR_p = P_t = \$4$. Therefore, the best level of output of the intermediate product is at $Q_p = 40$ and is given by point $E_{p'}$ at which $D_p = MR_p = P_t = MC_{p'} = \$4$. Since the marketing division can purchase the intermediate product (internally or externally) at $P_t = \$4$, the division's total marginal cost curve, MC_t, is equal to the vertical summation of its own marginal cost of assembling and marketing the product (MC_m) and the price of the intermediate product (P_t). Thus, the best level of output of the final product by the marketing division is 30 units and is given by point E_m, at which $MR_m = MC_t$, so that $P_m = \$9$ (as in Fig. 11-3).

11.5 PRICING IN PRACTICE

Because it may be too expensive or impossible to collect precise marginal revenue and marginal cost data, most firms use *cost-plus pricing*. This involves calculating the average variable cost of producing the normal or standard level of output (usually between 70 percent and 80 percent of capacity), adding an average overhead charge so as to get the *fully allocated average cost* for the product, and then adding to this a *markup on cost* for profit. The markup-on-cost formula is

$$m = \frac{P - C}{C} \qquad\qquad (11\text{-}3)$$

where m is the markup on cost, P is the product price, C is the fully allocated average cost of the product, and $P - C$ is the *profit margin*. Solving equation (*11-3*) for P, we get the price of the product in a cost-plus pricing scheme. That is,

$$P = C(1 + m) \qquad\qquad (11\text{-}4)$$

Cost-plus pricing has some important advantages and disadvantages (see Problem 11.18) but in view of its widespread use, the advantages must clearly outweigh the disadvantages. Since firms usually apply higher markups to products facing a less elastic demand than to products with a more elastic demand, cost-plus pricing can be shown to lead to approximately the profit-maximizing price (see Problem 11.19). However, correct pricing and output decisions by a firm involve *incremental analysis*, which should lead a firm to undertake a particular course of action only if the incremental revenue from the action exceeds the incremental cost (see Problem 11.20).

EXAMPLE 5.   Suppose that a firm considers 80 percent of its capacity output of 125 units as the normal or standard output, that it projects total variable and total overhead costs for the year to be, respectively, $1,000 and $600, and that it wants to apply a 25 percent markup on costs. Then the normal or standard output of the firm is 100 units, AVC = $10, and the average overhead cost is $6. Thus, $C = \$16$ and $P = 16(1 + 0.25) = \$20$, with $m = (\$20 - \$16)/\$16 = 0.25$

Glossary

Consumers' surplus   The difference between what consumers are willing to pay for a specific quantity of a product and what they actually pay.

Cost-plus pricing   The most common pricing practice by firms today, whereby a markup is added to the fully allocated average cost of the product.

Demand interrelationships   The relationship of substitutability or complementarity among the products produced by the firm.

First-degree price discrimination   The selling of each unit of product separately and charging the highest price possible for each unit sold.

Fully allocated average cost   The sum of the average variable cost of producing the normal or standard level of output plus an average overhead charge.

Incremental analysis   Comparison of incremental revenue with incremental cost in managerial decision making.

Markup on cost   The ratio of the profit margin to the fully allocated average cost of the product.

Price discrimination   The practice of charging different prices for different quantities of a product, at different times, to different customer groups, or in different markets, when these price differences are not justified by cost differences.

Profit margin   The difference between the price and the fully allocated average cost of the product.

Second-degree price discrimination   The charging of a uniform price per unit for a specific quantity or block of a product, a lower price per unit for an additional batch or block of the product, and so on.

Third-degree price discrimination   The charging of different prices for the same product in different markets until the marginal revenue of the last unit of the product sold in each market equals the marginal cost of the product.

Transfer pricing   The determination of the price of intermediate products sold by one semiautonomous division of a firm to another semiautonomous division of the same enterprise.

Review Questions

1.   If a firm produces products A and B and $\Delta TR_B/\Delta Q_A$ and $\Delta TR_A/\Delta Q_B$ are negative, products A and B are

   (*a*)   complements.

   (*b*)   substitutes.

   (*c*)   independent.

   (*d*)   any of the above.

   Ans.   (*b*) See Section 11.1.

2.   Which of the following statements is false?

   (*a*)   Firms produce multiple products in order to make fuller use of the production facilities.

   (*b*)   Firms usually introduce products in the order of their profitability.

   (*c*)   Successive products introduced by a firm are sold at higher prices and produced at lower marginal costs than previous products.

   (*d*)   To maximize profits a firm should produce the output level at which $MR_A = MR_B = MR_C$, where product C is the least profitable product.

   Ans.   (*c*) See Section 11.1.

3.   For a firm producing products jointly in fixed proportions that are unrelated in consumption,

   (*a*)   it is impossible to rationally allocate the total cost of producing the package to the individual products in the package.

   (*b*)   the total marginal revenue curve for the two products is obtained by horizontally summing the marginal revenue curves of the jointly produced products.

   (*c*)   the firm sells a jointly produced product only if its $MR < 0$.

   (*d*)   all of the above.

   Ans.   (*a*) See Section 11.2 and Example 1.

4.   A firm producing products jointly in fixed proportions

   (*a*)   may produce some units of the product for which MR is negative.

   (*b*)   will not sell any units of the product for which MR is negative.

   (*c*)   will receive revenues from the sale of each jointly produced product.

   (*d*)   all of the above.

   Ans.   (*d*) See Section 11.2 and Example 1.

5.   When products are produced in variable proportions, they are

   (*a*)   complementary in production.

   (*b*)   substitutes in production.

   (*c*)   always interdependent in demand.

   (*d*)   all of the above.

   Ans.   (*b*) See Section 11.2 and Problems 11.6 and 11.7.

6.   Which of the following is not an example of price discrimination?

   (*a*)   Lower prices for bulk than for small purchases because of cost savings to the firm in handling large orders

   (*b*)   Lower electricity charges to commercial than to residential users

   (*c*)   Lower medical fees for lower-income than for higher-income people

   (*d*)   Lower fares on public transportation for children and the elderly

   Ans.   (*a*) See Section 11.3.

7.   Which of the following conditions is required for a firm to be able to practice price discrimination?

   (*a*)   The firm must have some control over price.

   (*b*)   The price elasticity of demand for the product must be different in different markets.

   (*c*)   The markets must be separable.

   (*d*)   All of the above.

   Ans.   (*d*) See Section 11.3.

8.   Third-degree price discrimination refers to the charging of different prices (not justified by cost differences)

   (*a*)   for each unit of the product.

   (*b*)   for different batches of the product.

   (*c*)   in different markets.

   (*d*)   all of the above.

   Ans.   (*c*) See Section 11.3.

9.   Which of the following statements is false?

   (*a*)   The rapid rise of the modern large-scale corporation has been accompanied by decentralization and the establishment of semiautonomous profit centers.

   (*b*)   Decentralization and the establishment of semiautonomous profit centers in modern large-scale enterprises have led to the need for transfer pricing.

   (*c*)   Transfer pricing refers to the determination of the price of intermediate products produced by one semiautonomous division of the firm and sold to another semiautonomous division of the same firm.

   (*d*)   None of the above.

   Ans.   (*d*) See Section 11.4.

10.   When there is no external market for an intermediate product, its transfer price is given by the

   (*a*)   marginal cost of the marketing division.

   (*b*)   marginal cost of the production division.

   (*c*)   marginal revenue of the marketing division.

   (*d*)   price of the final product.

   Ans.   (*b*) See Section 11.4.

11.   When an external perfectly competitive market for an intermediate product exists, the quantity of the intermediate product produced by the production division in relation to the quantity produced of the final product by the marketing division of the firm is

(a) larger.

(b) smaller.

(c) equal.

(d) any of the above.

Ans.   (*d*) See Section 11.4 and Example 4.

12.   Which of the following statements is false with regard to cost-plus pricing?

(a) It is the most prevalent pricing method used by business firms.

(b) It involves adding a markup or profit margin to the fully allocated average cost to determine the price of the product.

(c) It is a form of incremental cost pricing.

(d) It completely disregards demand conditions in actual real-world applications.

Ans.   (*c*) See Section 11.5.

Solved Problems

PRICING OF MULTIPLE PRODUCTS WITH INTERDEPENDENT DEMANDS

11.1   (*a*) What is meant by demand interrelationships for a multiproduct firm? (*b*) How are demand interrelationships measured? (*c*) Why must a multiproduct firm take into consideration demand interrelationships in its pricing and output decisions?

(a) Demand interrelationships refer to the substitutability and complementarity relationships that exist among the products produced by a firm.

(b) Demand interrelationships are measured by the cross-marginal revenue effects in the marginal revenue function for each product sold by the firm. For a two-product (A and B) firm, the MR_A function includes a $\Delta TR_B / \Delta Q_A$ term and the MR_B function includes a $\Delta TR_A / \Delta Q_B$ term, which measure demand interrelationships. Products A and B are complements if the terms $\Delta TR_B / \Delta Q_A$ and $\Delta TR_A / \Delta Q_B$ are positive and substitutes if these cross-marginal revenue effects are negative.

(c) Optimal pricing and output decisions by the firm require it to take the total effect (i.e., the direct as well as the cross-marginal effects) into consideration. For example, if products A and B are complements but the firm disregards the term $\Delta TR_B / \Delta Q_A$ (which is positive) and produces at $MR_A = \Delta TR_A / \Delta Q_A = MC_A$, the firm will produce too little of product A to maximize profits. However, if products A and B are substitutes but the firm disregards the term $\Delta TR_B / \Delta Q_A$ (which is negative) and produces at $MR_A = \Delta TR_A / \Delta Q_A = MC_A$, the firm will produce too much of product A to maximize profits.

11.2   Draw a figure showing the best level of output and price of each of three products (A, B, and C) produced by the firm, where product A is the most profitable and product C is the least profitable.

See Fig. 11-5. D_A, D_B, and D_C are the demand curves for products A, B, and C sold by the firm, and MR_A, MR_B, and MR_C are the corresponding marginal revenue curves. The firm maximizes profits when $MR_A = MR_B = MR_C = MC$. This is shown by points E_A, E_B, and E_C, at which the equal marginal revenue (EMR) curve crosses the MR_A, MR_B, and MR_C curves at the level at which $MR_C = MC$. Thus, the best level of output of each product and price are, respectively, Q_A and P_A, $Q_B - Q_A$ and P_B, $Q_C - Q_B$ and P_C. Note that each successive demand curve is more elastic, and that the price of each successive product is lower, while its MC is higher.

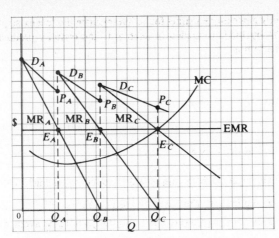

Fig. 11-5

11.3 For Fig. 11-5 in Problem 11.2, indicate (*a*) to what extent it would be profitable for the firm to introduce new products, (*b*) what assumption is made with respect to the adaptation of the firm's production facilities in the production of new products, (*c*) what demand interrelationships exist among the products produced by the firm, and (*d*) whether the firm would ever produce a product on which it makes no profit.

(*a*)   It would be profitable for the firm of Fig. 11-5 to introduce still other products until the price of the last product introduced is equal to its marginal cost (so that the firm would be a perfect competitor in the market for this product), or the firm's productive capacity has been reached.

(*b*)   The assumption made in the analysis and figure in Problem 11.2 is that the firm's production facilities can easily be adapted to the production of other products and that the firm's marginal cost curve reflects any increase in costs resulting from the introduction of additional products.

(*c*)   In Fig. 11-5 we implicitly assume that the demand curve for each product sold by the firm is independent rather than interrelated or that the figure shows the total and final effect of all demand interrelationships.

(*d*)   A firm may produce a product on which it makes little or no profit in order to offer a full range of products, to use as a "loss leader" (i.e., to attract customers), to retain customers' good will, to keep channels of distribution open, or to keep the firm's resources in use while awaiting more profitable opportunities (as in the case of construction companies).

PRICING AND OUTPUT OF JOINTLY PRODUCED PRODUCTS

11.4 The demand and marginal revenue functions of a firm producing products A and B jointly in fixed proportions are

$$Q_A = 180 - 10P_A \quad \text{or} \quad P_A = 18 - 0.1Q_A \quad \text{and} \quad MR_A = 18 - 0.2Q_A$$
$$Q_B = 100 - 10P_B \quad \text{or} \quad P_B = 10 - 0.1Q_B \quad \text{and} \quad MR_B = 10 - 0.2Q_B$$

Two alternative marginal cost functions for the joint production package are, respectively,

$$MC = 8 + 0.1Q \quad \text{or} \quad MC' = \frac{2Q}{35}$$

Determine graphically the best level of output and price of products A and B for each alternative MC function.

   See Fig. 11-6. With marginal cost curve MC [see part (*a*) of Fig. 11-6], the best level of output of products A and B is 40 units and is given by point E, at which $MR_T = MC$. For $Q = 40$, $P_A = \$14$ (on D_A) and $P_B = \$6$ (on D_B).

   With marginal cost curve MC' [see part (*b*) of Fig. 11-6], the best level of output of the joint production package is 70 units and is given by point E', at which $MR_T = MC'$. The firm sells 70 units of product A at

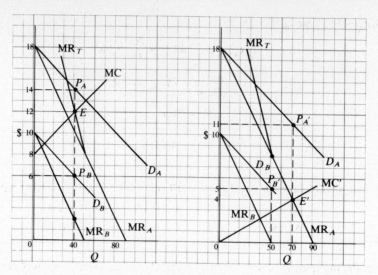

Fig. 11-6

$P_{A'} = \$11$ (on D_A). However, since $MR_B < 0$ for $Q > 50$, the firm sells only 50 units of product B at $P_{B'} = \$5$ (for which TR_B is maximum and $MR_B = 0$). The firm keeps from the market and disposes of the remaining 20 units of product B in order not to depress its price below the one for which $MR_B = 0$.

11.5   Solve Problem 11.4 mathematically.

Adding the MR_A and MR_B functions together, we get

$$MR_T = MR_A + MR_B = 18 - 0.2Q_A + 10 - 0.2Q_B = 28 - 0.4Q$$

Setting $MR_T = MC$, we have

$$MR_T = 28 - 0.4Q = 8 + 0.1Q = MC$$
$$0.5Q = 20$$
$$Q = 40$$

Since $Q = 40$ is the profit-maximizing level of output and sales of each product [see Fig. 11-6(a)],

$$MR_A = 18 - 0.2(40) = \$10 \quad \text{and} \quad MR_B = 10 - 0.2(40) = \$2$$
$$P_A = 18 - 0.1(40) = \$14 \quad \text{and} \quad P_B = 10 - 0.1(40) = \$6$$

On the other hand, with MC', we have

$$MR_T = 28 - 0.4Q = \frac{2Q}{35} = MC'$$

$$0.4Q + \frac{2Q}{35} = 28$$

$$\frac{(14 + 2)Q}{35} = 28$$

$$16Q = 980$$
$$Q = 61.25$$

However, setting $MR_B = 0$, we get

$$MR_B = 10 - 0.2Q_B = 0$$

$$Q_B = 50$$

Therefore, $MR_B < 0$ for $Q_B > 50$, and so $MR_T = MR_A$ for $Q = 50$.

Setting $MR_A = MC'$, we have

$$MR_A = 18 - 0.2Q = \frac{2Q}{35} = MC'$$

$$0.2Q + \frac{2Q}{35} = 18$$

$$\frac{(7 + 2)Q}{35} = 18$$

$$9Q = 630$$

$$Q = 70$$

Thus, the best level of output is 70 units of product A but only 50 units of product B [see Fig. 11-6(b)].

At sales of $Q_A = 70$, $P_{A'} = 18 - 0.1(70) = \$11$
At sales of $Q_B = 50$, $P_{B'} = 10 - 0.1(50) = \$5$

11.6 Answer the following questions with respect to Fig. 11-7: (a) What is another name for the curved total cost (TC) curves shown in the figure? Why do these curves refer to the case of products that are jointly produced in variable proportions? Why are these total cost curves concave to the origin? (b) What do the straight total revenue (TR) lines in the figure show? What prices of products A (P_A) and B (P_B) are implied by the TR lines shown in the figure? What is implied by TR lines that are straight? What is the slope of the TR lines in terms of P_A and P_B? (c) How is the level of the firm's maximum total profit (π) determined for each level of TC? What combinations of products A and B (i.e., Q_A and Q_B) lead to overall maximum total profits for the firm at any TC level?

(a) Another name for the curved total cost (TC) curves in Fig. 11-7 is *product transformation curve* or *production possibilities curve*. The TC curves refer to the case of products that are jointly produced in varying proportions; each curve shows the different combinations of products A and B that the firm can produce with a specific TC. For example, with TC = $100 (the lowest curve in Fig. 11-7), the firm can produce 40A and 60B (point G), 20A and 80B (point H), or any combination of products A and B shown on the TC = $100 curve. Note that in order to produce more of one product with a given TC, the firm must give up some units of the other product. The TC or production transformation curves are concave to the origin because the firm's production resources are not perfectly adaptable in (i.e., cannot be perfectly transferred between) the production of the two products.

(b) The straight isorevenue lines show the various combinations of sales of products A and B that result in a particular TR. For example, TR = $120 results when the firm sells 80A and 0B, 40A and 60B, 0A and

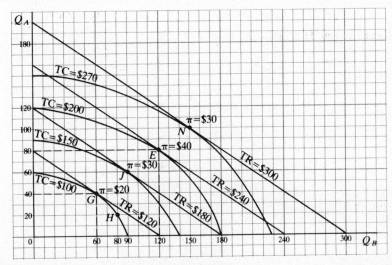

Fig. 11-7

$120B$, or any combination of products A and B on the TR = $120 line. This implies that P_A = $1.50 (from $120/80) and P_B = $1. Straight TR lines imply constant P_A and P_B. The absolute slope of the TR lines is P_B/P_A = $1.00/$1.50 = 2/3. Since the TR lines are parallel, their slopes are equal.

(c) The level of the firm's maximum total profits (π) for each level of TC is given by the point at which a TR or isorevenue line is tangent to the particular TC curve. For example, the TR = $120 isorevenue line is the highest that the firm can reach with TC = $100. The overall maximum profit of the firm is π = $40 (point E) and is obtained when the firm produces and sells $80A$ and $120B$, and thus reaches the TR = $240 isorevenue line, at which TC = $200.

11.7 Table 11.1 shows the various quantities of products A and B that a firm can produce with three different levels of total expenditures, i.e., total costs (TC). If the prices of products A and B are P_A = $1.00 and P_B = $0.50, draw a figure showing the maximum total profit (π) that the firm can earn at each level of TC and the overall maximum profit that the firm can earn at any of the three different levels of TC.

Table 11.1

TC = $70		TC = $90		TC = $140	
Product A	Product B	Product A	Product B	Product A	Product B
80	0	100	0	130	0
70	40	90	60	110	80
50	70	70	90	80	120
20	90	30	120	40	150
0	95	0	130	0	160

See Fig. 11-8. With P_A = $1.00 and P_B/P_A = $0.50, the isorevenue lines have absolute slopes of P_B/P_A = $0.50/$1.00 = $\frac{1}{2}$. With TC = $70, the maximum profit is π = $20, which the firm earns when it produces and sells $70A$ and $40B$ and thus reaches the TR = $90 isorevenue line at point G. With TC = $90, the maximum profit is π = $30, which the firm earns when it produces and sells $90A$ and $60B$ and thus reaches the TR = $120 isorevenue line at point E. With TC = $140, the maximum profit is π = $10, which the firm earns when it produces and sells $110A$ and $80B$ and thus reaches the TR = $150 isorevenue line at point H.

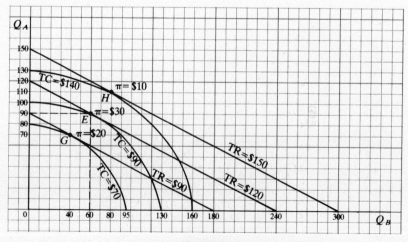

Fig. 11-8

PRICE DISCRIMINATION

11.8 Identify the conditions required for a firm to be able to practice price discrimination and explain why each condition is required. How are these conditions met in the real world?

    Three conditions are required for a firm to be able to practice price discrimination:

(1) The firm must have some control over the price of the product (i.e., the firm must be an imperfect competitor). A perfectly competitive firm has no control over the price of the product it sells (i.e., it is a price taker) and thus cannot possibly practice price discrimination.

(2) The price elasticity of demand for the product must differ for different quantities of the product, at different times, for different customer groups, or in different markets. If these price elasticities of demand are equal, the firm cannot increase its revenues and profits by practicing price discrimination.

(3) The quantities of the good or service, the times when they are used or consumed, and the customer groups, or markets, for the product must be separable (i.e., the firm must be able to segment the total market). Otherwise, individuals or firms will purchase the good or service where it is cheap and resell it where it is more expensive, thereby undermining the firm's effort to charge different prices for the same product (i.e., practice price discrimination).

    The above conditions are met in different ways in the real world. In the case of electricity, gas, and water consumption, meters on business premises or in homes keep the markets separate. Transportation costs and trade restrictions keep domestic and foreign markets separate. In the case of services, markets are naturally separated by the fact that most services (e.g., doctors' visits, legal advice, haircuts, public transportation passes for the elderly, etc.) cannot be easily, if at all, transferred or resold to other people.

11.9 A firm faces the demand function $Q = 80 - 10P$. (*a*) Plot the demand curve that the firm faces. (*b*) What is the firm's total revenue on sales of 60 units of the product? How much would consumers be willing to pay for 60 units of the product? What is the amount of the consumers' surplus? (*c*) How could the firm extract all of the consumers' surplus? What type of price discrimination is this? How common is this type of price discrimination? (*d*) How much of the consumers' surplus would the firm be able to extract from consumers by charging a price of $5 per unit for the first 30 units of the product sold and a price of $2 per unit on the next 30 units of the product sold? What type of price discrimination is this? In which markets is this type of price discrimination encountered most often?

(*a*) See Fig. 11-9.

(*b*) At $Q = 60$, $P = \$2$ and TR $= \$120$ (the area of rectangle *CFOG*). Consumers would be willing to pay *ACFO* $= \$300$ for 60 units of the product. Thus, the consumers' surplus is *ACFO* $-$ *CFOG* $= \$300 - \$120 = \$180$.

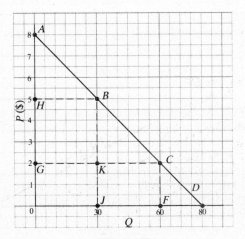

Fig. 11-9

(c) The firm could extract all of the consumers' surplus from consumers by selling each unit of the product separately and charging the highest price possible for each unit sold. This is first-degree price discrimination. To be able to practice first-degree price discrimination, however, the firm must have precise knowledge of the demand curve of each consumer and sell each unit of the product at the highest possible price. This is very difficult or impossible to do, and so first-degree price discrimination is not very common in the real world.

(d) If the firm sold 30 units of the product at a price of $5 per unit and another 30 units at a price of $2 per unit, the total revenue of the firm would be $210 (as compared with a TR of $120 from selling 60 units of the product at a price of $2 per unit). Thus, the firm would extract $BKGH = \$90$, or one-half, of the consumers' surplus. This is second-degree price discrimination. It is most common in markets in which usage of the good or service can be easily measured or metered, as in the case of electricity, gas, and water consumption.

11.10 Do (a) quantity discounts and (b) lower airfares for midweek travel represent price discrimination? Why?

(a) To the extent that quantity discounts reflect only cost savings on the part of the firm in handling large orders (e.g., lower costs for sales people, paperwork, transportation) they do not represent price discrimination. However, if the amount of the quantity discount exceeds the cost savings that result from handling large orders, then the difference represents second-degree price discrimination.

(b) Business travel is particularly heavy on Mondays, when managers leave home offices to meet clients, suppliers, and regional offices, and on Fridays, when the managers return home for the weekend. To encourage fuller use of capacity at midweek, airlines offer fare discounts for midweek travel. To the extent that the lower midweek airfares fully reflect the lower marginal costs per passenger for air travel during that period, these airfares do not represent third-degree price discrimination. The existing airfare differentials for midweek air travel, however, seem to be too large to reflect cost differences only. Thus, this pricing practice by the airlines may in fact reflect some price discrimination.

11.11 A firm produces one type of product and sells it directly to consumers and to wholesalers. The demand and marginal revenue functions of the firm from consumers (market 1) and from wholesalers (market 2) are, respectively,

$$Q_1 = 140 - 10P_1 \quad \text{or} \quad P_1 = 14 - 0.1Q_1 \quad \text{and} \quad MR_1 = 14 - 0.2Q_1$$
$$Q_2 = 160 - 20P_2 \quad \text{or} \quad P_2 = 8 - 0.05Q_2 \quad \text{and} \quad MR_2 = 8 - 0.1Q_2$$

The firm's total cost function is TC $= 180 + 4Q$. Draw a figure showing (1) the demand, marginal revenue, and marginal cost curves faced by the firm; (2) the best level of output of the firm and how the firm should distribute sales in each market in order to maximize total profits with third-degree price discrimination; (3) the price and total revenue of the firm in each market with third-degree price discrimination; (4) the profit per unit and in total with third-degree price discrimination; and (5) the output, price, total revenue, and profit per unit and in total in the absence of price discrimination.

See Fig. 11-10. D_1 and MR_1 in part (a) are the demand and marginal revenue curves that the firm faces in market 1, D_2 and MR_2 in part (b) are the demand and marginal revenue curves that the firm faces in market 2, and D and MR in part (c) are the overall total demand and marginal revenue curves faced by the firm for the two markets combined. $D = \Sigma D_{1+2}$ and MR $= \Sigma MR_{1+2}$, by horizontal summation. The total cost function, TC $= 180 + 4Q$, indicates that the firm faces total fixed costs of $90 and a marginal cost of $4. The best level of output of the firm is 90 units and is given by point E in part (c), at which MR $=$ MC $= \$4$. With third-degree price discrimination, the firm should sell 50 units of the product in market 1 and 40 units in market 2, so that $MR_1 = MR_2 =$ MR $=$ MC $= \$4$ (points E_1, E_2, and E). For $Q_1 = 50$, $P_1 = \$9$ (on D_1) in market 1, so that $TR_1 = \$450$. For $Q_2 = 40$, $P_2 = \$6$ (on D_2) in market 2, so that $TR_2 = \$240$. Thus, the overall total revenue of the firm is TR $= TR_1 + TR_2 = \$450 + \$240 = \$690$. For $Q = 90$, TC $= \$180 + \$4(90) = \$540$, so that ATC $=$ TC$/Q = \$540/90 = \$6$. Hence, the firm earns a profit of $P_1 -$ ATC $= \$9 - \$6 = \$3$ per unit and $150 in total in market 1, and a profit of $P_2 -$ ATC $= \$6 - \$6 = \$0$ per unit and in total in market 2. Thus, the overall total profit of the firm is $\pi = \pi_1 + \pi_2 = \$150 + \$0 = \$150$. In the absence of third-degree price discrimination, $Q = 90$, $P = \$7$, [in part (c)], TR $= (\$7)(90) = \$630$, and profits are $1 per unit and $90 in total.

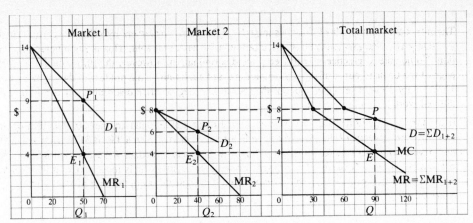

Fig. 11-10

11.12 Solve Problem 11.11 algebraically.

With TC $= 180 + 4Q$, MC $= \$4$ (the coefficient of Q). With third-degree price discrimination, the condition for profit maximization for the firm is

$$MR_1 = MR_2 = MR = MC$$

Setting $MR_1 = MC$ and $MR_2 = MC$, we get

$$MR_1 = 14 - 0.2Q_1 = 4 = MC \quad \text{and} \quad MR_2 = 8 - 0.1Q_2 = 4 = MC$$

so that

$$0.2Q_1 = 10 \quad \text{and} \quad 0.1Q_2 = 4$$
$$Q_1 = 50 \qquad\qquad Q_2 = 40$$

The price that the firm should charge in each market is then

$$P_1 = 14 - 0.1(50) = \$9 \quad \text{and} \quad P_2 = 8 - 0.05(40) = \$6$$

so that

$$TR_1 = P_1Q_1 = (\$9)(50) = \$450 \quad \text{and} \quad TR_2 = P_2Q_2 = (\$6)(40) = \$240$$

and

$$TR = TR_1 + TR_2 = \$450 + \$240 = \$690$$

For $Q = 90$,

$$TC = \$180 + \$4(90) = \$540 \quad \text{and} \quad ATC = \frac{TC}{Q} = \frac{\$540}{90} = \$6$$

Thus, the firm's profits per unit (π/Q) and in total (π) with third-degree price discrimination are

$$\frac{\pi_1}{Q_1} = P_1 - ATC = \$9 - \$6 = \$3 \quad \text{and} \quad \frac{\pi_2}{Q_2} = P_2 - ATC = \$6 - \$6 = \$0$$

and

$$\pi_1 = \left(\frac{\pi_1}{Q_1}\right)Q_1 = (\$3)(50) = \$150 \quad \text{and} \quad \pi_2 = \left(\frac{\pi_2}{Q_2}\right)Q_2 = (\$0)(40) = \$0$$

so that

$$\pi = \pi_1 + \pi_2 = \$150 + \$0 = \$150$$

The total profit of the firm can also be found as follows:

$$\pi = TR_1 + TR_2 - TC = \$450 + \$240 - \$540 = \$150$$

In the absence of price discrimination, the firm will sell the product at the same price in both markets (i.e., $P_1 = P_2 = P$). The total demand function faced by the firm for prices below $\$8$ (for which $Q_2 > 0$) is

$$Q = Q_1 + Q_2$$
$$= 140 - 10P_1 + 160 - 20P_2$$
$$= 300 - 30P$$

so that $\qquad\qquad\qquad\qquad P = 10 - 0.0333Q \quad$ and $\quad$ MR $= 10 - 0.0667Q$

Setting MR = MC, we get

$$\text{MR} = 10 - 0.0667Q = 4 = \text{MC}$$

so that $\qquad\qquad\qquad 0.0667Q = 6 \quad$ and $\quad Q = 89.96 \cong 90$

At $Q = 90$

$$P = 10 - 0.0333(90) = 10 - 2.997 \cong \$7$$

so that $\qquad\qquad\qquad\qquad$ TR $= (P)(Q) = (\$7)(90) = \$630$

(as compared with \$690 with third-degree price discrimination).

The profit per unit (π/Q) and in total (π) are

$$\frac{\pi}{Q} = P - \text{ATC} = \$7 - \$6 = \$1$$

and $\qquad\qquad \pi = \left(\frac{\pi}{Q}\right)Q = (\$1)(90) = \$90 \quad$ or $\quad \pi = \text{TR} - \text{TC} = \$630 - \$540 = \$90$

(as compared with $\pi = \$150$ with third-degree price discrimination).

These results are shown in Fig. 11.10, as described in Problem 11.11.

TRANSFER PRICING

11.13 A firm is composed of two semiautonomous divisions—a production division, which manufactures the intermediate product, and a marketing division, which assembles and markets the final product. There is no external demand for the intermediate product manufactured by the production division. The external demand and marginal revenue functions for the finished product are, respectively,

$$Q_m = 100 - 10P_m \quad \text{or} \quad P_m = 10 - 0.1Q_m \quad \text{and} \quad \text{MR}_m = 10 - 0.2Q_m$$

The marginal cost functions of the production and marketing divisions of the firm are, respectively,

$$\text{MC}_p = 2 + 0.1Q_p \quad \text{and} \quad \text{MC}_m = 0.1Q_m$$

Draw a figure showing the firm's best level of output and price for the finished product and the transfer price and output of the intermediate product.

See Fig. 11-11. In the figure, the marginal cost of the firm (MC) is equal to the vertical summation of MC_p and MC_m, the marginal cost curves of the production and the marketing divisions of the firm, respectively. D_m is the external demand for the final product faced by the firm's marketing division and MR_m is the corresponding marginal revenue curve. The firm's best level of output of the final product is 20 units and is given by point E_m, at which $\text{MR}_m = \text{MC}$, so that $P_m = \$8$. Since the production of each unit of the final product requires one unit of the intermediate product, the transfer price for the intermediate product, P_t, is set equal to MC_p at $Q_p = 20$. Thus, $P_t = \$4$. With $D_p = \text{MR}_p = P_t = \text{MC}_p = \$4$ at $Q_p = 20$ (see point E_p), $Q_p = 20$ is the best level of output of the intermediate product for the production division.

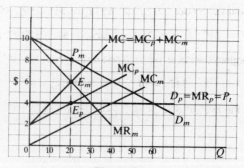

Fig. 11-11

11.14 Starting with the data given in Problem 11.13, except that $MC_{p'} = 1 + 0.1Q_p$ and that a perfectly competitive market exists for the intermediate product at $P_t = \$4$, (a) determine graphically the profit-maximizing output of the firm's production and marketing divisions, the optimal transfer price for the intermediate product, and the price of the final product. (b) What is the difference between the solution of this problem in part (a) and the solution of Problem 11.13? To what is the difference due?

(a) See Fig. 11-12. Fig. 11-12 is identical to Fig. 11-11, except that $MC_{p'}$ is lower than MC_p. At the perfectly competitive external price of $P_t = \$4$ for the intermediate product, the production division of the firm faces $D_p = MR_p = P_t = \$4$. Therefore, the best level of output of the intermediate product is $Q_p = 30$ and is given by point $E_{p'}$ at which $D_p = MR_p = P_t = MC_{p'} = \$4$. Since the marketing division can purchase the intermediate product (internally or externally) at $P_t = \$4$, its total marginal cost curve, MC_t, is equal to the vertical summation of MC_m and P_t. Thus, the best level of output of the final product by the marketing division is 20 units and is given by point E_m, at which $MR_m = MC_t$, so that $P_m = \$8$ (as in Fig. 11-11). Hence, when a perfectly competitive external market for the intermediate product exists, the transfer price is given by the external competitive price of the intermediate product.

(b) In Fig. 11-11 in Problem 11.13, $Q_m = Q_p = 20$, with $P_t = \$4$ and $P_m = \$8$. In Fig. 11-12, for part (a) of this problem, $Q_m = 20$, $Q_p = 30$, with $P_t = \$4$ and $P_m = \$8$. Thus, in Fig. 11-11 and Problem 11.13 (i.e., when no external market exists for the intermediate product), Q_p must necessarily be equal to Q_m. In Fig. 11-12, for part (a) of this problem (i.e., when a perfectly competitive external market exists for the intermediate product), Q_p is given by the point at which the competitive market price for the intermediate product, P_t, equals $MC_{p'}$, and this may involve an output for $Q_p \gtreqless Q_m$. If $Q_p > Q_m$, the production division sells the excess $(Q_p - Q_m)$ of the intermediate product on the external market at P_t. If, however, $Q_p < Q_m$, the marketing division of the firm purchases an additional quantity $(Q_m - Q_p)$ of the intermediate product on the external market at P_t.

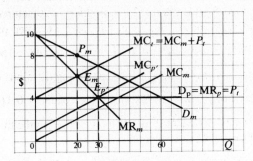

Fig. 11-12

11.15 Solve Problem 11.14 algebraically.

The demand and marginal revenue curves for the final product faced by the marketing division of the firm in Fig. 11-12 can be represented algebraically as

$$Q_m = 100 - 10P_m \quad \text{or} \quad P_m = 10 - 0.1Q_m \quad \text{and} \quad MR_m = 10 - 0.2Q_m$$

The marginal cost functions of the production and marketing divisions are, respectively,

$$MC_{p'} = 1 + 0.1Q_p \quad \text{and} \quad MC_m = 0.1Q_m$$

Since $P_t = \$4$, the total marginal cost function of the marketing division (MC_t) is

$$MC_t = MC_m + P_t = 0.1Q_m + 4$$

The best level of output of the intermediate product by the production division is given by the point at which $MC_{p'} = P_t$. Thus,

$$MC_{p'} = 1 + 0.1Q_p = 4 = P_t$$

so that

$$0.1Q_p = 3 \quad \text{and} \quad Q_p = 30$$

The best level of output of the *final product* by the marketing division is given by the point at which $MC_t = MR_m$. Thus,

$$MC_t = 0.1Q_m + 4 = 10 - 0.2Q_m = MR_m$$

so that

$$0.3Q_m = 6 \quad \text{and} \quad Q_m = 20$$

Hence,

$$P_m = 10 - 0.1(20) = \$8$$

These results are the same as those obtained graphically in Fig. 11-12 in Problem 11.14.

11.16 Given Fig. 11-13, determine (*a*) what the $MR_m - MC_p$ curve measures, (*b*) how the MR_p curve is derived, (*c*) the best level of output of the production division of the firm, (*d*) the distribution of the output of the production division between the marketing division and the external market, (*e*) the internal transfer price, and (*f*) the price of the intermediate product in the external market.

(*a*)   The $MR_m - MC_p$ curve in part (*a*) of the figure measures the marketing division's net marginal revenue from sales of the final product. The curve is given by the marginal revenue of the marketing division minus the transfer price, P_t, which is equal to MC_p.

(*b*)   The MR_p (i.e., the marginal revenue) curve of the production division of the firm, in part (*c*), is obtained by the horizontal summation of the net marginal revenue curve of the marketing division of the firm and the marginal revenue curve for sales of the intermediate product on the external market (MR_e). That is, $MR_p = MR_m - MC_p + MR_e$.

(*c*)   The best level of output of the intermediate product by the firm's production division is 40 units and is given by point E_p in part (*c*), at which $MR_p = MC_p$.

(*d*)   The optimal distribution of $Q_p = 40$ by the production division of the firm is 20 units to the marketing division and 20 units to the external market (given by points P_t and E_e, respectively), at which $MR_m - MC_p = MR_e = MR_p = MC_p = \$4$.

(*e*)   The internal transfer price is $P_t = MC_t = \$4$ because that amount ensures that the marketing division of the firm [shown in part (*a*)] will demand 20 units of the intermediate product, which leads to profit maximization for the marketing division and for the firm as a whole.

(*f*)   With optimal sales of 20 units of the intermediate product in the external market [given by point E_e in part (*b*)], the market-clearing price for the intermediate product is $P_e = \$6$.

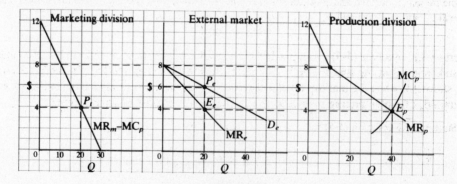

Fig. 11-13

PRICING IN PRACTICE

11.17 Suppose that a firm considers 80 percent of its capacity output of 2,000 units as the normal or standard output, that it projects total variable and overhead costs for the year to be, respectively, $8,000 and $4,800, and that it wants to apply a 20 percent markup on cost. Determine the price that the firm should charge for the product.

The price that the firm should charge for the product is given by

$$P = C(1 + m)$$

where P is the price of the product, C is the fully allocated average cost of the product for the normal or standard level of output, and m is the markup on cost. The normal or standard level of output is 80 percent of the capacity output of 2,000 units, or 1,600 units. The fully allocated average cost for the product is

$$C = AVC + \text{average overhead charge}$$

$$AVC = \frac{TVC}{Q} = \frac{\$8,000}{1,600} = \$5$$

$$\text{Average overhead charge} = \frac{\text{total overhead charge}}{Q} = \frac{\$4,800}{1,600} = \$3$$

Thus, $C = \$5 + \$3 = \$8$ and $P = 8(1 + 0.2) = \$9.60$

11.18 What are (a) the advantages and (b) the disadvantages of cost-plus pricing? (c) Why is incremental-cost pricing the correct pricing method? When is full-cost pricing equal to incremental-cost pricing?

(a) The advantages of cost-plus pricing are that (1) it requires less information than the MR = MC rule, (2) it is relatively simple and easy to use, (3) it usually results in relatively stable prices, and (4) it provides a clear indication of the need for price increases when costs rise.

(b) The disadvantages of cost-plus pricing are as follows: (1) It is often based on accounting and historical costs rather than on replacement or opportunity costs. (Cost-plus pricing could, however, be based on the appropriate cost concepts.) (2) It is based on average rather than on marginal costs. (To the extent, however, that AC = MC over the normal or standard level of output, this does not create much of a problem.) (3) It ignores conditions of demand. (Since firms usually apply higher markups to products with a less elastic demand than to products with a more elastic demand, however, cost-plus pricing leads to approximately the profit-maximizing price.)

(c) Correct pricing and output decisions by a firm involve incremental analysis, that is, the firm lowers the price of a product, introduces a new product, accepts a new order, etc., only if the incremental revenue from the action exceeds the incremental cost. When excess capacity exists in the short run, overhead or fixed costs are irrelevant in managerial decisions. Correct incremental analysis, however, involves taking into consideration both the short-run and the long-run implications of the managerial decision as well as all the important demand and production interrelationships. Only when the firm operates with no idle capacity will incremental-cost and full-cost pricing lead to the same results.

11.19 Starting with equation (5-5), which relates marginal revenue to price and to the price elasticity of demand, and assuming that the fully allocated average cost is approximately equal to the marginal cost, show that when the markup on cost that the firm applies is inversely related to the price elasticity of demand, cost-plus pricing results in approximately the profit-maximizing price.

Starting with equation (5-5) for

$$MR = P\left(1 + \frac{1}{E_p}\right)$$

and solving for P, we get

$$P = \frac{MR}{1 + (1/E_p)} = \frac{MR}{(E_p + 1)/E_p} = MR\left(\frac{E_p}{E_p + 1}\right)$$

Since profits are maximized where MR = MC, we can substitute MC for MR in the above equation and get

$$P = MC\left(\frac{E_p}{E_p + 1}\right)$$

To the extent that the firm's MC is constant over the normal or standard level of output, MC = C, where C is the fully allocated average cost of the product. Substituting C for MC in the above equation, we get

$$P = C\left(\frac{E_p}{E_p + 1}\right)$$

Substituting the right-hand side of equation (11-4) for P in the above equation, we get

$$C(1 + m) = C\left(\frac{E_p}{E_p + 1}\right)$$

so that the optimal markup is

$$m = \frac{E_p}{E_p + 1} - 1$$

From the above equation we can conclude that if $E_p = -1.5$, $m = 2$, or 200 percent; if $E_p = -2$, $m = 1$, or 100 percent; if $E_p = -3$, $m = 0.5$, or 50 percent, and if $E_p = -4$, $m = 0.33$, or 33 percent. Since firms usually apply higher markups to products facing a less elastic demand than to products with a more elastic demand, cost-plus pricing leads to approximately the profit-maximizing price.

11.20 Suppose that a firm's average variable cost of producing a product is $12, the overhead charge per unit is $8, and the firm is producing below capacity. What is the minimum price that the firm should accept for the product in (a) the short run and (b) the long run?

(a) Since the firm is operating with idle capacity, the minimum price that the firm should accept for the product in the short run is $12. That is, the product price should at least cover the firm's AVC for the product in the short run. Any amount by which the price of the product exceeds $12 can then be applied toward the firm's overhead costs. This is an example of incremental analysis in pricing.

(b) In the long run, all costs (variable and overhead, or fixed) must be covered. Thus, the minimum price that the firm should accept for the product in the long run is $20. Thus, in the long run, there is no conflict between incremental-cost and full-cost pricing.

Chapter 12

Regulation and Antitrust: The Role of Government in the Economy

12.1 GOVERNMENT REGULATION TO SUPPORT BUSINESS AND TO PROTECT CONSUMERS, WORKERS, AND THE ENVIRONMENT

According to the *economic theory of regulation* expounded by George Stigler and others, regulation arises from the actions of pressure groups and results in laws and policies in support of business and to protect consumers, workers, and the environment. Some of the policies designed to support business restrict entry and competition. These are *licenses*, *patents*, restrictions on price competition, import restrictions (*tariffs* and *quotas*), as well as subsidies and special tax treatments to aid such sectors as agriculture, railroads, airlines, and energy. Consumers are protected by regulations requiring truthful disclosure by firms and forbidding misrepresentation of products, as well as by laws requiring truth in lending, fairness in evaluating credit applications, clarity in warranties, safety on highways, and many other consumer-protective practices. Workers are protected by laws that specify safety standards, equal employment opportunity, and minimum wages, while regulation of air, water, and other aspects of the environment is carried out by the Environmental Protection Agency.

EXAMPLE 1. Government restrictions on price competition include government-guaranteed parity prices in agriculture and control of trucking freight rates and airline fares (before deregulation) and of ocean shipping rates, as well as restrictions on many other prices and pricing practices. One part of the Robinson-Patman Act, which was passed in 1936 to amend the Clayton Antitrust Act, also restricted price competition by forbidding firms from selling more cheaply to one buyer or in one market than to other buyers or in other markets and from selling at "unreasonably low prices" with the intent of destroying competition or eliminating a competitor. The act sought to protect small retailers (primarily grocery stores and drug stores) from price competition from large chain-store retailers, whose power was based on their ability to obtain lower prices and brokerage concession fees on bulk purchases from suppliers. Judging from the continuous decline in the number of small independent grocers, drug stores, and other retail businesses, and the expansion in the number and size of supermarkets, however, the act was not very successful.

EXAMPLE 2. Some of the laws, regulations, and agencies that protect consumers from unfair business practices are these:

1. The *Food and Drug Act of 1906* and the subsequent amendments to it, which forbid adulteration and mislabeling of foods, drugs, and cosmetics. Other requirements are that drugs and chemical additives to foods be proved safe for human use and that herbicides and pesticides be tested for their toxicity.

2. The *Federal Trade Commission Act of 1914* and its 1938 amendment, the *Wheeler-Lea Act*, which protects firms against unfair business practices by competitors and which also protects consumers against such practices as claiming to have slashed prices after having first raised them and other types of false advertising.

3. The *Consumer Credit Protection Act of 1968*, which requires truth in lending.

4. The *Consumer Product Safety Commission*, established in 1972, which protects consumers against the risk of injury associated with the use of a product.

5. The *Fair Credit Reporting Act of 1971*.

6. The *Warranty Act of 1975*.

7. The *National Highway Safety Traffic Administration*.

Workers are protected by the Occupational Safety and Health Administration, the Equal Employment Opportunity Commission, and minimum wage laws, among others, while the environment is protected by the Environmental Protection Agency.

12.2 EXTERNALITIES AND REGULATION

According to the *public interest theory*, government regulation is undertaken to overcome *market failures*, so that the economic system can operate in a manner consistent with the public interest. One type of market failure is due to *externalities*. These refer to beneficial or harmful effects received or borne by firms or individuals other than those producing or consuming the product or service. We have external economies and diseconomies of production and consumption. *External economies of production* are uncompensated benefits received by firms other than those involved in the production of the good or service. *External diseconomies of production* are uncompensated costs imposed on firms other than those involved in production of the good or service. *External economies of consumption* are uncompensated benefits received by individuals other than those consuming the good or service. *External diseconomies of consumption* are uncompensated costs imposed on individuals other than those consuming the good or service. Market failures due to externalities can be overcome by prohibitions or regulations, taxes or subsidies, voluntary payments, mergers, or the sale of pollution rights.

EXAMPLE 3. Figure 12-1(*a*) shows that the best number of hours of typing per evening for individual A is 4 and is given by point E_A, at which A's marginal private benefit (MPB_A) and marginal private cost (MPC_A) are equal. Evening typing by individual A, however, creates noise and a cost for individual B (who is driven to eat out or go to a movie or a bar). The marginal social cost (MSC) is thus given by the vertical summation of the MPC_A and MPC_B curves. From society's point of view, the best level of typing by individual A is 3 hours per evening and is given by point E_S, at which $MPB_A = MSC = \$8$. The socially optimal level of 3 hours of evening typing is reached when the government imposes a tax of $t = \$3$ per hour of evening typing on individual A. This shifts the MPC_A curve up by \$3 so that the $MPC_A + t$ curve (not shown in the figure) intersects the MPB_A curve at point E_S, at which $MPB_A = MSB = MSC$. In part (*b*), the best number of hours for individual A to work in his or her yard is 6 hours per week and is given by point E_A, at which $MPB_A = MPC_A$. Individual A's yardwork, however, generates an external benefit to individual B (i.e., the work increases the value of individual B's home also). Thus, the marginal social benefit, MSB, equals $MPB_A + MPB_B$. Therefore, the best level of yardwork by individual A is 10 hours per week, as shown by point E_S, at which $MSB = MPC_A = MSC = \$9$. Individual A can be induced to tend the yard for 10 hours per week by giving the person a consumption subsidy of $s = \$3$ per hour. This shifts the MPB_A curve up by \$3 so that the $MPB_A + s$ curve intersects the MPC_A curve at point E_S, at which $MSB = MPC_A = MSC$. (The same result can be reached by shifting the $MPC_A - s$ curve down by \$3.)

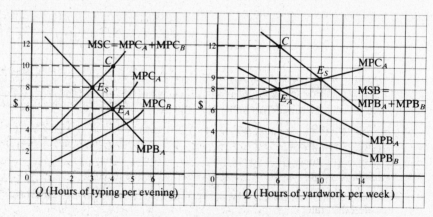

Fig. 12-1

12.3 PUBLIC UTILITY REGULATION

In some industries, economies of scale operate continuously as output expands, so that a single firm could supply the entire market more efficiently than any number of smaller firms. Such *natural monopolies* are common in the provision of electric, gas, water, local telephone, and local transportation services (*public utilities*). In cases such as these, the government usually allows a single firm to supply the entire market but sets $P = LAC$ so that the firm breaks even (i.e., earns only a normal return on investment). Economic efficiency, however, requires that P = LMC. But this would result in a loss, and the company would not supply the service in the long run without a subsidy (see Example 4).

EXAMPLE 4. In Fig. 12-2 the D and MR curves are, respectively, the market demand and marginal revenue curves faced by the public utility company for the service, while the LAC and LMC curves are the company's long-run average and marginal cost curves. If unregulated, the company's best level of output in the long run would be 5 million units per time period and is given by point E, at which the LMC and MR curves intersect. For Q = 5 million units, the company would charge \$11 (point A on the D curve) so that LAC = \$9 (point B on the LAC curve), thereby earning a profit of \$2 (line segment AB) per unit and \$10 million (the area of rectangle $ABCF$) in total. To ensure that the public utility company earns only a normal rate of return on investment, the regulatory commission usually sets P = LAC. This is given by point G, at which P' = LAC = \$6 and Q = 10 million units per time period. The best level of output from society's point of view, however, is 13 million units, given by point H, at which P = LMC = \$3. At Q = 13 million, however, the public utility would incur a loss of \$2 (line segment HJ) per unit and \$26 million per time period. As a result, the company would not supply the service in the long run without a per-unit subsidy of \$2 per unit. There are many other difficulties with public utility regulation. (See Problem 12-12.)

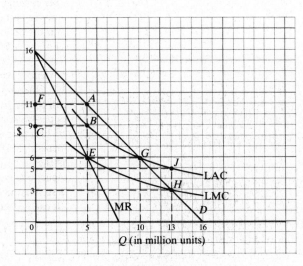

Fig. 12-2

12.4   ANTITRUST: GOVERNMENT REGULATION OF MARKET STRUCTURE AND CONDUCT

Starting with the Sherman Act of 1890, a number of antitrust laws were passed to prevent monopoly or undue concentration of economic power, protect the public against the abuses and inefficiencies resulting from monopoly or the concentration of economic power, and maintain a workable degree of competition in the U.S. economy. The *Sherman Act (1890)* prohibits monopolization and restraints of trade in commerce among the states and with foreign nations. The *Clayton Antitrust Act (1914)* prohibits price discrimination, exclusive and tying contracts, and intercorporate stock holdings if they substantially lessen competition or tend to create a monopoly, and unconditionally prohibits interlocking directorates. The *Federal Trade Commission Act (1914)*, passed to supplement the Clayton Antitrust Act, makes unfair methods of competition illegal and also established the Federal Trade Commission (FTC) to prosecute violators of the antitrust laws and protect the public against false and misleading advertisements. The *Robinson-Patman Act (1936)* protects small retailers from unfair price competition from large chain-store retailers, based on the latter's ability to obtain lower prices and brokerage concession fees on bulk purchases from suppliers, if the intent is to destroy competition or eliminate a competitor. The *Wheeler-Lea Act (1938)* amended the Federal Trade Commission Act and forbids false or deceptive advertising of foods, drugs, corrective devices, and cosmetics entering interstate commerce. The *Celler-Kefauver Antimerger Act (1950)* closed a loophole in the Clayton Antitrust

Act by making it illegal to acquire not only the stock but also the assets of competing corporations if such a purchase substantially lessens competition or tends to create a monopoly.

12.5 ENFORCEMENT OF ANTITRUST LAWS AND THE DEREGULATION MOVEMENT

Enforcement of antitrust laws has been the responsibility of the Antitrust Division of the Department of Justice and the Federal Trade Commission (FTC). Antitrust violations have been resolved by (1) dissolution and divestiture, (2) injunction, and (3) consent decree [see Problem 12.17(b)]. Fines and jail sentences have also been imposed. Starting with the 1945 Alcoa case, the U.S. Supreme Court ruled that size per se is an offense, irrespective of illegal acts. Today, however, both size and some anticompetitive behavior seem to be required for successful prosecution. The Court has generally challenged horizontal mergers between large direct competitors, but has not challenged vertical and conglomerate mergers unless they would lead to increased horizontal market power. The Court has used the Sherman Act to prosecute not only attempts to set up a cartel, but also any informal collusion to share the market, fix prices, or establish price leadership schemes. The Court has ruled that *conscious parallelism* (i.e., the adoption of similar policies by oligopolists in view of their recognized interdependence) is illegal when it reflects collusion. The Court has also attacked *predatory pricing* (i.e., selling at below average variable cost in a particular market in order to drive a competitor out or to discourage new entrants) and price discrimination and other price behavior when it substantially lessens competition or tends to create a monopoly. Since the mid-1970s, the government has deregulated airlines and trucking, and reduced the level of regulation for financial institutions, telecommunications, and railroads in order to increase competition and avoid some of the heavy compliance costs of regulation. While the full impact of deregulation has yet to be felt, deregulation seems to have led to increased competition and lower prices, but it has also resulted in some problems.

EXAMPLE 5. In 1974 the Justice Department filed suit against AT&T under Section 2 of the Sherman Antitrust Act for illegal practices to eliminate competitors in the markets for telephone equipment and long-distance telephone service. In 1982, after eight years of litigation and at a cost of $25 million to the government (and $360 million incurred by AT&T to defend itself), the case was settled. By consent decree, AT&T agreed to divest itself of the 22 local telephone companies (which represented two-thirds of its total assets) and relinquish its monopoly on long-distance telephone service. In return, AT&T was allowed to retain Bell Laboratories and its manufacturing arm, Western Electric, and to enter the rapidly growing fields of cable TV, electronic data transmission, videotext communications, and computers. The agreement also led to an increase in local telephone charges (which had been subsidized by AT&T's long-distance telephone service) and to a reduction in long-distance telephone charges.

EXAMPLE 6. In 1961 General Electric, Westinghouse, and a number of smaller companies producing electrical equipment pleaded guilty to violations of antitrust laws because of price fixing and division of the market. The companies were fined a total of $2 million and had to pay over $400 million in damages to customers; 7 of their executives were sent to jail, and 23 others received suspended sentences. The conspiracy (which occurred from 1956 to 1959) took the following form: company executives met at conventions or trade associations, and wrote or called to decide which of them would submit the lowest (sealed) bid on a particular contract. The executives involved in the conspiracy knew that they were breaking the law, since they usually met in secret, used code words, did not register at hotels under their own names, sent letters without return addresses, used only first names, etc. While most of the agreements lasted only a short time, and the defendants argued that the profitability of their firms was less during than before the conspiracy, they were found guilty because the prosecution proved that a conspiracy, whether successful or not, had in fact taken place.

Glossary

Celler-Kefauver Antimerger Act (1950) Closed a loophole in the Clayton Act by making it illegal to acquire not only the stock but also the assets of competing corporations if such a purchase substantially lessens competition or tends to create a monopoly.

Clayton Antitrust Act (1914)   Prohibits price discrimination, exclusive and tying contracts, and intercorporate stock holdings if they substantially lessen competition or tend to create a monopoly, and unconditionally prohibits interlocking directorates.

Conscious parallelism   The adoption of similar policies by oligopolistic firms in view of their recognized interdependence.

Economic theory of regulation   The theory that regulation results from pressure-group action to support business and to protect consumers, workers, and the environment.

External diseconomies of consumption   Uncompensated costs imposed on some individuals by the consumption expenditures of some other individual.

External diseconomies of production   Uncompensated costs imposed on some firms by the expansion of output by other firms.

External economies of consumption   Uncompensated benefits conferred on some individuals by the consumption expenditures of some other individual.

External economies of production   Uncompensated benefits conferred on some firms by the expansion of output by other firms.

Externalities   Harmful or beneficial effects borne or received by firms or individuals other than those producing or consuming a product or service.

Federal Trade Commission Act (1914)   A supplement to the Clayton Act; made unfair methods of competition illegal and established the Federal Trade Commission (FTC) to prosecute violators of the antitrust laws and protect the public against false and misleading advertisements.

Licensing   The requirement that a franchise or other formal permission must be secured from a recognized source in order to enter or remain in a business, profession, or a trade.

Market failure   Economic inefficiencies arising because of the existence of monopoly power in imperfectly competitive markets, externalities, and the existence of public goods.

Natural monopoly   The case in which economies of scale results in a single firm supplying the entire market.

Patent   The right granted to an inventor by the federal government for the exclusive use of an invention for a period of 17 years.

Predatory pricing   Selling at below average variable cost in order to drive a competitor out of the market or discourage new entrants.

Public interest theory of regulation   The theory that regulation is undertaken to overcome market failures and to ensure that the economic system operates in a manner consistent with the public interest.

Public utilities   Natural monopolies supplying electric, water, gas, local telephone, and local transportation services.

Quota   A quantitative restriction on imports.

Robinson-Patman Act (1936)   Protects small retailers from price competition by large chain-store retailers, based on the latter's ability to obtain lower prices and brokerage concession fees on bulk purchases from suppliers, if the intent is to destroy competition or eliminate a competitor.

Sherman Antitrust Act (1890)   Prohibits monopolization and restraints of trade in commerce among the states and with foreign nations.

Tariff   A tax on imports.

Wheeler-Lea Act (1938)   An amendment to the Federal Trade Commission Act; forbids false or deceptive advertisement of foods, drugs, corrective devices, and cosmetics entering interstate commerce.

Review Questions

1. Government restricts entry and competition by

   (a) licensing.

   (b) patents.

   (c) tariffs and quotas.

   (d) all of the above.

   Ans. (d) See Section 12.1.

2. Which of the following laws does not protect consumers?

   (a) The Federal Trade Commission Act

   (b) The Robinson-Patman Act

   (c) The Food and Drug Act

   (d) The Fair Credit Reporting Act

   Ans. (b) See Example 2.

3. Externalities are

   (a) uncompensated costs borne by firms other than those producing a product.

   (b) uncompensated benefits received by firms other than those producing the product.

   (c) uncompensated costs or benefits imposed or conferred on individuals other than those consuming the product or service.

   (d) all of the above.

   Ans. (d) See Section 12.2.

4. When maintenance personnel trained by American Airlines go to work for Continental, the latter is the recipient of an external

   (a) diseconomy of production.

   (b) economy of production.

   (c) diseconomy of consumption.

   (d) economy of consumption.

   Ans. (b) See Section 12.2.

5. When a paper mill discharges refuse into a stream, a brewery downstream faces an external

   (a) diseconomy of production.

   (b) economy of production.

   (c) diseconomy of consumption.

   (d) economy of consumption.

   Ans. (a) See Section 12.2.

6. When individuals improve the appearance of their house, they confer on their neighbors an external

    (*a*) diseconomy of production.

    (*b*) economy of production.

    (*c*) diseconomy of consumption.

    (*d*) economy of consumption.

    Ans. (*d*) See Section 12.2.

7. A market failure due to externalities can be overcome by

    (*a*) prohibition or regulation.

    (*b*) taxes or subsidies.

    (*c*) voluntary payments, merger, or the sale of pollution rights.

    (*d*) all of the above.

    Ans. (*d*) See Section 12.2.

8. Public utility companies are

    (*a*) unregulated monopolies.

    (*b*) regulated natural monopolies.

    (*c*) oligopolistic firms.

    (*d*) monopolistically competitive firms.

    Ans. (*b*) See Section 12.3.

9. Which of the following statements is false with respect to a public utility company?

    (*a*) Its LAC curve continues to decline when it supplies the entire market.

    (*b*) Its best level of output from society's point of view is at $P = \text{LMC}$.

    (*c*) It breaks even at the best level of output from society's point of view.

    (*d*) None of the above.

    Ans. (*c*) See Section 12.3 and Example 4.

10. Which of the following antitrust acts seeks to protect small retailers from unfair price competition from large chain-store retailers?

    (*a*) Sherman Act

    (*b*) Clayton Antitrust Act

    (*c*) Federal Trade Commission Act

    (*d*) Robinson-Patman Act

    (*e*) Wheeler-Lea Act

    (*f*) Celler-Kefauver Antimerger Act

    Ans. (*d*) See Section 12.4.

11. Which of the following antitrust acts makes it illegal for a corporation to acquire the assets of a competing corporation if the acquisition substantially lessens competition or tends to create a monopoly?

   (a)   Sherman Act

   (b)   Clayton Antitrust Act

   (c)   Federal Trade Commission Act

   (d)   Robinson-Patman Act

   (e)   Wheeler-Lea Act

   (f)   Celler-Kefauver Antimerger Act

   Ans.   (f) See Section 12.4.

12. In the interpretation of the Sherman Act, the U.S. Supreme Court has consistently ruled that

   (a)   size per se is illegal.

   (b)   size per se is not illegal.

   (c)   price collusion is illegal.

   (d)   vertical mergers between large firms are illegal.

   Ans.   (c) See Section 12.5.

Solved Problems

GOVERNMENT REGULATION TO SUPPORT BUSINESS AND TO PROTECT CONSUMERS, WORKERS, AND THE ENVIRONMENT

12.1   Which two theories seek to explain the rationale for government intervention in the economy? What do they postulate? Which is the prevailing theory today?

Two theories that seek to explain the rationale for government intervention in the economy are: (1) the economic theory of regulation and (2) the public interest theory. The economic theory of regulation postulates that regulation is the result of pressures brought to bear on the government by businesses, consumers, workers, and environmental groups to pass legislation to protect them or their cause. According to the public interest theory, however, regulation results from the desire on the part of elected government officials to eliminate or correct market failures (i.e., situations in which private and social benefits or costs diverge or in which efficient operation requires a monopoly). The public interest theory provided the traditional rationale for government intervention in the economy. Today, however, the economic theory of regulation seems to be preferred by a growing number of economists.

12.2   (a) In what way do licensing, patents, import taxes, and import quotas restrict competition? (b) What are some of the direct restrictions on price competition resulting from government regulation?

   (a)   Licensing restricts entry and competition by limiting the number of franchises granted to enter and/or to remain in a business, profession, or trade. A patent restricts entry and competition by forbidding anyone but the inventor to make use of an invention for a period of 17 years. Tariffs are taxes on imports and, hence, restrict competition that domestic firms face from abroad. A quota is an even stronger restriction on competition from abroad which limits the quantity of a product that is allowed to be imported into a nation.

   (b)   Some examples of direct restrictions on price competition resulting from government regulation include government-guaranteed parity prices on agricultural products, control of trucking freight rates and airfares (before deregulation), control of ocean shipping rates, and the provision of the Robinson-Patman Act forbidding firms to sell more cheaply to one buyer or in one market than to other buyers or in other markets or to sell at "unreasonably low prices" with the intent of destroying competition or eliminating a competitor.

12.3 Using your managerial text or library resources, indicate some of the most important provisions of the Federal Trade Commission Act of 1914 and its amendment by the Wheeler-Lea Act of 1938.

Among the most important practices forbidden by the Federal Trade Commission Act are misrepresenting (1) the prices of products (such as claiming that prices have been slashed after first artificially raising them, or falsely claiming to be selling at below cost), (2) the origin of products (such as claiming that a product was manufactured in the United States when in fact it was produced abroad), (3) the usefulness of the products (such as claiming that a product can prevent arthritis when it does not), (4) the quality of the product (such as claiming that glass is crystal). The act was amended by the Wheeler-Lea Act of 1938, which forbids false or deceptive advertising of foods, drugs, corrective devices, and cosmetics entering interstate commerce. The federal laws have been supplemented by similar state and local laws and regulations.

EXTERNALITIES AND REGULATION

12.4 (a) How much of a tax of $3 per hour for evening typing imposed on individual A in part (a) of Fig. 12-1 (Example 3) actually falls on (i.e., is actually paid by) A, and how much of the tax does, in fact, fall on those who demand A's typing services? (b) On what does the incidence of a per-unit tax (i.e., the relative share of the tax burden) depend in general?

(a) Even though the government collects the tax of $3 per hour from individual A for evening typing, A is able to shift part of the burden of the tax onto those who demand the typing services. In part (a) of Fig. 12-1, we can see that individual A receives $6 per hour for evening typing in the absence of the tax and $8 per hour with the tax of $3 per hour. Thus, with the tax, individual A receives a net payment of $5 per hour for evening typing, as compared with $6 in the absence of the tax. Individual A is thus able to shift two-thirds of the burden of the tax (i.e., $2) onto those who demand the typing services, so that the actual burden, or incidence, of the tax on A is only one-third, or $1.

(b) The incidence, or relative burden, of a per-unit tax depends on the price elasticity of demand for the product or service [the MPB$_A$ curve in part (a) of Fig. 12-1]. The more inelastic is the demand curve, the greater is the relative burden of the tax on those who demand the good or service. At one extreme, when the price elasticity of demand is zero (i.e., when the demand curve is vertical), the burden of the tax falls entirely on those demanding the good or service (by having to pay a price that is higher by the exact amount of the tax). At the opposite extreme (i.e., when the demand curve is infinitely elastic, or horizontal), the price of the product or service will remain the same after the imposition of the tax. This means that the tax falls entirely on the supplier of the product or service (who will receive an after-tax price that is lower, by the exact amount of the tax, than the pretax price).

12.5 (a) Why can a per-hour subsidy given to individual A for tending his or her yard be shown by a downward shift in the MPC$_A$ curve in Fig. 12-1(b)? (b) Explain why the result of a subsidy of $3 per hour given to individual A for yardwork, shown by shifting the MPC$_A$ curve down by $3, is the same as the result obtained by shifting the MPB$_A$ curve up by $3.

(a) Since individual A receives the benefit (i.e., the increase in the value of his or her home) from tending the yard and also incurs the cost of such an activity, a per-unit (hour) subsidy can be shown graphically either by an upward shift in the MPB$_A$ curve or by a downward shift in the MPC$_A$ curve by the amount of the subsidy in Fig. 12-1(b).

(b) If the subsidy of $3 per hour is shown by shifting the MPC$_A$ curve down by $3 in Fig. 12-1(b), the new MPC$_A - s$ curve would intersect the MPB$_A$ curve so as to indicate that individual A will spend 10 hours per week tending the yard. This is the socially optimal number of hours per week for individual A to tend the yard (since MSB = MSC) and is the same as the result obtained by shifting the MPB$_A$ curve up by $3.

12.6 The demand and supply functions for a product in a perfectly competitive market are, respectively,

$$QD = 16 - P \quad \text{and} \quad QS = -8 + 2P$$

where P is in dollars. The production of each unit of the product, however, results in a pollution cost of $0.50 per unit. Draw a figure showing the equilibrium price and quantity for this product, as well as the socially optimal price and quantity.

Figure 12-3 shows that the equilibrium price is $8 and the equilibrium quantity is 8 units. These are given by point E, at which the D and S curves intersect. The socially optimal price (which takes into consideration the external diseconomy of production resulting from pollution) is, however, $10, and the socially optimal quantity is 6 units. These are given by point E', at which the D and S' curves intersect. Point E' cannot be reached, however, without government intervention.

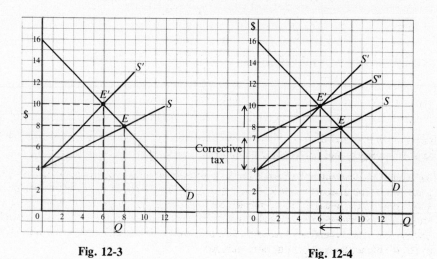

Fig. 12-3   Fig. 12-4

12.7 Draw a figure showing the corrective tax or subsidy that would induce the industry in Problem 12.6 to produce the socially optimal quantity of the product. What would be the net price received by producers?

Figure 12-4 shows that a corrective tax of $3 per unit collected from producers will make S'' the new industry supply curve. With S'', $P = \$10$ and $Q = 6$ (given by the intersection of D and S'' at point E'). Producers now receive a net price of $7 ($P = \$10$ minus the $3 tax per unit).

12.8 Suppose that the market demand and supply curves for a product in a perfectly competitive market are, respectively,

$$QD = 30 - 2P \quad \text{and} \quad QS = -6 + 2P$$

where P is in dollars. If the demand curve showing the marginal social benefit of consuming the product has the same vertical intercept but twice the absolute slope of D, draw a figure showing (1) the equilibrium price and quantity, (2) the socially optimal price and quantity, and (3) the tax or subsidy per unit that would induce consumers to consume the socially optimal quantity of the product. What is the net price paid by consumers with the tax or subsidy?

Figure 12-5 shows that the equilibrium price is $9 and the equilibrium quantity is 12 units. These are given by point E, at which the D and S curves intersect. The socially optimal price (which takes into consideration the external diseconomy of consumption resulting from consuming each unit of the product) is, however, $7, and the socially optimal quantity is 8 units. These are given by point E', at which the D' and S curves intersect. Point E' can be reached by imposing a corrective tax of $4 per unit on consumers. This will make D'' the new demand curve. Consumers now pay $7 plus $2 of the $4 tax per unit on the product, or a net price of $11 (as compared with the price of $9 before the imposition of the tax).

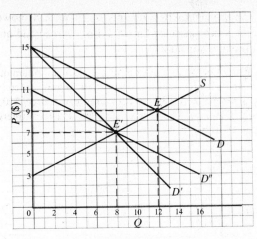

Fig. 12-5

12.9 Explain how an external diseconomy can be overcome by (*a*) prohibition or regulation (*b*) voluntary payment, (*c*) merger, and (*d*) the sale of pollution rights.

(*a*)   An external diseconomy of production can be overcome simply by forbidding or regulating the activity that gives rise to the diseconomy. For example, auto emission can be eliminated by prohibiting the use of automobiles. This, however, also eliminates the much larger benefits that arise from the use of automobiles. More practical, therefore, is a regulation that requires the installment of emission-control equipment in automobiles. This is generally less cost-efficient, however, than taxation, since the latter will also stimulate more efficient methods of limiting auto emission.

(*b*)   An external diseconomy can sometimes be overcome by voluntary payment. For example, if a firm pollutes the air and produces a foul odor, the residents of the area can get together and contribute to the firm's cost of installing pollution-abatement equipment, or the firm can contribute to the cost of relocating the area residents. The latter method, however, is impractical when there are many people residing in an area.

(*c*)   Still another method of overcoming external diseconomies imposed by some firms is to allow or foster mergers, so that the external diseconomies are internalized and explicitly taken into consideration by the merged firm. For example, if a paper mill is located upstream from a brewery, the discharges of the paper mill into the stream represent an external diseconomy for the brewery, since the latter incurs the additional cost of purifying the water that it uses in beer making. If the paper mill and the brewery merge, however, the cost of purifying the water for beer making becomes an explicit and direct cost that the merged firm will take into consideration in its production (milling and brewing) decisions.

(*d*)   A radically different method of limiting the amount of a negative externality to the level that is socially optimal is achieved by the sale of pollution rights by the government. Under such a system, the government decides on the amount of pollution that it thinks is socially acceptable (based on the benefits that result from the activities that generate the pollution) and then auctions off licenses to firms to pollute up to the specified amount. Pollution costs are thus internalized (i.e., considered as part of regular production costs) by firms, and the allowed amount of pollution is utilized in activities which provide the greatest service.

PUBLIC UTILITY REGULATION

12.10 Suppose that the market demand curve for the public utility service shown in Fig. 12-2 shifts to the right by 2 million units at each price level, but the LAC and LMC curves remain unchanged. Draw a figure showing the price that the public utility commission would set for the service and the quantity of the service that would be supplied to the market at that price.

See Fig. 12-6. In the figure, D and D' are, respectively, the original and new market demand curves. With the new demand curve D' and the unchanged LAC curve, the regulatory commission would set $P' = \text{LAC} =$

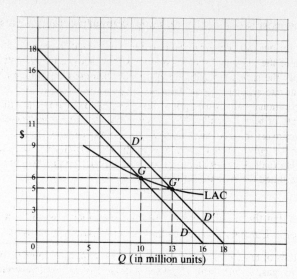

Fig. 12-6

$5 (point G') and the public utility company would supply 13 million units of the service per time period (as compared with $P = LAC = \$6$ with $Q = 10$ million units per time period shown by point G with D). In either case, the public utility company breaks even.

12.11 Suppose that the market demand curve for the public utility service shown in Fig. 12-2 shifts to the right by 2 million units at each price and, at the same time, the LAC curve of the public utility company shifts up by $2 throughout because of production inefficiencies that escape detection by the public utility commission. Draw a figure showing the price that the commission would set for the service and the quantity of the service that would be supplied to the market at that price.

See Fig. 12-7. In the figure, D and D' are, respectively, the original and the new market demand curves, and LAC and LAC' are the original and new long-run average cost curves facing the public utility company. With D' and LAC', the public utility commission would set $P'' = LAC' = \$8$ (point G'') and the public utility company would supply 10 million units of the service per time period. This is based on the assumption that the commission does not realize that the upward shift in the company's LAC curve is due to production inefficiencies rather than to legitimate increases in costs of production.

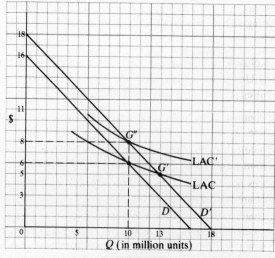

Fig. 12-7

12.12 What are some of the most serious difficulties arising in public utility regulation?

> Some of the most serious difficulties arising in public utility regulation are as follows: (1) It is very difficult to determine the value of the plant or fixed assets on which to allow a normal rate of return. (2) Since public utility companies supply the service to different classes of customers, each with a different price elasticity of demand, many different rate schedules could be used to allow the company to break even. (3) It is impossible to allocate costs in any rational way to the various services provided, since they are jointly produced. (4) With a guaranteed normal rate of return, public utilities have little incentive to keep costs down. (5) Public utilities will overinvest or underinvest in fixed assets if rates are set, respectively, too high or too low. (This is called the *Averch-Johnson or A-J effect*, after Harvey Averch and Leland Johnson, who first identified this problem.) (6) There is usually a lag (called a *regulatory lag*) of from 9 to 12 months between the time that the need for a rate change is recognized and the time it is granted.

12.13 Given the difficulties that the regulation of public utilities faces, would it not be better to nationalize public utilities, as some European countries have done? Explain your answer.

> Given the difficulties of regulating public utilities, many European countries have nationalized the companies that supply electric, gas, water, local telephone, and local transportation services. The difficulty with this policy is that it removes, even more than regulation does, any incentive for economic efficiency in supplying these basic services. Specifically, in the absence of any competition and facing even less scrutiny than the managers of regulated public utility companies, the public servants who manage the nationalized public utility companies have less incentive than the managers of regulated public utilities to produce the best quality of service at the lowest possible price. Nationalization, therefore, does not seem to be the answer to the efficiency problems faced by public utilities.

ANTITRUST: GOVERNMENT REGULATION OF MARKET STRUCTURE AND CONDUCT

12.14 (*a*) What is meant by a "trust" in economics? What is its function? (*b*) What are antitrust laws? Why were they passed?

> (*a*) A trust is an agreement to transfer the voting rights of the stock of the firms in an oligopolistic industry to a body that will manage the firms as a cartel: restricting output, charging monopoly prices, and earning monopoly profits. The most notorious of these trusts were the Standard Oil Trust, the Tobacco Trust, and several railroad and coal trusts, all of which operated in the United States in the 1880s.

> (*b*) Antitrust laws are laws that seek to prevent monopoly or undue concentration of economic power, protect the public against the abuses and inefficiencies resulting from monopoly or the concentration of economic power, and maintain a workable degree of competition in the U.S. economy. Public indignation over the rapid increase in the concentration of economic power and the abuses that resulted from it led to the passage of antitrust laws, starting with the Sherman Act of 1890.

12.15 What is meant by (*a*) exclusive and tying contracts, (*b*) intercorporate stock holdings, and (*c*) interlocking directorates? (*d*) Under what conditions are they illegal? (*e*) When and under what antitrust law were they declared illegal?

> (*a*) Exclusive and tying contracts refer to the leasing or sale of a commodity on condition that the lessee or buyer does not purchase, lease, or deal in the commodity of a competitor.

> (*b*) Intercorporate stock holdings are holdings by a corporation of the stocks of a competing corporation or of the stocks of two or more corporations that compete with one another.

> (*c*) Interlocking directorates refer to cases in which the same individual is on the board of directors of two or more corporations that are in competition with one another.

> (*d*) Exclusive and tying contracts and intercorporate stock holdings are illegal only if they substantially lessen competition or tend to create a monopoly. However, interlocking directorates are illegal per se, that is, there is no need to show that they lead to a reduction in competition.

> (*e*) The above actions were declared illegal under the Clayton Antitrust Act of 1914.

12.16 (*a*) How does the government decide whether to subject a very large firm to regulation or antitrust action? (*b*) Which are the basic antitrust laws? Why were other laws passed subsequently?

(*a*) If economies of scale are so pervasive that a single firm can supply a service to the entire market much more efficiently than any number of smaller firms (as in the case of public utilities), the government is likely to allow a single firm (a natural monopoly) to operate in the given market, subject to regulation of the price the firm can charge for the service (so that the firm earns only a normal return on investment) and of the type and quality of service it provides. However, if economies of scale are not so pervasive as to justify the operation of only a single firm in the market, the government is likely to apply antitrust laws to break up the monopoly or restrain the firms supplying the good or service from anticompetitive behavior and unfair business practices.

(*b*) The basic antitrust laws are the Sherman Act of 1890 and the Clayton Act of 1914. They prohibit "monopolization," "restraints of trade," and "unfair competition." Being very broad in nature, however, the Sherman and Clayton acts left a great deal to judicial interpretation based on economic analysis. The result was the passage of further legislation that spells out more precisely what business behavior is in fact prohibited by the antitrust laws and that closes loopholes in the original law.

ENFORCEMENT OF ANTITRUST LAWS AND THE DEREGULATION MOVEMENT

12.17 (*a*) What have been the most difficult problems in enforcing the antitrust laws? (*b*) What is meant by the terms dissolution and divestiture, injunction, and consent decree? (*c*) What other types of penalties have been imposed on violators of the antitrust laws?

(*a*) Since U.S. antitrust laws are often broad and general, a great deal of judicial interpretation based on economic analysis has often been required in their enforcement. This gave rise to problems of defining what is meant by "substantially lessening competition," in defining the relevant product and geographical markets, in deciding when competition is "unfair," and in proving tacit collusion.

(*b*) Dissolution and divestiture refer to a court order under which the firm is ordered either to dissolve (thereby losing its identity) or to divest itself of (i.e., sell) some of its assets. An injunction is a court order requiring that the defendant refrain from certain anticompetitive actions or take some specified competitive actions. A consent decree is an agreement, without a court trial, between the defendant (without, however, admitting guilt) and the Justice Department, under which the defendant agrees to abide by the rules of business behavior set down in the decree. Most antitrust actions have been settled with consent decrees.

(*c*) Antitrust violations have also been punished by fines in civil suits and by fines and jail sentences in criminal cases.

12.18 Has the Supreme Court interpreted size as illegal per se in enforcing the antitrust laws? Explain.

From the passage of the Sherman Act in 1890 until 1945, the Supreme Court held that size per se was not illegal. The illegal use of monopoly power was required for successful prosecution. Thus, in the 1911 Standard Oil case, the Supreme Court argued that Standard Oil of New Jersey had acquired and used a 90 percent controlling interest in the refining and sale of petroleum products by illegal actions (such as using profits from one market to sell at below cost in another market in order to drive competitors out) and ordered the company's dissolution into 30 independent firms. However, in the 1920 U.S. Steel case, the Supreme Court ruled that size in and of itself was no offense, and in the absence of conclusive proof of illegal actions refused to order the dissolution of U.S. Steel. The same was true in the International Harvester case in 1927.

Starting with the 1945 Alcoa case, however, the Supreme Court ruled that size per se was an offense, irrespective of illegal acts. The fact that Alcoa has achieved 90 percent control of the aluminum market by efficient operation and by maintaining low profit margins was no defense. In the 1982 IBM and AT&T cases, however, the Court took an intermediate position in its interpretation of Section 2 of the Sherman Act. While the Court backed away from the ruling that size per se was illegal, it held that practices that did not represent an offense by themselves, or when used by smaller firms, were illegal when used by a very large firm. Thus, the Court ordered AT&T to divest itself of its 22 local telephone companies under a consent decree, but decided to drop its case against IBM.

12.19 Using your text or newspaper articles, indicate the most important aspects of the IBM antitrust case (settled on January 8, 1982).

In 1969, the Justice Department filed suit against IBM under Section 2 of the Sherman Act for monopolizing the computer market, using exclusive and tying contracts, and selling new equipment at below cost. The government sought the dissolution of IBM. In 1982, however, after 13 years of litigation, more than 104,000 trial transcript pages, a cost of $26 million to the government (and $300 million incurred by IBM to defend itself), the Justice Department dropped its suit. The reason for doing so was that rapid technological change, increased competition in the field of computers, and changed marketing methods since the filing of the suit had so weakened the government case that the Justice Department felt it could no longer win.

12.20 What antitrust guidelines does the Supreme Court apply in ruling on (*a*) merger cases, (*b*) collusion, and (*c*) price discrimination?

(*a*)   The Supreme Court generally challenges horizontal mergers between large direct competitors, but not vertical and conglomerate mergers, unless they would lead to increased horizontal market power. For example, in the 1962 Brown Shoe case, the Court ruled against the proposed merger between the Brown Shoe Company and the Kinney Shoe Company, both of which manufactured shoes and operated retail shoe outlets. Even though the merged firm would have had only a 1.6 percent share of retail shoe sales, the Court cited the existence of a trend toward vertical and horizontal concentration in the industry which, if unchecked, would have substantially lessened competition.

(*b*)   The Court is likely to rule against any type of collusion (formal or informal) to share the market, fix prices, or establish price leadership schemes. The Court ruled against the three largest tobacco companies in the 1946 Tobacco case, in which the Court inferred that conscious parallelism was the result of collusion (price leadership), but ruled to drop the 1954 Theater Enterprises case, in which conscious parallelism did not seem to result from collusion.

(*c*)   The Court is likely to rule against price discrimination or other types of price behavior that would substantially lessen competition or would tend to create a monopoly. The Court would most likely rule aginst predatory pricing.

12.21 (*a*) What are the reasons for the deregulation movement since the mid-1970s? (*b*) Which industries were affected and to what extent have they been deregulated? (*c*) What has been the result of the deregulation?

(*a*)   According to the *economic theory of regulation* expounded by George Stigler and others (see Section 12.1), regulation is the result of pressure-group action and leads to laws and policies that restrict competition and promote the interest of the firms that are supposed to be regulated. (This is sometimes called the "capture theory" of regulation.) It was to increase competition and reduce some of the heavy burdens of compliance that the deregulation movement came into existence in the 1970s.

(*b*)   The *Airline Deregulation Act of 1978* removed all restrictions on entry, scheduling, and pricing in domestic air travel in the United States, and so did the *Motor Carrier Act of 1980* in the trucking industry. The *Depository Institutions and Monetary Control Act of 1980* allowed banks to pay interest on checking accounts and increased competition for business loans. The *Railroad Revitalization and Regulatory Reform Act of 1976* greatly increased the flexibility of railroads to set prices, determine levels of service, and areas of operation. The settlement of the *AT&T antitrust case in 1982* opened competition in long-distance telephone service and in telecommunications. Natural gas pipelines are now deregulated, and there is talk of deregulating the electric power generation industry.

(*c*)   Although it is too early to assess the full impact of deregulation, most observers would probably conclude that, on balance, the net effect has been positive. Competition has generally increased and prices have fallen in the industries that were deregulated. As expected, however, deregulation has also resulted in some difficulties and strains in the industries affected, to the point at which some consumer groups and some firms in recently deregulated industries are asking Congress to reregulate the industries.

12.22 Using articles in the *New York Times* (see, for example, September 7, 1987, p. 1, and September 23, 1987, p. D1) or in other newspapers and magazines, evaluate the effects of airline deregulation to date.

By 1987 most of the airlines that had been established since the 1978 deregulation had either gone out of business or had merged with established carriers. Several large mergers also took place during 1986 and 1987 among large, established carriers. The result was that by the end of 1987, eight carriers controlled 94 percent of all domestic air travel in the United States. Instead of the large number of small and highly competitive airlines envisioned by deregulation, the airline industry exhibited much less vigorous price competition in 1987 than in the years soon after deregulation and began to look more and more like an oligopoly. It has been estimated that to start a new airline now requires more than $100 million, and with established carriers ready to meet price competition head on in order to retain their share of the market, few investors are ready to risk their money in a new venture in this industry. Thus, entry seems virtually closed.

It is true that increases in airfares since deregulation have been smaller than the rate of inflation for the economy as a whole and that airlines could not possibly continue to charge fares so low as to incur losses continuously. Nevertheless, lack of vigorous price competition is beginning to worry even the staunchest supporters of deregulation. Furthermore, while safety does not seem to have suffered, and many small cities have not lost air service (as the opponents of deregulation had warned), delays at airports and passenger complaints about lost luggage, cancelled flights, and general declines in the quality of service have increased significantly since deregulation. This has recently led to some talk in Congress of reregulating the industry.

Chapter 13

Capital Budgeting, Public Goods, and Benefit-Cost Analysis

13.1 CAPITAL BUDGETING: AN OVERVIEW

Capital budgeting refers to the process of planning expenditures that give rise to revenues or returns over a number of years. Investment projects can be undertaken to replace worn-out equipment, reduce costs, expand output of traditional products in traditional markets, expand into new products and/or markets, or meet government regulations. The firm's profitability, growth, and its very survival in the long run depend on how well management accomplishes these tasks. Capital budgeting integrates the operation of all the major divisions of the firm. The basic principle involved in capital budgeting is that the firm undertakes additional investment projects until the marginal return on an investment is equal to its marginal cost (see Example 1).

EXAMPLE 1. In Fig. 13-1 the various lettered bars indicate the amount of capital required for each investment project and the rates of return on the investments. Thus, the top of each bar, represents the firm's demand for capital. The marginal cost of capital (MCC) curve shows the rising costs that the firm faces in raising additional amounts of capital. The firm will undertake projects A, B, and C because the expected rates of return on these projects exceed the 10 percent cost of raising the capital to make these investments. However, the firm will not undertake projects D and E because the expected rates of return on these projects are lower than their capital cost.

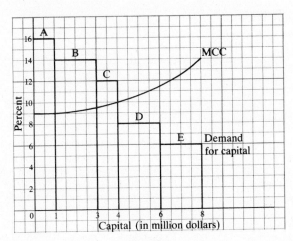

Fig. 13-1

13.2 THE CAPITAL BUDGETING PROCESS

The first step in capital budgeting is the estimation of the *net cash flow from the project*. This is the difference between cash receipts and cash expenditures over the life of the project. Net cash flows should be measured on an incremental and after-tax basis, and depreciation charges should be used only to calculate taxes (see Problem 13.6). A firm should undertake a project only if the net present value of the project is positive. The *net present value (NPV) of a project* is given by

$$\text{NPV} = \sum_{t=1}^{n} \frac{R_t}{(1+k)^t} - C_0 \tag{13-1}$$

where R_t is the estimated net cash flow in each of the n years of the project, k is the risk-adjusted discount rate, Σ stands for the "sum of," and C_0 is the initial cost of the project.

Alternatively, the project should be undertaken only if the *internal rate of return* (*IRR*) on the project exceeds the marginal cost of capital to the firm. As indicated in equation (*13-2*), the IRR is the rate of discount (k^*) that equates the present value of the project's net cash flow to its initial cost.

$$\sum_{t=1}^{n} \frac{R_t}{(1 + k^*)^t} = C_0 \tag{13-2}$$

EXAMPLE 2. Suppose that the cash flows from a project are those given in Table 13.1. If the initial cost of the project is $100,000 and the firm uses a risk-adjusted discount rate of 12 percent, the net present value of the project is

$$\text{NPV} = \frac{\$26,000}{(1 + 0.12)^1} + \frac{\$28,400}{(1 + 0.12)^2} + \frac{\$31,040}{(1 + 0.12)^3} + \frac{\$33,944}{(1 + 0.12)^4} + \frac{\$82,138}{(1 + 0.12)^5} - \$100,000$$

$$= \$136,127 - \$100,000$$

$$= \$36,127$$

This project would thus add $36,127 to the value of the firm. This corresponds to an IRR (k^*) of about 24 percent as compared to the marginal cost of capital, or risk-adjusted discount rate (k), of 12 percent used by the firm, and so the firm should undertake the project.

For a single or independent project, the NPV and IRR methods will always lead to the same accept/reject investment decision. For mutually exclusive projects, however, the two methods may give contradictory signals (see Problem 13.11). In that case the project with the higher NPV should be chosen. With capital rationing (i.e., when all the projects with positive NPV cannot be undertaken), the firm should rank and choose projects according to their *profitability index* (*PI*). This is given by the ratio of the present value of a project's net cash flows to its initial cost.

Table 13.1

	Year				
	1	2	3	4	5
Sales	$100,000	$110,000	$121,000	$133,100	$146,410
Less: Variable costs	60,000	66,000	72,600	79,860	87,846
Fixed costs	10,000	10,000	10,000	10,000	10,000
Depreciation	20,000	20,000	20,000	20,000	20,000
Profit before taxes	$ 10,000	$ 14,000	$ 18,400	$ 23,240	$ 28,564
Less: Income tax	4,000	5,600	7,360	9,296	11,426
Profit after tax	$ 6,000	$ 8,400	$ 11,040	$ 13,944	$ 17,138
Plus: Depreciation	20,000	20,000	20,000	20,000	20,000
Net cash flow	$ 26,000	$ 28,400	$ 31,040	$ 33,944	$ 37,138

Plus: Salvage value of equipment = $ 30,000
Recovery of working capital = 15,000

Net cash flow in year 5 = $ 82,138

13.3 THE COST OF CAPITAL

A firm can raise investment funds internally (i.e., from undistributed profits) or externally (i.e., by borrowing and by selling stocks). The cost of using internal funds is their opportunity cost, or the forgone return on these funds if they were invested outside the firm. The cost of external funds is the lowest rate of return that lenders and stockholders require to lend to, or invest their funds in, the firm. Since interest payments on borrowed funds are tax-deductible, the after-tax *cost of debt* (k_d) is the interest paid (r) times 1 minus the firm's marginal tax rate (t):

$$k_d = r(1 - t) \qquad (13\text{-}3)$$

One method of estimating the cost of equity capital (k_e) to the firm is by using the risk-free rate (r_f) plus a risk premium (r_p). That is,

$$k_e = r_f + r_p \qquad (13\text{-}4)$$

The U.S. Treasury bill rate is usually used for r_f. The risk premium (r_p) has two components: the excess of the rate of interest on the firm's bonds above the rate on government bonds (p_1) and the additional risk of holding the firm's stocks rather than its bonds (p_2). Historically, the value of p_2 has been about 4 percent.

The equity cost of capital can also be estimated by the *dividend valuation model*, given by

$$k_e = \frac{D}{P} + g \qquad (13\text{-}5)$$

where D is the dividend per share paid to stockholders, P is the price of a share of the stock, and g is the expected growth rate of dividend payments. The value of g used is the firm's historic growth rate or the earnings growth forecasted by security analysts.

A third method of estimating the cost of equity capital is the *capital asset pricing model (CAPM)*. This is given by

$$k_e = r_f + \beta(k_m - r_f) \qquad (13\text{-}6)$$

where the *beta coefficient*, β, measures the variability in the return on the common stock of the firm in relation to the variability in the return on the average stock and k_m is the return on the average stock. Multiplying β by ($k_m - r_f$) gives the risk premium on holding the common stock of the firm. Firms generally use more than one method to estimate the cost of equity capital and usually raise capital both by borrowing and by selling stocks.

The *composite cost of capital* to the firm (k_c) is the weighted average of the cost of debt capital (k_d) and equity capital (k_e). That is,

$$k_c = w_d k_d + w_e k_e \qquad (13\text{-}7)$$

where w_d and w_e are, respectively, the proportion of debt and equity capital in the firm's capital structure. Review of projects after they have been implemented, or *post audit*, can greatly improve managerial decisions.

EXAMPLE 3. Suppose that a firm pays an interest rate of 8.67 percent on its bonds (i.e., $r = 8.67$), the marginal income tax rate that the firm faces is 40 percent (i.e., $t = 0.4$), the rate on government bonds (r_f) is 6 percent, the return on the average stock (k_m) is 12 percent, the beta coefficient (β) is 1.2, and the firm raises 40 percent of its capital by borrowing (i.e., $w_d = 0.4$). The cost of debt (k_d) to the firm is then

$$k_d = r(1 - t) = 8.67\%(1 - 0.4) = 5.2\%$$

The equity cost of capital to the firm (k_e), found with the CAPM, is

$$k_e = r_f + \beta(k_m - r_f) = 6\% + 1.2(12\% - 6\%) = 13.2\%$$

The composite cost of capital to the firm (k_c) is then

$$k_c = w_d k_d + w_e k_e = 0.4(5.2\%) + 0.6(13.2\%) = 10\%$$

This is the composite marginal cost of capital that we have used to evaluate all the proposed investment projects the firm faced in Section 13.1 and Fig. 13-1.

13.4 PUBLIC GOODS

Public goods are those that are *nonrival in consumption*. That is, the use of the good or service by someone does not reduce its availability to others. For example, one individual's watching of TV does not interfere with the reception of the same TV program by others. Some public goods (such as TV programs) are exclusive (i.e., the service can be confined to those paying for it, as in the case of cable TV), while others (such as national defense) are *nonexclusive* (i.e., it is impossible to confine the benefit to only those paying for it).

Public goods that are nonexclusive lead to the *free-rider problem*, i.e., the unwillingness of people to help pay for public goods in the belief that the goods would be provided anyway. Less than the optimal amount of these goods would then be provided without the government's raising money to pay for them through general taxation. Even this does not entirely eliminate the problem because individuals have no incentive to accurately reveal their preferences, or demand, for the public good. Since a given amount of a public good can be consumed by more than one individual at the same time, the aggregate or total demand for a public good is obtained by the vertical summation of the demand curves of all those who consume the public good (see Example 4).

EXAMPLE 4. In Fig. 13-2, D_A and D_B are, respectively, the demand curves for public good X of individuals A and B. If A and B are the only two individuals in the market, the aggregate demand curve for public good X, D_T, is obtained by the *vertical* summation of D_A and D_B. The reason is that each unit of the good can be consumed by both individuals at the same time. Given market supply curve S_X for public good X, the optimal amount of X is 4 units per time period (indicated by the intersection of D_T and S_X at point E). At point E, the sum of the individual's marginal benefits equals the marginal cost of producing the 4 units of the public good (i.e., $AB + BC = AE$).

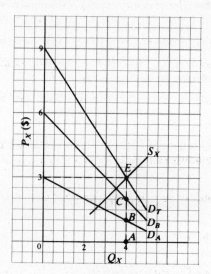

Fig. 13-2

13.5 BENEFIT-COST ANALYSIS

Benefit-cost analysis is a method or technique for estimating and comparing the social benefits and costs of a public project in order to determine whether or not the project should be undertaken. Benefit-cost analysis is, thus, the public-sector counterpart of the capital budgeting technique used by private firms. Benefit-cost analysis is generally more complex than capital budgeting because government agencies, as opposed to private firms, must consider the indirect as well as the direct benefits and costs of a proposed project, and also because there is less agreement about the appropriate *social discount rate* to use to calculate the present value of the benefits and costs of a public project. The theoretical justification for benefit-cost analysis rests on the *compensation principle*. That is, a public project is justified if gainers can fully compensate losers for their losses and still have some gain left. The principle holds regardless of whether such a redistribution actually takes place or not.

The steps involved in benefit-cost analysis are these: (1) estimate the net monetary value of the stream of direct and indirect benefits and costs resulting from the public project; (2) decide on the appropriate social discount rate to use; (3) make sure that the ratio of the present value of the benefits to the costs of the project exceeds 1. Since the resources for a public project must come from private consumption and/or investment, economists advocate the use of a social discount rate that reflects the opportunity cost, or alternatives forgone, of these funds in the private sector. In spite of the shortcomings facing benefit-cost analysis, its usefulness has been proved during the past two decades in a wide variety of undertakings ranging from water projects to defense, transportation, health, education, urban renewal, and recreational projects.

Glossary

Benefit-cost analysis   A technique for estimating and comparing the social benefits and costs of a public project in order to determine whether or not the project should be undertaken.

Beta coefficient (β)   The ratio of the variability in the return on the common stock of a firm to the variability in the average return on all stocks.

Capital asset pricing model (CAPM)   The method of measuring the equity cost of capital as the risk-free rate plus the product of the beta coefficient (β) times the risk premium on the average stock.

Capital budgeting   The process of planning expenditures that give rise to revenues or returns over a number of years.

Compensation principle   The principle that a project or policy improves social welfare if gainers can fully compensate the losers for their losses and still have some of the gain left.

Composite cost of capital   The weighted average of the cost of debt capital and equity capital to a firm.

Cost of debt   The net (after-tax) interest rate paid by a firm to borrow funds.

Dividend valuation model   The method of measuring the equity cost of capital to the firm by calculating the ratio of the dividend per share of the stock to the price of the stock and adding that ratio to the expected growth rate of dividend payments.

Free-rider problem   The problem that arises when people do not contribute to the payment for a public good in the belief that it will be provided anyway.

Internal rate of return (IRR) on a project   The rate of discount that equates the present value of the net cash flow to the initial cost of a project.

Net cash flow from a project   The difference between cash receipts and cash expenditures over the life of a project.

Net present value (NPV) of a project   The present value of the estimated stream of net cash flows from a project, discounted at the firm's cost of capital, minus the initial cost of the project.

Nonexclusion   The situation in which it is impossible or prohibitively expensive to confine the benefit or the consumption of a good to only those people paying for it.

Nonrival consumption   The distinguishing characteristic of a public good whereby its consumption by some individuals does not reduce the amount available to others.

Post audit   The review of projects after they have been implemented.

Profitability index (PI)   The ratio of the present value of the net cash flows from a project to its initial cost.

Public goods   Goods and services for which consumption by some individuals does not reduce the amount available for others. That is, once the goods or services are provided for someone, others can consume them at no additional cost.

Social discount rate   The opportunity cost of capital used in a public project.

Review Questions

1.   Capital budgeting refers to the

(a)   identification of the investment projects that a firm can undertake.

(b)   estimation of the expected rate of return on the investment projects open to a firm.

(c)   estimation of the cost of raising capital for various projects.

(d)   all of the above.

Ans. (d) See Section 13.1.

2.   Which of the following statements is false with respect to capital budgeting and the investment behavior of most large firms?

(a)   These decisions are critical to the profitability, growth, and the very survival of the firm in the long run.

(b)   Most large investment projects are reversible.

(c)   Investment projects should be undertaken as long as the expected return on the investments exceeds the cost of raising the capital to undertake them.

(d)   The cost of raising capital for additional investments eventually rises.

Ans. (b) See Section 13.1 and Example 1.

3.   In capital budgeting, the net cash flows from a project should be estimated

(a)   on an incremental basis.

(b)   on an after-tax basis.

(c)   by considering depreciation charges only for tax purposes.

(d)   all of the above.

Ans. (d) See Section 13.2

4.   A firm should undertake a project if the

(a)   net cash flow from the project is positive.

(b)   present value of the net cash flows is smaller than the cost of capital.

(c)   net present value of the project is positive.

(d)   marginal cost of capital exceeds the internal rate of return.

Ans. (c) See Section 13.2

5.   Which of the following statements is false with regard to capital budgeting?

(a)   The NPV and the IRR methods will always lead to the same investment decision.

(b)   When the NPV is positive the IRR exceeds the marginal cost of capital.

(c)   When the IRR is smaller than the marginal cost of capital the NPV is negative.

(d)   With capital rationing, projects should be undertaken according to their profitability index.

Ans. (a) See Section 13.2 and Example 2.

6.   Which of the following statements is false with regard to the cost of capital?

(a)   The interest that a firm pays on its bonds is tax-deductible.

(b)   The dividends that a firm pays on its stocks are not tax-deductible.

(c)   The cost of debt is usually less than the cost of equity capital.

(d)   None of the above.

Ans. (d) See Section 13.3.

7. Which of the following statements is false with regard to the cost of capital?

   (*a*) The cost of debt is equal to the interest that a firm pays on its bonds times 1 minus the marginal income tax rate of the firm.

   (*b*) The cost of equity capital can be found by adding a risk premium to the risk-free rate, by using the dividend valuation model, or by using the capital asset pricing model.

   (*c*) The cost of equity capital found by different methods must be the same.

   (*d*) The composite cost of capital is equal to the weighted average of the cost of debt and the cost of equity capital.

Ans.   (*c*) See Section 13.3.

8. Which of the following statements is true with regard to the composite cost of capital to a firm?

   (*a*) Since the cost of debt is usually smaller than the cost of equity capital, the firm should use only debt to raise additional capital.

   (*b*) The firm should raise additional capital by selling stocks because this is usually less risky than borrowing.

   (*c*) Even though the cost of debt is usually lower than the cost of equity capital, firms generally raise additional capital both by borrowing and by selling stocks.

   (*d*) None of the above.

Ans.   (*c*) See Section 13.3 and Example 3.

9. The distinguishing characteristic of public goods is

   (*a*) nonrival consumption.

   (*b*) nonexclusivity.

   (*c*) that they can be provided only by the government.

   (*d*) all of the above.

Ans.   (*a*) See Section 13.4.

10. The aggregate demand curve for a public good is obtained by adding the individuals' demand curves

   (*a*) horizontally.

   (*b*) vertically.

   (*c*) horizontally or vertically.

   (*d*) to the market supply curve of the good.

Ans.   (*b*) See Section 13.4 and Example 4.

11. Which of the following statements is false with respect to benefit-cost analysis?

   (*a*) It is the public-sector counterpart of capital budgeting.

   (*b*) It requires the estimation of the social benefits and costs of a public project.

   (*c*) It utilizes the social discount rate to find the present value of the stream of social benefits and costs of a project.

   (*d*) None of the above.

Ans.   (*d*) See Section 13.5.

12. The social discount rate used in benefit-cost analysis is equal to

   (*a*) the return on government securities.

   (*b*) the average return on the stock of private firms.

   (*c*) the opportunity cost of public funds in the private sector.

   (*d*) all of the above.

Ans.   (*c*) See Section 13.5.

Solved Problems

CAPITAL BUDGETING: AN OVERVIEW

13.1 (*a*) In what way can it be said that capital budgeting is nothing more than the application of the theory of the firm to investment projects? (*b*) Why are major capital investments for the most part irreversible?

(*a*) The theory of the firm postulates that in order to maximize total profits or the value of a firm, the firm should expand production as long as the marginal revenue from the sale of the product exceeds the marginal cost of producing it and until marginal revenue equals marginal cost. In a capital budgeting framework, this principle implies that the firm should undertake additional investment projects as long as returns on investments exceed the cost of raising the capital required to make the investments and until the marginal return from the last investment made is equal to its marginal cost.

(*b*) Major capital investment projects are for the most part irreversible because after a specialized type of machinery has been installed it has a very small second-hand value if the firm reverses its decision.

13.2 (*a*) How can the various investment projects that a firm could undertake be classified? (*b*) Which class of investments is likely to prove most complex?

(*a*) Investment projects can be classified into the following categories:

(1) *Replacement.* These are investments to replace equipment that is worn out in the production process.

(2) *Cost reduction.* These are investments (expenditures) to replace working but obsolete equipment with new and more efficient equipment, to conduct training programs that would reduce labor costs, or to move production facilities to areas where labor and other inputs are cheaper.

(3) *Output expansion of traditional products and markets.* These are investments to expand production facilities in response to increased demand for the firm's traditional products in traditional or existing markets.

(4) *Expansion into new products and/or markets.* These are investments to develop, produce, and sell new products and/or enter new markets.

(5) *Government regulation.* These are investments made to comply with government regulations. These include investment projects required to meet government health and safety regulations, pollution controls, and so on.

(*b*) The most complex investment projects that a firm is likely to face are those that involve producing new products and/or moving into new markets because lack of familiarity with the product and/or market results in much greater risks for the firm. These projects, however, are also likely to be the most essential and financially rewarding in the long run since a firm's product line tends to become obsolete over time and its traditional markets may shrink or even disappear.

13.3 (*a*) Who is responsible within the firm for the generation of ideas and proposals for new investment projects? (*b*) Why and in what way can it be said that capital budgeting usually involves all the major divisions of a firm?

(*a*) In well-managed and dynamic firms, all employees are encouraged to come up with new investment ideas. Most large firms, however, are likely to have a research and development division with the responsibility of coming up with proposals for new investment projects. Such a division is likely to be staffed by experts in product development, marketing research, industrial engineering, and so on, and they may regularly meet with the heads of other divisions in brainstorming sessions to examine new products, markets, and strategies.

(*b*) The capital budgeting process is likely to involve most of the firm's divisions. This is especially true for investment projects that involve entering into new product lines and markets. The marketing division will have to forecast the demand for the new or modified products that the firm plans to sell; the production, engineering, personnel, and purchasing departments must provide feasibility studies and estimates of the cost of the investment projects; and the finance department must determine how the required investment funds are to be raised and what their cost will be to the firm.

13.4 Suppose that a firm can undertake the projects indicated in Table 13.2, and it has estimated that it could raise $3.0 million of capital at a rate (cost) of 10 percent, an additional $2.5 million at 12 percent, $2.0 million at 15 percent, and still another $1.5 million at 18 percent. Draw a figure to show which projects the firm should undertake and which it should not.

Table 13.2

Capital Projects	Required Investment (millions)	Rate of Return
A	$1.5	19%
B	2.0	16
C	1.0	14
D	2.0	11
E	2.5	9

See Fig. 13-3. The top of the lettered bars in the figure gives the firm's demand for capitol, while the stepped MCC curve gives the marginal cost of capital to the firm. From the figure we can determine that the firm should undertake projects A, B, and C because the rates of return expected from them exceed the marginal cost (of 12 percent) of raising the capital required to undertake them. However, the firm would not undertake projects D and E because the rates of return these are expected to generate are below the cost of capital.

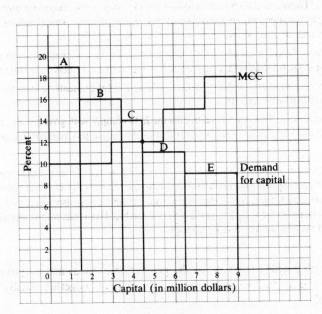

Fig. 13-3

13.5 (a) Redraw Fig. 13-3 and add to it smooth curves approximating the firm's demand curve for capital and its marginal cost curve of capital. (b) Under what conditions would these smooth curves hold? (c) How much would the firm invest if it faced these smooth curves? What would be the return on, and the cost of, the last dollar invested?

(a) See Fig. 13-4.

(b) Smooth curves for capital demand and for MCC are based on the assumption that the firm can make investments and raise funds in very small amounts in relation to the scale on the horizontal axis.

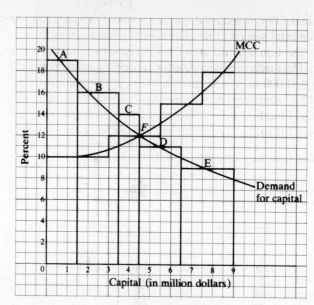

Fig. 13-4

(c) With the smooth curves for capital demand and MCC shown in Fig. 13-4, the firm would invest a total of $4.5 million and receive a return and incur a capital cost of 12 percent on the last dollar invested and raised. This is given by point F at the intersection of the demand and MCC curves.

THE CAPITAL BUDGETING PROCESS

13.6 (a) Why is the estimation of the net cash flow from a project a very important and difficult task of capital budgeting? (b) What guidelines should a firm follow in estimating the net cash flow from a project? (c) How are depreciation charges treated in estimating the net cash flow from a project? Why?

(a) The estimation of the net cash flow from a project is a very important task because an overestimate could lead a firm to undertake a project that would result in a loss and to a reduction in the value of the firm. However, an underestimate could lead the firm not to undertake a project that would increase the firm's value. Estimation of the net cash flow from a project is difficult because receipts and expenditures occur in the future and may be subject to a great deal of uncertainty.

(b) The general guidelines that a firm should follow in properly estimating the net cash flow from an investment project are as follows: (1) The net cash flow should be measured on an incremental basis (i.e., by the difference between the stream of the firm's net cash flow with and without the project). (2) The net cash flow must be estimated on an after-tax basis, using the firm's marginal tax rate. (3) Depreciation charges must be considered only in estimating the taxes that the firm has to pay.

(c) As noncash expenses, depreciation charges are subtracted from the sales revenues of the firm in order to calculate the taxes that the firm has to pay, but they are then added back to the firm's after-tax revenues to calculate the net cash flow from the project. The reason for doing this is that while depreciation charges are tax-deductible, they are available to the firm over the economic life of the machinery and equipment, i.e., until the machinery and equipment are replaced and the depreciation charges are actually disbursed.

13.7 A firm would like to introduce a new product. It has estimated that the cost of purchasing, delivering, and installing the new machinery required to manufacture the product is $150,000. The expected life of the product is six years. Incremental sales revenues are estimated to be $200,000 in the first year of operation, $240,000 in the second year, $220,000 in the third year, and $200,000 in each of the remaining three years. The incremental variable costs of producing the product are estimated to be 50 percent of incremental sales revenues. The firm is also expected to incur additional fixed costs of $30,000 per year. The firm uses the straight-line depreciation method. The marginal tax rate of the firm is 40 percent. The machinery purchased will have a salvage value of $30,000, and the firm also expects to recoup $10,000 of its working capital at the end of the six years. (*a*) Construct a table similar to Table 13.1, summarizing the cash flows from the project. (*b*) Calculate the net present value of the project if the firm uses a risk-adjusted discount rate of 20 percent. (*c*) Should the firm undertake the project? If so, by how much would the value of the firm increase?

(*a*)   The net cash flow from the project is summarized in Table 13.3.

Table 13.3

	Year					
	1	2	3	4	5	6
Sales	$200,000	$240,000	$220,000	$200,000	$200,000	$200,000
Less: Variable costs	100,000	120,000	110,000	100,000	100,000	100,000
Fixed costs	30,000	30,000	30,000	30,000	30,000	30,000
Depreciation	25,000	25,000	25,000	25,000	25,000	25,000
Profit before taxes	$ 45,000	$ 65,000	$ 55,000	$ 45,000	$ 45,000	$ 45,000
Less: Income tax	18,000	26,000	22,000	18,000	18,000	18,000
Profit after tax	$ 27,000	$ 39,000	$ 33,000	$ 27,000	$ 27,000	$ 27,000
Plus: Depreciation	25,000	25,000	25,000	25,000	25,000	25,000
Net cash flow	$ 52,000	$ 64,000	$ 58,000	$ 52,000	$ 52,000	$ 52,000

Plus: Salvage value of equipment = $ 30,000
Recovery of working capital =   10,000

Net cash flow in year 6 = $ 92,000

(*b*)   The net present value of the project is

$$\text{NPV} = \frac{\$52,000}{(1+0.20)^1} + \frac{\$64,000}{(1+0.20)^2} + \frac{\$58,000}{(1+0.20)^3} + \frac{\$52,000}{(1+0.20)^4} + \frac{\$52,000}{(1+0.20)^5} + \frac{\$92,000}{(1+0.20)^6}$$
$$- \$150,000$$

$$= \frac{\$52,000}{1.2} + \frac{\$64,000}{1.44} + \frac{\$58,000}{1.728} + \frac{\$52,000}{2.0736} + \frac{\$52,000}{2.48832} + \frac{\$92,000}{2.985984} - \$150,000$$

$$= \$43,333.33 + \$44,444.44 + \$33,564.82 + \$25,077.16 + \$20,897.63 + \$30,810.61 - \$150,000$$

$$= \$198,128 - \$150,000$$

$$= \$48,128$$

(*c*)   Since the NPV of the project is positive, the firm should undertake the project. This project would add $48,127 to the value of the firm.

13.8   Find the net present value of the project in Problem 13.7, using Table B.2 in Appendix B, if the firm uses a risk-adjusted discount rate of (*a*) 16 percent and (*b*) 24 percent. (*c*) What is the internal rate of return of this project?

(*a*)   Table B.2 in Appendix B gives the present value interest factors (PVIF) for various interest or discount rates ($i = k$) and years (n). For example, for $i = k = 16\%$ and $n = 1$, $\text{PVIF}_{16,1} = 0.8621$ (the first number under the column headed 16% in Table B.2). This gives the present value of $1/(1 + 0.16)^1$. For $i = k = 16$ and $n = 2$, $PVIF_{16,2} = $1/(1 + 0.16)^2 = 0.7432$, and so on. The present value of the net cash flow from the project is then obtained by *multiplying* the net cash flow from the project in each year by the appropriate present value interest factor. Specifically, the present value of a sum (R) received in year n and discounted at the rate i is equal to $R_n(PVIF_{i,n})$. The NPV of the project in Problem 13.7 for $i = k = 16\%$ is

$$NPV = \$52,000(0.8621) + \$64,000(0.7432) + \$58,000(0.6407) + \$52,000(0.5523)$$
$$+ \$52,000(0.4761) + \$92,000(0.4104) - \$150,000$$
$$= \$220,788.20 - \$150,000$$
$$= \$70,788.20$$

The same result, of course, could be obtained by direct calculation (i.e., without using Table B.2).

(b) If the firm used instead the risk-adjusted discount rate of 24 percent,

$$NPV = \$52,000(0.8065) + \$64,000(0.6504) + \$58,000(0.5245) + \$52,000(0.4230)$$
$$+ \$52,000(0.3411) + \$92,000(0.2751) - \$150,000$$
$$= \$179,027 - \$150,000$$
$$= \$29,027$$

Note that the higher the risk-adjusted discount rate used, the smaller is the NPV of the project.

(c) The internal rate of return (IRR) on a project is the rate of discount (k^*) that equates the present value of the net cash flow from the project to the initial cost of the project. This can be found by trial and error, using Table B.2 in Appendix B. That is, if at a given rate of discount the present value of the net cash flow exceeds the initial cost of the project, the discount rate is increased and the process is repeated. However, if at a given rate of discount the present value of the net cash flow is smaller than the initial cost of the project, the discount rate is reduced. The process is repeated until the discount rate is found that equates the present value of the net cash flow to the initial cost of the project. This discount rate (k^*) is the internal rate of return (IRR) on the project.

Using a discount rate of 32 percent for the project in Problem 13.7, we get

$$NPV = \$52,000(0.7576) + \$64,000(0.5739) + \$58,000(0.4348)$$
$$+ \$52,000(0.3294) + \$52,000(0.2495)$$
$$+ \$92,000(0.1890) - \$150,000$$
$$= \$148,834 - \$150,000$$
$$= -\$1,166$$

Since the NPV for $i = k = 32\%$ is close to zero, IRR $= k^* = 32\%$ for this project. The precise value of IRR (found with a calculator) is in fact 31.64 percent.

13.9. Suppose that the net cash flow from the investment project in Problem 13.8 is $60,000 in each year, the salvage value of the machinery purchased is zero and, furthermore, the firm does not recover any working capital at the end of the six years. Use Table B.4 in Appendix B to determine whether the firm should undertake the project if the risk-adjusted discount rate is 20 percent.

The net present value of the project is obtained from

$$NPV = \sum_{t=1}^{n} \frac{R_t}{(1+k)^t} - C_0$$
$$= \sum_{t=1}^{6} \frac{\$60,000}{(1+0.20)^t} - \$150,000$$
$$= \$60,000\,(PVIFA_{20,6}) - \$150,000$$
$$= \$60,000\,(3.3255) - \$150,000$$
$$= \$199,530 - \$150,000$$
$$= \$49,530$$

Note that $PVIFA_{20,6}$ refers to the present-value interest factor of an annuity of $1 for six years discounted at 20 percent (see Table B.4 of Appendix B).

13.10 (a) When can the NPV and the IRR methods of evaluating investment projects provide contradictory results? (b) How can this arise? (c) Which method should then be used? Why?

(a) Only when evaluating mutually exclusive investment projects can the NPV and the IRR methods provide contradictory signals as to which investment project the firm should undertake. For a single or independent project, the two methods will always give the same investment signal.

(b) The NPV and the IRR methods can provide contradictory investment signals because the NPV method implicitly and conservatively assumes that the net cash flows generated by the investment project are reinvested at the firm's cost of capital or risk-adjusted discount rate, while the IRR method implicitly assumes that the net cash flows are reinvested at the same higher IRR earned on the given project.

(c) When contradictory signals are provided by the NPV and the IRR methods, the former should be used because the firm cannot assume that it can reinvest the net cash flows from the project at the same higher IRR earned on the project.

13.11 Using a discount rate of 12 percent, determine (a) the net present value and (b) the internal rate of return on mutually exclusive investment projects A and B with the initial cost and net cash flows given in Table 13.4. (c) Which project should the firm undertake? Why?

Table 13.4

	Project A	Project B
Initial cost	$100,000	$100,000
Net cash flow (per year)		
Year 1	−20,000	33,000
Year 2	10,000	33,000
Year 3	40,000	33,000
Year 4	40,000	33,000
Year 5	150,000	33,000

(a) Using Table B.2 in Appendix B, the firm will find that the NPV of project A is $29,116 and the NPV of project B is $18,958.

(b) Using Table B.2, the firm can find by trial and error that the IRR on both projects lies between 18 percent and 20 percent, but the IRR is much closer to 18 percent (it is in fact 18.2 percent) on project A and closer to 20 percent (it is in fact 19.4 percent) on project B.

(c) Since investment projects A and B are mutually exclusive, and the NPV and IRR methods give contradictory results, the firm should undertake project A because its NPV is higher than for project B. The reason is that the firm cannot assume that it can reinvest the net cash flows generated by the project chosen at the same higher IRR that it will earn on that project.

13.12 A firm with $200,000 to invest faces the three projects indicated in Table 13.5. (a) Which project(s) would the firm undertake if it used the NPV investment criterion? (b) Is this the correct decision? Why? (c) Why might the capital available to the firm be limited to $200,000?

Table 13.5

	Project A	Project B	Project C
Present value of net cash flows (PVNCF)	$270,000	$150,000	$125,000
Initial cost of project (C_0)	200,000	110,000	90,000

(a) The NPV of each project is obtained by subtracting the initial cost of the investment (C_0) from the present value of the net cash flows (PVNCF). Thus, NPV = $70,000 for project A, $40,000 for project B, and $35,000 for project C. With capital rationing, the firm can undertake either project A only or projects B and C. Ranking projects according to their NPV, the firm would undertake project A.

(b) Since the firm faces capital rationing, however, it should use the profitability index (PI) as its investment criterion. The PI of each project is given by the ratio of the PVNCF to the C_0 of each project.

$$\text{For project A,} \quad \text{PI} = \frac{\$270,000}{\$200,000} = 1.35$$

$$\text{For project B,} \quad \text{PI} = \frac{\$150,000}{\$110,000} = 1.36$$

$$\text{For project C,} \quad \text{PI} = \frac{\$125,000}{\$90,000} = 1.39$$

The end results of the firm's use of the PI investment criteria indicates that the firm should undertake projects B and C. The reason is that these projects provide a higher rate of return per dollar invested than project A. Note that the sum of NPV for projects B and C exceeds NPV for project A.

(c) Capital rationing may result from top management's desire to avoid overexpansion, overborrowing, and possibly loss of control of the firm by selling more stocks to raise additional capital.

THE COST OF CAPITAL

13.13 Explain why (a) the cost of debt is usually lower than the cost of equity capital to a firm and (b) firms do not rely exclusively on debt financing.

(a) The cost to a firm of debt capital is usually lower than the cost of equity capital for two reasons. First, interest payments on borrowed funds (debt) are tax-deductible while dividends paid to stockholders are not. Secondly, the return (interest required to be paid) on bonds is usually lower than the return on equity capital (dividend plus capital gains) because firms must honor their commitment to pay interest and principal on loans before paying dividends to stockholders. Since lenders face a smaller risk than stockholders, the former naturally require a smaller average return than the latter.

(b) Firms do not rely exclusively on debt financing because they would probably be unable to borrow as many funds as they need. Of greater importance is that the more a firm borrows, the greater is the risk that lenders face and the higher is the rate of interest that they require. At some point, the cost of debt will exceed the cost of equity capital. In general, firms do not borrow up to the point at which the interest rate that they must pay on the marginal funds borrowed is equal to or larger than the cost of equity capital, but rather raise debt and equity capital simultaneously and calculate the cost of funds as the weighted average of the various types of funds that they utilize.

13.14 A firm can sell bonds at an interest rate of 10 percent. The interest rate on government securities is 6 percent. Calculate the cost of equity capital for this firm.

The cost of equity capital for the firm (k_e) can be calculated by finding the sum of the risk-free rate, or rate on government securities (r_f), plus the risk premium required to induce investors to buy the stock of the firm (r_p). That is,

$$k_e = r_f + r_p$$

The value of r_p is given by p_1 plus p_2, where p_1 is equal to $r - r_f$ and p_2 is the additional premium required in order to induce investors to purchase the firm's stock rather than its bonds. Historically, the value of p_2 has been about 4 percent. Thus, the cost of equity capital to this firm is

$$k_e = r_f + p_1 + p_2$$
$$= r_f + (r - r_f) + p_2$$
$$= 6\% + (10\% - 6\%) + 4\%$$
$$= 14\%$$

13.15 A firm expects to pay a $3 dividend to the holders of each share of its common stock during the current year. A share of the common stock of the firm sells for 12 times current earnings. Management and outside analysts expect the growth rate of earnings and dividends for the company to be 9 percent. Calculate the cost of equity capital to this firm.

The cost of equity capital to this firm (k_e) can be calculated with the dividend valuation model, as follows:

$$k_e = \frac{D}{P} + g$$

where D is the dividend paid per year on each share of the common stock of the firm, P is the price of a share of the common stock of the firm, and g is the expected yearly growth rate in dividend payments by the firm.

Since the dividend per share of the common stock of the firm is $3 per year and a share of the common stock of the firm sells for 12 times current earnings, the price of a share of the common stock of the firm is ($3)(12) = $36.

With the expected yearly growth of 9 percent for earnings and dividends of the firm, the cost of equity capital for this firm is

$$k_e = \frac{\$3}{\$36} + 0.09 = 0.0833 + 0.09 = 0.1733, \text{ or } 17.33\%$$

13.16 Suppose that a firm pays an interest rate of 11 percent on its bonds, the marginal income tax rate that the firm faces is 40 percent, the rate on government bonds is 7.5 percent, the return on the average stock is 11.55 percent, the beta coefficient for the common stock of the firm is 2, and the firm wishes to raise 40 percent of its capital by borrowing. Determine (a) the cost of debt, (b) the cost of equity capital, and (c) the composite cost of capital for this firm.

(a) The cost of debt (k_d) is given by the interest rate that the firm must pay on its bonds (r) times 1 minus the firm's marginal income tax rate (t). That is,

$$k_d = r(1 - t) = 11\%(1 - 0.4) = 6.6\%$$

(b) The cost of equity capital (k_e) found by the capital asset pricing model (CAPM) is given by

$$k_e = r_f + \beta(k_m - r_f)$$

where r_f is the risk-free rate (i.e., the interest rate on government securities), k_m is the return on the average stock of all firms in the market, and β is the estimated beta coefficient for the common stock of this firm. With $r_f = 7.5\%$, $k_m = 11.55\%$, and $\beta = 2$, the cost of this firm's equity capital, using the CAPM, is

$$k_e = 7.5\% + 2(11.55\% - 7.5\%) = 15.6\%$$

(c) The composite cost of capital (k_c) is given by

$$k_c = w_d k_d + w_e k_e$$

where w_d and w_e are, respectively, the proportion of debt and equity capital in the firm's capital structure. With $w_d = 0.4$, $w_e = 0.6$, $k_d = 6.6\%$, and a cost of equity capital of $k_e = 15.6\%$, the composite cost of capital for this firm is

$$k_c = 0.4(6.6\%) + 0.6(15.6\%) = 12.0\%$$

This is the composite marginal cost of capital that we have used to evaluate the investment projects open to the firm in Problems 13.4 and 13.5.

13.17 A firm estimates that it must pay a rate of interest of 13 percent on its bonds and faces a marginal income tax rate of 50 percent. The interest on government securities is 10 percent. During the current year, the firm expects to pay a dividend of $2 on each share of its common stock, which sells for 8 times current earnings. Management and outside analysts expect the growth rate of earnings and dividends of the firm to be 5 percent per year. The return on the average stock of all firms in the market is 15 percent and the estimated beta coefficient for the common stock of the firm is 1.4. The firm wants to maintain a capital structure of 30 percent debt. Calculate (a) the cost of equity capital faced by this firm as determined by each of the three methods discussed in Section 13.3 and (b) the composite cost of capital if the firm uses the cost of equity capital found by the capital asset pricing model.

(a) The cost of equity capital (k_e) calculated as the sum of the risk-free rate plus the risk premium is

$$k_e = r_f + r_p = r_f + p_1 + p_2 = r_f + (r - r_f) + 4\%$$
$$= 10\% + (13\% - 10\%) + 4\% = 17\%$$

The cost of equity capital calculated with the stock valuation model is

$$k_e = \frac{D}{P} + g = \frac{\$2}{\$16} + 0.05 = 0.125 + 0.05 = 0.175, \text{ or } 17.5\%$$

The cost of equity capital by the capital asset pricing model (CAPM) is

$$k_e = r_f + \beta(k_m - r_f) = 10\% + 1.4(15\% - 10\%) = 17\%$$

(b) The composite cost of capital is equal to the weighted average of the cost of debt and the cost of equity capital.

$$k_d = r(1 - t) = 13\%(1 - 0.5) = 6.5\%$$

Hence, with $k_e = 17\%$ and $w_d = 0.3$

$$k_c = w_d k_d + w_e k_e = 0.3(6.5\%) + 0.7(17\%) = 13.85\%$$

13.18 Explain (a) what a post audit involves and (b) how it can improve managerial decisions.

(a) It is very important to review projects after they have been implemented. Such a post-audit review involves comparing the actual cash flow and return from a project with the expected or predicted cash flow and return on the project, as well as providing an explanation of the observed differences between predicted and actual results.

(b) A post-audit review can improve managerial decisions because if decision makers know that their investment projects will be reviewed and evaluated after implementation, they are likely to draw up investment plans more carefully and to work harder to ensure that their predictions are in fact fulfilled.

PUBLIC GOODS

13.19 (a) How do the goals of public and not-for-profit organizations differ from those of private firms? (b) In what way are the principles applied by public and not-for-profit organizations in the pursuit of their goals similar to those used by private firms?

(a) The goal of private firms is to maximize profits or the value of the firm. However, the goals of public and not-for-profit organizations (such as hospitals, schools, foundations) are to provide a service to the largest possible number of people, achieve a more equitable distribution of income, prevent environmental deterioration, or a combination of these and other "social" goals.

(b) Both public and not-for-profit organizations, on the one hand, and private firms, on the other, seek to achieve their respective goals in the face of the specific constraints they face. While their objectives differ, both types of organization use the same general principles and employ the same general types of tools of analysis in striving to achieve their goals.

13.20 Given the following information, draw a figure showing the aggregate or total demand curve for good Y, and its equilibrium price and quantity if it is a public good. How much of good Y do individuals A and B consume?

$$QD_A = 18 - 3P_Y \qquad QD_B = 15 - \frac{3}{2}P_Y \qquad QS_Y = 1 + \frac{3}{2}P_Y$$

where P_Y is given in dollars.

See Fig. 13-5. The figure shows that the market demand curve for good Y when it is a public good is obtained by the *vertical* summation of the demand curves of individuals A and B for good Y. This is given by D_T in the figure. With D_T and S_Y, the equilibrium price for good Y is $6 and the equilibrium quantity is 10. This is given by the intersection of D_T and S_Y at point E. From Fig. 13-5 we can see that when good Y is a public good, individuals A and B each consume 10 units of it.

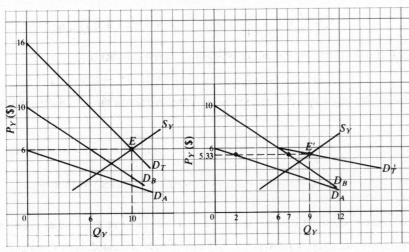

Fig. 13-5   **Fig. 13-6**

13.21 Answer Problem 13.20 if good Y is a private rather than a public good.

See Fig. 13-6. The figure shows that the market demand curve for good Y when it is a private rather than a public good is obtained by the *horizontal* summation of the demand curves of individuals A and B for the good. This is given by D_T' in the figure. With D_T' and S_Y, the equilibrium price for good Y is $5.33 and the equilibrium quantity is 9. This is given by the intersection of D_T' and S_Y at point E'. These compare with $P_Y = 6 and $Q_Y = 10$ when good Y is a public good (see Fig. 13-5). From Fig. 13-6 we can see that when good Y is a private good, individual A consumes 2 units and individual B consumes 7 units of the good (as compared with 10 units of the good consumed by each individual when good Y is a public good).

13.22 (*a*) Explain the distinction between public goods and goods supplied by the government, and give some examples. (*b*) What type of public goods can be provided only by the government? How can the government provide these goods?

(*a*) All goods and services provided by the government are public goods (i.e., are nonrival in consumption), but not all public goods are, or need be, provided by the government. Those public goods that do not exhibit nonexclusion (i.e., those for which each user can be charged) can be, and in fact often are, provided by the private sector. An example of a public good that is provided by the government and exhibits nonexclusion is national defense. An example of a public good that does not exhibit nonexclusion and is provided by private firms is cable TV programming. An example of a public good that does not exhibit nonexclusion (so that it could be provided by private firms but is often provided by the government) is garbage collection.

(*b*) Public goods that exhibit nonexclusion can be provided only by the government. Private firms will not provide these goods because they cannot exclude nonpaying users of these goods. The government generally raises the funds needed to pay for the public goods it provides by taxing the general public. The government can then either produce the goods itself or, more likely in the United States, it can pay private firms to produce those goods (as, for example, most items of national defense).

BENEFIT-COST ANALYSIS

13.23 Why is it generally more difficult to estimate (*a*) the benefits and costs of a public than of a private project and (*b*) the benefits than the costs of a public project?

(*a*) Estimating the benefits and costs of public projects is generally much more difficult than estimating the benefits and costs of a private project because while private firms need consider only the direct benefits and costs resulting from a project, public agencies must consider the indirect benefits and costs as well. *Indirect* benefits and costs accrue to people and firms other than those directly involved in the project or transaction. Since private firms usually cannot charge for indirect benefits or be charged for indirect costs, the firms need not consider indirect benefits and costs in their capital budgeting analysis.

However, since public agencies seek to maximize social rather than private welfare, they must consider all indirect benefits and costs in addition to the direct ones. The indirect benefits and costs of a public project are generally even more difficult to estimate than the direct benefits and costs because the former are even further removed from the market pricing system than direct benefits and costs, and may also involve such intangibles as the esthetic effect of a project on a locality, to which a monetary value cannot be assigned.

(*b*) Estimating the benefits of a public project is generally more difficult than estimating its costs because the prices of public goods and services are usually not market-determined. However, the cost of public projects can be determined from the market price of the equipment and services and the opportunity cost of the capital used in the project.

13.24. (*a*) How should the social discount rate be estimated according to most economists? (*b*) Has this procedure actually been followed in the past by public agencies?

(*a*) Since public funds must come (i.e., must be transferred) from the private sector of the economy, William Baumol and most other economists advocate the use of a social discount rate that reflects the opportunity cost of these funds, or what the funds would have earned in the private sector. The opportunity cost of funds withdrawn from personal consumption can be measured by the return on government securities that these funds could have earned (when consumers save part of their disposable income). The opportunity cost of funds withdrawn from private investments can be measured by the return on the average stock of private firms. Since public funds are likely to come partly from consumption expenditures and partly from private investments, the social discount rate to be used to evaluate public projects should be the weighted average rate of return on private funds, with the weights being given by the proportion in which funds are withdrawn from consumption expenditures and from private investments.

(*b*) Public agencies have seldom if ever used the opportunity cost of public funds as the social discount rate in evaluating public projects. The social discount rate that they used was almost invariably much too low in relation to the opportunity cost of public funds. In fact, some public agencies, such as the departments of the Treasury and Labor, actually used no discount rate at all in the evaluation of their public projects until the late 1960s. When a social discount rate was used, the rate differed widely among different agencies and projects. The very low, wide array of social discount rates used by public agencies to evaluate public projects almost certainly involved a gross misallocation of investment funds between the private and public sectors of the economy and within the public sector itself.

13.25 What are the most serious shortcomings of benefit-cost analysis?

Benefit-cost analysis faces a number of serious conceptual and measurement problems. One of the most serious is the measurement of the net social benefits and costs of a public project. The estimation of the direct benefits of a public project is generally more difficult than the measurement of the direct costs, especially when there is no market-determined price for the public good provided (the usual case). The estimation of the indirect or external benefits and costs is even more difficult. There are also many intangible benefits and costs, such as esthetic considerations, which often cannot be assigned a monetary value.

A second shortcoming of benefit-cost analysis is that there is disagreement on the appropriate social discount rate to use. While most economists advocate the use of a social discount rate that reflects the opportunity cost of public funds based on what these funds could have earned in similarly risky undertakings in the private sector, not everyone subscribes to this approach, and even when they do, it may still be difficult to determine what the precise social discount rate should be for evaluating a particular public project.

Benefit-cost analysis can also lead to very erroneous conclusions when it is used to compare public projects in widely different fields in which the degree by which social benefits and costs are overestimated or underestimated can vary greatly. Furthermore, when investment projects are interrelated, so that the outcome of one project affects the outcome of another project, the projects must be evaluated jointly, and this compounds the problems of measurement and evaluation.

13.26 In spite of its serious shortcomings, benefit-cost analysis retains a great deal of usefulness in the evaluation of public projects. (*a*) What useful functions does benefit-cost analysis serve? (*b*) What real-world considerations lead you to believe that the usefulness of benefit-cost analysis has been established?

(*a*)   One of the great advantages of using benefit-cost analysis to evaluate public projects is that it forces government officials to make explicit all the assumptions underlying the analysis. Since investment decisions must be made, it is generally better to base them on some information and analysis than on none. Scrutiny of the assumptions has sometimes led to decision reversals. For example, in 1971 the Federal Power Commission (now the Federal Energy Regulatory Commission) approved the construction of a hydroelectric dam on the Snake River, which flows from Oregon to Idaho and forms Hell's Canyon (the deepest in North America). The decision was based on a benefit-cost analysis that ignored some environmental costs. Because of this, the Supreme Court, on appeal from the Secretary of the Interior, revoked the order to build the dam pending a new benefit-cost analysis that properly included *all* benefits and costs. Finally, Congress passed a law prohibiting the construction of the dam.

(*b*)   Although benefit-cost analysis is still more of an art than a science and is somewhat subjective, its usefulness has been proved in a wide variety of undertakings ranging from water projects to defense, transportation, health, education, urban renewal, and recreational projects. In fact, in 1965 the federal government formally began to introduce benefit-cost analysis for its budgetary procedures under the Planning-Programming-Budgeting System (PPBS). While the PPBS system failed because of its high cost and because it generated much more information than the Budget Bureau could handle, the concept of justifying public projects by benefit-cost analysis survived and even spread to state and local governments.

Appendix A

Mathematical Appendix

A.1 THE CONCEPT OF THE DERIVATIVE

Optimization analysis, which was conducted graphically in Section 2.3, can be performed much more efficiently and precisely with differential calculus. This relies on the concept of the *derivative*, which can be explained in terms of the TR curve of Fig. 2-1, reproduced here with some modifications as Figure A-1.

In Section 2.2, we defined the *marginal revenue* (MR) as the change (Δ) in the total revenue per unit change in output. For example, when output (Q) increases from 2 to 3 units, total revenue (TR) increases from \$12 to \$15. Thus,

$$MR = \frac{\Delta TR}{\Delta Q} = \frac{\$15 - \$12}{3 - 2} = \frac{\$3}{1} = \$3$$

This is the slope of chord BC on the total revenue curve. However, when the quantity is infinitesimally divisible (i.e., when Q assumes values smaller than unity and as small as we want, and even approaching zero in the limit), then MR is given by the slope of shorter and shorter chords and, in the limit, approaches the slope of the TR curve at a point. Thus, starting from point B, as the change in quantity approaches zero, the change in total revenue or marginal revenue approaches the slope of the TR curve at point B. That is, $MR = \Delta TR/\Delta Q = \$4$ (the slope of tangent BK to the TR curve at point B) as the change in output approaches zero in the limit. Note that the derivative or MR (i.e., the slope of the TR curve) declines as we move farther up the total revenue curve to reflect its concave shape and declining slope.

More generally, if we let $TR = Y$ and $Q = X$, *the derivative of* Y *with respect to* X is given by the change in Y with respect to X as the change in X approaches zero. That is,

$$\frac{dY}{dX} = \lim_{\Delta X \to 0} \frac{\Delta Y}{\Delta X}$$

This reads: The derivative of Y with respect to X is equal to the limit of the ratio $\Delta Y/\Delta X$, as ΔX approaches zero. Geometrically, this corresponds to the slope of the curve at the point at which we want to find the limit. Note that the smaller the change in X, the closer is the value of the derivative to the slope of the curve at a point. For example, for ΔX between 2 and 4 in Fig. A-1, the average $dY/dX = \$2$ (the slope of chord BD). For the smaller ΔX between 2 and 3, the average $dY/dX = \$3$ (the slope of chord BC), which is closer to

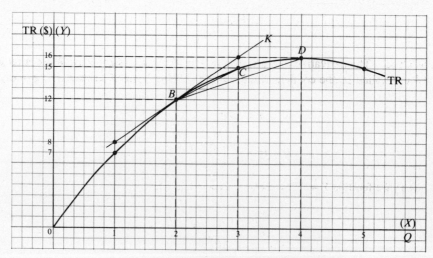

Fig. A-1

250

the slope of the curve at point B (i.e., $dY/dX = \$4$). The concept of the limit is extremely important in marginal and optimization analysis.

A.2 RULES OF DIFFERENTIATION

Differentiation is the process of determining the derivative of a function, i.e., finding the change in Y for a change in X, when the change in X approaches zero. In this section, we present the rules of differentiation. A more extensive treatment of these rules as well as their proofs may be found in any introductory calculus text, or by consulting *Schaum's Outline of Calculus*.

Constant Function Rule.   The derivative of a constant function, $Y = f(X) = a$, is zero for all values of a (the constant). That is, for the function

$$Y = f(X) = a$$
$$\frac{dY}{dX} = 0$$

EXAMPLE 1.   For the function

$$Y = 2$$
$$\frac{dY}{dX} = 0$$

This is graphed in Fig. A-2(a). Since Y is defined to be a constant, its value does not change for any value of X, and so dY/dX (the slope of the Y line) is zero.

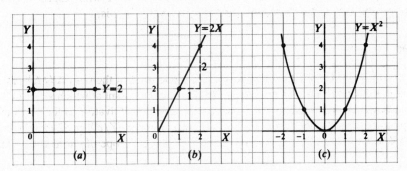

Fig. A-2

Power Function Rule.   The derivative of a power function, $Y = aX^b$, where a and b are constants, is equal to the exponent b multiplied by the coefficient a times the variable X raised to the $b - 1$ power. That is, for the function

$$Y = aX^b$$
$$\frac{dY}{dX} = b \cdot a \cdot X^{b-1}$$

EXAMPLE 2.   Given the function $Y = 2X$, where $a = 2$, $b = 1$ (implicit)

$$\frac{dY}{dX} = 1 \cdot 2 \cdot X^{1-1}$$
$$= 2X^0$$
$$= 2(1) = 2$$

That is, for

$$Y = 2X$$
$$\frac{dY}{dX} = 2$$

This is graphed in Fig. A-2(b). Note that the slope of the line (dY/dX) is constant at the value of 2 over any range of X values.

EXAMPLE 3. For the function $Y = X^2$

$$\frac{dY}{dX} = 2 \cdot 1 \cdot X^{2-1}$$
$$= 2X^1$$
$$= 2X$$

That is, for the function

$$Y = X^2$$
$$\frac{dY}{dX} = 2X$$

This is graphed in Fig. A-2(c). Note that the slope of the curve (dY/dX) varies at every value of X and is negative for $X < 0$, zero at $X = 0$, and positive for $X > 0$.

Sums and Differences Rule. The derivative of a sum (difference) is equal to the sum (difference) of the derivatives of the individual terms. Thus, if

$$U = g(X) \quad \text{and} \quad V = h(X)$$

where U is an unspecified function g of X, while V is another unspecified function h of X, then for the function

$$Y = U \pm V$$
$$\frac{dY}{dX} = \frac{dU}{dX} \pm \frac{dV}{dX}$$

EXAMPLE 4. If $U = g(X) = 2X$ and $V = h(X) = X^2$, so that

$$Y = U + V = 2X + X^2$$
$$\frac{dY}{dX} = 2 + 2X$$

Since $dU/dX = 2$ and $dV/dX = 2X$ (by the power function rule), the derivative of the total function (dY/dX) is equal to the derivative of the sum of its parts ($2 + 2X$).

EXAMPLE 5. For

$$Y = 0.04X^3 - 0.9X^2 + 10X + 5$$
$$\frac{dY}{dX} = 0.12X^2 - 1.8X + 10$$

Note that the derivatives of the first three terms of the Y function are obtained by the power function rule, while the derivative of the constant, 5, is equal to zero by the constant function rule.

Product Rule. The derivative of the product of two expressions is equal to the first expression multiplied by the derivative of the second *plus* the second expression multiplied by the derivative of the first. Thus, for the function

$$Y = U \cdot V$$

where, $U = g(X)$ and $V = h(X)$

$$\frac{dY}{dX} = U\frac{dV}{dX} + V\frac{dU}{dX}$$

EXAMPLE 6.   For the function

$$Y = 2X^2(3 - 2X)$$

and letting $U = 2X^2$ and $V = 3 - 2X$

$$\frac{dY}{dX} = 2X^2\left(\frac{dV}{dX}\right) + (3 - 2X)\frac{dU}{dX}$$
$$= 2X^2(-2) + (3 - 2X)(4X)$$
$$- 4X^2 + 12X - 8X^2$$
$$= 12X - 4X^2$$

Quotient Rule.   The derivative of the quotient of two expressions is equal to the denominator multiplied by the derivative of the numerator *minus* the numerator multiplied by the derivative of the denominator, all divided by the denominator squared. Thus, for the function

$$Y = \frac{U}{V}$$

and letting $U = g(X)$ and $V = h(X)$

$$\frac{dY}{dX} = \frac{V\dfrac{dU}{dX} - U\dfrac{dV}{dX}}{V^2}$$

EXAMPLE 7.   For the function

$$Y = \frac{3 - 2X}{2X^2}$$

and letting $U = 3 - 2X$ and $V = 2X^2$

$$\frac{dY}{dX} = \frac{2X^2(-2) - (3 - 2X)4X}{(2X^2)^2} = \frac{-4X^2 - 12X + 8X^2}{4X^4}$$
$$= \frac{4X^2 - 12X}{4X^4} = \frac{4X(X - 3)}{4X(X^3)} = \frac{X - 3}{X^3}$$

Function of a Function (Chain) Rule.   If $Y = f(U)$ and $U = g(X)$, then the derivative of Y with respect to X is equal to the derivative of Y with respect to U multiplied by the derivative of U with respect to X. That is, if

$$Y = f(U) \quad \text{and} \quad U = g(X)$$

then

$$\frac{dY}{dX} = \frac{dY}{dU} \cdot \frac{dU}{dX}$$

EXAMPLE 8.   If

$$Y = U^3 + 10 \quad \text{and} \quad U = 2X^2$$

then

$$\frac{dY}{dU} = 3U^2 \quad \text{and} \quad \frac{dU}{dX} = 4X$$

Therefore,

$$\frac{dY}{dX} = \frac{dY}{dU} \cdot \frac{dU}{dX} = (3U^2)4X$$

Substituting the expression for U (i.e., $U = 2X^2$) into the previous expression, we get

$$\frac{dY}{dX} = 3(2X^2)^2(4X) = 3(4X^4)4X = 48X^5$$

EXAMPLE 9.   To find the derivative of

$$Y = (3X^2 + 10)^3$$

let

$$U = 3X^2 + 10 \quad \text{and} \quad Y = U^3$$

then

$$\frac{dY}{dU} = 3U^2 \quad \text{and} \quad \frac{dU}{dX} = 6X$$

Thus,

$$\frac{dY}{dX} = \frac{dY}{dU} \cdot \frac{dU}{dX} = (3U^2)6X$$

Substituting the value of U (i.e., $3X^2 + 10$) into the previous expression, we get

$$\frac{dY}{dX} = 3(3X^2 + 10)^2(6X) = 3(9X^4 + 60X^2 + 100)(6X)$$

$$= 162X^5 + 1{,}080X^3 + 1{,}800X = 2X(81X^4 + 540X^2 + 900)$$

Table A.1 summarizes the above rules for differentiating functions.

Table A.1   Rules for Differentiating Functions

Function	Derivative
1. Constant function $Y = a$	$\dfrac{dY}{dX} = 0$
2. Power function $Y = aX^b$	$\dfrac{dY}{dX} = b \cdot a \cdot X^{b-1}$
3. Sums and differences of functions $Y = U \pm V$	$\dfrac{dY}{dX} = \dfrac{dU}{dX} \pm \dfrac{dV}{dX}$
4. Product of two functions $Y = U \cdot V$	$\dfrac{dY}{dX} = U\dfrac{dV}{dX} + V\dfrac{dU}{dX}$
5. Quotient of two functions $Y = \dfrac{U}{V}$	$\dfrac{dY}{dX} = \dfrac{V\dfrac{dU}{dX} - U\dfrac{dV}{dX}}{V^2}$
6. Function of a function $Y = f(U)$, where $U = g(X)$	$\dfrac{dY}{dX} = \dfrac{dY}{dU} \cdot \dfrac{dU}{dX}$

A.3   DETERMINING A MAXIMUM OR A MINIMUM BY CALCULUS

Optimization often requires finding the maximum or minimum value of a function. For example, a firm may want to maximize its revenue, minimize the cost of producing a given output or, more likely, maximize its profits. For a function to be at its maximum or minimum, the derivative of the function must be zero. Geometrically, this corresponds to the point at which the curve has zero slope.

EXAMPLE 10. For total revenue function

$$TR = 8Q - Q^2 \qquad\qquad (A\text{-}1)$$
$$\frac{d(TR)}{dQ} = 8 - 2Q$$

Setting $d(TR)/dQ = 0$, we get

$$8 - 2Q = 0$$

Therefore,
$$Q = 4$$

That is, for total revenue function $(A\text{-}1)$, $d(TR)/dQ = 0$ (i.e., its slope is zero) and total revenue is at its maximum at an output level of 4 units (see Fig. A-1).

A.4 DISTINGUISHING BETWEEN A MAXIMUM AND A MINIMUM: THE SECOND DERIVATIVE

To distinguish between a maximum and a minimum point we use the *second derivative*. For the general function $Y = f(X)$, the second derivative is written as d^2Y/dX^2. The second derivative is the derivative of the derivative and is found by applying to the (first) derivative the rules of differentiation presented in Section A.2 and summarized in Table A.1.

EXAMPLE 11. For

$$Y = X^3$$
$$\frac{dY}{dX} = 3X^2 \quad \text{and} \quad \frac{d^2Y}{dX^2} = 6X$$

Similarly, for

$$TR = 8Q - Q^2$$
$$\frac{d(TR)}{dQ} = 8 - 2Q \quad \text{and} \quad \frac{d^2(TR)}{dQ^2} = -2$$

Geometrically, the first derivative gives the slope of the function, while the second derivative gives the *change* in the slope of the function. The value of the second derivative can thus be used to determine whether we have a maximum or a minimum at the point at which the first derivative (slope) is zero. The rule is that *if the second derivative is positive, we have a minimum, and if the second derivative is negative, we have a maximum*. We have already encountered the geometric equivalent of this rule in Problem 2.9 when dealing with the total profit (π) function at the bottom of Fig. 2-8. That function has a zero slope (i.e., $d\pi/dQ = 0$) at $Q = 0.5$ and $Q = 2$. But in the neighborhood of $Q = 0.5$, the slope of the π function increases (i.e., $d^2\pi/dQ^2 > 0$) from a negative value before $Q = 0.5$, to zero at $Q = 0.5$, to a positive value after $Q = 0.5$, so that the function faces up and we have a minimum. However, in the neighborhood of $Q = 2$, the slope of the π function decreases (i.e., $d^2\pi/dQ^2 < 0$) from positive values to zero and then to negative values, so that the function faces down and we have a maximum. A few applications follow.

EXAMPLE 12. A comprehensive and important illustration of the use of the second derivative is provided by determining the profit maximization by a firm. Suppose that the total revenue and total cost functions of the firm are, respectively,

$$TR = 45Q - 0.5Q^2$$
$$TC = Q^3 - 8Q^2 + 57Q + 2$$

Then
$$\begin{aligned}\pi &= TR - TC \\ &= 45Q - 0.5Q^2 - (Q^3 - 8 + 57Q + 2) \\ &= 45Q - 0.5Q^2 - Q^3 + 8 - 57Q - 2 \\ &= -Q^3 + 7.5Q^2 - 12Q - 2\end{aligned}$$

To determine the level of output at which the firm maximizes profits, we proceed as follows:

$$\frac{d\pi}{dQ} = -3Q^2 + 15Q - 12 = 0$$

$$= (-3Q + 3)(Q - 4) = 0$$

therefore, at $Q = 1$ and $Q = 4$

$$\frac{d^2\pi}{dQ^2} = -6Q + 15$$

At $Q = 1$, $d^2\pi/dQ^2 = -6(1) + 15 = 9$, and π is at a minimum.

At $Q = 4$, $d^2\pi/dQ^2 = -6(4) + 15 = -9$, and π is at a maximum.

Therefore, π is maximized at $Q = 4$, and from the original π function we can determine that

$$\pi = -(4)^3 + 7.5(4)^2 - 12(4) - 2$$

$$= -64 + 120 - 48 - 2$$

$$= \$6$$

The geometric equivalent of the above analysis is found in Fig. 2-3. Note that if we set $d(\text{TR})/dQ$, or MR, equal to $d(\text{TC})/dQ$, or MC, we would find that MR = MC at $Q = 1$ and $Q = 4$. However, only at $Q = 4$ does the MC curve intercept the MR curve from below, so that π is maximized. (See Fig. 2-3.)

A.5 PARTIAL DERIVATIVES

Until now we have examined the relationship between two variables only. For example, variable Y (say total revenue, total cost, or total profit) was assumed to be a function of, or to depend on, only the value of variable X (total output or quantity). Most economic relationships, however, involve more than two variables. For example, total revenue may be a function of, or depend on, both output and advertising; total costs may depend on expenditures on both labor and capital; and total profit may depend on sales of commodities X and Y. Thus, it becomes important to determine the marginal effect on the dependent variable, say total profit, resulting from changes in the quantities of each individual variable, say the quantities of commodities X and Y sold *separately*. These marginal effects are measured by the *partial derivative*, which is indicated by the symbol ∂ (as compared to d for the derivative). The partial derivative of the *dependent*, or left-hand, variable with respect to each of the *independent*, or right-hand, variables is found by the same rules of differentiation presented earlier, *except that all independent variables other than the one with respect to which we are finding the partial derivative are held constant.*

EXAMPLE 13. Suppose that the total profit (π) function of a firm depends on sales of commodities X and Y as follows:

$$\pi = f(X, Y) = 80X - 2X^2 - XY - 3Y^2 + 100Y \tag{A-2}$$

To find the partial derivative of π with respect to X, $\partial\pi/\partial X$, we hold Y constant and obtain

$$\frac{\partial\pi}{\partial X} = 80 - 4X - Y$$

This isolates the marginal effect on π from changes in the quantity sold of commodity X only (i.e., while holding the quantity of commodity Y constant). Note that the derivative of the third term of the π function is $-Y$ (since the implicit exponent of X is 1) and that Y is treated as a constant. The fourth and fifth terms of the π function drop out in the partial differentiation because they contain no X term. Similarly, to isolate the marginal effect of a change in Y on π, we hold X constant and obtain

$$\frac{\partial\pi}{\partial Y} = -X - 6Y + 100$$

We can visualize the concept of the partial derivative geometrically with a three-dimensional figure in which π is on the vertical axis and the X and Y axes form the base of the figure, which is now a plane surface, rather than a line. Then, $\partial\pi/\partial X$ measures the marginal effect of X on π in the cross section of the three-dimensional figure along the X axis. Similarly, $\partial\pi/\partial Y$ examines the marginal effect of Y on π in the cross section of the three-dimensional figure along the Y axis. Note that the value of $\partial\pi/\partial X$ depends also on the level at which Y is held constant. Similarly, the value of $\partial\pi/\partial Y$ depends also on the level at which X is held constant. This is the reason that the expression for $\partial\pi/\partial X$ found above also contains a Y term, while the expression for $\partial\pi/\partial Y$ also contains an X term.

A.6 MAXIMIZING A MULTIVARIABLE FUNCTION

To maximize or minimize a multivariable function, we must set each partial derivative equal to zero and solve the resulting set of simultaneous equations for the optimal value of the independent, or right-hand, variables.

EXAMPLE 14.   To maximize the total profit function shown in equation (A-2), i.e.,

$$\pi = 80X - 2X^2 - XY - 3Y^2 + 100Y$$

we set $\partial\pi/\partial X$ and $\partial\pi/\partial Y$ (found earlier) equal to zero and solve for X and Y. Specifically,

$$\frac{\partial\pi}{\partial X} = 80 - 4X - Y = 0$$

$$\frac{\partial\pi}{\partial Y} = -X - 6Y + 100 = 0$$

Multiplying the first of the above expressions by -6, rearranging the second, and adding, we get

$$-480 + 24X + 6Y = 0$$
$$\underline{100 - \quad X - 6Y = 0}$$
$$-380 + 23X \qquad\quad = 0$$

Therefore, $X = \frac{380}{23} = 16.52$. Substituting $X = 16.52$ into the first expression of the partial derivative set equal to zero, and solving for Y, we get

$$80 - 4(16.52) - Y = 0$$
$$Y = 80 - 66.08 = 13.92$$

Thus, the firm maximizes π when it sells 16.52 units of commodity X and 13.92 units of commodity Y. Substituting these values into the π function, we get the maximum total profit of the firm:

$$\pi = 80(16.52) - 2(16.52)^2 - (16.52)(13.92) - 3(13.92)^2 + 100(13.92) = \$1,356.52$$

The condition for distinguishing between a maximum and minimum is based on the value of the second-order partial derivative. This condition is much more complex than for a function of a single independent variable and is beyond the scope of this appendix. Here, we simply assume that the second-order condition for maximization is satisfied. The interested reader should consult any calculus text.

A.7 CONSTRAINED OPTIMIZATION

Until now we have examined unconstrained optimization, or the maximization or minimization of an objective function subject to no constraints. Most of the time, however, managers face constraints in their optimization decisions. For example, a firm may face a limitation on its production capacity or on the availability of skilled personnel and crucial raw materials. It may also face legal and environmental constraints. In such cases, we have a *constrained optimization* problem, i.e., the maximizing or minimizing of an objective function subject to some constraints. The existence of such constraints reduces the freedom of action of the firm and usually prevents it from attaining its unconstrained optimum. Constrained optimization problems can be solved by substitution or by the Lagrangian multiplier method. These are examined in turn.

A constrained optimization problem may be solved by first solving the *constraint equation* for one of the decision variables and then substituting the expression for this variable into the *objective function* that the firm seeks to maximize or minimize. This procedure converts a constrained optimization problem into an unconstrained one, which can then be solved as indicated in the previous section.

EXAMPLE 15. Suppose that the firm seeks to maximize its total profit function as given by equation (*A-2*):

$$\pi = 80X - 2X^2 - XY - 3Y^2 + 100Y$$

but faces the constraint that the output of commodity X plus the output of commodity Y must be 12. That is,

$$X + Y = 12 \qquad\qquad (A\text{-}3)$$

To solve this optimization problem by substitution, we solve the constraint function for X, substitute the value of X into the objective function (π) that the firm seeks to maximize, and then apply the procedure (shown in the previous section) for maximizing an unconstrained objective function. Specifically, solving the constraint function for X, we get

$$X = 12 - Y$$

Substituting the above constraint expression for X into the objective profit function, we obtain

$$\begin{aligned}
\pi &= 80(12 - Y) - 2(12 - Y)^2 - (12 - Y)Y - 3Y^2 + 100Y \\
&= 960 - 80Y - 2(144 - 24Y + Y^2) - 12Y + Y^2 - 3Y^2 + 100Y \\
&= 960 - 80Y - 288 + 48Y - 2Y^2 - 12Y + Y^2 - 3Y^2 + 100Y \\
&= -4Y^2 + 56Y + 672
\end{aligned}$$

To maximize the above (unconstrained) profit function, we find the first derivative of π with respect to Y, set it equal to zero, and solve for Y. That is,

$$\frac{d\pi}{dY} = -8Y + 56 = 0$$

Therefore, $Y = 7$. Substituting $Y = 7$ into the constraint function, we get

$$\begin{aligned}
X &= 12 - Y \\
&= 12 - 7 = 5
\end{aligned}$$

Thus, the firm maximizes total profits when it produces 5 units of commodity X and 7 units of commodity Y (as compared with $X = 16.52$ and $Y = 13.92$ found earlier when the firm faced no output constraint). With $X = 5$ and $Y = 7$,

$$\begin{aligned}
\pi &= 80(5) - 2(5)^2 - (5)(7) - 3(7)^2 + 100(7) \\
&= \$868
\end{aligned}$$

as compared with $1,356.52 (see Example 14) in the absence of any output constraint.

A.8 CONSTRAINED OPTIMIZATION BY THE LAGRANGIAN MULTIPLIER METHOD

When the constraint equation is too complex or cannot be solved for one of the decision variables as an explicit function of the other(s), the technique of substitution to solve a constrained optimization problem can become burdensome or impossible. In such cases we may resort to the *Lagrangian multiplier* method. The first step in this method is to form a *Lagrangian function*. This is given by the original objective function that the firm seeks to maximize or minimize plus λ (the Greek letter lambda, which is conventionally used for the Lagrangian multiplier) times the constraint function set equal to zero. Because it incorporates the constraint function set equal to zero, the Lagrangian function can also be treated as an unconstrained optimization problem, and its solution will always be identical to the original constrained optimization problem.

EXAMPLE 16. The constrained profit-maximization problem that was solved in Example 15 by substitution can be solved by the Lagrangian multiplier method. To do so, we first set the constraint function, equation (*A-3*) (i.e., $X + Y = 12$) equal to zero and obtain

$$X + Y - 12 = 0$$

We then multiply this form of the constraint function by λ and add it to the original profit function, equation $(A\text{-}2)$, which we seek to maximize (i.e., $\pi = 80X - 2X^2 - XY - 3Y^2 + 100Y$) so as to form the Lagrangian function (L_π). That is,

$$L_\pi = 80X - 2X^2 - XY - 3Y^2 + 100Y + \lambda(X + Y - 12) \qquad (A\text{-}4)$$

The above function can be treated as an unconstrained function in three unknowns: X, Y, and λ. Now the solution that maximizes L also maximizes π.

To maximize L_π, we set the partial derivative of L_π with respect to X, Y, and λ equal to zero, and solve the resulting set of simultaneous equations for the values of X, Y, and λ. Finding the partial derivatives of L_π with respect to each of the three unknowns, and setting the derivatives equal to zero, we get

$$\frac{\partial L_\pi}{\partial X} = 80 - 4X - Y + \lambda = 0 \qquad (A\text{-}5)$$

$$\frac{\partial L_\pi}{\partial Y} = -X - 6Y + 100 + \lambda = 0 \qquad (A\text{-}6)$$

$$\frac{\partial L_\pi}{\partial \lambda} = X + Y - 12 = 0 \qquad (A\text{-}7)$$

Note that equation $(A\text{-}7)$ is equal to the constraint imposed on the original profit function of the firm [equation $(A\text{-}2)$]. Indeed, Lagrangian function $(A\text{-}4)$ was specifically set up so that when the partial derivative of L_π with respect to λ (the Lagrangian multiplier) is set equal to zero, not only the constraint of the problem is satisfied but the Lagrangian function (L_π) reduces to the original unconstrained profit function (π), so that the optimal solution of both functions is identical.

To find the values of X, Y, and λ that maximize L_π and π, we solve equations $(A\text{-}5)$, $(A\text{-}6)$, and $(A\text{-}7)$ simultaneously. To do this, we subtract equation $(A\text{-}6)$ from equation $(A\text{-}5)$ and get

$$-20 - 3X + 5Y = 0 \qquad (A\text{-}8)$$

Multiplying equation $(A\text{-}7)$ by 3 and adding to it equation $(A\text{-}8)$, we obtain

$$\begin{aligned} 3X + 3Y - 36 &= 0 \\ \underline{-3X + 5Y - 20} &= 0 \\ 8Y - 56 &= 0 \end{aligned}$$

Therefore, $Y = 7$ and $X = 5$, so that $\pi = \$868$ (as in the previous example). Finally, by substituting the values of $X = 5$ and $Y = 7$ into equation $(A\text{-}6)$, we get the value of λ. That is,

$$-5 - 42 + 100 = -\lambda$$

Thus, $\lambda = -53$.

The value of λ has an important economic interpretation. It is the marginal effect on the objective-function solution associated with a 1-unit change in the constraint. In the problem shown in the above example, this means that a decrease in the output capacity constraint from 12 to 11 units or an increase to 13 units will reduce or increase, respectively, the total profit (π) of the firm by \$53.

Appendix B

Interest Factor Tables

Table B.1 Compound Value of $1: $FVIF_{i,n} = (1 + i)^n$

Period	1%	2%	3%	4%	5%	6%	7%	8%	9%	10%
1	1.0100	1.0200	1.0300	1.0400	1.0500	1.0600	1.0700	1.0800	1.0900	1.1000
2	1.0201	1.0404	1.0609	1.0816	1.1025	1.1236	1.1449	1.1664	1.1881	1.2100
3	1.0303	1.0612	1.0927	1.1249	1.1576	1.1910	1.2250	1.2597	1.2950	1.3310
4	1.0406	1.0824	1.1255	1.1699	1.2155	1.2625	1.3108	1.3605	1.4116	1.4641
5	1.0510	1.1041	1.1593	1.2167	1.2763	1.3382	1.4026	1.4693	1.5386	1.6105
6	1.0615	1.1262	1.1941	1.2653	1.3401	1.4185	1.5007	1.5869	1.6771	1.7716
7	1.0721	1.1487	1.2299	1.3159	1.4071	1.5036	1.6058	1.7138	1.8280	1.9487
8	1.0829	1.1717	1.2668	1.3686	1.4775	1.5938	1.7182	1.8509	1.9926	2.1436
9	1.0937	1.1951	1.3048	1.4233	1.5513	1.6895	1.8385	1.9990	2.1719	2.3579
10	1.1046	1.2190	1.3439	1.4802	1.6289	1.7908	1.9672	2.1589	2.3674	2.5937
11	1.1157	1.2434	1.3842	1.5395	1.7103	1.8983	2.1049	2.3316	2.5804	2.8531
12	1.1268	1.2682	1.4258	1.6010	1.7959	2.0122	2.2522	2.5182	2.8127	3.1384
13	1.1381	1.2936	1.4685	1.6651	1.8856	2.1329	2.4098	2.7196	3.0658	3.4523
14	1.1495	1.3195	1.5126	1.7317	1.9799	2.2609	2.5785	2.9372	3.3417	3.7975
15	1.1610	1.3459	1.5580	1.8009	2.0789	2.3966	2.7590	3.1722	3.6425	4.1772
16	1.1726	1.3728	1.6047	1.8730	2.1829	2.5404	2.9522	3.4259	3.9703	4.5950
17	1.1843	1.4002	1.6528	1.9479	2.2920	2.6928	3.1588	3.7000	4.3276	5.0545
18	1.1961	1.4282	1.7024	2.0258	2.4066	2.8543	3.3799	3.9960	4.7171	5.5599
19	1.2081	1.4568	1.7535	2.1068	2.5270	3.0256	3.6165	4.3157	5.1417	6.1159
20	1.2202	1.4859	1.8061	2.1911	2.6533	3.2071	3.8697	4.6610	5.6044	6.7275
21	1.2324	1.5157	1.8603	2.2788	2.7860	3.3996	4.1406	5.0338	6.1088	7.4002
22	1.2447	1.5460	1.9161	2.3699	2.9253	3.6035	4.4304	5.4365	6.6586	8.1403
23	1.2572	1.5769	1.9736	2.4647	3.0715	3.8197	4.7405	5.8715	7.2579	8.9543
24	1.2697	1.6084	2.0328	2.5633	3.2251	4.0489	5.0724	6.3412	7.9111	9.8497
25	1.2824	1.6406	2.0938	2.6658	3.3864	4.2919	5.4274	6.8485	8.6231	10.834
26	1.2953	1.6734	2.1566	2.7725	3.5557	4.5494	5.8074	7.3964	9.3992	11.918
27	1.3082	1.7069	2.2213	2.8834	3.7335	4.8223	6.2139	7.9881	10.245	13.110
28	1.3213	1.7410	2.2879	2.9987	3.9201	5.1117	6.6488	8.6271	11.167	14.421
29	1.3345	1.7758	2.3566	3.1187	4.1161	5.4184	7.1143	9.3173	12.172	15.863
30	1.3478	1.8114	2.4273	3.2434	4.3219	5.7435	7.6123	10.062	13.267	17.449
40	1.4889	2.2080	3.2620	4.8010	7.0400	10.285	14.974	21.724	31.409	45.259
50	1.6446	2.6916	4.3839	7.1067	11.467	18.420	29.457	46.901	74.357	117.39
60	1.8167	3.2810	5.8916	10.519	18.679	32.987	57.946	101.25	176.03	304.48

Table B.1 (*Continued*)

Period	12%	14%	15%	16%	18%	20%	24%	28%	32%	36%
1	1.1200	1.1400	1.1500	1.1600	1.1800	1.2000	1.2400	1.2800	1.3200	1.3600
2	1.2544	1.2996	1.3225	1.3456	1.3924	1.4400	1.5376	1.6384	1.7424	1.8496
3	1.4049	1.4815	1.5209	1.5609	1.6430	1.7280	1.9066	2.0972	2.3000	2.5155
4	1.5735	1.6890	1.7490	1.8106	1.9388	2.0736	2.3642	2.6844	3.0360	3.4210
5	1.7623	1.9254	2.0114	2.1003	2.2878	2.4883	2.9316	3.4360	4.0075	4.6526
6	1.9738	2.1950	2.3131	2.4364	2.6996	2.9860	3.6352	4.3980	5.2899	6.3275
7	2.2107	2.5023	2.6600	2.8262	3.1855	3.5832	4.5077	5.6295	6.9826	8.6054
8	2.4760	2.8526	3.0590	3.2784	3.7589	4.2998	5.5895	7.2058	9.2170	11.703
9	2.7731	3.2519	3.5179	3.8030	4.4355	5.1598	6.9310	9.2234	12.166	15.916
10	3.1058	3.7072	4.0456	4.4114	5.2338	6.1917	8.5944	11.805	16.059	21.646
11	3.4785	4.2262	4.6524	5.1173	6.1759	7.4301	10.657	15.111	21.198	29.439
12	3.8960	4.8179	5.3502	5.9360	7.2876	8.9161	13.214	19.342	27.982	40.037
13	4.3635	5.4924	6.1528	6.8858	8.5994	10.699	16.386	24.758	36.937	54.451
14	4.8871	6.2613	7.0757	7.9875	10.147	12.839	20.319	31.691	48.756	74.053
15	5.4736	7.1379	8.1371	9.2655	11.973	15.407	25.195	40.564	64.358	100.71
16	6.1304	8.1372	9.3576	10.748	14.129	18.488	31.242	51.923	84.953	136.96
17	6.8660	9.2765	10.761	12.467	16.672	22.186	38.740	66.461	112.13	186.27
18	7.6900	10.575	12.375	14.462	19.673	26.623	48.038	85.070	148.02	253.33
19	8.6128	12.055	14.231	16.776	23.214	31.948	59.567	108.89	195.39	344.53
20	9.6463	13.743	16.366	19.460	27.393	38.337	73.864	139.37	257.91	468.57
21	10.803	15.667	18.821	22.574	32.323	46.005	91.591	178.40	340.44	637.26
22	12.100	17.861	21.644	26.186	38.142	55.206	113.57	228.35	449.39	866.67
23	13.552	20.361	24.891	30.376	45.007	66.247	140.83	292.30	593.19	1178.6
24	15.178	23.212	28.625	35.236	53.108	79.496	174.63	374.14	783.02	1602.9
25	17.000	26.461	32.918	40.874	62.668	95.396	216.54	478.90	1033.5	2180.0
26	19.040	30.166	37.856	47.414	73.948	114.47	268.51	612.99	1364.3	2964.9
27	21.324	34.389	43.535	55.000	87.259	137.37	332.95	784.63	1800.9	4032.2
28	23.883	39.204	50.065	63.800	102.96	164.84	412.86	1004.3	2377.2	5483.8
29	26.749	44.693	57.575	74.008	121.50	197.81	511.95	1285.5	3137.9	7458.0
30	29.959	50.950	66.211	85.849	143.37	237.37	634.81	1645.5	4142.0	10143.
40	93.050	188.88	267.86	378.72	750.37	1469.7	5455.9	19426.	66520.	*
50	289.00	700.23	1083.6	1670.7	3927.3	9100.4	46890.	*	*	*
60	897.59	2595.9	4383.9	7370.1	20555.	56347.	*	*	*	*

*FVIF > 99,999.

INTEREST FACTOR TABLES

Table B.2 Present Value of \$1: $PVIF_{i,n} = 1/(1 + i)^n = 1/FVIF_{i,n}$

Period	1%	2%	3%	4%	5%	6%	7%	8%	9%	10%
1	.9901	.9804	.9709	.9615	.9524	.9434	.9346	.9259	.9174	.9091
2	.9803	.9612	.9426	.9246	.9070	.8900	.8734	.8573	.8417	.8264
3	.9706	.9423	.9151	.8890	.8638	.8396	.8163	.7938	.7722	.7513
4	.9610	.9238	.8885	.8548	.8227	.7921	.7629	.7350	.7084	.6830
5	.9515	.9057	.8626	.8219	.7835	.7473	.7130	.6806	.6499	.6209
6	.9420	.8880	.8375	.7903	.7462	.7050	.6663	.6302	.5963	.5645
7	.9327	.8706	.8131	.7599	.7107	.6651	.6227	.5835	.5470	.5132
8	.9235	.8535	.7894	.7307	.6768	.6274	.5820	.5403	.5019	.4665
9	.9143	.8368	.7664	.7026	.6446	.5919	.5439	.5002	.4604	.4241
10	.9053	.8203	.7441	.6756	.6139	.5584	.5083	.4632	.4224	.3855
11	.8963	.8043	.7224	.6496	.5847	.5268	.4751	.4289	.3875	.3505
12	.8874	.7885	.7014	.6246	.5568	.4970	.4440	.3971	.3555	.3186
13	.8787	.7730	.6810	.6006	.5303	.4688	.4150	.3677	.3262	.2897
14	.8700	.7579	.6611	.5775	.5051	.4423	.3878	.3405	.2992	.2633
15	.8613	.7430	.6419	.5553	.4810	.4173	.3624	.3152	.2745	.2394
16	.8528	.7284	.6232	.5339	.4581	.3936	.3387	.2919	.2519	.2176
17	.8444	.7142	.6050	.5134	.4363	.3714	.3166	.2703	.2311	.1978
18	.8360	.7002	.5874	.4936	.4155	.3503	.2959	.2502	.2120	.1799
19	.8277	.6864	.5703	.4746	.3957	.3305	.2765	.2317	.1945	.1635
20	.8195	.6730	.5537	.4564	.3769	.3118	.2584	.2145	.1784	.1486
21	.8114	.6598	.5375	.4388	.3589	.2942	.2415	.1987	.1637	.1351
22	.8034	.6468	.5219	.4220	.3418	.2775	.2257	.1839	.1502	.1228
23	.7954	.6342	.5067	.4057	.3256	.2618	.2109	.1703	.1378	.1117
24	.7876	.6217	.4919	.3901	.3101	.2470	.1971	.1577	.1264	.1015
25	.7798	.6095	.4776	.3751	.2953	.2330	.1842	.1460	.1160	.0923
26	.7720	.5976	.4637	.3607	.2812	.2198	.1722	.1352	.1064	.0839
27	.7644	.5859	.4502	.3468	.2678	.2074	.1609	.1252	.0976	.0763
28	.7568	.5744	.4371	.3335	.2551	.1956	.1504	.1159	.0895	.0693
29	.7493	.5631	.4243	.3207	.2429	.1846	.1406	.1073	.0822	.0630
30	.7419	.5521	.4120	.3083	.2314	.1741	.1314	.0994	.0754	.0573
35	.7059	.5000	.3554	.2534	.1813	.1301	.0937	.0676	.0490	.0356
40	.6717	.4529	.3066	.2083	.1420	.0972	.0668	.0460	.0318	.0221
45	.6391	.4102	.2644	.1712	.1113	.0727	.0476	.0313	.0207	.0137
50	.6080	.3715	.2281	.1407	.0872	.0543	.0339	.0213	.0134	.0085
55	.5785	.3365	.1968	.1157	.0683	.0406	.0242	.0145	.0087	.0053

Table B.2 (Continued)

Period	12%	14%	15%	16%	18%	20%	24%	28%	32%	36%
1	.8929	.8772	.8696	.8621	.8475	.8333	.8065	.7813	.7576	.7353
2	.7972	.7695	.7561	.7432	.7182	.6944	.6504	.6104	.5739	.5407
3	.7118	.6750	.6575	.6407	.6086	.5787	.5245	.4768	.4348	.3975
4	.6355	.5921	.5718	.5523	.5158	.4823	.4230	.3725	.3294	.2923
5	.5674	.5194	.4972	.4761	.4371	.4019	.3411	.2910	.2495	.2149
6	.5066	.4556	.4323	.4104	.3704	.3349	.2751	.2274	.1890	.1580
7	.4523	.3996	.3759	.3538	.3139	.2791	.2218	.1776	.1432	.1162
8	.4039	.3506	.3269	.3050	.2660	.2326	.1789	.1388	.1085	.0854
9	.3606	.3075	.2843	.2630	.2255	.1938	.1443	.1084	.0822	.0628
10	.3220	.2697	.2472	.2267	.1911	.1615	.1164	.0847	.0623	.0462
11	.2875	.2366	.2149	.1954	.1619	.1346	.0938	.0662	.0472	.0340
12	.2567	.2076	.1869	.1685	.1372	.1122	.0757	.0517	.0357	.0250
13	.2292	.1821	.1625	.1452	.1163	.0935	.0610	.0404	.0271	.0184
14	.2046	.1597	.1413	.1252	.0985	.0779	.0492	.0316	.0205	.0135
15	.1827	.1401	.1229	.1079	.0835	.0649	.0397	.0247	.0155	.0099
16	.1631	.1229	.1069	.0930	.0708	.0541	.0320	.0193	.0118	.0073
17	.1456	.1078	.0929	.0802	.0600	.0451	.0258	.0150	.0089	.0054
18	.1300	.0946	.0808	.0691	.0508	.0376	.0208	.0118	.0068	.0039
19	.1161	.0829	.0703	.0596	.0431	.0313	.0168	.0092	.0051	.0029
20	.1037	.0728	.0611	.0514	.0365	.0261	.0135	.0072	.0039	.0021
21	.0926	.0638	.0531	.0443	.0309	.0217	.0109	.0056	.0029	.0016
22	.0826	.0560	.0462	.0382	.0262	.0181	.0088	.0044	.0022	.0012
23	.0738	.0491	.0402	.0329	.0222	.0151	.0071	.0034	.0017	.0008
24	.0659	.0431	.0349	.0284	.0188	.0126	.0057	.0027	.0013	.0006
25	.0588	.0378	.0304	.0245	.0160	.0105	.0046	.0021	.0010	.0005
26	.0525	.0331	.0264	.0211	.0135	.0087	.0037	.0016	.0007	.0003
27	.0469	.0291	.0230	.0182	.0115	.0073	.0030	.0013	.0006	.0002
28	.0419	.0255	.0200	.0157	.0097	.0061	.0024	.0010	.0004	.0002
29	.0374	.0224	.0174	.0135	.0082	.0051	.0020	.0008	.0003	.0001
30	.0334	.0196	.0151	.0116	.0070	.0042	.0016	.0006	.0002	.0001
35	.0189	.0102	.0075	.0055	.0030	.0017	.0005	.0002	.0001	*
40	.0107	.0053	.0037	.0026	.0013	.0007	.0002	.0001	*	*
45	.0061	.0027	.0019	.0013	.0006	.0003	.0001	*	*	*
50	.0035	.0014	.0009	.0006	.0003	.0001	*	*	*	*
55	.0020	.0007	.0005	.0003	.0001	*	*	*	*	*

*The factor is zero to four decimal places.

Table B.3 Future Value of an Annuity of $1 for *n* Periods:
$$\text{FVIFA}_{i,\,n} = \Sigma_{t=1}^{n}\,(1 + i)^{t-1}$$

Number of Periods	1%	2%	3%	4%	5%	6%	7%	8%	9%	10%
1	1.0000	1.0000	1.0000	1.0000	1.0000	1.0000	1.0000	1.0000	1.0000	1.0000
2	2.0100	2.0200	2.0300	2.0400	2.0500	2.0600	2.0700	2.0800	2.0900	2.1000
3	3.0301	3.0604	3.0909	3.1216	3.1525	3.1836	3.2149	3.2464	3.2781	3.3100
4	4.0604	4.1216	4.1836	4.2465	4.3101	4.3746	4.4399	4.5061	4.5731	4.6410
5	5.1010	5.2040	5.3091	5.4163	5.5256	5.6371	5.7507	5.8666	5.9847	6.1051
6	6.1520	6.3081	6.4684	6.6330	6.8019	6.9753	7.1533	7.3359	7.5233	7.7156
7	7.2135	7.4343	7.6625	7.8983	8.1420	8.3938	8.6540	8.9228	9.2004	9.4872
8	8.2857	8.5830	8.8923	9.2142	9.5491	9.8975	10.259	10.636	11.028	11.435
9	9.3685	9.7546	10.159	10.582	11.026	11.491	11.978	12.487	13.021	13.579
10	10.462	10.949	11.463	12.006	12.577	13.180	13.816	14.486	15.192	15.937
11	11.566	12.168	12.807	13.486	14.206	14.971	15.783	16.645	17.560	18.531
12	12.682	13.412	14.192	15.025	15.917	16.869	17.888	18.977	20.140	21.384
13	13.809	14.680	15.617	16.626	17.713	18.882	20.140	21.495	22.953	24.522
14	14.947	15.973	17.086	18.291	19.598	21.015	22.550	24.214	26.019	27.975
15	16.096	17.293	18.598	20.023	21.578	23.276	25.129	27.152	29.360	31.772
16	17.257	18.639	20.156	21.824	23.657	25.672	27.888	30.324	33.003	35.949
17	18.430	20.012	21.761	23.697	25.840	28.212	30.840	33.750	36.973	40.544
18	19.614	21.412	23.414	25.645	28.132	30.905	33.999	37.450	41.301	45.599
19	20.810	22.840	25.116	27.671	30.539	33.760	37.379	41.446	46.018	51.159
20	22.019	24.297	26.870	29.778	33.066	36.785	40.995	45.762	51.160	57.275
21	23.239	25.783	28.676	31.969	35.719	39.992	44.865	50.422	56.764	64.002
22	24.471	27.299	30.536	34.248	38.505	43.392	49.005	55.456	62.873	71.402
23	25.716	28.845	32.452	36.617	41.430	46.995	53.436	60.893	69.531	79.543
24	26.973	30.421	34.426	39.082	44.502	50.815	58.176	66.764	76.789	88.497
25	28.243	32.030	36.459	41.645	47.727	54.864	63.249	73.105	84.700	98.347
26	29.525	33.670	38.553	44.311	51.113	59.156	68.676	79.954	93.323	109.18
27	30.820	35.344	40.709	47.084	54.669	63.705	74.483	87.350	102.72	121.09
28	32.129	37.051	42.930	49.967	58.402	68.528	80.697	95.338	112.96	134.20
29	33.450	38.792	45.218	52.966	62.322	73.639	87.346	103.96	124.13	148.63
30	34.784	40.568	47.575	56.084	66.438	79.058	94.460	113.28	136.30	164.49
40	48.886	60.402	75.401	95.025	120.79	154.76	199.63	259.05	337.88	442.59
50	64.463	84.579	112.79	152.66	209.34	290.33	406.52	573.76	815.08	1163.9
60	81.669	114.05	163.05	237.99	353.58	533.12	813.52	1253.2	1944.7	3034.8

Table B.3 (*Continued*)

Number of Periods	12%	14%	15%	16%	18%	20%	24%	28%	32%	36%
1	1.0000	1.0000	1.0000	1.0000	1.0000	1.0000	1.0000	1.0000	1.0000	1.0000
2	2.1200	2.1400	2.1500	2.1600	2.1800	2.2000	2.2400	2.2800	2.3200	2.3600
3	3.3744	3.4396	3.4725	3.5056	3.5724	3.6400	3.7776	3.9184	4.0624	4.2096
4	4.7793	4.9211	4.9934	5.0665	5.2154	5.3680	5.6842	6.0156	6.3624	6.7251
5	6.3528	6.6101	6.7424	6.8771	7.1542	7.4416	8.0484	8.6999	9.3983	10.146
6	8.1152	8.5355	8.7537	8.9775	9.4420	9.9299	10.980	12.135	13.405	14.798
7	10.089	10.730	11.066	11.413	12.141	12.915	14.615	16.533	18.695	21.126
8	12.299	13.232	13.726	14.240	15.327	16.499	19.122	22.163	25.678	29.731
9	14.775	16.085	16.785	17.518	19.085	20.798	24.712	29.369	34.895	41.435
10	17.548	19.337	20.303	21.321	23.521	25.958	31.643	38.592	47.061	57.351
11	20.654	23.044	24.349	25.732	28.755	32.150	40.237	50.398	63.121	78.998
12	24.133	27.270	29.001	30.850	34.931	39.580	50.894	65.510	84.320	108.43
13	28.029	32.088	34.351	36.786	42.218	48.496	64.109	84.852	112.30	148.47
14	32.392	37.581	40.504	43.672	50.818	59.195	80.496	109.61	149.23	202.92
15	37.279	43.842	47.580	51.659	60.965	72.035	100.81	141.30	197.99	276.97
16	42.753	50.980	55.717	60.925	72.939	87.442	126.01	181.86	262.35	377.69
17	48.883	59.117	65.075	71.673	87.068	105.93	157.25	233.79	347.30	514.66
18	55.749	68.394	75.836	84.140	103.74	128.11	195.99	300.25	459.44	700.93
19	63.439	78.969	88.211	98.603	123.41	154.74	244.03	385.32	607.47	954.27
20	72.052	91.024	102.44	115.37	146.62	186.68	303.60	494.21	802.86	1298.8
21	81.698	104.76	118.81	134.84	174.02	225.02	377.46	633.59	1060.7	1767.3
22	92.502	120.43	137.63	157.41	206.34	271.03	469.05	811.99	1401.2	2404.6
23	104.60	138.29	159.27	183.60	244.48	326.23	582.62	1040.3	1850.6	3271.3
24	118.15	158.65	184.16	213.97	289.49	392.48	723.46	1332.6	2443.8	4449.9
25	133.33	181.87	212.79	249.21	342.60	471.98	898.09	1706.8	3226.8	6052.9
26	150.33	208.33	245.71	290.08	405.27	567.37	1114.6	2185.7	4260.4	8233.0
27	169.37	238.49	283.56	337.50	479.22	681.85	1383.1	2798.7	5624.7	11197.9
28	190.69	272.88	327.10	392.50	566.48	819.22	1716.0	3583.3	7425.6	15230.2
29	214.58	312.09	377.16	456.30	669.44	984.06	2128.9	4587.6	9802.9	20714.1
30	241.33	356.78	434.74	530.31	790.94	1181.8	2640.9	5873.2	12940.	28172.2
40	767.09	1342.0	1779.0	2360.7	4163.2	7343.8	22728.	69377.	*	*
50	2400.0	4994.5	7217.7	10435.	21813.	45497.	*	*	*	*
60	7471.6	18535.	29219.	46057.	*	*	*	*	*	*

*FVIFA > 99,999.

Table B.4 Present Value of an Annuity of $1 for *n* Periods:
$$\text{PVIFA}_{i,n} = \Sigma_{t=1}^{n}\left[1/(1+i)^{t}\right]$$

Number of Payments	1%	2%	3%	4%	5%	6%	7%	8%	9%
1	0.9901	0.9804	0.9709	0.9615	0.9524	0.9434	0.9346	0.9259	0.9174
2	1.9704	1.9416	1.9135	1.8861	1.8594	1.8334	1.8080	1.7833	1.7591
3	2.9410	2.8839	2.8286	2.7751	2.7232	2.6730	2.6243	2.5771	2.5313
4	3.9020	3.8077	3.7171	3.6299	3.5460	3.4651	3.3872	3.3121	3.2397
5	4.8534	4.7135	4.5797	4.4518	4.3295	4.2124	4.1002	3.9927	3.8897
6	5.7955	5.6014	5.4172	5.2421	5.0757	4.9173	4.7665	4.6229	4.4859
7	6.7282	6.4720	6.2303	6.0021	5.7864	5.5824	5.3893	5.2064	5.0330
8	7.6517	7.3255	7.0197	6.7327	6.4632	6.2098	5.9713	5.7466	5.5348
9	8.5660	8.1622	7.7861	7.4353	7.1078	6.8017	6.5152	6.2469	5.9952
10	9.4713	8.9826	8.5302	8.1109	7.7217	7.3601	7.0236	6.7101	6.4177
11	10.3676	9.7868	9.2526	8.7605	8.3064	7.8869	7.4987	7.1390	6.8052
12	11.2551	10.5753	9.9540	9.3851	8.8633	8.3838	7.9427	7.5361	7.1607
13	12.1337	11.3484	10.6350	9.9856	9.3936	8.8527	8.3577	7.9038	7.4869
14	13.0037	12.1062	11.2961	10.5631	9.8986	9.2950	8.7455	8.2442	7.7862
15	13.8651	12.8493	11.9379	11.1184	10.3797	9.7122	9.1079	8.5595	8.0607
16	14.7179	13.5777	12.5611	11.6523	10.8378	10.1059	9.4466	8.8514	8.3126
17	15.5623	14.2919	13.1661	12.1657	11.2741	10.4773	9.7632	9.1216	8.5436
18	16.3983	14.9920	13.7535	12.6593	11.6896	10.8276	10.0591	9.3719	8.7556
19	17.2260	15.6785	14.3238	13.1339	12.0853	11.1581	10.3356	9.6036	8.9501
20	18.0456	16.3514	14.8775	13.5903	12.4622	11.4699	10.5940	9.8181	9.1285
21	18.8570	17.0112	15.4150	14.0292	12.8212	11.7641	10.8355	10.0168	9.2922
22	19.6604	17.6580	15.9369	14.4511	13.1630	12.0416	11.0612	10.2007	9.4424
23	20.4558	18.2922	16.4436	14.8568	13.4886	12.3034	11.2722	10.3711	9.5802
24	21.2434	18.9139	16.9355	15.2470	13.7986	12.5504	11.4693	10.5288	9.7066
25	22.0232	19.5235	17.4131	15.6221	14.0939	12.7834	11.6536	10.6748	9.8226
26	22.7952	20.1210	17.8768	15.9828	14.3752	13.0032	11.8258	10.8100	9.9290
27	23.5596	20.7069	18.3270	16.3296	14.6430	13.2105	11.9867	10.9352	10.0266
28	24.3164	21.2813	18.7641	16.6631	14.8981	13.4062	12.1371	11.0511	10.1161
29	25.0658	21.8444	19.1885	16.9837	15.1411	13.5907	12.2777	11.1584	10.1983
30	25.8077	22.3965	19.6004	17.2920	15.3725	13.7648	12.4090	11.2578	10.2737
35	29.4086	24.9986	21.4872	18.6646	16.3742	14.4982	12.9477	11.6546	10.5668
40	32.8347	27.3555	23.1148	19.7928	17.1591	15.0463	13.3317	11.9246	10.7574
45	36.0945	29.4902	24.5187	20.7200	17.7741	15.4558	13.6055	12.1084	10.8812
50	39.1961	31.4236	25.7298	21.4822	18.2559	15.7619	13.8007	12.2335	10.9617
55	42.1472	33.1748	26.7744	22.1086	18.6335	15.9905	13.9399	12.3186	11.0140

Table B.4   (*Continued*)

Number of Payments	10%	12%	14%	15%	16%	18%	20%	24%	28%	32%
1	0.9091	0.8929	0.8772	0.8696	0.8621	0.8475	0.8333	0.8065	0.7813	0.7576
2	1.7355	1.6901	1.6467	1.6257	1.6052	1.5656	1.5278	1.4568	1.3916	1.3315
3	2.4869	2.4018	2.3216	2.2832	2.2459	2.1743	2.1065	1.9813	1.8684	1.7663
4	3.1699	3.0373	2.9137	2.8550	2.7982	2.6901	2.5887	2.4043	2.2410	2.0957
5	3.7908	3.6048	3.4331	3.3522	3.2743	3.1272	2.9906	2.7454	2.5320	2.3452
6	4.3553	4.1114	3.8887	3.7845	3.6847	3.4976	3.3255	3.0205	2.7594	2.5342
7	4.8684	4.5638	4.2883	4.1604	4.0386	3.8115	3.6046	3.2423	2.9370	2.6775
8	5.3349	4.9676	4.6389	4.4873	4.3436	4.0776	3.8372	3.4212	3.0758	2.7860
9	5.7590	5.3282	4.9464	4.7716	4.6065	4.3030	4.0310	3.5655	3.1842	2.8681
10	6.1446	5.6502	5.2161	5.0188	4.8332	4.4941	4.1925	3.6819	3.2689	2.9304
11	6.4951	5.9377	5.4527	5.2337	5.0286	4.6560	4.3271	3.7757	3.3351	2.9776
12	6.8137	6.1944	5.6603	5.4206	5.1971	4.7932	4.4392	3.8514	3.3868	3.0133
13	7.1034	6.4235	5.8424	5.5831	5.3423	4.9095	4.5327	3.9124	3.4272	3.0404
14	7.3667	6.6282	6.0021	5.7245	5.4675	5.0081	4.6106	3.9616	3.4587	3.0609
15	7.6061	6.8109	6.1422	5.8474	5.5755	5.0916	4.6755	4.0013	3.4834	3.0764
16	7.8237	6.9740	6.2651	5.9542	5.6685	5.1624	4.7296	4.0333	3.5026	3.0882
17	8.0216	7.1196	6.3729	6.0472	5.7487	5.2223	4.7746	4.0591	3.5177	3.0971
18	8.2014	7.2497	6.4674	6.1280	5.8178	5.2732	4.8122	4.0799	3.5294	3.1039
19	8.3649	7.3658	6.5504	6.1982	5.8775	5.3162	4.8435	4.0967	3.5386	3.1090
20	8.5136	7.4694	6.6231	6.2593	5.9288	5.3527	4.8696	4.1103	3.5458	3.1129
21	8.6487	7.5620	6.6870	6.3125	5.9731	5.3837	4.8913	4.1212	3.5514	3.1158
22	8.7715	7.6446	6.7429	6.3587	6.0113	5.4099	4.9094	4.1300	3.5558	3.1180
23	8.8832	7.7184	6.7921	6.3988	6.0442	5.4321	4.9245	4.1371	3.5592	3.1197
24	8.9847	7.7843	6.8351	6.4338	6.0726	5.4510	4.9371	4.1428	3.5619	3.1210
25	9.0770	7.8431	6.8729	6.4642	6.0971	5.4669	4.9476	4.1474	3.5640	3.1220
26	9.1609	7.8957	6.9061	6.4906	6.1182	5.4804	4.9563	4.1511	3.5656	3.1227
27	9.2372	7.9426	6.9352	6.5135	6.1364	5.4919	4.9636	4.1542	3.5669	3.1233
28	9.3066	7.9844	6.9607	6.5335	6.1520	5.5016	4.9697	4.1566	3.5679	3.1237
29	9.3696	8.0218	6.9830	6.5509	6.1656	5.5098	4.9747	4.1585	3.5687	3.1240
30	9.4269	8.0552	7.0027	6.5660	6.1772	5.5168	4.9789	4.1601	3.5693	3.1242
35	9.6442	8.1755	7.0700	6.6166	6.2153	5.5386	4.9915	4.1644	3.5708	3.1248
40	9.7791	8.2438	7.1050	6.6418	6.2335	5.5482	4.9966	4.1659	3.5712	3.1250
45	9.8628	8.2825	7.1232	6.6543	6.2421	5.5523	4.9986	4.1664	3.5714	3.1250
50	9.9148	8.3045	7.1327	6.6605	6.2463	5.5541	4.9995	4.1666	3.5714	3.1250
55	9.9471	8.3170	7.1376	6.6636	6.2482	5.5549	4.9998	4.1666	3.5714	3.1250

Statistical Tables

Table C.1 Areas under the Standard Normal Distribution

z	.00	.01	.02	.03	.04	.05	.06	.07	.08	.09
0.0	.0000	.0040	.0080	.0120	.0160	.0199	.0239	.0279	.0319	.0359
0.1	.0398	.0438	.0478	.0517	.0557	.0596	.0636	.0675	.0714	.0753
0.2	.0793	.0832	.0871	.0910	.0948	.0987	.1026	.1064	.1103	.1141
0.3	.1179	.1217	.1255	.1293	.1331	.1368	.1406	.1443	.1480	.1517
0.4	.1554	.1591	.1628	.1664	.1700	.1736	.1772	.1808	.1844	.1879
0.5	.1915	.1950	.1985	.2019	.2054	.2088	.2123	.2157	.2190	.2224
0.6	.2257	.2291	.2324	.2357	.2389	.2422	.2454	.2486	.2517	.2549
0.7	.2580	.2611	.2642	.2673	.2704	.2734	.2764	.2794	.2823	.2852
0.8	.2881	.2910	.2939	.2967	.2995	.3023	.3051	.3078	.3106	.3133
0.9	.3159	.3186	.3212	.3238	.3264	.3289	.3315	.3340	.3365	.3389
1.0	.3413	.3438	.3461	.3485	.3508	.3531	.3554	.3577	.3599	.3621
1.1	.3643	.3665	.3686	.3708	.3729	.3749	.3770	.3790	.3810	.3830
1.2	.3849	.3869	.3888	.3907	.3925	.3944	.3962	.3980	.3997	.4015
1.3	.4032	.4049	.4066	.4082	.4099	.4115	.4131	.4147	.4162	.4177
1.4	.4192	.4207	.4222	.4236	.4251	.4265	.4279	.4292	.4306	.4319
1.5	.4332	.4345	.4357	.4370	.4382	.4394	.4406	.4418	.4429	.4441
1.6	.4452	.4463	.4474	.4484	.4495	.4505	.4515	.4525	.4535	.4545
1.7	.4554	.4564	.4573	.4582	.4591	.4599	.4608	.4616	.4625	.4633
1.8	.4641	.4649	.4656	.4664	.4671	.4678	.4686	.4693	.4699	.4706
1.9	.4713	.4719	.4726	.4732	.4738	.4744	.4750	.4756	.4761	.4767
2.0	.4772	.4778	.4783	.4788	.4793	.4798	.4803	.4808	.4812	.4817
2.1	.4821	.4826	.4830	.4834	.4838	.4842	.4846	.4850	.4854	.4857
2.2	.4861	.4864	.4868	.4871	.4875	.4878	.4881	.4884	.4887	.4890
2.3	.4893	.4896	.4898	.4901	.4904	.4906	.4909	.4911	.4913	.4916
2.4	.4918	.4920	.4922	.4925	.4927	.4929	.4831	.4932	.4934	.4936
2.5	.4938	.4940	.4941	.4943	.4945	.4946	.4948	.4949	.4951	.4952
2.6	.4953	.4955	.4956	.4957	.4959	.4960	.4961	.4962	.4963	.4964
2.7	.4965	.4966	.4967	.4968	.4969	.4970	.4971	.4972	.4973	.4974
2.8	.4974	.4975	.4976	.4977	.4977	.4978	.4979	.4979	.4980	.4981
2.9	.4981	.4982	.4983	.4984	.4984	.4985	.4985	.4986	.4986	.4986
3.0	.4987	.4987	.4987	.4988	.4988	.4989	.4989	.4989	.4990	.4990

Example: For z = 1.96, shaded area is 0.4750 out of the total area of 1.

Table C.2　Areas under the Tails of the *t* Distribution

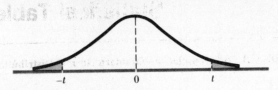

Degrees of Freedom	Probabilities							
	.80	.60	.40	.20	.10	.05	.02	.01
1	0.325	0.727	1.376	3.078	6.314	12.706	31.821	63.657
2	0.289	0.617	1.061	1.886	2.920	4.303	6.965	9.925
3	0.277	0.584	0.978	1.638	2.353	3.182	4.541	5.841
4	0.271	0.569	0.941	1.533	2.132	2.776	3.747	4.604
5	0.267	0.559	0.920	1.476	2.015	2.571	3.365	4.032
6	0.265	0.553	0.906	1.440	1.943	2.447	3.143	3.707
7	0.263	0.549	0.896	1.415	1.895	2.365	2.998	3.499
8	0.262	0.546	0.889	1.397	1.860	2.306	2.896	3.355
9	0.261	0.543	0.883	1.383	1.833	2.262	2.821	3.250
10	0.260	0.542	0.879	1.372	1.812	2.228	2.764	3.169
11	0.260	0.540	0.876	1.363	1.796	2.201	2.718	3.106
12	0.259	0.539	0.873	1.356	1.782	2.179	2.681	3.055
13	0.259	0.538	0.870	1.350	1.771	2.160	2.650	3.012
14	0.258	0.537	0.868	1.345	1.761	2.145	2.624	2.977
15	0.258	0.536	0.866	1.341	1.753	2.131	2.602	2.947
16	0.258	0.535	0.865	1.337	1.746	2.120	2.583	2.921
17	0.257	0.534	0.863	1.333	1.740	2.110	2.567	2.898
18	0.257	0.534	0.862	1.330	1.734	2.101	2.552	2.878
19	0.257	0.533	0.861	1.328	1.729	2.093	2.539	2.861
20	0.257	0.533	0.860	1.325	1.725	2.086	2.528	2.845
21	0.257	0.532	0.859	1.323	1.721	2.080	2.518	2.831
22	0.256	0.532	0.858	1.321	1.717	2.074	2.508	2.819
23	0.256	0.532	0.858	1.319	1.714	2.069	2.500	2.807
24	0.256	0.531	0.857	1.318	1.711	2.064	2.492	2.797
25	0.256	0.531	0.856	1.316	1.708	2.060	2.485	2.787
26	0.256	0.531	0.856	1.315	1.706	2.056	2.479	2.779
27	0.256	0.531	0.855	1.314	1.703	2.052	2.473	2.771
28	0.256	0.530	0.855	1.313	1.701	2.048	2.467	2.763
29	0.256	0.530	0.854	1.311	1.699	2.045	2.462	2.756
30	0.256	0.530	0.854	1.310	1.697	2.042	2.457	2.750
40	0.255	0.529	0.851	1.303	1.684	2.021	2.423	2.704
60	0.254	0.527	0.848	1.296	1.671	2.000	2.390	2.660
120	0.254	0.526	0.845	1.289	1.658	1.980	2.358	2.617
∞	0.253	0.524	0.842	1.282	1.645	1.960	2.326	2.576

Note: The probabilities given in the table are for two-tailed tests. Thus, a probability of 0.05 allows for 0.025 in each tail. For example, for a probability of 0.05 and 21 degrees of freedom, $t = 2.080$. This means that 2.5 percent of the area under the *t* distribution lies to the right of $t = 2.080$ and 2.5 percent to the left of $t = -2.080$.

Source: From Table III of R. A. Fisher and F. Yates, *Statistical Tables for Biological, Agricultural and Medical Research*, 6th ed., London: Longman Group Ltd., 1974; previously by Oliver & Boyd, Edinburgh, by permission of the authors and publishers.

Table C.3 F Distribution for 5% Significance

Degrees of Freedom for Denominator	\ Degrees of Freedom for Numerator																		
	1	2	3	4	5	6	7	8	9	10	12	15	20	24	30	40	60	120	∞
1	161	200	216	225	230	234	237	239	241	242	244	246	248	249	250	251	252	253	254
2	18.5	19.0	19.2	19.2	19.3	19.3	19.4	19.4	19.4	19.4	19.4	19.4	19.5	19.5	19.5	19.5	19.5	19.5	19.5
3	10.1	9.55	9.28	9.12	9.01	8.94	8.89	8.85	8.81	8.79	8.74	8.70	8.66	8.64	8.62	8.59	8.57	8.55	8.53
4	7.71	6.94	6.59	6.39	6.26	6.16	6.09	6.04	6.00	5.96	5.91	5.86	5.80	5.77	5.75	5.72	5.69	5.66	5.63
5	6.61	5.79	5.41	5.19	5.05	4.95	4.88	4.82	4.77	4.74	4.68	4.62	4.56	4.53	4.50	4.46	4.43	4.40	4.37
6	5.99	5.14	4.76	4.53	4.39	4.28	4.21	4.15	4.10	4.06	4.00	3.94	3.87	3.84	3.81	3.77	3.74	3.70	3.67
7	5.59	4.74	4.35	4.12	3.97	3.87	3.79	3.73	3.68	3.64	3.57	3.51	3.44	3.41	3.38	3.34	3.30	3.27	3.23
8	5.32	4.46	4.07	3.84	3.69	3.58	3.50	3.44	3.39	3.35	3.28	3.22	3.15	3.12	3.08	3.04	3.01	2.97	2.93
9	5.12	4.26	3.86	3.63	3.48	3.37	3.29	3.23	3.18	3.14	3.07	3.01	2.94	2.90	2.86	2.83	2.79	2.75	2.71
10	4.96	4.10	3.71	3.48	3.33	3.22	3.14	3.07	3.02	2.98	2.91	2.85	2.77	2.74	2.70	2.66	2.62	2.58	2.54
11	4.84	3.98	3.59	3.36	3.20	3.09	3.01	2.95	2.90	2.85	2.79	2.72	2.65	2.61	2.57	2.53	2.49	2.45	2.40
12	4.75	3.89	3.49	3.26	3.11	3.00	2.91	2.85	2.80	2.75	2.69	2.62	2.54	2.51	2.47	2.43	2.38	2.34	2.30
13	4.67	3.81	3.41	3.18	3.03	2.92	2.83	2.77	2.71	2.67	2.60	2.53	2.46	2.42	2.38	2.34	2.30	2.25	2.21
14	4.60	3.74	3.34	3.11	2.96	2.85	2.76	2.70	2.65	2.60	2.53	2.46	2.39	2.35	2.31	2.27	2.22	2.18	2.13
15	4.54	3.68	3.29	3.06	2.90	2.79	2.71	2.64	2.59	2.54	2.48	2.40	2.33	2.29	2.25	2.20	2.16	2.11	2.07
16	4.49	3.63	3.24	3.01	2.85	2.74	2.66	2.59	2.54	2.49	2.42	2.35	2.28	2.24	2.19	2.15	2.11	2.06	2.01
17	4.45	3.59	3.20	2.96	2.81	2.70	2.61	2.55	2.48	2.45	2.38	2.31	2.23	2.19	2.15	2.10	2.06	2.01	1.96
18	4.41	3.55	3.16	2.93	2.77	2.66	2.58	2.51	2.46	2.41	2.34	2.27	2.19	2.15	2.11	2.06	2.02	1.97	1.92
19	4.38	3.52	3.13	2.90	2.74	2.63	2.54	2.48	2.42	2.39	2.31	2.23	2.16	2.11	2.07	2.03	1.98	1.93	1.88
20	4.35	3.49	3.10	2.87	2.71	2.60	2.51	2.45	2.39	2.35	2.28	2.20	2.12	2.08	2.04	1.99	1.95	1.90	1.84
21	4.32	3.47	3.07	2.84	2.68	2.57	2.49	2.42	2.37	2.32	2.25	2.18	2.10	2.05	2.01	1.96	1.92	1.87	1.81
22	4.30	3.44	3.05	2.82	2.66	2.55	2.46	2.40	2.34	2.30	2.23	2.15	2.07	2.03	1.98	1.94	1.89	1.84	1.78
23	4.28	3.42	3.03	2.80	2.64	2.53	2.44	2.37	2.32	2.27	2.20	2.13	2.05	2.01	1.96	1.91	1.86	1.81	1.76
24	4.26	3.40	3.01	2.78	2.62	2.51	2.42	2.36	2.30	2.25	2.18	2.11	2.03	1.98	1.94	1.89	1.84	1.79	1.73
25	4.24	3.39	2.99	2.76	2.60	2.49	2.40	2.34	2.28	2.24	2.16	2.09	2.01	1.96	1.92	1.87	1.82	1.77	1.71
30	4.17	3.32	2.92	2.69	2.53	2.42	2.33	2.27	2.21	2.16	2.09	2.01	1.93	1.89	1.84	1.79	1.74	1.68	1.62
40	4.08	3.23	2.84	2.61	2.45	2.34	2.25	2.18	2.12	2.08	2.00	1.92	1.84	1.79	1.74	1.69	1.64	1.58	1.51
60	4.00	3.15	2.76	2.53	2.37	2.25	2.17	2.10	2.04	1.99	1.92	1.84	1.75	1.70	1.65	1.59	1.53	1.47	1.39
120	3.92	3.07	2.68	2.45	2.29	2.18	2.09	2.02	1.96	1.91	1.83	1.75	1.66	1.61	1.55	1.50	1.43	1.35	1.25
∞	3.84	3.00	2.60	2.37	2.21	2.10	2.01	1.94	1.88	1.83	1.75	1.67	1.57	1.52	1.46	1.39	1.32	1.22	1.00

Source: M. Merrington and C. M. Thompson, "Tables of Percentage Points of the Inverted Beta (F) Distribution," *Biometrica*, vol. 33, 1943, p. 73.

Table C.3 F Distribution for 1% Significance

Degrees of Freedom for Numerator

Degrees of Freedom for Denominator	1	2	3	4	5	6	7	8	9	10	12	15	20	24	30	40	60	120	∞
1	4,052	5,000	5,403	5,625	5,746	5,859	5,928	5,982	6,023	6,056	6,106	6,157	6,209	6,235	6,261	6,287	6,313	6,339	6,366
2	98.5	99.0	99.2	99.2	99.3	99.3	99.4	99.4	99.4	99.4	99.4	99.4	99.4	99.5	99.5	99.5	99.5	99.5	99.5
3	34.1	30.8	29.5	28.7	28.2	27.9	27.7	27.5	27.3	27.2	27.1	26.9	26.7	26.6	26.5	26.4	26.3	26.2	26.1
4	21.2	18.0	16.7	16.0	15.5	15.2	15.0	14.8	14.7	14.5	14.4	14.2	14.0	13.9	13.8	13.7	13.7	13.6	13.5
5	16.3	13.3	12.1	11.4	11.0	10.7	10.5	10.3	10.2	10.1	9.89	9.72	9.55	9.47	9.38	9.29	9.20	9.11	9.02
6	13.7	10.9	9.78	9.15	8.75	8.47	8.26	8.10	7.98	7.87	7.72	7.56	7.40	7.31	7.23	7.14	7.06	6.97	6.88
7	12.2	9.55	8.45	7.85	7.46	7.19	6.99	6.84	6.72	6.62	6.47	6.31	6.16	6.07	5.99	5.91	5.82	5.74	5.65
8	11.3	8.65	7.59	7.01	6.63	6.37	6.18	6.03	5.91	5.81	5.67	5.52	5.36	5.28	5.20	5.12	5.03	4.95	4.86
9	10.6	8.02	6.99	6.42	6.06	5.80	5.61	5.47	5.35	5.26	5.11	4.96	4.81	4.73	4.65	4.57	4.48	4.40	4.31
10	10.0	7.56	6.55	5.99	5.64	5.39	5.20	5.06	4.94	4.85	4.71	4.56	4.41	4.33	4.25	4.17	4.08	4.00	3.91
11	9.65	7.21	6.22	5.67	5.32	5.07	4.89	4.74	4.63	4.54	4.40	4.25	4.10	4.02	3.94	3.86	3.78	3.69	3.60
12	9.33	6.93	5.95	5.41	5.06	4.82	4.64	4.50	4.39	4.30	4.16	4.01	3.86	3.78	3.70	3.62	3.54	3.45	3.36
13	9.07	6.70	5.74	5.21	4.86	4.62	4.44	4.30	4.19	4.10	3.96	3.82	3.66	3.59	3.51	3.43	3.34	3.25	3.17
14	8.86	6.51	5.56	5.04	4.69	4.46	4.28	4.14	4.03	3.94	3.80	3.66	3.51	3.43	3.35	3.27	3.18	3.09	3.00
15	8.68	6.36	5.42	4.89	4.56	4.32	4.14	4.00	3.89	3.80	3.67	3.52	3.37	3.29	3.21	3.13	3.05	2.96	2.87
16	8.53	6.23	5.29	4.77	4.44	4.20	4.03	3.89	3.78	3.69	3.55	3.41	3.26	3.18	3.10	3.02	2.93	2.84	2.75
17	8.40	6.11	5.19	4.67	4.34	4.10	3.93	3.79	3.68	3.59	3.46	3.31	3.16	3.08	3.00	2.92	2.83	2.75	2.65
18	8.29	6.01	5.09	4.58	4.25	4.01	3.84	3.71	3.60	3.51	3.37	3.23	3.08	3.00	2.92	2.84	2.75	2.66	2.57
19	8.19	5.93	5.01	4.50	4.17	3.94	3.77	3.63	3.52	3.43	3.30	3.15	3.00	2.92	2.84	2.76	2.67	2.58	2.49
20	8.10	5.85	4.94	4.43	4.10	3.87	3.70	3.56	3.46	3.37	3.23	3.09	2.94	2.86	2.78	2.69	2.61	2.52	2.42
21	8.02	5.78	4.87	4.37	4.04	3.81	3.64	3.51	3.40	3.31	3.17	3.03	2.88	2.80	2.72	2.64	2.55	2.46	2.36
22	7.95	5.72	4.82	4.31	3.99	3.76	3.59	3.45	3.35	3.26	3.12	2.98	2.83	2.75	2.67	2.58	2.50	2.40	2.31
23	7.88	5.66	4.76	4.26	3.94	3.71	3.54	3.41	3.30	3.21	3.07	2.93	2.78	2.70	2.62	2.54	2.45	2.35	2.26
24	7.82	5.61	4.72	4.22	3.90	3.67	3.50	3.36	3.26	3.17	3.03	2.89	2.74	2.66	2.58	2.49	2.40	2.31	2.21
25	7.77	5.57	4.68	4.18	3.86	3.63	3.46	3.32	3.22	3.13	2.99	2.85	2.70	2.62	2.54	2.45	2.36	2.27	2.17
30	7.56	5.39	4.51	4.02	3.70	3.47	3.30	3.17	3.07	2.98	2.84	2.70	2.55	2.47	2.39	2.30	2.21	2.11	2.01
40	7.31	5.18	4.31	3.83	3.51	3.29	3.12	2.99	2.89	2.80	2.66	2.52	2.37	2.29	2.20	2.11	2.02	1.92	1.80
60	7.08	4.98	4.13	3.65	3.34	3.12	2.95	2.82	2.72	2.63	2.50	2.35	2.20	2.12	2.03	1.94	1.84	1.73	1.60
120	6.85	4.79	3.95	3.48	3.17	2.96	2.79	2.66	2.56	2.47	2.34	2.19	2.03	1.95	1.86	1.76	1.66	1.53	1.38
∞	6.63	4.61	3.78	3.32	3.02	2.80	2.64	2.51	2.41	2.32	2.18	2.04	1.88	1.79	1.70	1.59	1.47	1.32	1.00

Source: M. Merrington and C. M. Thompson, "Tables of Percentage Points of the Inverted Beta (F) Distribution," Biometrica, vol. 33, 1943, p. 73.

Table C.4 Durbin-Watson Statistic for 5% Significance Points of d_L and d_U

n	$k' = 1$		$k' = 2$		$k' = 3$		$k' = 4$		$k' = 5$	
	d_L	d_U	d_L	d_U	d_L	d_U	d_L	d_U	d_L	d_U
15	1.08	1.36	0.95	1.54	0.82	1.75	0.69	1.97	0.56	2.21
16	1.10	1.37	0.98	1.54	0.86	1.73	0.74	1.93	0.62	2.15
17	1.13	1.38	1.02	1.54	0.90	1.71	0.78	1.90	0.67	2.10
18	1.16	1.39	1.05	1.53	0.93	1.69	0.82	1.87	0.71	2.06
19	1.18	1.40	1.08	1.53	0.97	1.68	0.86	1.85	0.75	2.02
20	1.20	1.41	1.10	1.54	1.00	1.68	0.90	1.83	0.79	1.99
21	1.22	1.42	1.13	1.54	1.03	1.67	0.93	1.81	0.83	1.96
22	1.24	1.43	1.15	1.54	1.05	1.66	0.96	1.80	0.86	1.94
23	1.26	1.44	1.17	1.54	1.08	1.66	0.99	1.79	0.90	1.92
24	1.27	1.45	1.19	1.55	1.10	1.66	1.01	1.78	0.93	1.90
25	1.29	1.45	1.21	1.55	1.12	1.66	1.04	1.77	0.95	1.89
26	1.30	1.46	1.22	1.55	1.14	1.65	1.06	1.76	0.98	1.88
27	1.32	1.47	1.24	1.56	1.16	1.65	1.08	1.76	1.01	1.86
28	1.33	1.48	1.26	1.56	1.18	1.65	1.10	1.75	1.03	1.85
29	1.34	1.48	1.27	1.56	1.20	1.65	1.12	1.74	1.05	1.84
30	1.35	1.49	1.28	1.57	1.21	1.65	1.14	1.74	1.07	1.83
31	1.36	1.50	1.30	1.57	1.23	1.65	1.16	1.74	1.09	1.83
32	1.37	1.50	1.31	1.57	1.24	1.65	1.18	1.73	1.11	1.82
33	1.38	1.51	1.32	1.58	1.26	1.65	1.19	1.73	1.13	1.81
34	1.39	1.51	1.33	1.58	1.27	1.65	1.21	1.73	1.15	1.81
35	1.40	1.52	1.34	1.58	1.28	1.65	1.22	1.73	1.16	1.80
36	1.41	1.52	1.35	1.59	1.29	1.65	1.24	1.73	1.18	1.80
37	1.42	1.53	1.36	1.59	1.31	1.66	1.25	1.72	1.19	1.80
38	1.43	1.54	1.37	1.59	1.32	1.66	1.26	1.72	1.21	1.79
39	1.43	1.54	1.38	1.60	1.33	1.66	1.27	1.72	1.22	1.79
40	1.44	1.54	1.39	1.60	1.34	1.66	1.29	1.72	1.23	1.79
45	1.48	1.57	1.43	1.62	1.38	1.67	1.34	1.72	1.29	1.78
50	1.50	1.59	1.46	1.63	1.42	1.67	1.38	1.72	1.34	1.77
55	1.53	1.60	1.49	1.64	1.45	1.68	1.41	1.72	1.38	1.77
60	1.55	1.62	1.51	1.65	1.48	1.69	1.44	1.73	1.41	1.77
65	1.57	1.63	1.54	1.66	1.50	1.70	1.47	1.73	1.44	1.77
70	1.58	1.64	1.55	1.67	1.52	1.70	1.49	1.74	1.46	1.77
75	1.60	1.65	1.57	1.68	1.54	1.71	1.51	1.74	1.49	1.77
80	1.61	1.66	1.59	1.69	1.56	1.72	1.53	1.74	1.51	1.77
85	1.62	1.67	1.60	1.70	1.57	1.72	1.55	1.75	1.52	1.77
90	1.63	1.68	1.61	1.70	1.59	1.73	1.57	1.75	1.54	1.78
95	1.64	1.69	1.62	1.71	1.60	1.73	1.58	1.75	1.56	1.78
100	1.65	1.69	1.63	1.72	1.61	1.74	1.59	1.76	1.57	1.78

Note: n = number of observations; k' = number of independent variables.

Source: J. Durbin and G. S. Watson, "Testing for Serial Correlation in Least Squares Regression," *Biometrica*, vol. 38, 1951, pp. 159–177. Reprinted with the permission of the authors and trustees of *Biometrica*.

Table C.4 Durbin-Watson Statistic for 1% Significance Points of d_L and d_U

n	$k' = 1$		$k' = 2$		$k' = 3$		$k' = 4$		$k' = 5$	
	d_L	d_U	d_L	d_U	d_L	d_U	d_L	d_U	d_L	d_U
15	0.81	1.07	0.70	1.25	0.59	1.46	0.49	1.70	0.39	1.96
16	0.84	1.09	0.74	1.25	0.63	1.44	0.53	1.66	0.44	1.90
17	0.87	1.10	0.77	1.25	0.67	1.43	0.57	1.63	0.48	1.85
18	0.90	1.12	0.80	1.26	0.71	1.42	0.61	1.60	0.52	1.80
19	0.93	1.13	0.83	1.26	0.74	1.41	0.65	1.58	0.56	1.77
20	0.95	1.15	0.86	1.27	0.77	1.41	0.68	1.57	0.60	1.74
21	0.97	1.16	0.89	1.27	0.80	1.41	0.72	1.55	0.63	1.71
22	1.00	1.17	0.91	1.28	0.83	1.40	0.75	1.54	0.66	1.69
23	1.02	1.19	0.94	1.29	0.86	1.40	0.77	1.53	0.70	1.67
24	1.04	1.20	0.96	1.30	0.88	1.41	0.80	1.53	0.72	1.66
25	1.05	1.21	0.98	1.30	0.90	1.41	0.83	1.52	0.75	1.65
26	1.07	1.22	1.00	1.31	0.93	1.41	0.85	1.52	0.78	1.64
27	1.09	1.23	1.02	1.32	0.95	1.41	0.88	1.51	0.81	1.63
28	1.10	1.24	1.04	1.32	0.97	1.41	0.90	1.51	0.83	1.62
29	1.12	1.25	1.05	1.33	0.99	1.42	0.92	1.51	0.85	1.61
30	1.13	1.26	1.07	1.34	1.01	1.42	0.94	1.51	0.88	1.61
31	1.15	1.27	1.08	1.34	1.02	1.42	0.96	1.51	0.90	1.60
32	1.16	1.28	1.10	1.35	1.04	1.43	0.98	1.51	0.92	1.60
33	1.17	1.29	1.11	1.36	1.05	1.43	1.00	1.51	0.94	1.59
34	1.18	1.30	1.13	1.36	1.07	1.43	1.01	1.51	0.95	1.59
35	1.19	1.31	1.14	1.37	1.08	1.44	1.03	1.51	0.97	1.59
36	1.21	1.32	1.15	1.38	1.10	1.44	1.04	1.51	0.99	1.59
37	1.22	1.32	1.16	1.38	1.11	1.45	1.06	1.51	1.00	1.59
38	1.23	1.33	1.18	1.39	1.12	1.45	1.07	1.52	1.02	1.58
39	1.24	1.34	1.19	1.39	1.14	1.45	1.09	1.52	1.03	1.58
40	1.25	1.34	1.20	1.40	1.15	1.46	1.10	1.52	1.05	1.58
45	1.29	1.38	1.24	1.42	1.20	1.48	1.16	1.53	1.11	1.58
50	1.32	1.40	1.28	1.45	1.24	1.49	1.20	1.54	1.16	1.59
55	1.36	1.43	1.32	1.47	1.28	1.51	1.25	1.55	1.21	1.59
60	1.38	1.45	1.35	1.48	1.32	1.52	1.28	1.56	1.25	1.60
65	1.41	1.47	1.38	1.50	1.35	1.53	1.31	1.57	1.28	1.61
70	1.43	1.49	1.40	1.52	1.37	1.55	1.34	1.58	1.31	1.61
75	1.45	1.50	1.42	1.53	1.39	1.56	1.37	1.59	1.34	1.62
80	1.47	1.52	1.44	1.54	1.42	1.57	1.39	1.60	1.36	1.62
85	1.48	1.53	1.46	1.55	1.43	1.58	1.41	1.60	1.39	1.63
90	1.50	1.54	1.47	1.56	1.45	1.59	1.43	1.61	1.41	1.64
95	1.51	1.55	1.49	1.57	1.47	1.60	1.45	1.62	1.42	1.64
100	1.52	1.56	1.50	1.58	1.48	1.60	1.46	1.63	1.44	1.65

Note: n = number of observations; k' = number of independent variables.

Source: J. Durbin and G. S. Watson, "Testing for Serial Correlation in Least Squares Regression," *Biometrica*, vol. 38, 1951, pp. 159–177. Reprinted with the permission of the authors and trustees of *Biometrica*.

INDEX

The letter p following a page number refers to a solved problem